John D. Conley III

SAMS
Teach Yourself
Object-Oriented
Programming
with Visual
Basic®

in 21 Days

SAMS

A Division of Macmillan Computer Publishing
201 West 103rd St., Indianapolis, Indiana, 46290 USA

Sams Teach Yourself Object-Oriented Programming with Visual Basic® in 21 Days

Copyright © 1998 by Sams Publishing

International Standard Book Number: 0-672-31299-9

Library of Congress Catalog Card Number: 97-81425

Printed in the United States of America

First Printing: June, 1998

01 00 99 98   4 3 2 1

Trademarks

All terms mentioned in this book that are known to be trademarks or service marks have been appropriately capitalized. Sams Publishing cannot attest to the accuracy of this information. Use of a term in this book should not be regarded as affecting the validity of any trademark or service mark.

Visual Basic is a registered trademark of Microsoft Corporation.

EXECUTIVE EDITOR
Chris Denny

ACQUISITIONS EDITOR
Sharon Cox

DEVELOPMENT EDITOR
Tony Amico

MANAGING EDITOR
Jodi Jensen

PROJECT EDITOR
Dana Rhodes Lesh

COPY EDITORS
Kate Talbot
Margaret Berson
Carolyn Linn
Anne Owen
San Dee Phillips

INDEXER
Kelly Talbot

TECHNICAL EDITORS
Sundar Rajan
Jeff Perkins
Ricardo Birmele

SOFTWARE DEVELOPMENT SPECIALIST
John Warriner

PRODUCTION
Michael Henry
Linda Knose
Tim Osborn
Staci Somers
Mark Walchle

Overview

Contents

About the Author

JOHN D. CONLEY III is the president and chief system architect of Samsona Software Co., Inc., a firm that specializes in developing custom software for organizations and creating development tools. He is the coauthor of several books, including *Visual Basic 5 Development Unleashed*, *Visual Basic 5 Fundamentals Unleashed*, *Special Edition Using Oracle Web Application Server 3.0*, and *Working with Cartridges*. A graduate of the University of Oklahoma and former student at U.C. Berkeley, he has over eleven years of professional software development experience and 17 years total experience. He can be reached at samsona@dallas.net, http://www.samsona.com, or (972) 394-3983.

Contact Information:

John Conley
Chief System Architect
Samsona Software Co., Inc.
P.O. Box 117354
Carrollton, TX 75011
samsona@dallas.net
Phone: (972) 394-3983
Fax: (972) 394-0845

Dedication

*To my Savior Jesus Christ who strengthens me, to my wife, Vivian, and our children, John IV and Tiara.
To my parents and siblings, as well as my very supportive friends who encouraged me along the way.*

Acknowledgments

I'd like to thank the Sams editing staff for their diligent efforts and helpful advice. Also, thanks to those hard-working Visual Basic developers who have access to one of the best development tools on the market. Finally, thanks to the Microsoft development staff for making the latest version of Visual Basic a real winner.

Introduction

Welcome to Object-Oriented Programming with Visual Basic

Greetings, fellow developer. Over the next twenty-one days, you will learn how to effectively implement object-oriented programming in Visual Basic. Along the way, you will examine a great deal of sample code, including fully functional classes, subsystems, and components. These structures will help you develop reusable applications much more quickly than if you had to start from scratch. The lessons on design patterns will also help you develop extensible application architectures so that constructing complete applications is as simple as plugging in subsystems with their interdependencies already mapped out in terms of methods calling methods.

The lessons start out with the basics of object-oriented programming. They then progress to a relatively straightforward treatment of more complex concepts. After that, the chapters cover in detail the actual subsystems commonly used—and reused—in many Visual Basic applications.

Who Should Read This Book

Any Visual Basic developer who needs to quickly learn how to implement the powerful object-oriented programming paradigm in Visual Basic should definitely read this book. Pay close attention to each lesson because object-oriented programming is complex, although not impossible to learn. Developers who have some knowledge of modularization of code and information hiding will progress through the lessons pretty quickly. If you're new to programming in general, I strongly advise that you give serious attention to the lessons in the first week. Although this book is certainly geared towards Visual Basic developers, developers in other languages such as Java, Visual C++, PowerBuilder, and Delphi can also benefit from the treatment of subsystems, classes, and design patterns because these structures are universal for all programming languages.

Why You Need to Use This Book

If you've developed Visual Basic applications for a while, you might have developed applications very quickly by placing code in forms and maybe one or two code modules. This works fine on one project, but as soon as you started another project, you might have quickly noticed that you had to almost reinvent the wheel in order to reuse some of the code in your applications. After a number of projects, this becomes very tedious. What's more, the code samples that ship with Visual Basic itself are form-intensive, meaning that the bulk of the code is embedded predominantly in the forms. Such practices, although rapid for one project, become nightmarish over several projects.

This book contains effective lessons for helping you leverage your hard labor so that you can fairly painlessly reuse it for many projects. Your coding habits will be such that when Microsoft releases newer versions of Visual Basic, your code will be well encapsulated enough to be minimally affected by the change. This also applies to upgraded versions of controls and components, as well as business or domain rule changes you encounter. You need this book to better leverage your work and your return on investment.

Imagine having the ability to develop and refine classes and subsystems over a few projects and then being able to reuse the work you put into those structures perpetually into the future. For you commercial developers, this is the law of increasing returns (not diminishing returns). You can be quite competitive on the market and with your peers who haven't harnessed the reuse power behind object-oriented programming.

A Quick Course Summary

The following synopses give you some ideas about the powerful lessons you'll learn in this book.

Week 1

The lessons for Week 1 get you started in object-oriented programming concepts in Visual Basic. You learn object-oriented analysis, design, and programming, as well as class inheritance, building ActiveX components, and incorporating third-party components.

Week 2

In Week 2, you learn about self-testing objects, breaking up applications into subsystems, and refining use cases. This week's lessons also teaches you about the subsystems for the graphical user interface, workgroup and security, and internal application management.

Week 3

In Week 3's lessons, you learn about the subsystems for business rules, reporting and printing, error processing and exception handling, and database access. You also learn how each subsystem generally communicates with other subsystems in the entire application.

What's Not Covered in This Book

This book is full of helpful lessons on object-oriented programming. However, there are some concepts that are not covered in full detail. The full specifications for the Unified Modeling Language (UML), which is the leading modeling language in object-oriented programming, aren't exhaustively covered in this book. The topics of workgroup modeling and security can be quite complex, so although the book gives some fundamental coverage of these, the complexities are not fully covered. Also, a detailed treatment of Data Access Objects (DAO) isn't included, although the classes that encapsulate your application's interaction with them is covered. Day 7, "Incorporating Third-Party Components," covers third-party controls in a general sense, but no detailed coverage of any specific third-party control is included. What you do learn about third-party controls, however, is how to effectively encapsulate your application from changes and failures in the controls so that you can easily replace them as needed. As with any book on object-oriented programming, there are more advanced concepts and modeling techniques such as the Object Constraint Language that are not covered, although you certainly learn enough in this book to effectively use the technology in Visual Basic. However, because UML is used in this book, further learning into other techniques should not prove to be difficult. Finally, not every possible subsystem or component you can develop is covered here. Instead, the most popular application subsystems are presented to you, and from there, you can extend your learning and experience into designing and implementing whatever subsystems you need for your special projects.

What's on the CD-ROM

All the extensive code examples you read in this book are included on the CD-ROM in the back of the book. The Samsona Bank Teller System example is broken up into several subsystems and placed on the CD-ROM so that you can examine it and use it for your own needs.

Recommended Files

The code files on the CD-ROM will help you solve your particular development problems. However, you will need the files for Active Data Objects (ADO) if you don't already have them. If you don't, you can download them free at www.microsoft.com/oledb. If you want to use Microsoft Access for reporting, you'll need that application installed.

Online Resources

After going through the helpful lessons in this book, you might need to keep abreast on object-oriented programming concepts as they evolve. Feel free to visit my Web site at www.samsona.com for ongoing assistance and for free components you can use in your applications.

WEEK 1

At a Glance

The lessons for Week 1 get you started in object-oriented programming concepts in Visual Basic. You learn object-oriented analysis, design, and programming, as well as class inheritance and building ActiveX components.

The week begins with a survey of fundamental concepts in object-oriented programming that provides the foundation for the remaining lessons in the book. Then you progress through the essentials of object-oriented analysis; you learn how to discover important entities or abstractions in your user requirements and other sources in your domain. You then move into the fundamentals of object-oriented design. This includes the creation of class diagrams that reflect the Visual Basic class modules you'll discover you need, as well as interaction diagrams that show how these classes interact to carry out user requirements.

In the middle of the week, you begin to apply the concepts of object technology and receive a lesson on object-oriented programming. In this lesson, you're going to take your learning a step further. You learn how to construct actual Visual Basic code from the simple sequence diagrams you created in previous lessons.

Toward the end of the week, you learn about class interface inheritance, in which one class implements the interface (public methods and properties) of another class. From there it's a short step to learning to build simple ActiveX components. The week wraps up with a look into the adaptation and reuse of third-party components, which allows you to reduce your development requirements.

1

2

3

4

5

6

7

DAY 1

Object-Oriented Programming: A Primer

Congratulations on your decision to implement object-oriented programming in Visual Basic. After reading this book, you will find creating classes and objects and implementing them in Visual Basic both quick and quite fun. This first chapter is a primer on object-oriented programming (OOP). Today you'll learn about the following:

- Migrating from legacy programming practices
- Creating a Visual Basic class, collections and aggregation of objects, sub-systems/packages, and more
- Effectively using the discovery-oriented nature of the object-oriented process
- Taking the guesswork out of programming by using analysis and design activities

As you read this chapter, you'll develop a fundamental understanding of object-oriented programming. If you feel you already know some OOP fundamentals, you can skip to Day 2, "Fundamental Object-Oriented Analysis."

Migrating from Legacy Programming Practices

Before you venture knee-deep into solid, experienced-based object-oriented programming in Visual Basic, you need a primer on OOP. Object-oriented programming is a complex technology. Programmers new to object technology should view OOP as an important, new computer programming paradigm. That is, decisions about application design are made before programming (or construction) even begins. Ad hoc assumptions about an application's design during construction are no longer valid. In fact, if such assumptions do occur, this indicates that the application's architecture has not been properly planned using object technology. Object technology requires much more organized work up front in problem assessment, analysis, and design for relatively complex problems. After reading this book, you'll know why it is important to plan your object-oriented application before you begin programming.

Object-oriented programming is the process of developing one-to-many lines of programming instructions, based on well-defined design models. Such design models are graphical illustrations that represent different aspects of objects, those objects' classes (from which they derive functions and property variables), and their interactions with each other.

NEW TERM   A *design model* is a graphical illustration that represents different aspects of objects, their parents, and their interactions with each other. Through inheritance, child classes derive their functions and properties from parent classes that can be modeled in a design model artifact known as a *class diagram*.

With all the hoopla surrounding the emergence and increasing acceptance of object-oriented programming, you might be saying to yourself, "Oh, boy!" Every week there seems to be some new technology pronouncing itself the guardian of true object orientation: Java/CORBA, C++/Visual Basic/ActiveX/MFC, and so on. That's the dynamic nature of new discoveries in the object technology community. Object technology companies are scrambling to find better and easier ways for designers and programmers of all backgrounds to migrate to the object-oriented paradigm.

Databases are becoming more object-oriented, and even the Internet is moving away from the common gateway interface (CGI) services to more robust distributed object architectures. The seasoned object-oriented practitioner merely folds useful technologies into his or her mind with a minimal learning curve. For those unaccustomed to object technology, though, whose skills might still depend on more traditional development technologies, the steady rise of object-oriented programming is a frightening, unfamiliar menace to the status quo. "What does all this mean?" you might ask.

Significant shifts in technology always seem to produce fear. When you stop to think about this, the fear usually derives from not knowing the technology from the ground up. Many books explain OOP, but there are new groups of professionals who are unaware of these. Also, many OOP novices are trying to learn it through Visual Basic.

To understand how to use object-oriented programming, you must re-evaluate past programming habits. Nearly gone are the days when developers can try to successfully make ad hoc assumptions about business processes, intimate software design, and expected application behavior.

Note If you are experienced in OOP, you might still want to read this section for information to pass on to other programmers trying to migrate to OOP.

Without the use of a proven object-oriented methodology, the complexities of a given project tend to lead to increased risk of failure or goals that are not fully achieved. In other words, it is more difficult to measure whether project goals have been achieved if critical assumptions about the application's architecture are made on-the-fly. Such ad hoc designs typically add more uncontrollable complexity to the application than originally expected. One fundamental idea behind object-oriented programming is to control the chaos normally associated with software development projects in order to promote reuse of objects. Reuse is achieved, in part, through well-designed classes. Well-designed classes are created by breaking down a complex problem into simpler abstractions. By iterating through one or more solutions to that problem, you can design classes with good attributes and methods, thus creating a strong class interface. You will learn about classes, their methods, and their attributes (including public class interfaces) in this book.

On-the-Fly Programming

On-the-fly programming (OTFP) is the easiest, most popular programming style that ever evolved in the software development community. For the most part, it has developed over the years as a response to growing expectations of computers by end users who want their software immediately. In OTFP, almost every function or sub is public and global. This idiom represents a higher level of abstraction absent in older programming practices. At least with Structured Analysis and Structured Design (SA/SD) methods, thought is given to creating well-defined functions and subroutines. Rapid Application Development (RAD) seeks to organize the industry's best practices into methods for rapidly providing turnkey solutions to end users. However, both SA/SD and RAD still do not fully address the need to break down problems documented in a requirements document into well-defined abstractions with grouped operations and attributes that can be

reused over the long term. Contrary to the opinion that object-
oriented methodologies take too long to rapidly develop software, object-oriented programming can indeed be fast. The main difference between OOP and non-OOP methods
is that object technology generally treats applications and components as long-term capital assets of companies large and small. For individual programmers, OOP represents a
better-organized way to reuse code in chunks called *objects*.

Even in small, cozy environments where everyone knows your name, OTFP tends to represent wasted opportunities to save development costs in the long run. The resulting
OTFP program is very dependent on both the original programmer and the programming
language technology it uses at a point in time. This means two things:

- If the programmer dies or quits, the often undocumented program must be rewrit-
  ten, and the person who usually rewrites it will likely use OTFP in order to satisfy
  rapid development requirements.

- If the technology becomes extinct or greatly changes (which happens often), the
  programmer will have to surf through the entire code base to find every reference
  to members of that technology (that is, API calls, object references, and so on).

The unfortunate result of both these side effects is what is commonly referred to as
spaghetti code. That is, OTFP generally (but not always) leads to a body of code that is
disorganized and exclusively understood in the short term by the original programmer. In
OTFP, all code is perfect to the original programmer, but beauty is in the eyes of the
beholder. If you work in a small, informal environment, you can probably get away with
OTFP because it takes far less analysis and design and might provide increased job security (which provides little benefit to the client). With this approach, though, there still
remains the risk of changes in technology, as well as changes in user requirements now
and in the future. In OTFP, you have to change every line of code—which can be hundreds
or thousands of lines—to accommodate such changes. However, in OOP, you simply go
to the object responsible for that technology or behavior and modify it accordingly, with
little or no effect on the rest of the application code.

In learning OOP, you'll likely use object technology in a team setting. On project teams,
objects and groups of objects can be easily assigned to each member of a team as long as
the objects' interfaces are well defined. This is one of the chief benefits of object technology. However, OTFP does not lend itself well to team development, in which a team
can consist of two or more developers. The common response to this statement is, "Well,
there are only two developers—Frank and I. We know each other well, and we just get
together and hammer out our differences." This seldom works because of the following:

1

- This represents on-the-fly design (OTFD) by compromise; there is no program architecture on which this compromise is based. Without some organized methodology for the programming process, one person's spaghetti coding style can take precedence over that of the other programmer. This is especially damaging when the other programmer is timid and nonconfrontational (a prevalent behavior in the programming community). More often than not, one of these programmers usually quits or in some way is removed from the project when things go wrong (and with OTFP, they often do).

- In some cases, it gives the project manager a false sense of security. For some curious reason, some project management styles tend to prefer one state of the project life cycle in the absence of all others: programming. Seldom is serious treatment given to analysis and design, much less to a formal methodology for the programming process as well as to the formulation of an architecture for the program.

From OTFP to OOP

OOP, and the entire object-oriented process, provides greater and longer lasting benefits to every project stakeholder (programmer, manager, end user, and so on). As mentioned earlier, one chief benefit of OOP is that it facilitates better team development. This is important for users of Visual Basic. Visual Basic offers enough features to enable with ease the implementation of object technology and formal object-oriented analysis and design methodologies. Team development is also easier in Visual Basic and facilitates the creation of projects that incorporate the individual talents of each developer. Visual Basic's support of an object repository (MS Repository) adds a good framework for team development as well. A Visual Basic project, in any size of corporate enterprise, also reflects the competence of its team members. In this context, a project represents a group of people who have as a common goal the development of an application or suite of applications to carry out some business process.

Another way that OOP lends itself well to project team development is by supporting the ability to break down a complex system into simpler abstractions (or understandable portions). Each abstraction, then, can be more easily assigned to team members for better definition and construction (application design and programming). Without an OOP background, novices in Visual Basic tend to revert to traditional waterfall techniques (or similar) as soon as the first problem in the project emerges. This chapter helps you avoid these mistakes by helping you to embrace OOP.

A Primer on Classes

A class is an abstract entity that carries out a subset of your user's requirements. Each abstraction has *behavior,* which is a set of functions or methods, and *attributes,* which are variables or properties that identify the class. Let's look at abstract entity, behavior, and attributes more closely.

NEW TERM A *class* is an abstract entity, a "thing," that carries out a subset of your user's requirements. It represents a classification of key abstractions you discover while assessing a given problem.

Abstract Entity

You might say that a class is a template. Some people call classes *cookie cutters* because each use of the cutter results in an edible cookie. Each cookie you eat is an instance of the cookie class. An instantiated object is brought into your computer's memory. It is a *concrete object*—an object with which you can interact in your application. Although this is true of concrete classes, this is not completely true of every class. However, for starters, this might help you grasp the concept of a class.

NEW TERM A *concrete class* is a child of a parent class whose instances provide runtime behavior for an application system. A concrete class is similar to a cookie cutter and the cookie it creates. An abstract class, by contrast, is the mold used to create the cookie cutter.

A class is much more than a mere cookie cutter or template. It is more than just a convenient way to organize code. Understanding the very nature of a class is difficult for many programmers new to OOP, as I discovered after several interviews with programmer candidates. As mentioned earlier, a class is an abstract entity.

Another more general term for abstract entity is *abstraction*. In his classic book *Object-Oriented Analysis and Design with Applications, Second Edition*, Grady Booch defines an abstraction as "one of the fundamental ways that we as humans cope with complexity." Notice that Booch did not use programming jargon or technical idioms in describing abstraction. His definition strikes a more human tone, potentially leaving you with the idea that the programming world is starting to learn from other human experiences.

Now for a more technical definition. Booch further defines an abstraction as denoting "the essential characteristics of an object that distinguish it from all other kinds of objects and thus provides crisply defined conceptual boundaries, relative to the perspective of the viewer." When you're starting to discover a solution to a common problem, then—no matter what scale—you have to look for descriptions of concepts and ideas in the problem that are important to the person who will use the solution you develop. In the pursuit of these concepts and ideas, you will discover the key abstractions that define the early boundaries of your system's types of classes. Notice the use of the term *bound-aries*. As you iterate through the process of developing your solution, these boundaries evolve into one or more interfaces for your classes. Interfaces provide a public facade by which clients of the class request services without knowing the internal details of how these services are carried out. This lack of knowledge of internal operation details is called encapsulation.

NEW TERM   *Encapsulation* describes the hiding of an object's private information and opera-tions. Requests for information and services (via operations or methods) must occur by invoking public methods, including Visual Basic's property methods.

Classes define the behavior and identity of objects. Some classes can also define the behavior and identity of other classes. Such classes are called *base classes*. Base classes that cannot be instantiated into concrete objects are called *abstract classes*. Objects implement—that is, provide runtime code logic for—the behavior of concrete classes. Because Visual Basic is not as object-oriented as C++ (not C) or Smalltalk, your classes will generally be concrete or *pure virtual*. This means that classes that inherit the inter-face of another class must implement every one of its methods and properties.

Behavior

By now, you should have an understanding of how classes represent key abstractions from the context of the problem you're studying. As part of your research into a given problem, you will discover that the abstractions tend to exhibit some form of behavior. These behaviors are not clearly defined early in the process of developing a solution, but their conceptual representations start to take shape. These conceptual behaviors evolve into methods from the verbs your users choose in describing a problem.

NEW TERM   *Behavior* is the anticipated response of an object when it receives stimuli in the form of a request from a client. A request for certain behavior usually results in the change of the object's state (attribute values).

A conceptual behavior eventually provides the foundation for actual class methods. An object's action or reaction is a manifestation of that object's behavior. Behavior exhibited by an object at any given time can lead to changes in the object's state. For example, given the class `Woman`, an instance of `Woman` would be someone named `Jan Doe`. One of her operations would be made manifest in the method `getMarried`. If she married an instance of `Man` named `John Smith`, the behavioral definition of the method `getMarried` might include a call to some method `setLastName` to change the last name from `Doe` to `Smith` (or `Doe-Smith`). You probably get the picture.

Behavior is in the eyes of the beholder. That is, it is meaningful to the client of the object. For example, you, as a medical "client" of your doctor, know that she can perform surgery on a bad knee. You don't know exactly how she does what she does, but you know she can repair your knee and heal any associated pain in the process. Therefore, you care only about the surgery behavior she exhibits when your knee is hurt.

Attribute

Attributes are, in part, what make a class of objects unique from another class of objects. They are variables, in a sense, that hold an object's current state. For example, given a `BankCustomer` class with a `Name` attribute, this class's state of object could be represented by a name value of `John Doe`. The state of an object is the value of its attributes at a given point in time. In Visual Basic, attributes are represented as properties.

NEW TERM   *State* is the value of an object's attributes at a given point in time.

The Visual Basic Class

The structure of a class is physically deployed differently in different programming languages, though the structure itself remains the same. For instance, in C++, the class is usually separated into a header file—for definitions of the class itself as well as its methods and properties (attributes)—and an implementation file that shows how each member (method or property) of the class is used in a particular domain. In Visual Basic, there is no such distinction—at least, not quite (more on this in a moment).

The Visual Basic class module is virtually the same as the familiar form module, a fact that has, unfortunately, led to some confusion over the difference between the graphical user interface form object and the class module. For example, both a form module and a class module can implement (inherit) the interface (public methods and properties) of another class. You can add properties and methods to both types of modules. Both have a constructor and destructor (`Form_Load`, `Form_Unload`, `Class_Initialize`, `Class_Terminate`). As a result, many Visual Basic developers place lots of business logic code into forms that make it difficult to try to reuse such code, much less partition the application into packages that can then be assigned to individual developers on a team. Figure 1.1 shows what a typical class module looks like.

A class module consists of both the definition and implementation of class members. These class members are methods (functions or subs) and properties (variables that hold information about an object whose type is defined by a class). The members of a class can be defined as either public, private, or friend.

FIGURE 1.1.

This is an example of a class module in Visual Basic.

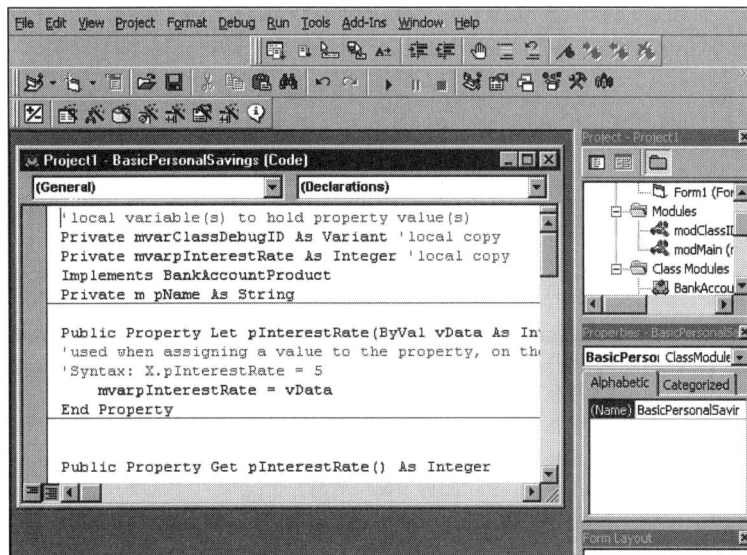

The keyword Public means that the member is accessible to all modules, both within the project and in external projects. If you don't want any members to be public outside the project, you can insert the following line of code in the General Declarations section of the class module:

Option Private

The keyword Private means that the member is accessible only by other members within the class module. This does not mean that you can't pass the value of the private property to an external module via a public property or method. For instance, let's say you have a class called CheckingAccount with the members in Listing 1.1.

LISTING 1.1. MEMBERS OF THE CheckingAccount CLASS.

```
 1: 'General Declarations
 2: Private mvarpAccountNumber As String
 3:
 4: Public Property Get pAccountNumber() As String
 5:     pAccountNumber = mvarpAccountNumber
 6: End Property
 7:
 8: Public Property Let pAccountNumber(ByVal sNewAccountNumber As String)
 9:     mvarpAccountNumber = sNewAccountNumber
10: End Property
```

Because the property pAccountNumber is publicly available, the value of the private mod-ule-level variable mvarpAccountNumber is also publicly available, even though the vari-able mvarpAccountNumber itself is not. This public availability of an attribute is an exam-ple of encapsulation.

Forms as Classes

Are forms in Visual Basic really classes? Technically speaking, they are. They have methods and properties like other classes. For many programmers, they have also become convenient modules for housing vast amounts of complex business processing logic, algorithmic engines, and the heart of the application architecture in general. In the Visual Basic community, this is the norm rather than the exception.

Programmers who have used forms as all-purposes classes should keep in mind that Microsoft did not add classes to Visual Basic out of the blue. There's actually a nice par-adigm shift in the industry away from simply sticking tons of code into forms and global code modules to thinking through, and documenting, how to partition the complexities of software specifications into simpler, nicely encapsulated classes that are responsible for carrying out a particular application behavior. These classes maintain information about their own state as each public and private method is invoked.

Yes, Microsoft's Visual Basic team made forms appear in order to exhibit characteristics of classes. In fact, you can add methods and properties to forms just as you would with classes. However, because this feature is available does not mean that programmers should pack a bunch of methods and variables into it. Each individual programmer might know which application behavior the form carries out, but there's a good chance that no one else on the team does. Forms are only responsible for gathering information from human actors (users) and, as the result of a series of internal processes, displaying expected information to those same actors. Classes acting together as subsystems carry out the core behavior of the application.

NEW TERM   A group of classes that collaborate within a subsystem to carry out a broader application behavior is known as a *package*.

Forms delegate non-form-like functionality to classes, more specifically, the public meth-ods of classes. Private class methods are used by the class as ancillary methods to carry out the publicly available method's interface. The simplest way to see how forms dele-gate behavior to classes is through the following code snippet, entered in the General Declarations section of a code module:

```
Global clsMyClass As CMyClass 'Declared, but now memory allocation with
                              'New
```

clsMyClass is the runtime object instance of CMyClass. Implied with this idea are a runtime architecture and a design-time architecture. CMyClass can be instantiated any number of times at runtime into objects. As stated earlier, objects are cookies. Classes (specifically, concrete classes) are cookie cutters. At design time, a method for CMyClass might be displayMessage. This method accepts two arguments: One is the text box control; the other is a string variable that has the value you want to display. Now let's continue. Assume that Form1 has a text control, Text1, in which you want to display some data. In some Click event, you would do the following:

```
Private Sub Form_Click
    Dim vReturns As Variant 'Some return variable. Explicitly declared
                            'Variant
    Set clsMyClass = New CMyClass 'Memory alloc
    vReturns = clsMyClass.displayMessage(Text1, "Hello, mom")
End Sub
```

In CMyClass, you might implement displayMessage as follows:

```
Public Function displayMessage(ByRef argTextBox, argDisplayString As
➥String)
    On Error GoTo displayMessageErr
    If TypeOf argTextBox Is TextBox Then
        argTextBox.Text = argDisplayString
    End If
    Exit Function
displayMessageErr:
    Err.Raise vbError + 1001, Err.Description 'Something like this to
                                              'raise errors
End Function
```

Here, the only thing the form cares about is that as long as CMyClass received a text box and a string, the class will deliver the promised goods via the displayMessage method. What actually goes on inside the method is none of the form's business. This is encapsulation, which evolved from information hiding. This greatly minimizes the risk of spaghetti code, makes the code easier to read, and encourages reuse throughout the enterprise in case other teams need similar class behavior. Keep in mind that not every class will always be easy to identify and create. You must continually refine classes to carry out clear duties and maximize chances of reuse.

Note The lowercase d in the method displayMessage is an idiom in the OOP community for naming methods.

Time and again, I have seen spaghetti Visual Basic code in which the forms do everything. It's hard to decipher what's going on and to make wise project decisions based on the resulting spaghetti code. This is one reason why Visual Basic and other 4GLs have acquired such a bad reputation. In Java and Visual C++, the dialog and implementation class functionality are separate, which forces you to create nonvisual classes. The larger the project, the more important it is to strictly practice this rule. By *small*, I mean projects in which you are the only one who will use the software. If one other person is involved, you greatly increase project risks by not practicing well-planned application partitioning.

Note

If you need more information, browse to http://www.samsona.com periodically. Using the Object Technology link, you will find helpful information on Visual Basic and object-oriented programming.

An Example of Class Identities

Good! You made it. Now for some interesting illustrations to help you remember the object-oriented concepts just discussed. The automotive industry provides one of the best analogies for understanding OOP. Take Chrysler, for instance. Think of it as a base class for the Sebring class of cars. Now, when you go to the Chrysler dealer, you don't actually buy a Sebring, but an instance of it. The instance you buy is the actual Sebring object because you can interact with it by driving it. The Sebring class, then, is a concrete class because with it, the assembly plant knows how to make real-world cars (objects) based on the Sebring class specification (behavior and attributes).

The Sebring class has methods (ways of operating) such as ignite the engine, turn the wheels, go in reverse, open doors, adjust speed, and so on. Its properties (or variables or attributes) would be color of car, current speed, maximum speed, light status (off or on), wheel base, wheel size, window tint, cabin style (sunroof, convertible, hardtop), retail price, and so on. When you instantiate a Sebring class into an actual Sebring car, these properties will be filled in by an *actor* (a human who interacts with a system, such as the automotive engineer or assembly person in the example). Thus, the color might be red, window tint might be dark smoke, wheel size might be 15″, price might be $25,000, and so on. These values, taken together, represent the current state of the object.

Did you notice something interesting about the Sebring class? Some of its methods and properties have something in common with other cars Chrysler makes. For instance, all Chrysler cars ignite engines, turn wheels, go in reverse, open doors, adjust speed, and so on. Also, they each have color, wheel size, wheel base, and so on. Instead of re-creating these methods and properties for each subclassed car (*subclass* means child class), Chrysler created abstract classes such as the H-Body cars, among others. This is a good example of what an abstract class means. That is, you can't go to the Chrysler dealer and pay for an H-Body car itself. The dealer, instead, will recommend H-Body car classes, such as the Sebring. If you insist on buying the H-Body itself, the puzzled dealer might call a Chrysler plant and tell them that some weirdo wants an H-Body skeleton car. The point is that H-Body is abstract (and might be purely abstract because certain behavior might be implemented at a finer level for certain subclasses). The Sebring class implements the H-Body abstract class. These are entities that are more important to the automotive engineer and repair technician than the buyer (end user). The actual Sebring car is the object that you, the end user, buys.

Creating Visual Basic Classes

By now, you should be comfortable with the idea of classes and objects and their interrelationships. Let's revisit the Visual Basic development environment where you'll actually create a class and observe simple class behaviors at runtime.

There are four ways (also known as *development processes*) to create classes in Visual Basic. In the Learning, Professional, and Enterprise editions of Visual Basic, you can add a new class module from the standard menu or the right-click pop-up menu or add a new class module that is based on an existing class template in the \Vb\Template folder. In the Enterprise edition, you can use the Class Builder to create a new class or use a modeling tool such as Rational Rose/Visual Basic or Microsoft Visual Modeler. Because these tools are principally for automating the design phase/iteration of the object-oriented software engineering life cycle, they will be discussed in more detail on Day 3, "Fundamental Object-Oriented Design." Today you will concentrate on the first three development processes. The following sections familiarize you with the OOP facilities in Visual Basic.

Adding a Class

By far, the easiest way to add a new class to a Visual Basic project is to add a new class module from the menu. Supporting this menu-driven approach are two implementations of this process. You can either choose Project | Add Class Module from the standard menu at the top of the Visual Basic IDE or right-click in the Project browser on the right side of the Visual Basic IDE. If you use the standard menu approach, you will see a dialog box like the one in Figure 1.2.

Double-click the Class Module icon. Visual Basic will add a new class module with the default name Class1 to your project.

If you take the right-click pop-up menu approach, you will need to right-click in the Project Browser. A pop-up menu displays. Choose Add Class Module. At this point, you will also see the Add Class Module dialog box (refer to Figure 1.2). Double-click the

Class Module icon. Visual Basic will add a new class module with the default name
`Class1` to your project.

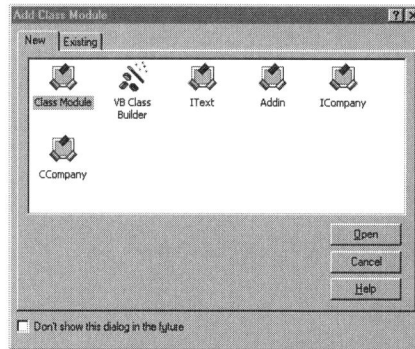

Building a Class with the Class Builder

If you have the Enterprise Edition of Visual Basic, you can create classes from scratch
using the helpful Class Builder. This utility is a distant cousin of Rational Rose/Visual
Basic and Microsoft Visual Modeler in that it lets you build classes in an automated
fashion.

If you haven't done so already, make sure Class Builder is available in the Add-In
Manager. To make it available, choose Add-Ins | Add-In Manager from the menu. You
will see the Add-In Manager dialog box (see Figure 1.3). Select the Visual Basic Class
Builder utility by clicking the check box associated with this item. Click OK.

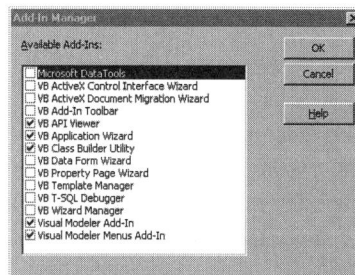

Now you're ready to work with Class Builder. To start this utility, choose Add-Ins Class
Builder from the menu. You will see the Class Builder utility, as illustrated in Figure 1.4.

FIGURE 1.4.

*Class Builder auto-
mates the process of
creating classes in
Visual Basic
Enterprise Edition.*

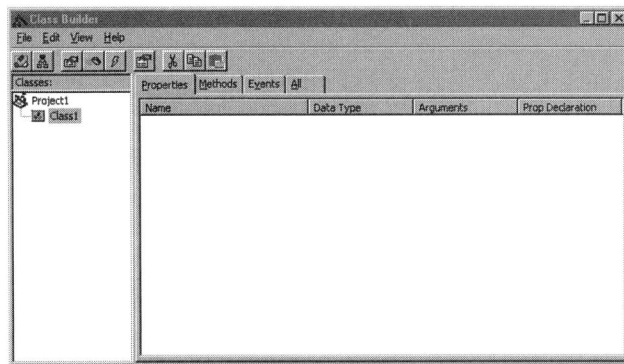

1

Note

If you added a class module to the existing project before using Class
Builder, you will see an informational dialog box indicating that the hierarchy of the classes created outside Class Builder can be incorporated into
Class Builder. You also cannot edit or delete members of that class. If this
dialog box appears, click OK. You can always edit existing classes manually
or in design tools such as Rational Rose/Visual Basic or Microsoft Visual
Modeler.

Not only does Class Builder automate the process of creating classes, but it also tracks
the hierarchy of all your classes and collections. Class Builder also generates the skeleton code you'll need in order to implement the classes and collections, including the
properties, methods, and events of each class.

Note

An event is similar to a method or function but is triggered by a human
actor or an external system action. Visual Basic forms have built-in events.
However, you can raise your own events as well, using the `RaiseEvent`
keyword. Events are particularly useful in ActiveX controls.

On examining the Class Builder utility environment, you'll notice the Windows Explorer–
style visual representation. The standard menu and toolbar reside at the top. Below these
are the Object Model pane on the left and the Properties, Methods, and Events pane on
the right.

The Object Model pane displays the hierarchy of the classes and collections in your project. If you click on a class in this pane, you make it available for editing in the

Properties, Methods, and Events pane. In turn, if you click on a method, property, or event in the Properties, Methods, and Events pane, that class member becomes available for editing.

Classes and collections that existed in previous sessions of the Class Builder can't be edited or deleted in later Class Builder sessions. Therefore, you must manually edit or delete unwanted members that survived (or persisted) beyond a previous Class Builder session.

You can also modify classes by using drag-and-drop features to, for instance, copy a property from one class to another.

The Menu

The Class Builder Menu is standard. If you choose File | New, you have the option of adding a new class, collection, property, method, or event. File | Delete deletes the currently selected class, collection, or class member. File | Rename enables you to rename the currently selected class, collection, or class member. File | Update Project immediately updates your current Visual Basic project with the new or modified class and collection information. File | Exit closes Class Builder after making sure to save current changes not previously updated.

Edit | Cut and Edit | Copy work functions like any other Windows application. You can either cut or copy the currently selected item. Choosing Edit | Properties displays an edit dialog box for the currently selected class or class member.

The View menu at first seems insignificant. Choosing View | Toolbar toggles the display of the toolbar on (displayed) and off (not displayed). Simple enough. However, choosing View | Options opens an unimposing yet far-reaching dialog box called Class Builder Options. Figure 1.5 shows this dialog box.

FIGURE 1.5.

The Class Builder Options dialog box has far-reaching implications for your Visual Basic project.

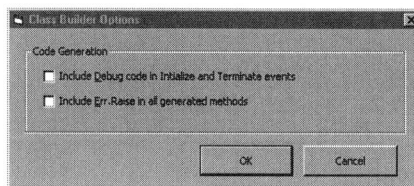

The Class Builder Options dialog box gives you two code generation options:

- Include Debug Code in Initialize and Terminate events
- Include Err.Raise in all generated methods

1

Because these two options are tightly coupled with development processes related to the design phase/iteration of the project life cycle, detailed discussions of them will be taken up on Day 3. For now, suffice it to say that these options let you track the creation and destruction of objects at runtime, as well as trap and raise errors in each object's methods at runtime. Keep in mind that objects are runtime copies (or instances) of classes.

The Help Menu is straightforward, enabling you to access information about the Class Builder utility. The toolbar contains buttons that are shortcuts to the operations already available in the menu.

In the Properties, Methods, and Events pane on the right, you see an index tab control with four tabs: Properties, Methods, Events, and All.

The Properties tab shows all the properties of the currently selected class (see Figure 1.6). With it, you can add, edit, and delete properties from the currently selected class. The container area is divided into four columns: Name, Data Type, Arguments, and Prop Declaration. The Name column shows the name of a given property in the class. The Data Type column shows the data type for each property. The Arguments column lists the arguments that the property method accepts (remember that properties in Visual Basic can be implemented as property methods). Finally, the Prop Declaration column indicates what type of operation the property method performs on the property. The Get type enables clients (other modules needing a value or service) to access the current value or object reference of the property. The Let type enables other modules to change the value of the property. The Set type is similar to the Let type, but other modules can change only the object reference (assuming the class property was declared as either Variant or Object).

FIGURE 1.6.

The Properties tab enables you to add, edit, and delete properties from the currently selected class.

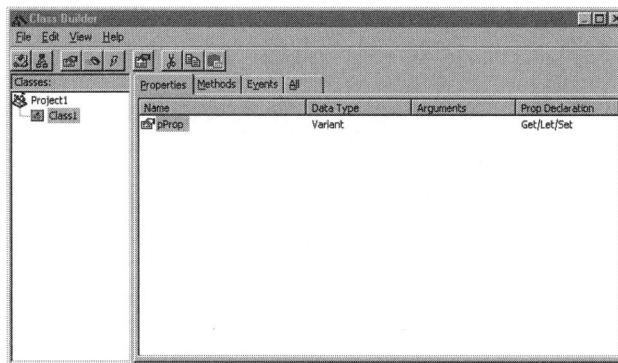

If you right-click anywhere in the tab container area, a pop-up menu will appear that gives you the ability to add a new property, delete a property, perform cut and copy operations, rename the property, and display the detailed specification of each property.

Figure 1.7 illustrates this specification. The specification is housed in the Property
Builder dialog box. Double-clicking in the tab container area also opens this dialog box.

FIGURE 1.7.

*The Property Builder
dialog box enables you
to view and modify
information about each
property.*

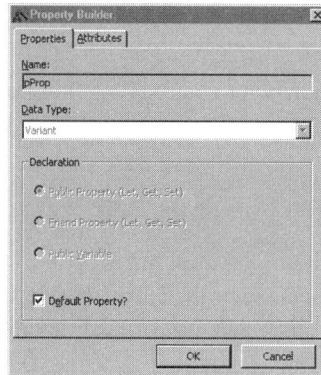

Using the Property Builder, you can specify a name and data type for the property, as
well as declare its scope (Public Property, Friend, Public Variable). You can also specify
that one of the properties is the default property of the class. This way, when you use the
class variable in code, like any other variable, the value of the default property is set or
returned.

The Methods tab is similar to the Properties tab. The Methods tab displays the methods
of the currently selected class or collection. You access it the same way you access the
Property Builder. Using the Method Builder (see Figure 1.8), you can perform the same
maintenance operations as with the Property Builder. The key differences are as follows:

FIGURE 1.8.

*The Method Builder
dialog box enables you
to view and modify
information about each
method.*

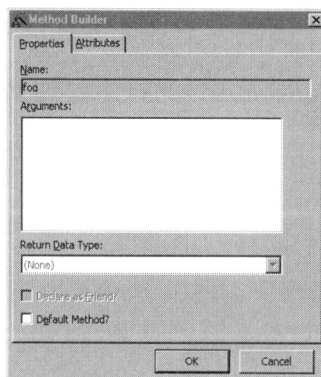

- You can specify a return value. The absence of a return value means that the method is a sub. Otherwise, it is a function.
- You can specify that the method is a friend. This means that it is available to all modules in the project but not to those modules outside the project.
- You can specify whether the current method should be the default method. Thus, if you use the class variable in code as you would a function or a sub, the Visual Basic compiler will use the default method to provide the requested service.
- There is no Prop Declaration column.

The Events tab shows all the events associated with the current class or collection. Because the creation and maintenance of events is the same as that of methods, double-clicking the Events tab opens the Method Builder as well. The difference between a method and event, as far as Class Builder is concerned, is that an event does not require a data type. Finally, the All tab combines the specifications for every member of the current class into one convenient list.

> **Tip**
>
> To convert a class in the Object Model pane into a collection, right-click on the class, and choose Set As Collection. To convert back to a class, right-click on the collection, and choose Set As Class.

Collections and Aggregations of Objects

In the earlier discussion of Class Builder, you came across the word *collection* and probably wondered what it meant. The word *collection* is synonymous with the expression *object collection*. An *object collection* is, well, a collection of objects. It is a list of objects, you might say. By that, you should understand that a collection is, itself, an object. This object holds references to other objects and has methods for adding, accessing, and deleting objects within it. You might view a collection as an inventory of related objects. For instance, borrowing from the banking theme, a collection class AllAccounts might contain a reference to all active accounts that a teller has to process at the end of a day. In code, you would simply iterate through each object reference until the teller processed the last one. Then you could store each object in a database, either as relational records or objects.

An *aggregation* of objects is an object that contains other objects, but not in the sense of a collection. In Visual Basic, a collection is a nice object mechanism for manipulating the similarly named methods and properties of objects. There is no sense of the purpose for using objects in the collection, other than for bundling them into a collection for easy access. With aggregation, though, there is a reason that the aggregate object has other objects. That is, the purpose of the *subordinate object* (contained object) is to serve the aggregate object for some special purpose known only by the aggregate. In a stricter sense of aggregation, a *composite object* determines when an object comes into existence and when it goes out of existence. The lifetime of the composed object is dependent on the composite object. Whew! Let's look at the Sebring example again.

> **Note**
>
> Some more astute object technologists might dispute the definition of the terms *aggregation*, *composition*, and *collection* here. The finer points of these concepts are a matter of intense discussion in some circles. Nevertheless, the fundamental ideas are explained here for simplicity's sake and seldom create a huge problem in practice.

NEW TERM An *aggregate object* is composed of one or more objects that are an integral part of that composite object. Thus, a tree class is composed of branch objects, which are then composed of leaf objects. These branch and leaf objects are said to be tightly coupled to the tree object because if the tree dies, they die. A *collection* of objects holds references to one or more objects that are loosely coupled. That is, a collection can hold references to any kind of object, and the lifetime of those objects isn't dependent on the collection itself. You create collections by using the `Collection` type in Visual Basic.

> **Note**
>
> Of course, you can create a special collection class that serves as a wrapper to an object declared as `Collection`. You can then customize this collection class to create and destroy objects as they are respectively added to and deleted from the collection. However, the wrapper class itself then begins to exhibit the behavior of an aggregate object more than a wrapper.

On further examination, have you noticed that the Sebring is actually composed of other objects? These objects include the tire, the steering wheel, the door, the window, the brake, headlights, and so on. You can say that the Sebring is an aggregate of all these objects. A collection of objects—sometimes hard to identify in the real world—might include the fuse box under the dashboard (another object) or under the hood (another object). Each fuse is an object, and the fuse box is a collection of fuse objects. A key method of each fuse would be to shut down a car's electrical system to avoid major problems.

Objects Talking to Each Other

Humans talk to each other through interfaces (such as mouths for delivering a message and ears for receiving messages). The protocol for communicating is determined by the formal or informal grammatical rules of the language. Likewise, objects talk to each other via their interfaces and the protocols set forth by the designer for carrying out this communication. The public methods and properties of an object together compose the object's interface. This interface implements the protocol of the object. A *protocol* is the rule by which two objects communicate with each other to properly carry out some goal. One object's interface, then, dispatches a message to another object's interface. A *message* is a stimulus in the form of an event, value, an object, or a pointer to a method. Messages are the result of dynamic interaction between objects and actors at runtime. Again, the Sebring class will help you understand the interface.

NEW TERM   An *interface* describes the public methods and properties of an object. It is the facility by which clients communicate with the serving object.

NEW TERM   *Protocol* is the rule by which two objects communicate with each other to properly carry out some goal.

NEW TERM   A *message* is a stimulus in the form of an event, value, an object, or a pointer to a method.

In your fuse box collection, you find that the fuses all interact with the same interface to relay electrical information to the engine (another object). In particular, the information flows to the engine's computer, which is another object, thereby making the engine an aggregate. The fuse box itself has an interface to each electrical component in the Sebring. The protocol is based on the fact that each component expects a particular voltage (message) of electricity through the fuse in order to shut itself down when a problem is encountered. (By *problem*, I mean the state of the car. The subsequent activities related to this state would be the *scenario* for defining how these objects interact.) If the voltage is the one the component expects for normal operations, the electrical message is ignored.

Was that straightforward? In case it wasn't, let's look at another example: the automatic transmission as an object. The usual methods for an automatic transmission are park, drive on normal roads, drive on slight incline, drive on steep incline, drive in reverse, and free the transmission (neutral). Together, these selections (which would be modeled as methods in your models) represent the interface to the transmission. The protocol (gulp!) would involve the nasty details of the stick interaction with the gears, among others.

Let's try another one to be safe. The air conditioner is an object whose behavior is to supply cool air when the weather is hot (forget cold weather for this example—sorry, Northerners). Of course, you don't simply tell the AC to turn itself on and adjust itself to your favorite temperature (but that technology is not far off). The high-level protocol calls for you to push some buttons and slide some levers. These buttons and levers are the interface to the AC. When you push the On button, this event (pushing the button) causes the button's internal methods to send an electric message to the AC to power up. Another way of explaining this power up process is that the AC initializes itself to either default (factory) settings or your previous settings. Other real-world objects have interfaces as well, such as your thermostat in your home, your microwave, and your television, among others. In turn, these objects interface with the object that supplies electricity. Because the real world operates with classes, objects, and their interfaces, why not use the same paradigm in software development?

Understanding Subsystems/Packages

Now that you've become familiar with the nature of classes and objects, it's time to introduce another concept. In the real world, or at least in theory, every object is made up of smaller objects. For instance, humans are made up of organs. In turn, these organs are made up of atoms. Likewise, a well-developed, object-oriented application comprises subsystems (or categories or packages), which are composed of classes (or sometimes other subsystems).

Definition

A *subsystem* is a portion of the application/system that carries out a particular behavior of the entire application/system. This portion can consist of classes as well as other subsystems. For instance, you can design a portion of an application to manage all database retrieval and storage (database subsystem), another to handle the display of data in and retrieval of data from GUI objects (GUI subsystem), and yet another to handle printing and reporting (printing and reporting subsystem). Going back to the Sebring example, the portion of the car (synonymous with *application* for your purposes) that handles the movement energy is the engine. The portion that handles stopping is the braking mechanism. The portion that handles air flow and temperature control is the AC. The engine subsystem (or portion), in turn, consists of different classes of nuts and bolts, as well as other subsystems, such as timing, cooling, starting (ignition), and so on. On another front, your house would be like an application, and it, too, has portions. Your house contains the AC subsystem (with some abstract similarities to the car's AC), the plumbing subsystem, the electrical subsystem, and so on. Get the idea? The class, then, would be the atomic unit (assuming it did not contain other objects).

Subsystems Talking to Each Other

Subsystems (or categories) communicate with each other through classes that play the role of subsystem brokers/agents or subsystem interfaces. If you think of subsystems as themselves being big classes, a class within it would act as an agent on behalf of the subsystem. You might also view this agent class as a diplomat or an ambassador. When two subsystems need to communicate, one dispatches an ambassador's envoy (a message) to the other's ambassador. The hosting ambassador validates the message (making sure it's not a package bomb that might blow up and crash your system). If the ambassador feels the message has come to the right place, it will pass the message on to the proper authorities (some delegated class) for further processing.

For instance, say a user of your application enters some personal information, such as name, address, and so on, and clicks a button to save the data to the database. At a high level, this is simple: Save it to the database straight from the form (or dialog box, for you C++ transplants). However, in OOP, the process is more method-based and organized. The form actually sends a message (packed with the data) to the GUI subsystem, which in turn separates the data from the form objects (that is, text box, list box, and so on) and sends it to a business layer class. This business layer class places each data value to its attributes (or properties), does some business rule processing, and if all is okay, sends this data to the database subsystem, which then saves this data to the database. (This process of saving class property values to the database is called *persistence* because the data persists beyond the current application session.) After you finish reading this book, you will be able to think your applications through in this manner (oops, didn't mean to scare you so soon). The idea of dividing an application into subsystems (or packages) is the core of object-oriented methods.

Working with Design Models

Quite naturally, when you plan the logic behind your object-oriented programming code, you'll need to properly model the relationships between objects. Design models provide pictures that represent an architectural overview of the application you're developing. You can create models and diagrams in Microsoft Visual Modeler, which I'll discuss on Day 3.

A design model you'll work with is the class model. Class models show each class's structure as well as the relationships between classes. Microsoft published a popular three-tier class model that you might find helpful when first learning OOP. The three-tier architecture partitions your application as follows:

- *User Services*, which encapsulate the mechanisms for providing interactivity between the user and the application
- *Business Services*, which encapsulate the business process logic and serve as a bridge between the user and the information repository (or database)
- *Data Services*, which encapsulate the connection between business services and the information repository

Summary

In this chapter, you learned about the fundamentals of object-oriented programming. At the center of this evolving technology are the class and its runtime equivalent, the object. A class is a design-time template that determines the behavior of objects based on it. Visual Basic enables you to perform OOP, using the class module and the Class Builder utility.

The fundamental idea to keep in mind in OOP is that the Visual Basic project must be viewed as a round-trip (or cyclical), evolving process, meaning that the artifacts of the analysis phase will need to be synchronized with the design and construction phases. Without this periodic synchronization process, you will lose the ability to trace the classes you create from the analysis phase down to the construction phase. This is where novice object-oriented programmers, often impatient, become confused and discouraged. When requirements need to be revisited, novice object-oriented programmers can't tell what class corresponds to what entity in the analysis and design models. Traceability, then, is of fundamental importance to object-oriented programming.

Day 2 shows you how to discover and evolve class identities from user requirements (even if you, the developer, will be the primary user) into a use-case model that is the foundation for the class model. Day 3 shows you how to iterate/evolve from the analysis phase to the design phase, meaning that you'll learn how to evolve your project from the use case model to the class and object models. Design tools such as Class Builder, Rational Rose/Visual Basic, and Microsoft Visual Modeler are discussed. Finally, Day 4, "Fundamental Object-Oriented Programming," teaches you how to make classes and sub-systems (class packages) communicate with each other properly. This communication-building process is also associated with the software development (or construction or programming) phase of the project life cycle.

Q&A

Q What is a class?

A A class is an abstract entity that carries out a subset of your user's requirements.

Q What is an abstraction?

A An abstraction is the hiding of an object's private information and operations. Requests for information and services (via operations or methods) must occur by invoking public methods, including Visual Basic's property methods.

Q What is the purpose of class attributes?

A The purpose of attributes is to hold the current state of a class instance.

Workshop

The workshop includes quiz questions to help gauge your grasp of the material. Even if you feel that you totally understand the concepts presented here, you should work through the quiz anyway. The last section is an exercise or two to help reinforce your learning. You'll find the answers to the quiz in Appendix A, "Answers."

Quiz

1. What is one of the chief benefits of object-oriented programming?
2. What is the importance of behavior?
3. Describe the roles that the keywords `Public` and `Private` play in encapsulation?

Exercises

1. Borrowing from the Sebring example, create a list of other subsystems in cars that might be applicable.
2. Again borrowing from the Sebring example, create a list of other properties a car might have. Also, describe what events might change the property values of a car. For instance, the event of driving makes the property `Gas Level` decrease until the gas tank is empty.

DAY 2

Fundamental Object-Oriented Analysis

Yesterday you received a primer on object-oriented programming. Today you learn the fundamentals of object-oriented analysis (OOA). The topics covered include the following:

- OOA's role in solution development
- Realizing the importance of using analysis methods
- Building the foundation for object-oriented analysis
- Identifying user requirements
- Version control for use cases
- Developer training issues
- The schedule-oriented approach to the use-case methodology
- Notating use cases for specific Visual Basic issues
- A sample analysis for the Samsona Bank Teller System

OOA's Role in Solution Development

In the most basic terms, analysis is the series of acts carried out by project team members to break down complex concepts into simpler abstractions. You examine the problem domain in order to formulate a solution.

For many, many years, many programmers have gone through each project life cycle with an enduring and possibly natural enmity toward the analysis process. Programmers who develop applications at home tend to refrain from thorough analysis. The standard thinking is that users don't know how to tell programmers what they want, so programmers assume they themselves know. There is real-world precedence for this. In the days before business management gurus Edward Deming and Peter Drucker came on the scene, most companies often ignored the wants of their customers. (For that matter, monopolies have a natural tendency to ignore customers; think of your utility monopolies' response to your billing complaints.) Then Deming and Drucker came along and led the corporate world toward more customer- and employee-oriented management styles.

Likewise, the three leading figures of the object-oriented software development paradigm shift—Jacobson, Booch, and Rumbaugh (among notable others)—have also led the software development community toward not only object-oriented styles of programming but also user-oriented project planning. That is, the central idea behind object-oriented systems is that objects respond to human users at some point in the execution of a business process. The stimuli are events or messages from the human actor to the application. The response of the objects can incorporate issuing client requests to other external systems, which makes the client system an actor as well (more on actors in a moment).

The important thing to understand about the analysis process is that you must be able to effectively translate the initial set of user requirements into a model or foundation on which your design models can be properly implemented. Such a translation occurs within the context of a project. Planning the development of a solution to an assessed problem cannot occur in a vacuum. You cannot guess at the completion date for a project. Object-oriented analysis provides the best early gauge of the feasibility of successfully completing an object-oriented programming project.

Realizing the Importance of Using Analysis Methods

Now that you've read through the object-oriented programming aspects (there will be plenty more on OOP later), let's step back a bit and discuss analysis. Some think that analysis is a waste of time, and this sentiment is sometimes justified. Most newcomers to

OOP bring an anti-analysis attitude with them into object-oriented projects. This is the favored approach for many programmers because each programmer decides for himself how the application will work and avoids becoming caught up in analysis paralysis. If there is a team of developers, they divide up the user requirements document, code in isolation, and come back together to argue over who is wrong or right, what should be hacked from the current release, and so on. Because of the complexity of user requirements, such an approach is prone to errors, and the user typically ends up with a system he did not ask for or want. To accommodate (or out of sympathy for) the developers (who probably stayed up all night for a whole week), the user says something like "Yeah, this looks okay. I guess I can do my work with this." The application is seldom used or is full of major bugs; eventually, the user returns to the manual way of doing business.

Note

> *Analysis paralysis* is a phase in a project when problem analysis seems to be performed endlessly and without hope of finding a solution.

The same thing applies when you try to implement OOP without doing the necessary analysis. In general, analysis helps find a solution to a business problem; someone's dream can become a high-level, often user-friendly model that evolves into an application. Using a methodology or carrying out some goal(s) to cultivate this evolutionary process is crucial. Perhaps the most widely used methodology is the Objectory method introduced by Ivar Jacobson. It's also generally known as *object-oriented software engineering* (OOSE). With it, you initiate a process of identifying what the current problem is and then help the user identify how she sees herself using the proposed application.

NEW TERM *Methodology* is an organized, disciplined system for doing something in an orderly manner. It's the implementation of a body of methods to achieve a measurable goal.

Pivotal Team Roles in Object-Oriented Analysis

To effectively use OOA to create a solid, easily extensible system using Visual Basic, you should have an understanding of the overall approach to the project. This means that every activity you expect to undertake in creating a Visual Basic application should be reasonably thought out beforehand. That is, you as a Visual Basic developer must accept that you will usually (but not always) wear many hats on a typical development project. These hats (or roles) should be identified and specified. Further, in performing these roles, you will perform tasks related to each role. These tasks, too, must be identified and quantified.

The pivotal players or roles about which you'll be concerned in this chapter are the requirements gatherer, object-oriented analyst, and architect.

The Requirements Gatherer

As a requirements gatherer, you typically interrogate end users, business managers (or domain experts), project managers, or anyone else who has the misfortune of coming across your path. Usually, there is no predefined method for gathering these requirements; you simply draft an almost ad hoc list of questions centered on mouse clicks instead of business processes executed by users. A requirements model is never generated. However, as a requirements gatherer, that's exactly what you want to do. A requirements model captures all the ways the user will use the Visual Basic system you're developing. Figure 2.1 shows a typical requirements model.

FIGURE 2.1.

A requirements model (the initial use-case model) illustrates how the end user will use your system from a business processing perspective.

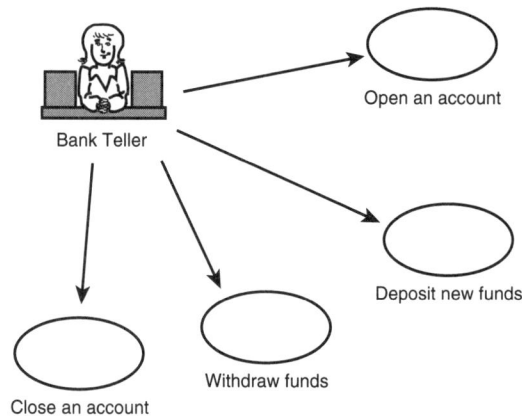

Bank Teller

Open an account

Deposit new funds

Withdraw funds

Close an account

In gathering requirements, you ask both yourself and the user how the system will be used. Initial requirements-gathering activities should shy away from inquiries such as "When you click such and such a button on the screen, what happens next?" You're forcing the user to think like a machine instead of like a business process user. Requirements gathering centered on graphical user interface (GUI) objects focuses on the semantics of clicking controls and moving a mouse, as opposed to the business tasks that the user must accomplish. When centered on GUI objects, requirements gathering often misses the big picture, and the foundation for further analysis activities becomes inefficient as the project evolves.

The Object-Oriented Analyst

As analysts in a traditional project, some developers are probably driven by a simplified focus on making the gathered requirements fit into the Visual Basic project. They quickly produce a list of global or form-level functions that seem to roughly provide the expected system behavior; analysis is over in a heartbeat. Analysis is really design, if that. It becomes quite tempting to grab some programming tips-and-tricks books and start forcing this analysis and design model of functions to incorporate ideas of how the system should work. This is a common concern and is known as fly-by-the-seat-of-your-pants development, or programming by chaos.

Quoting noted object-oriented methodologist Jim Rumbaugh, analysis "is the careful examination of the requirements for a system with the intent of understanding them, exploring their implications, and removing inconsistencies and omissions." Effective analysis builds on the mature (or evolved) requirements model by evolving an ideal structure that endures throughout the life cycle of the proposed system under development. During the early iterations of your analysis processes, you don't want to formulate a detailed list of low-level functions to rush out the door without concern for how the user uses the system and how the system responds to those uses. By *low-level*, I mean that you don't want to worry about which database you're using, which neat trick you want to incorporate to make a MAPI or Windows API call, or similar notions. This is important because changes in vendors, for instance, can necessitate a change in tools or even operating systems. Also, by avoiding the detailed design stuff early in the analysis iteration, you can better concentrate on the activities of the business process user because the analysis model is far simpler than the design model(s).

A mature design model provides direct guidance to your programming activities, whereas an analysis model provides a solid foundation for your design model(s). Figure 2.2 gives you an example of a simple analysis model. Note how it's focused only on high-level business objects when initially created. In the User Services layer of the proposed system, a Teller Interface class encapsulates your understanding of the interaction between the user and the system. Don't worry about button clicks or mouse movements. Also, a Checking Account class and a Savings Account class encapsulate your knowledge of each type of account. You could easily have one class called Account at this stage; it depends on your particular environment. Finally, there's a Persistence class, which is responsible for storing and retrieving information created or modified in your application, as well as eliminating information the user wants destroyed. In the analysis model, it's called *persistence*, as opposed to *database management*, because you don't know whether the data repository will be a database or a flat file (regular text or a binary file you store anywhere on your hard disk). That kind of detail is left to your design model.

The Architect

The role of the architect is to formulate and facilitate the elaboration of the system's architectural foundation. The advantage of understanding this role is that you're able to abstract the project tasks that apply only to architects. This, in turn, helps you focus on those tasks, should such duties be required of you. Without understanding this role, you risk not concentrating on the architecture elaboration process, which often leads to a faulty, pseudo-architecture. As a pseudo-architect in a traditional shop, a developer does what you might call detailed analysis, but it really is ad hoc design. Such developers take the list of functions and manipulate each one to communicate with another. Often, the code for some functions is hidden behind GUI control events (for example, `Command1_Click`) for the sake of convenience (ad-hoc spaghetti architecture). Such architecture makes it extremely difficult to trace application behavior back to the requirements and analysis models.

FIGURE 2.2.

A service model.

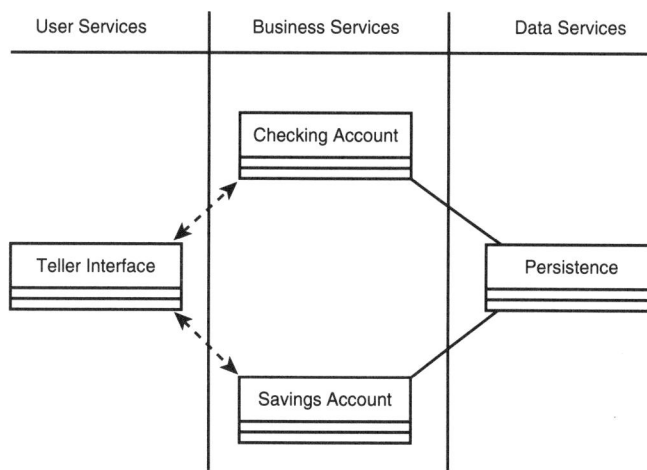

Object-oriented architects work with analysts—and sometimes are the analysts—to ensure that project team members can trace the names of business objects between the requirements and analysis models. Architects also work with designers and developers, but your main concern here is analysis. In traditional analysis, end users and managers assume that programmer-analysts have a nearly perfect understanding of the problem domain. This inevitably results in a decreased emphasis on analysis and increased emphasis on construction activities. Because the gap in knowledge between the users and developers isn't adequately addressed in the beginning, all the members and beneficiaries of the project teams (also known as *stakeholders*) experience levels of stress much higher than necessary as the project approaches its deadline.

NEW TERM   The *problem domain* is the business need being addressed by the proposed system under development.

The driving assumption behind object-oriented analysis, on the other hand, is that the analyst doesn't possess anything close to a perfect knowledge of the problem domain. That is, an acknowledged gap in knowledge exists between the users ordering the application and the manufacturers of that system. To ultimately bridge this gap, all stakeholders in the project depend on the round-trip development process offered by object-oriented technology. Given that, the benefits of the object-oriented analysis approach to Visual Basic developers become clear.

Key Activities in Object-Oriented Development

For any given project, no matter how large or small, you identify or assess a problem and develop a solution to it. Therefore, your projects incorporate a period of time for problem assessment and solution development. Each of these consists of some level of analysis and modeling activities, with solution development exclusively containing design activities. The activities in object-oriented projects typically include (sometimes in a slightly different order) the following:

- Problem assessment (statement)
- Project inception
- Business domain research
- Identification of candidate classes and actors in the problem statement
- Identification of candidate verbs and verb phrases in the problem statement
- Creation of the use-case model
- Creation of the sequence diagram
- Elaboration and construction (with testing)

Problem Assessment

Every application you develop seeks to solve a problem. If you have a problem doing financial calculations by hand, you can use the financial functions in Visual Basic to create a helpful financial calculation application. If you have a problem keeping track of all your clients, you can develop a contact management application. In every software development endeavor, you as a developer seek to assess a given problem.

Problem assessment is the analytical act of identifying the nature of a problem in a given context. For companies large and small, the act of identifying a problem usually coincides with the need to either cut costs or increase revenues. For personal hobbyists, identifying problems might be much more spontaneous, almost whimsical. To properly assess a problem, you have to ask yourself how important the problem is and why you must assess it. Corporate developers must have a reasonable understanding of workgroup-specific business processes and sometimes corporatewide workflow patterns. This knowledge helps provide boundaries around the problem so that any further development activity stays within a well-defined scope.

NEW TERM *Problem assessment* is the act of identifying the nature of a problem in a given context.

Project Inception

For any kind of software development project you undertake, you will undergo a phase known as Inception. The Inception Phase of a project establishes the justification for proceeding further with the development of a solution. You define the scope of the project in the Inception Phase after assessing the problem.

This phase is very important. In it, you honestly assess whether the problem can be adequately solved. For simple, individual projects, the decision might come down to whether you personally have the time and motivation to develop a solution. For larger enterprise applications, however, the decision is much more critical and usually involves hundreds of thousands or millions of dollars. In the latter case, true honesty can save money if the solution seems cost prohibitive. By *true honesty*, I mean that determining whether a problem is worth solving requires adequately analyzing the problem and identifying key abstractions (or initial business concepts) before making a decision about proceeding with a project. Deciding to proceed with the design of a solution because it feels right doesn't justify spending millions of dollars on solution development.

For corporate and commercial projects, the Inception Phase is crucial. In fact, given that such projects are prone to budgetary constraints, the best way to gauge success factors is to iterate through problem assessment and partial analysis for a solution. On many corporate projects, project managers make ad hoc guesses about how long it takes to develop an application. Usually, there is little reasoning behind these guesses, yet companies pour millions of dollars into such projects. This is akin to the old days when wildcatters sunk huge amounts of money into locating oil on the basis of speculation—and usually went bankrupt from these gambles. For corporate projects, schedule gambling is written off, and unwitting programmers are usually blamed for schedule slips. This is particularly true for Visual Basic developers, who must live up to managerial expectation of Visual Basic's ease of use.

Undergoing problem assessment and analysis as a precondition for Inception helps managers make a more realistic estimate about the project's completion. Yes, this is more expensive and probably goes against much of what you've learned about development projects, but it minimizes the unnecessary risks associated with project scheduling.

The Inception Phase for personal projects is much less formal than for corporate projects. Yet it's still a good idea to size up the specific tasks necessary to accomplish your solutions. A model of the business processes affected by the solution you propose provides a common basis of understanding between you, your team members, managers, and your users.

Note

When you develop a Visual Basic application for a company, you are developing a tool that enables a worker to accomplish some task that helps complete a business process. A *business process* is a collection of one or more tasks that provides some value for the company. A *business process model* represents one or more business processes that interact to carry out a goal. Workers who are responsible for carrying out these processes are *task owners*, and their manager is the *process owner*. These personnel are also represented in the business process model. For instance, in a bank, there would be a loan application acceptance and entry process, a loan approval process, and a loan acceptance and delivery process.

Business Domain Research

Whether you develop software in-house for a client or commercially as an entrepreneur, you need to understand how the intended user will use the system within his or her environment. Normally, you would conduct this kind of research in the Elaboration Phase of the project. During this phase, not only are you doing domain or market research, but you're also establishing the foundation of your system's application in the least risky manner possible. However, when projects are sensitive to monetary constraints or time-to-market scheduling, you should do domain research as part of Inception. This gives you a better idea of what's at stake for your project and provides an intelligence report on customer psychology, the extent that customers will use the system (use cases), and the visibility of the project to executives.

Tip

In the Visual Basic community, it has become normal practice to insert hundreds of lines of code into forms, use highly publicized tips and tricks, and slap together a nice graphical user interface with slick features. The resulting system, typically based on ad hoc assumptions, is deemed to have an architecture. However, this process of developing doesn't lend itself to

> establishing a sound architectural foundation for a valuable application. A good architecture isn't only valuable to you as a developer, but it's also crucial for your customer, especially if that customer happens to be a large corporation.

Companies generally implement software systems as corporate assets. Some other Visual Basic programmer will likely need to evolve the system long after you're gone. An architecture that has a clear separation of concerns in the form of objects and components, together with artifacts such as class models and design diagrams, represents a project that has a high chance of success in the short and long term. This book itself was developed with an architecture in which chapters are treated as components and sections as objects. The best lesson you could learn is that a good architecture is beneficial for your reputation and the viability of the customer.

Sample Problem: A Bank Teller Information System

One of six branches of the Second Bank of Carrollton, a city in Texas, has a team of bank tellers who have been manually performing tasks under the retail banking process umbrella. To open a new checking or savings account, a teller does the following tasks:

- Physically gather the necessary paperwork.
- Have the customer decide on a preferred type of account by reading from several brochures.
- Fill out a paper application in the customer's presence.
- Have the customer fill out a signature card.
- Establish a session on a mainframe host terminal with a check account history verification system.
- On approval, call a central retail banking worker to obtain an available account number. That worker establishes a mainframe session on a system that tracks all accounts for the bank across the city.

The branch manager finds this process too time-consuming. The average time to open a new account is a little more than an hour. She calls Samsona Software Company for help. Samsona uses object-oriented methodologies to solve such problems.

As a consultant for Samsona, you're given the job. You ask questions about the customer's domain, taking notes on your notebook computer. You discover that the check account history verification system sometimes takes five to ten minutes to respond to the teller. You also find that bank policy requires that new account applications be done in

▼ pencil to avoid the mess of correcting pen-based writing on applications. There are six tellers total for each branch. By now, you're sweating a bit, and you roll up your sleeves.

NEW TERM A *domain*, in this context, represents the set of business tasks and users affected by the solution you design and develop.

The branch manager likes your diligence. She takes you aside and mentions that if you can develop an application for this branch within three months, she will make a recommendation to bank executives to deploy the application citywide. You ask her how she arrived at three months. "It's a guess. We need it as soon as possible. Can you do it?" You tell her that you'll need time to ask the tellers questions. "Well, I don't have the luxury of having a teller answer too many questions. Can you just ask me? I know what

▲ they do." You agree, although you still want to question the hands-on tellers.

Elaboration and Construction

After you have decided that you understand what's at stake in solving a problem, you can begin to *elaborate* your knowledge into a solution. Solution development builds on the analysis activities you perform during the Inception Phase and is also known as the *Elaboration* and *Construction Phases*. During solution development, you elaborate through analysis and design in an iterative and incremental manner. This means that any discoveries about the context of the problem will cause you to loop through the artifacts of your knowledge and update them. You will identify additional use cases, create and revise analysis and design models, and re-interview customers. After you have iterated through analysis and design to the point where new discoveries are trivial, you can begin Construction. The Construction Phase is that point in the project when you develop the actual Visual Basic code, using the design models you created. The project plan is based on the activities necessary for solution development.

Tip

In many industries, especially the telecommunications and engineering industries, business terminology is often vague or conflicting. Terms are confusingly interchangeable. Confusing terminology is a major factor in the failure of a software development project. The nouns in use-case documentation identify candidate class types and business concepts. This terminology is one of the pillars of the proposed system's architecture. As part of your separation of concerns, you must find clear, distinct definitions of business terms so that your classes and components can be properly built. Without making this distinction, you will find it difficult to communicate with customers, new project personnel you hire, and even yourself, when you are thinking through a problem and solution.

Use Cases and the Jacobson Methodology

When Microsoft released version 5 of Visual Basic Enterprise, the Visual Basic language moved into the ballpark of object-oriented languages (although only as a pinch hitter perhaps, but close enough). The capability to create classes whose interfaces can be implemented by other classes and the capability to create complex ActiveX components have made Visual Basic a serious commercial development tool. Added to that is the automation of the design process with the help of Microsoft Visual Modeler. However, Visual Basic doesn't help with the discovery and identification of classes, actors (human and external system), and use cases. To compound this situation, most Visual Basic programmers don't have an object-oriented background, which leaves the programmers resorting to traditional, familiar ways of developing software.

In reality, solid system architectures and class structures never evolve or mature properly when programmers don't know how to discover use cases and classes—it's like pouring new wine into old wineskin bottles. As a result, Visual Basic, which is a strong development tool for implementing object technology, will continue to be maligned. The remainder of this chapter explains how to use object-oriented analysis techniques—specifically use case identification and modeling—to help you successfully initiate the analysis process and give Visual Basic a better name in the development community.

The Problem Statement

▼ REAL WORLD

Figure 2.1, earlier in the chapter, illustrates a simple use case model. Of course, the elements within a use case model don't appear out of thin air. As an analyst, you ask the user, "In what ways do you want to use the system?" The user, who is a teller within your development context, responds that she wants to be able to open an account, close an account, deposit new funds, and withdraw funds. Because the teller uses the system, that teller is an actor in your system. Notice how each phrase includes an important verb, such as *open*, *close*, *deposit*, and *withdraw*. These verb phrases, taken together with the actor performing these verbs, provide the context for your system. When formally written down, these phrases become the core verbiage in what's called the *problem statement*. In other words, a problem statement provides the formal boundaries (or context) for the foundation of your Visual Basic application. Figure 2.3 illustrates a problem statement.

When the problem statement has matured over one or more sessions with *domain experts* (users who are knowledgeable about a particular area of concern), you'll want to peruse this document to identify key nouns and verbs. The list of nouns becomes a list of candidate actors or classes, whereas the list of verbs provides a candidate list of business processes carried out by actors. (Keep in mind that actors are human users of your system or external systems that interact with your system.) These verbs can also indicate

▼

and verbs require further analysis to determine whether they are truly actors, classes, business processes (or use cases), and/or methods.

FIGURE 2.3.

Using a word processor such as Microsoft Word, you can document a plain English, high-level description of how the user(s) will use the system you're developing with Visual Basic.

Problem Statement

Samsona Bank Teller System

The teller will use the Samsona Bank Teller System to better facilitate the process of maintaining bank accounts. Each teller needs to be able to open an account, close an account, deposit new funds, and withdraw funds.

2

Identifying Candidate Classes and Actors in the Problem Statement

Based on your problem statement, the following list represents candidate classes and actors:

Teller

Samsona Bank Teller System

Process

Bank accounts

Account

Funds

In analyzing each actor/class candidate, you and/or your team determine whether each item is meaningful to the context of the business processes being addressed by your system. By *meaningful*, I mean something that represents a role performed by the user or external system, helps the user produce a product or service that is valuable to the business, and isn't too vaguely defined within the context of your proposed system. For instance, the word *funds* is too vague for your system because the teller doesn't create the funds nor place the funds into your system. She merely accepts funds from her customer or gives funds to him. Therefore, funds are eliminated from your list of candidates.

If you're a beginning or intermediate object-oriented practitioner (an architect, analyst, designer, programmer, and tester), you might ask yourself why there is no mention of the customer in the problem statement. Answer: The customer isn't in the context of your system (your problem domain). The exchanging of cash or information between the teller

▼ and the customer is outside the scope of the Samsona Bank Teller System. Recall from the problem statement that your system helps the teller "to better facilitate the process of maintaining bank accounts." The teller interfaces with her customer in one context and then interfaces with your system in another. Your problem domain is concerned only with the second context. Business process engineering (the designing and modeling of business tasks/responsibilities and events at the enterprise or workgroup level) would likely be concerned with the first context.

Tip

> If you encounter new, possibly helpful requirements that are outside the scope of your current project increment or iteration, the team's architect and project manager should decide in which increment/iteration of the software the requirements should be incorporated. An *increment* incorporates a new feature or subsystem to the application. An *iteration* results in an EXE file being released to users or another project team.

Returning to your list of candidate actors/classes, you'll notice that *teller* is obviously an important noun because this is the main actor who will use your system. Therefore, you now have your first actor. The noun *Samsona Bank Teller System* is the name of your system, and at this point, let's assume that you don't have a compelling reason to model it as an actor or a class. Therefore, it's no longer a viable candidate.

Note

> In general, you wouldn't model your application as an actor or a class. However, it could be modeled as a subsystem or package if it were part of a suite of applications.

The noun *process* describes the act of maintaining accounts and is too vague to be anything more than a descriptive noun that helps express the problem statement more fully for the system developers. It, too, is no longer a viable candidate.

The noun *bank accounts* is a collection of accounts. Within the sentence that mentions bank accounts, you see that they are the main objects that the teller manages and, as a collection, are a strong candidate for a class (or more specifically, a collection class).

Tip

> If you discover plural nouns in your problem statement that are of significance to your system, make a design note to yourself that such nouns might be a collection class, which Visual Basic supports. An example of plural nouns is a noun with an *s* at the end that implies more than one of the noun.

▼

▼ Along similar lines, the noun *account* is also a strong candidate for a class. Again, the noun *funds* doesn't fit within your context and is therefore not a viable candidate. Now you have a more streamlined, definitive list of actors and candidates that resembles Table 2.1.

TABLE 2.1. STRONG CANDIDATE ACTORS AND CLASSES.

Noun	Type
Teller	Actor
Bank Accounts	Class
Account	Class

You might also want to journalize the reasons for rejecting a candidate. This list becomes an artifact that might help future stakeholders on this project or other enterprise projects so that even the process of analyzing requirements and use cases can be reused throughout the company.

Identifying Candidate Verbs and Verb Phrases in the Problem Statement

Your candidate list of verbs and verb phrases includes the following:

Use

Facilitate

Maintaining bank accounts

Needs

Open an account

Close an account

Deposit new funds

Withdraw funds

Again, you want to model only meaningful verbs that provide value to the problem domain. This list of verbs and verb phrases eventually provides the context for a use case model, which is roughly similar to the functional model of the Object Modeling Technique (OMT); a class model; and an object model. (The class model and sequence diagram are discussed on Day 3, "Fundamental Object-Oriented Design," and Day 4, "Fundamental Object-Oriented Programming.") Some verbs in your list of candidate verbs will be superfluous. Identifying such verbs might seem an elusive goal to begin-
▼ ners, but with only a few practice runs you should develop a good feel for the process.

▼ The verb *use* is too generic. It restates what you already know: The user will use your system. Hence, you discard this verb from the list.

The verb *facilitate* is merely an expression of how the user uses the system; it doesn't convey any behavior that is meaningful for the actor (teller) or the system.

Maintaining bank accounts sounds meaningful because, within the context of your system, the teller will do something with bank accounts, which at first glance might include some sort of management of such accounts. Let's keep it.

The verb *needs* conveys only that the following information is a requirement. Therefore, although the information that follows could very well pass from candidate to real verb, the verb *needs* itself doesn't mean anything to the behavior of the system. Let's discard this verb.

Open an account, *close an account*, *deposit new funds*, and *withdraw funds* sound like actions the teller needs to perform with your system. A normal part of the teller's business processes is to open and close accounts, as well as deposit and withdraw funds. Let's keep these.

> **IDENTIFYING TRUE ACTORS**
> Keep in mind that within the requirements context of your system, a human teller uses your system, not a customer. If it were a customer, the teller would need to be an automated teller machine, and, therefore, opening and closing accounts would not be meaningful to your system for logistical and legal reasons.

This is your list of verb phrases:

Maintaining bank accounts

Open an account

Close an account

Deposit new funds

Withdraw funds

Here is a gray area for most object-oriented (OO) novices. At this point, you could continue on to the use case model and then on to design. However, the trained practitioner will notice that there is a potential conflict or overlapping of verbs. You have just identified that your actor, the teller, can maintain accounts, as well as open and close accounts, and withdraw and deposit funds. Therefore, a question arises: Exactly what does *main-*
▼ *taining bank accounts* mean? Is it not the operation (within your context) of opening and

▼ closing accounts and withdrawing and depositing funds? The intermediate object-oriented practitioner might say that it is and proceed to eliminate the phrase *maintaining bank accounts* from the list of system uses. However, the advanced practitioner might say that *maintaining bank accounts* could be a high-level description of the grouping of operations represented as *open account*, *close account*, *withdraw funds*, and *deposit funds*. The assessment you choose is entirely up to you; however, for the sake of simplicity, let's discard *maintaining bank accounts* because it's a grouping of the other verbs. Now your list looks like this:

Open an account

Close an account

Deposit new funds

Withdraw funds

Do	Don't
DO create a list of candidate nouns and verbs, based on key concepts in the problem statement and/or other existing requirements documents.	DON'T move beyond the problem statement until all ambiguous nouns and verbs are resolved.
DO double-check to ensure that candidates that you decide to remove from your list are indeed unworthy.	DON'T spend more than a few hours figuring out a list of candidate classes and verbs for most applications. For all applications, DON'T spend more than four or five days total.
DO create a journal of all candidates that you removed from your list, for future reference.	

The Use-Case Model

The use-case model captures the meaningful verbs you discovered, together with the actor and business domain classes that support each *use case*. A use case is an identified use by the actor of the system under development. In its simplest form, a use case is a description of one of many ways, called *transactions*, that a user uses your system. The user (or human actor) performs a sequence of steps (or events) from beginning to end; that is what a use case captures. A use case can be *customized* (or instantiated) to capture how the user executes the use case for a given scenario.

For instance, the teller can open an account (which is a use case), but how does the teller open an account when the customer wants to open it with more than $10,000 in cash? As
▼ you might know, in this situation the teller's bank must file some paperwork with the

▼ federal government to comply with laws that govern bank transactions involving cash amounts of more than $10,000. This scenario, then, is a different instance (or customization) of the use case Open Account. It's certainly different than opening an account with less than $10,000 in cash. Use case scenarios (and their corresponding sequence diagrams) describe each path (or instantiation) the use case can take.

Now you should re-examine the use-case model in Figure 2.1. This use-case model is the end result (or artifact) of your initial analysis process. At this point, you're proud to have completed your first use-case model—so proud, in fact, that you race off to display your stroke of genius to the domain experts (expert users or managers) who own the business process(es) behind this model.

At first, the experts are pleasantly surprised and impressed. They brag about you to a teller who will use the system. The teller is pleased that progress is being made, but he notices something missing. He needs to be able to look up the customer's account information before closing the account to make sure that the customer doesn't owe money to the bank and is authorized to close the account. Also, he might want to view the account information to answer a customer's questions.

In the traditional analysis process, you would have to restructure the data flow diagrams in various places and redo the program code (because you probably already started coding the requirements). This rework usually involves patching in the new functionality, meaning that new global functions are inserted in some module somewhere or the code is tucked behind a button on a form. Some programmers are not even this nice; they might growl that the requested feature was not in the original specs and therefore cannot be incorporated.

With the object-oriented analysis approach, such crucial change requests are easily incorporated, provided they fit naturally within the context of your problem domain. Clearly, the viewing of account information is a mission-critical feature (as each of the project's stakeholders agree) and, as such, needs to be added to your use case model. Because you have done no coding, the only extra time you need is for inserting another use case into your model and updating the problem statement (another often overlooked step). Figure 2.4 shows your updated problem statement. Figure 2.5 represents the updated use case model. In Figure 2.5, I've added a use case, *View Account Information*, that captures the activity in which the teller needs to view his or her customer's account information.

The Sequence Diagram

As alluded to earlier, a *sequence diagram* (also known as an *interaction diagram* or *event trace diagram*) is a diagrammatic representation of a specific instance of a use case. This
▼ specific use case instance is called a *scenario*. A scenario is a sequence of steps taken by

▼ a human actor while performing a given use case. There are two types of scenarios: a *normal scenario* and an *abnormal scenario*. A sequence diagram captures the interactions of an actor and objects in your application for a given scenario.

FIGURE 2.4.

The updated problem statement.

Problem Statement

Samsona Bank Teller System

The teller will use the Samsona Bank Teller System to better facilitate the process of maintaining bank accounts. Each teller needs to be able to open an account, view account information, close an account, deposit new funds, and withdraw funds.

FIGURE 2.5.

The updated use-case model.

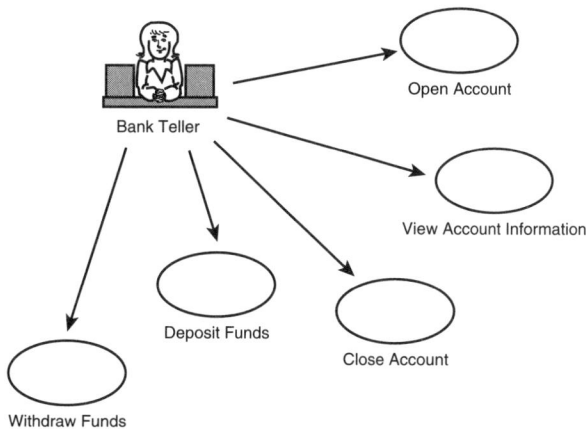

The normal scenario captures the normal interaction between the actor and the system. At the analysis level, the system is represented by the main domain object that is the object affected by the actor's activities. You don't care about forms or buttons or interfaces at this point. These objects will be exposed during the design iteration (or phase). In diagramming a normal scenario, you're asking yourself and your project stakeholders what actions the actor will normally carry out when there are no anomalies or error conditions.

A use case can take alternative paths, each of which is still normal. For instance, the use case Open Account could have at least two alternative normal scenarios: Open Savings Account and Open Checking Account.

Abnormal scenarios capture use case paths that take into consideration anomalies and error conditions. For instance, an abnormal path for Close Account might be "The account being closed does not exist." Also, for the Withdraw Funds use case, you'll have
▼ a scenario that deals with the situation in which there are not enough funds to withdraw.

▼ To build a list of normal and abnormal scenarios to illustrate in your sequence diagrams, you need to interview domain experts and end users. Assuming this has been done, let's list the current scenarios (see Table 2.2).

TABLE 2.2. A LIST OF USE CASES AND THEIR RESPECTIVE SCENARIOS.

Use Case	Scenario
Open an Account	The customer is a new customer with no previous accounts and has the minimum required balance.
	The customer has an existing account that is active.
	The customer has an existing account that is inactive.
	The customer is new but doesn't have the minimum required balance.
	The customer is a new customer with no previous accounts but wants to deposit more than $10,000 in cash.
Close an Account	An active account exists, and the customer is authorized to close it.
	The account being closed is inactive.
	The customer isn't authorized to close the account.
	The customer is authorized to close the account, but the account is deficient, or the customer owes money to the bank.
Deposit New Funds	An active account exists, and the customer is authorized to deposit money in it.
	The customer isn't authorized to deposit money in the account.
	The amount being deposited exceeds $10,000 in cash.
Withdraw Funds	An active account exists, and the customer is authorized to withdraw money from it.
	The customer isn't authorized to withdraw money from the account.
	The teller tries to withdraw, at the customer's request, more money than is available.

For simplicity's sake, you'll concentrate on the first sequence diagram for the Open an Account use case. Assume that you had a use case meeting with the users and domain experts, who then elaborated on the steps involved.

The First Sequence Diagram

As noted in Table 2.2, the first scenario is the normal path that reads "The customer is a new customer with no previous accounts and has the minimum required balance." Before
▼ diagramming this scenario, you should elaborate on the steps involved. A good format

▼ for proceeding would be to identify the scenario that belongs to the use case. You assign a unique identifier to the use case as well as the scenario, as follows:

Use Case 001: Open an Account

Scenario 01: The customer is a new customer with no previous accounts and has the minimum required balance.

Step 1: The teller provides the customer information to the system.

Step 2: The teller wants to check the customer's checking history with Telecheck.

Step 3: When the teller sees that the customer has a good checking history, the teller provides the opening deposit balance to the system.

Step 4: The teller prints out the new account information.

Notice that in elaborating on the steps involved in this use case, you uncovered some more significant nouns and verbs. They are as follows:

Nouns

Customer information

Customer

System

Checking history

Telecheck

Opening deposit balance

Account information

Verbs

Provide the customer information to the system

Check the customer's checking history

Provide the opening deposit balance to the system

Print out the new account information

Before creating the sequence diagram, you must again determine which nouns and verbs are significant.

Each of the nouns *customer information* and *account information* contains a word that provides a strong clue as to its importance in your proposed system: *information*. When users use words such as *customer information* or *account information*, these almost
▼ always imply properties (or attributes) of classes in your system. They certainly imply

▼   relational database tables. Because the words *customer* and *account* are so pivotal in your domain, the architects, analysts, and lead designers agree that these should be nominal domain classes. Let's keep them.

The noun *customer* is another representation of *customer information*. You already decided to incorporate a nominal class named *customer*, so this is a repetition. You can discard it.

The noun *system* is a more generic reference to your application name, which is *Samsona Bank Teller System*. If you want the analysis-view use case to remain generic enough to be reused across your enterprise, it's probably best to leave it as *system*. However, if you decide that the actual application name is more meaningful, by all means use the full system name. Because you have already identified the system as the Samsona Bank Teller System, let's use the full name. Thus, you just replace the word *system* with *Samsona Bank Teller System*.

The noun *checking history* is an interesting one. For simplicity's sake, you have omitted the fact that there is more than one kind of account in banking systems. Furthermore, in your domain (or context), the domain experts and users did not mention any particular type of account. After a quick meeting with these stakeholders, you agree that for this release of the system, you will not consider the various kinds of accounts. Therefore, *checking history* becomes a nominal class, but not a specialization of the `Account` class you already identified in your earlier analysis. This is a very, very important point that many OO novices miss entirely. Do not create classes and actors simply because it seems logical. Stick to the project plan. Such deviations, although thoughtful, usually slow down the object-oriented process, which prompts many to exaggerate the length of time OO projects typically take. However, with practice or a good mentor, the project will soon fall into a rhythm, and slowness will give way to deliveries of the system in increments and iterations.

The noun *Telecheck* is, in English grammar, an indirect object; it's on the receiving end of the action initiated by the teller. However, you don't know exactly what Telecheck means, so you ask the experts. They tell you that it's a vendor who provides research services to the bank. The teller views the information supplied by Telecheck to determine whether the customer can establish an account. On further investigation, you discover that there is an electronic interface between the bank teller's machine and the vendor. Through this interface, the teller sends customer information to Telecheck for verification and research. The research results are returned directly to the terminal screen in the current system. Based on this behavior, you conclude that Telecheck is an actor you can stereotype as an *external system*. Therefore, you promote it from noun to distinct actor. You'll have to update your use-case model with your new actor. Figure 2.6 shows the
▼   new use-case model, including the Telecheck external system actor.

▼ **FIGURE 2.6.**

The external system actor Telecheck is incorporated into your use-case model.

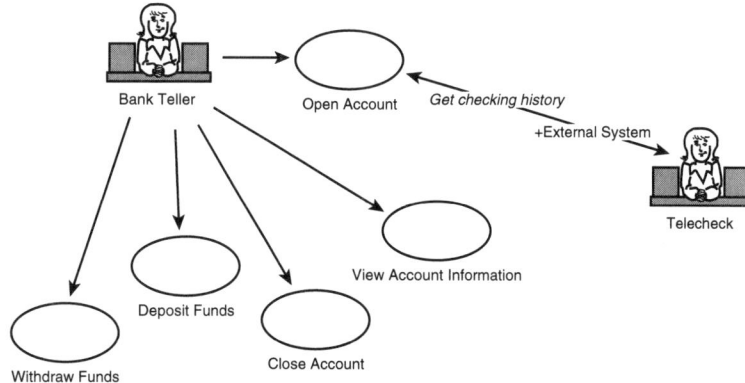

2

The noun *opening deposit balance* is a monetary amount. You might be tempted to model it as a class, but does it really exhibit behavior or have attributes? If it were a candidate class, it would have only one attribute (or property), and that would be Value. Identifying classes and members of classes (properties and methods) isn't always an easy process, and even the very best object technologists admit that sometimes they don't correctly identify classes the first time. On further analysis, you discover that *opening deposit balance* is actually a property of your Account class. How did you gather this? The adjective *opening* provides a big clue. It implies that something other than the object *balance* is going to fluctuate at some point in time. Balances fluctuate, but so do accounts. Then you remember that when you receive a monthly account statement from your bank, there is a beginning balance and an ending balance. Because the account statement is merely a snapshot (or instance) of your account information, you finally decide that Balance is an attribute of the Account class. In general, a good rule of thumb to use (loosely) is that if a candidate class has only one property (or attribute) and no methods, it can be a property of a larger class.

The verb phrase *provides the customer information to the system* (*system* now being *Samsona Bank Teller System*) indicates an action taken by the teller against the system. This action is also known as an *event*. You decide that this is a valid event, and, therefore, you incorporate this verb phrase into your sequence diagram.

The verb phrase *check the customer's checking history* is an action the teller carries out, using the interface to the Telecheck system. Therefore, you should incorporate it into your sequence diagram.

The verb phrase *provides the opening deposit balance to the system* (system now being *Samsona Bank Teller System*) specifies information about the new account, supplied by ▼ the teller. You should incorporate it into your sequence diagram.

▼ The verb phrase *prints out the new account information* is also an event initiated by the teller against the system. Therefore, you should incorporate it into your sequence diagram.

> **Note**
>
> Because the teller is specifying that account information be printed out, this suggests that *print* is a possible method for your `Account` class. This is true of each of your verbs and verb phrases; they become possible methods for the class indicated in the indirect object part of the sentence or phrase.

Now you are ready to create your sequence diagram. Note that *Samsona Bank Teller System* will be represented by some class that implements one of its behaviors. Your lists of nominal nouns and verb phrases look like this:

Nouns

Customer

Samsona Bank Teller System

Checking history

Telecheck

Account (Property: Balance)

Verbs

Provide the customer information to the Samsona Bank Teller System

Check the customer's checking history

Provide the opening deposit balance to the Samsona Bank Teller System

Print out the new account information

Figure 2.7 shows your sequence diagram. You can use stick man figures, the Jacobson symbol for actors, for the teller and Telecheck. Although Telecheck is a machine-based system, you still model it as a stick man actor. The lines with the arrow at one end represent events and actions being carried out by actors and domain class instances (or objects). The rectangle preceding each line is called the *focus of control bar*. These bars indicate that each line protruding from it is part of the same event or action. For instance, the `Teller`-initiated event `Provide Info` is the only event in the teller's focus of control (or duration of a single event or action). However, both `Check` lines, as well as the `Supply History` and `Display History` lines, are all part of the check history event initiated by the `Teller`. Rational Rose/Visual Basic enables you to do this type of modeling
▼ in an automated fashion.

▼ **FIGURE 2.7.**

The sequence diagram shows the stimuli being sent from one object to another. The main actor, the Teller, initiates the events in the diagram and therefore is the first object displayed on the left.

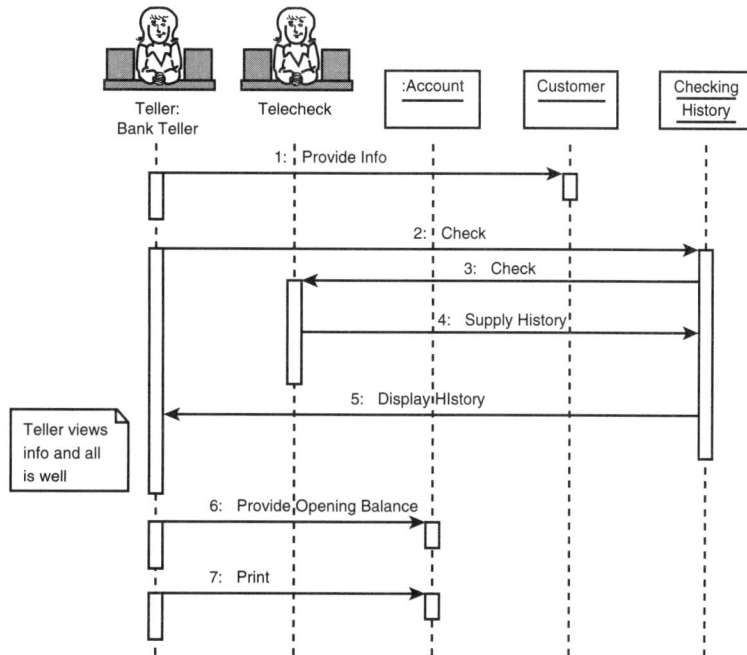

Note

Rational Rose/Visual Basic, which is based on the Unified Modeling Language (UML), is available for a hefty price from Rational Corporation (www.rational.com). At Microsoft's Web site (www.microsoft.com), Visual Modeler is available free to owners of Visual Basic Enterprise; however, it doesn't incorporate use cases, so you can't do sequence diagrams in it.

If you don't have the resources to purchase Rational Rose, do it by hand. There are some rumors that Visio's latest version offers features for the UML.

The Analysis Class Model

By now you've identified a collection class (BankAccounts) and several classes (Account, Customer, CheckingHistory). The initial class model will have these three classes as model items, as shown in Figure 2.8.

Notice that the collection class BankAccounts contains many Account class instances (or objects). The darkened black diamond indicates this relationship, which in Visual Basic would be represented as ByVal (as opposed to just ByRef). This relationship is named *Has*, which is another way of saying that BankAccounts contains many Account objects.

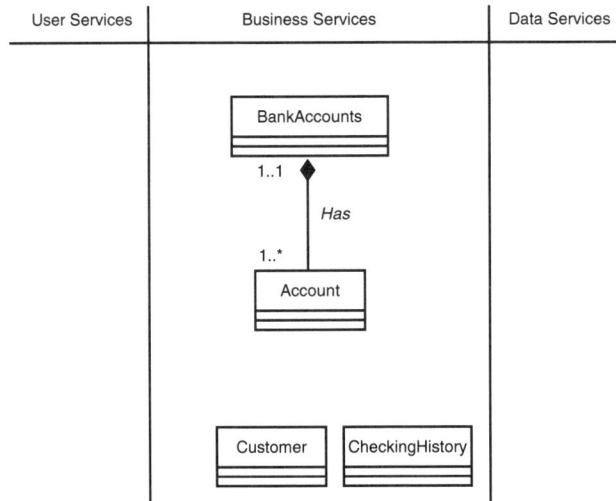

FIGURE 2.8.

The initial class model.

The notations 1..1 and 1..* together are known as the relationship's *cardinality*. That is, because there is only one BankAccounts object, its cardinality is 1..1; because you can have one to an unlimited number of Account objects in your collection, Account's cardinality in the relationship is 1..*. The asterisk (*) represents an unlimited number. The Customer and CheckingHistory classes are relationships that have meaning only with respect to the actors in your system. These actors' events can be formalized in your system through *control objects*, a subject you will examine on Day 3. Day 3 covers the concept of the HasA, IsA, and Uses relationships in more detail.

Summary

Today you learned that the three primary roles usually involved in the use case identification process are the requirements gatherer, the object-oriented analyst, and the architect. You saw that the requirements gatherer typically interrogates end users, business managers (or domain experts), and project managers to draft both a problem statement and optionally an initial requirements model. The object-oriented analyst then carefully examines the requirements model to understand the requirements and elaborate on the requirements model, to assess the implications of each requirement, and to remove inconsistencies and requirements that have been discovered to be no longer valid. Object-oriented architects work with analysts and designers to ensure that project team members can trace the names of business objects between the list of requirements, analysis models, and design models. Architects sometimes perform the roles of both the analyst and designer; otherwise, the architect is a mediator and final decision-maker of the system architecture. With the advent of the software reuse structure of the business organization, these roles will become more specialized (partitioned into smaller roles).

You next learned that the problem statement is used to capture, in plain English, how the users see the system helping them complete their business processes. From this problem statement, the analyst and architect identify and list meaningful nouns and verbs, which helps the technicians identify potential actors, classes, class behavior, and use cases. After a list of these objects is drafted, the superfluous or vague items are discarded in favor of those with stronger meaning in the current problem domain (or business context). The main artifacts of the analysis process are the problem statement, the use-case model, and an analysis class model.

On Day 3, you will learn how to take the artifacts of the analysis process and create a more refined design class model, design-view scenario diagrams, and other design artifacts.

Q&A

Q Are there distinct transitions between the phases of a project, or do the phases overlap?

A They typically overlap.

Q What is analysis?

A Analysis is the series of acts carried out by project team members to break down complex concepts into simpler abstractions.

Q What's the central idea behind object-oriented systems?

A The central idea behind object-oriented systems is that objects respond to human users at some point in the execution of a business process.

Q What is an important goal of object-oriented analysis?

A The important thing to understand about the analysis process is that you must effectively translate the initial set of user requirements into a model or foundation on which your design models can be properly implemented.

Workshop

The workshop includes quiz questions to help gauge your grasp of the material. Even if you feel that you totally understand the concepts presented here, you should work through the quiz anyway. The last section is an exercise that you might work through to help reinforce your learning. You'll find the answers to the quiz in Appendix A, "Answers."

Quiz

1. What is at least one benefit of object-oriented analysis?
2. What is a methodology?
3. Describe the importance of use cases in analysis.
4. What are the three primary roles performed during analysis?

Exercise

You've been asked by a local insurance company to help it manage its large piles of paperwork. The manager with whom you interface says she wants to keep the application simple. She explains that she wants to place bar codes on each document and scan them in as images. Using a wand to read it, she and her staff of five employees could use the bar code to help access the stored image corresponding to the hard copy document. She doesn't want each worker to have access to another worker's stored images after they have been archived. Stored documents flagged as having problems should be electronically brought to the manager's attention. The project was funded based on the manager's and boss's conviction, and they both estimated it should take only two weeks to develop. There are no written requirements documents, but the manager wants you to document the specifications for the system.

(a) Determine how you would approach the Inception Phase.

(b) What use cases and scenarios have you identified?

(c) What actors have you discovered?

(d) Is this project feasible? Why or why not?

DAY 3

Fundamental Object-Oriented Design

Yesterday you learned the fundamental concepts of object-oriented analysis. Today you'll learn fundamental object-oriented design (OOD). In particular, this chapter discusses the following:

- Understanding OOD's role in solution development
- Using Rational Rose/Visual Basic and Microsoft Visual Modeler
- Dividing a proposed Visual Basic application into subsystem packages
- Naming subsystem packages, classes, and objects
- Understanding advanced design issues: design patterns
- Gearing up for code implementation

OOD's Role in Solution Development

Like analysis, design is usually a whirlwind process for many developers. Decisions about the detail architecture of the proposed system under development are made, for the most part, on an ad hoc basis. Typically, one individual arrives at such crucial decisions in an isolated setting, using his thought processes from a previous whirlwind design process to dictate the design process for the current domain. There is no sanity check (or organized feedback) from fellow developers, analysts (if any), and domain experts.

This isn't entirely the programmer's fault, however. Executives and managers, accustomed to the mainframe application development processes, have seldom established their IS and IT departments as they would other business groups—that is, with no separation between a designer's role and a programmer's role, between the architect and the project manager. Generally, programmers are expected to double as designers (and sometimes analysts, architects, testers, documenters, and so on). For commercial and independent entrepreneurial developers, you will undoubtedly wear all these hats.

Solution development, and particularly system design, should be a very careful, methodical process. Because Visual Basic isn't quite object-oriented (OO), you have to be even more careful—without excessive worry, though. During the design phase, you want to pursue different pattern and coding strategies, based on the initial architecture exposed by the analysis phase. Architectural flaws discovered during design are far less costly than those discovered during the actual development phase. This is because during design, no coding is done (except for evolving a prototype as a sanity check for proof of concept). The artifacts of design are nonprogramming models, meaning that when logic flaws are discovered, those flaws can be easily corrected by modifying the corresponding document. When you skip or skim past design, the inevitable flaws you encounter during programming cost you the following:

- Many extra hours of overtime
- Unnecessarily increased levels of stress
- Abnormally high levels of impatience among users and managers
- Personnel turnover
- Faulty programmer assumptions about the system, made in isolation
- Excessive cost overruns
- An unusually high increase in the risk of project failure

Programmers who have never tried implementing design in their software development repertoire criticize this phase as wasteful, time-consuming, and pointless. Such nonbelievers are usually new to the methodology or have never given thought to the historical problems of the software development process. Unfortunately, many of these programmers hail from the Visual Basic camp because Visual Basic makes development work seem deceptively simple and straightforward (thanks, Microsoft Visual Basic marketing staff). However, it must be stressed time and time again that the design phase is absolutely critical to the development of high quality software. Incorporating object-oriented design principles in your development efforts will pay off in the long run in the following ways:

- Increased productivity
- Lower project costs on average
- Greater respect for your productive abilities among peers and managers

This chapter helps you on your way toward these ends.

Using object-oriented design helps you identify classes and objects you've discovered in the analysis phase, as well as those not yet discovered. During design, you also elaborate on the architecture of the system, including the identification of possible design patterns and frameworks. *Design patterns*, in simple terms, are repeated ways that objects communicate with each other to carry out a system goal. Keep in mind that patterns occur in everyday life outside the computer programming industry.

Note

Although I discuss design patterns in the last section of this chapter, there isn't enough time to cover all the design patterns discovered thus far. For information on the Internet, find `http://hillside.net/patterns/`. It's mainly for C++, but some patterns can be translated for Visual Basic. Also, browse to `www.samsona.com` (the "Object Technology" link) for more design patterns adapted to Visual Basic.

When you finish the last design iteration (there can be many iterations through the design phase, depending on the complexity of your proposed system), your system specification will be detailed enough for you to develop the system without having to make assumptions about the system architecture or user motivations. The problems discovered during the actual development phase should be minor and should require minor iterations through the design phase to update the corresponding models. At the same time, minor updates in design models should lead to very minor updates in the analysis models—such as changes in the name of a class or class member or the addition of an argument to a private method. Major changes—such as drastic changes in the way objects communicate, the addition of a new subsystem or package, changes to the graphical user interface

(GUI) or interfaces between systems—should not occur during the development phase. If such changes are not addressed during design, before development, this might suggest inadequate skill sets among domain experts, analysts, architects, or designers. In any event, such modifications should be deferred until a future release of the system, if possible. If not possible, the development phase must be postponed while the design flaws are revisited in the design phase.

> **Tip**
>
> Always remember that the object-oriented development process is discovery-oriented and is analogous to a whirlwind. Each discovery adds force to the whirling winds until the whirlwind reaches its peak strength. At that point, the discoveries become fewer and fewer until the whirlwind finally subsides. Thus, during design, discoveries about business processes, application features, and so on, will cause you to loop back to (iterate through) analysis to verify that they are within your project's scope. This is also true for commercial and entrepreneurial developers because control of product enhancements reduces product deployment and marketing expenses. In general, placing discoveries within their proper context lessens the complexities of developing software, no matter what the purpose of the development effort.

Design Example: Second Bank of Carrollton

REAL WORLD ▼

After a couple of long days spent assessing the needs of your client, including the development of an initial use-case model, you and your boss at Samsona agree that the project should take, at most, eight months. The worst case would be twelve months. You two base this decision on the following:

- More than one legacy mainframe system is involved.

- Two previous bank automation projects with similar needs required between eight and twelve months.

You were unexpectedly frustrated on another project at another company when you didn't properly anticipate the problems your client wanted solved. This time, you want to be certain that the project is feasible, which is why you sought the advice of your boss.

After drinking some coffee (it's morning, you know), you decide to call your client, the branch manager. You explain that your initial analysis and estimations show that the project should take eight to twelve months. "No, no, we need it sooner than that. As I said, our customer attrition rates are horrible, a result of declining customer satisfaction directly related to our slow responsiveness and manual processes. Can we do anything to

▼ speed it up?" You pause a bit, thinking through your options. After some time, your

▼ client is worried. "Hello, you still there?" You finally advise her that you could plan to implement the most important behavior and features in the initial increments, rolling out the remaining behaviors in successive increments. The first increment could be installed within three to four months, depending on how smoothly the iterations go through analysis, design, and construction. That explanation seems to do the trick. "Well, though I'd like to have all my required functionality in place during that same time period, I also don't want to disrupt my operations with a low-quality system. Let's go with that plan and see how it goes." You agree and offer to fax her a copy of the requirements, as well as a consulting agreement for her to sign and return, which she later does.

In Table 2.1 on Day 2, "Fundamental Object-Oriented Analysis," you created a list of candidate classes, based on the initial problem statement. Recall that a *problem statement* is the requirements document that provides the foundation for all your project's models and other object-oriented artifacts. That list of candidate classes includes `Teller`, `Bank Accounts`, and `Account`. Throughout this chapter, you will elaborate through the artifacts of design, including the interaction diagrams (sequence and collaboration) and class models. These artifacts will not only help you develop your system but also help you
▲ provide full explanations of the project's progress to your client.

The Three Amigos of Object Technology

These days there are many flavors of object-oriented design in the OO community. This section briefly introduces the most pervasive methodologies that include design processes. They are the following:

- Object-oriented software engineering (Objectory)
- Object Modeling Technique (OMT)
- Booch

Object-Oriented Software Engineering (Objectory)

Noted OO methodologist Ivar Jacobson is the brains behind the Objectory method. Because of its ease of use and effectiveness in accurately representing document and model requirements (via the use-case model), it has become the foundation for object-oriented design efforts in general. However, Jacobson also offers the object-oriented software engineering (OOSE) approach to software construction (or design and programming).

The OOSE design approach models the behavior of the system, as documented by the use cases, into logical parts (classes). At the core of the design model in OOSE are three types of classes (whose instances are objects):

- Entity
- Interface
- Control

Entity Classes

Entity classes represent the types of objects whose data needs to be stored persistently beyond the lifetime of the application session. This persistent storage is usually realized in the form of a database or flat file. Because you aren't always sure which storage approach a project will incorporate, you want to logically refer to these storage media as *information repositories* or *information persistence*. Thus, as storage media changes over time, your project artifacts (models and documentation) better stand the test of time and are reusable for future projects.

An example of an entity class is in order here:

Class:

        SavingsAccount

Properties:

        Number

        CurrentBalance

        DepositAmount

        WithdrawalAmount

        InterestRate

Methods:

        depositFunds

        withdrawFunds

        viewTransactionHistory

Given a Visual Basic entity class of this structure, you might, as part of your domain-specified requirements, need to persistently store the savings account number, current balance, deposit amount, withdrawal amount, and interest rate. As an alternative, you might feel that the current balance is a derived property value, meaning that an accumulative query of your persistent storage media would render the current balance. Derived properties are typically borderline issues that must be addressed on a case-by-case basis. Nevertheless, you should understand what constitutes an entity class.

Entity classes are usually the first class type discovered during the earliest stages of analysis. For instance, if you're developing a system for a defense contract firm, you

▼ might discover a class called `ProcurementRuleEnforcement` or `GovernmentCustomer`. If your client is a bank, a key entity class would be `Account` or `Customer`. Many times, such entity classes become subsystems (or packages). Use cases provide the justification for entity classes. Any entity class not addressed in a use-case model should be eliminated to avoid scope creep, when projects go off track and fall behind schedule.

Interface Classes

Interface classes represent the types of objects that enable the actor (human or external system) to interact with your proposed system. As Jacobson mentions in several books and magazine articles, object instances of interface classes convert inputs from the actor into events and method invocations within your system. For instance, one of your use cases for the Second Bank of Carrollton Bank Teller System is *Open a New Account*. After several design reviews with the users, you find that you need to have a GUI button captioned `Open New Account`. That button is an interface object with an associated `Click` event, among others. In turn, the `Click` event can trigger the invocation of several class methods. Because these method invocations can become complex, it isn't unusual to have a control object handle the details of invoking the proper methods.

Control Classes

Control classes represent the types of objects that don't easily fit into entity or interface classes. More complex systems (and, therefore, more complex use cases) require the inclusion of control objects in your domain. Control classes can translate user inputs into method invocations on more than one entity class. For instance, if your user needs the ability to cancel an in-process request for checking account and credit history information for a particular banking customer, the user would click a Cancel button, which would then call a control object possibly named `CustomerVerification`, which would then invoke the appropriate methods on entity objects named `CheckingAccountHistoryInfo`, `CreditHistoryInfo`, `Account`, and `Customer` (among
▲ many possible others). Control objects control the flow of events for complex use cases.

OMT

The Object Modeling Technique (OMT) was developed by Jim Rumbaugh to help developers capture the design specification of a proposed system. OMT is primarily based on entity/relationship modeling (Rumbaugh's background is database design) and emphasizes modeling classes, inheritance, and encapsulated behavior. The cornerstone of the OMT process includes

- Analysis
- System design

- Object design
- Coding
- Testing

The analysis phase is similar to that discussed on Day 2. System design is concerned with the initial versions of the Object model, the Dynamic model, and the Functional model. The *Object model* shows the relationships (or links) between classes. The *Dynamic model* elaborates on states of objects and events associated with changes in state. The *Functional model* shows how the invoking of methods (or class operations) generates resulting values from a set of input values. The object design phase is an elaboration of the system design phase. Coding and testing aren't unlike that discussed on Day 4, "Fundamental Object-Oriented Programming." Much OMT notation has been captured in the Unified Modeling Language (UML), which I'll explain in a moment.

Booch

The Booch method, fathered by Grady Booch, proposes statements for designers to use in the elaboration of class structures and relationships. The statements follow this format:

- Candidate Class A "is a" type of Class B.
- Candidate Class A "has a" Class B type of object.
- Candidate Class A "uses" Class B.

The "is a" relationship suggests that A is everything that B represents (and possibly more). This is called *inheritance*. For instance, a checking account *is a* type of account.

The "has a" relationship suggests that A owns B for its own purposes, meaning that B's lifetime depends on A's lifetime. There has been much heated discussion on this very topic in the OO community. The idea is that, for instance, a bank customer *has* several accounts with the bank. When the customer stops being a bank customer, these accounts also cease as the customer closes them (at least in most cases).

The "uses" relationship suggests that A *uses* B for a particular task or activity but doesn't own B. For instance, in the Second Bank of Carrollton Bank Teller System, the `Account` class might use the `CheckingAccountHistoryInfo` class to verify the customer's checking account history before opening a new account. The `Account` class doesn't own `CheckingAccountHistoryInfo`; `Account` just uses it for this verification process. In Visual Basic, a "uses" relationship might look like the following:

```
cmdVerifyCheckAccountHistory_Click()
     theAcount.verifyCheckAccountHistory(SomeCustomerSSN)
End Sub
```

▼ In the `Account` class, this method call would then have the following "uses" relationship:

```
Public Sub verifyCheckAccountHistory(SomeCustomerSSN)
    theCheckingAccountHistoryInfo.verify(SomeCustomerSSN)
End Sub
```

In most cases, the "uses" relationship resembles delegation, in which an object delegates one or all of its responsibilities to another object.

The Booch method is primarily concerned with discovering the chief abstractions (or areas of specialized focus) of classes and objects as parts of the overall system in your problem domain. The identification process examines the vocabulary of the business domain, much the way OOSE does. Booch also looks at the contextual meaning of these classes and objects and how they are used by others. Grasping the meaning of classes and objects is by no means an easy process and requires many iterations through design and analysis. Thus, domain experts become critical stakeholders in the production of analysis and design models and other artifacts.

Finally, Booch divides the system into several views and models. Among the views are the Logical View and the Physical View (which are the basis of Microsoft's Visual Modeler). The *Logical View* encompasses the structure of and relationships between classes and objects. The *Physical View* encompasses the actual file location of the classes in the Logical View.

3

UML

UML stands for Unified Modeling Language. Its notation represents the combination of the most important object-oriented methodologies in the software development community today. The three top methodologists—Ivar Jacobson, Jim Rumbaugh, and Grady Booch—are the chief architects of UML. The UML creation process began in late 1994 when Booch and Rumbaugh collaborated to unify their respective methodologies. Jacobson joined them shortly thereafter.

The UML doesn't represent an elimination of OOSE, OMT, or the Booch method, as some have suggested. Instead, it represents a unified way of modeling elements in each. Of course, the UML creation process has led to some version upgrades in the top three methodologies, but the UML only represents a standard way to express each one.

The UML is wholly encapsulated within the Rational Rose automation tool. This should not be surprising because Jacobson, Booch, and Rumbaugh are the joint chiefs of Rational Corporation. Because UML and Rational Rose 4.0 are so tightly intertwined, I'll discuss more details of the UML in the section on Rational Rose later. For now, suffice it to say that the UML incorporates four views of the system:

- Use Case View
- Logical View

▼

- Component View
- Deployment View

The *Use Case View* encompasses all the use-case models, including the actors. The *Logical View* encompasses the classes and objects needed to support the use-case models. The *Component View*, like Booch's Physical View, shows the actual location of the files for each class and component (that is, ActiveX controls, other third-party tools, and so on). The *Deployment View* encompasses the physical locations of key processors and hardware devices in your system domain. Examples of these appear later in this chapter.

Using Rational Rose/Visual Basic and Microsoft Visual Modeler

As seasoned software developers will tell you (if you don't already know), having automation tools that ease the process of developing sophisticated software is a must in today's technology-intensive environment. Two tools stand out in this arena: Rational Rose/Visual Basic and Microsoft Visual Modeler.

Similarities and Differences

Many of you are probably saying, "Hey, these tools look alike." Not surprising. There is a reason for this: Microsoft, the master of the graphical user interface, and Rational, the ruler of automated object-oriented software development, joined forces to provide a much needed facelift to Rational Rose. For those readers who remember the previous versions of Rose, you are probably glad the GUI was brought up to speed.

Although there are quite a number of similarities between Visual Modeler and Rational Rose/Visual Basic, using both will quickly bring to light the obvious differences. The following are the obvious similarities:

- Both tools support Microsoft's three-tier (or three-partition) approach to application architecture. The three tiers are User Services (GUI-centered objects), Business Services (rules and entity objects), and Data Services (database objects, recordset objects, flat file interfaces, and so on).
- Both tools support the Logical and Physical Views of the application.

The key difference is that Rational Rose/Visual Basic supports the Use Case View. This critical view is missing from Visual Modeler, possibly because of licensing restrictions negotiated by Rational. Whatever the reason, the lack of the Use Case View in Visual Modeler makes it more difficult to enforce traceability from the use cases to the detail design class models. Thus, project risks must be assessed appropriately and allocated to this situation.

▼ Common Uses

The most important project activity you'll engage in with either Rational Rose/Visual Basic or Visual Modeler is the creation of architecture models, diagrams, and documentation. In addition, you'll be able to create the necessary class modules and class utilities (or general code modules) to support the evolving system architecture as you iterate and increment through the various project phases. With either tool, you can also reverse-engineer an existing Visual Basic project, thereby automatically creating a model.

The Importance of Traceability

Traceability is that attribute of a project artifact that enables following business-related entity classes from the actual code to the lowest class models up to the high analysis models and the project documentation itself. Master test cases and test scripts also refer to the same class, object, and actor names as other artifacts of the project life cycle. Unfortunately, too many projects give little attention to the necessity of traceability. It might seem like extra work, but make sure to keep all artifacts (documents, models, diagrams, and code files) in sync when it comes to business domain terminology. Failing to do so very often results in unnecessary confusion and stress down the road.

The Design-View Class Model

When you begin modeling your classes in the design phase, the resulting models will become more detailed with each iteration. Figure 3.1 shows how your class model from the analysis phase now appears.

FIGURE 3.1.

The updated class model has two more classes because of your new discoveries about the domain. Notice that traceability is still evident.

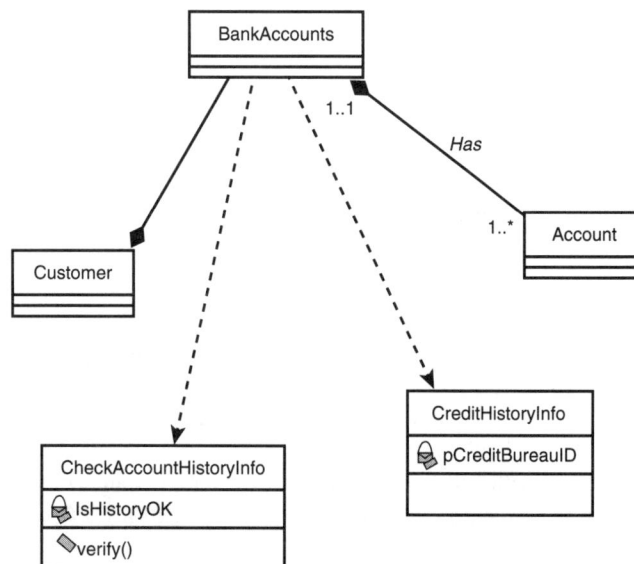

▼ As you can see in Figure 3.1, two more classes appear in the class model: `CreditHistoryInfo` and `CheckAccountHistoryInfo`. Each rectangle is an icon representing a class. The line between the `Customer` class and the `BankAccounts` class indicates an association between the two classes. The black diamond means that the `Customer` class has an instance of the `BankAccounts` class. The same relationship exists between the `BankAccounts` class and the `Account` class, with the single `BankAccounts` class (`1..1`, meaning a minimum of one to a maximum of 1) having one or more instances (`1..*`, or one to many) of the `Account` class. The broken lines with arrows, between the `BankAccounts` class and the two new classes, indicate that the `BankAccounts` class depends on (uses) the two classes. The icon to the left of the `isHistoryOK` property in the `CheckAccountHistoryInfo` class indicates this property is private. The purple icon next to the `verify` method in the same class means it's a public method. For the sake of simplicity, let's decide that each of these classes has a method called `verify` to handle customer information processing. That both classes can have a method with the same name but different implementations is an example of a form of polymorphism.

Your modeling tools (Visual Modeler and Rational Rose/Visual Basic) enable you to show the methods for each class. Figure 3.2 shows each class with its methods and properties displayed. Note that, in most cases, you don't want to show more class members than is necessary to explain a particular scenario. Otherwise, the models become cluttered with model elements and almost unreadable.

FIGURE 3.2.

Now the class diagram has more expressive classes with properties and methods. As a rule, try not to show every member of every class for a given scenario (or application context or situation).

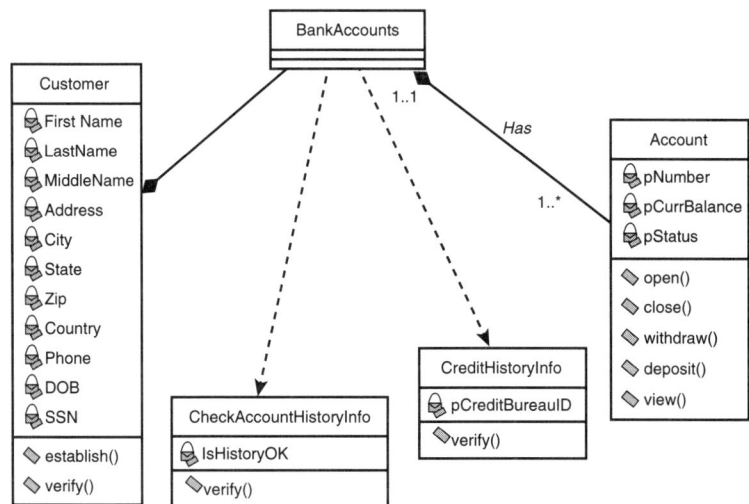

Why is avoiding the clutter of models important? Because readability is an obvious ben-
▼ efit of object-oriented models. Certain scenarios call for different views of your class

▼ model. For instance, if you have a scenario that deals with the opening of an account for a customer with a valid Social Security number and good credit and checking account histories, your class model view would show only the members of the Account and Customer classes. All other classes would display only a name and possibly a single method that is meaningful to the context.

Sequence Diagrams

Sequence diagrams literally show a sequence of interactions between actors and objects in your system. It's tempting to immediately associate sequence diagrams with data flow diagrams (DFDs), but they aren't the same. DFDs show only dimly defined paths of function calls. Sequence diagrams show the interaction between actors and objects for a given scenario, with focus on state changes and timing issues.

Take a look at Figure 3.3. The sequence diagram from Day 2's Figure 2.7 is updated to include the two new classes (CreditHistoryInfo and CheckAccountHistoryInfo).

FIGURE 3.3.

The sequence diagram has been updated to incorporate the new classes.

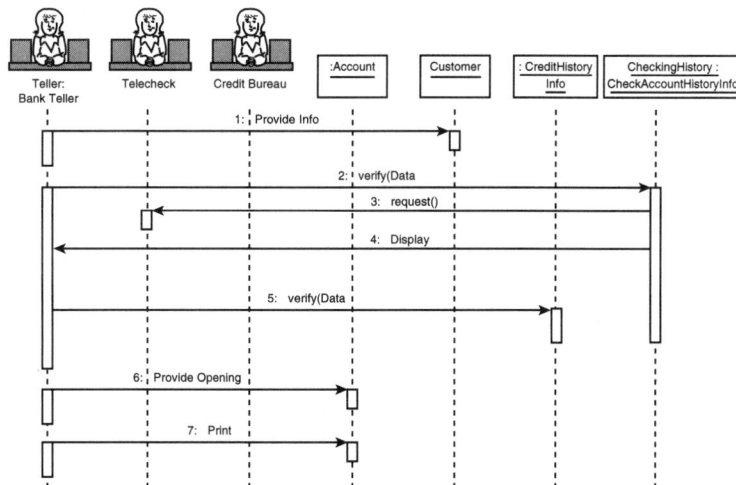

Collaboration Diagrams

Collaboration diagrams are similar to sequence diagrams, except they don't look as sequential and structured. Figure 3.4 shows how your sequence diagram would appear as a collaboration diagram.

Collaboration diagrams aren't as popular with some OO camps as sequence diagrams. Nevertheless, in some situations, a collaboration diagram captures views of the system that better show method invocations on objects. The choice is a matter of preference
▼ more than science, generally speaking.

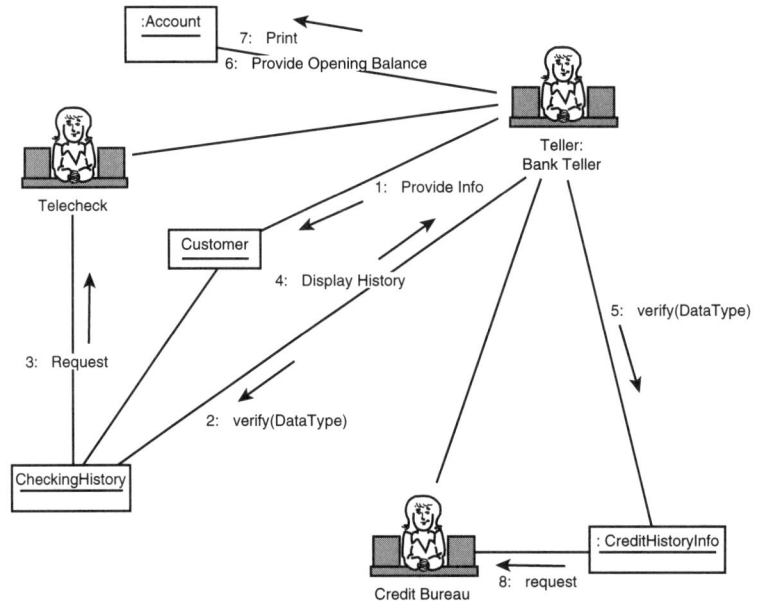

FIGURE 3.4.

This is how your sequence diagram would appear as a collaboration diagram.

Dividing a Proposed Visual Basic Application into Subsystem Packages

As if the concept of classes and objects weren't difficult enough, you must also become familiar with the idea of dividing your applications into logical subapplications or subsystems. A subsystem is composed of one to many classes whose object instances interact with each other to carry out a common application behavior. Groupings of classes are also called *packages*. To give you an example, you will have a subsystem that handles communications between the data repository (database, flat file, and so on) and the application. There's no sense in every form needing to communicate directly with the data repository, which has become the norm in the Visual Basic development community. This flattens the system architecture, graying the lines between the User, Business, and Data Services layers, and thus can cause spaghetti code. What's more, code reuse is next to impossible to hope for when all the layers of the application code are embedded within forms. Delegating key functionality to subsystems not only helps avoid spaghetti code but also greatly increases the readability of the code and the ability to assign parts of the application to each member of a team of developers.

Naming Subsystem Packages, Classes, and Objects

Naming and coding standards aren't pervasive among newcomers to programming (and sometimes among seasoned developers who have managed to skirt the issue of implementing such standards). Microsoft's naming suggestions, of course, are fine, but I'll mention the ones that apply to classes and objects:

- *Class names* can start with a capital C (CAccount), as is the case with MS Visual C++, or you can opt to capitalize the first letter of the class, such as Account. Class names should be nouns and should adequately and briefly describe the types of functionality and attributes the classes will encapsulate. The same naming convention holds true for subsystems (or packages) that also are classes that are aggregates of one to many classes.

- *Object names* start with cls (clsAccount), or you can prefix object names with the or rep. Examples include theAccount or repAccount.

- *Methods* start with lowercase verbs (openAccount). Avoid using nouns for names of methods because you might confuse them with properties. Also, method names with verb forms accurately convey that an action will be carried out by the class (which is a noun).

- *Class properties* start with lowercase p (pName), unless you're able to differentiate between methods and properties (which is possible with the suggestion on naming methods).

- *Implementation variables* at the module level start with either a lowercase m or m_. If you use Class Builder, it will prefix implementation property variables with mvar. Implementation variables are variables used internally within a class.

As for coding standards, whole books have been written on this topic (by authors including Jacobson, Booch, and Rumbaugh). At a high level, you use a mix of limited inheritance and delegation to express "is a," "has a," and "uses" relationships (discussed earlier in this chapter); delegation would be the default in your Visual Basic design models. You'll want to develop your interfaces (or protocols) so that they don't change—only the implementation changes. You can have newer versions of an interface, meaning that during some overlapping period, you'll support both the old and new interfaces for compatibility, but compatibility isn't your immediate concern. You'll want to break your application model into nice categories (or subsystems) so that each developer has an island of classes with which to work. The idea here is that while these categories are being worked on, no two developers need to try to develop together. Only when the interfaces of each category are well developed will the two come together for integration—which shouldn't take much time, depending on the complexity of the behavior being carried out. If one finishes before the other, the slower developer (for lack of a better term) could check out the category with which to work.

Advanced Design Issues: Design Patterns

Although the identification of patterns isn't a new science, the concept of design patterns has been gaining rapid popularity in the object-oriented software development community over the past several years. The purpose of design patterns within the OO community is to make available a repository of problems and solutions to help software deal with common redundant issues. Identifying design patterns facilitates communication of in-depth knowledge and experience about these recurring problems and deciding how best to implement solutions. Having this at the disposal of developers, especially Visual Basic developers, results in well-structured system architectures that provide rapid reuse for the client and are understandable to fellow developers.

The idea of object-oriented design patterns is a very complex one, suitable for intermediate to advanced object technologists. The premier book on design patterns is *Design Patterns: Elements of Reusable Object-Oriented Software* by Erich Gamma, Richard Helm, Ralph Johnson, and John Vlissides. Several others exist. It's advisable to acquire such books to familiarize yourself with the idea of design patterns. However, be forewarned that current design patterns books are written with C++ in mind because many design patterns deal with inheritance, an area in which Visual Basic isn't yet capable.

Christopher Alexander, a noted scientist and building architect/theorist, describes a pattern as "a three-part rule, which expresses a relation between a certain context, a problem, and a solution. The pattern is, in short, at the same time a thing, which happens in the world, and the rule that tells us how to create that thing, and when we must create it. It is both a process and a thing; both a description of a thing that is alive, and a description of the process that will generate that thing." Because the term *design pattern* has become immensely popular, to the point of being a buzzword, some vanity patterns have entered the community that are not quite solutions.

Interested in writing a design pattern? Doug Lea, a pattern author at `http://st-www.cs.uiuc.edu/users/patterns/patterns.html`, wrote a checklist for documenting patterns. The following list paraphrases what Lea suggests a pattern should reflect:

- A specific kind of problem
- The context in which a given problem occurs

- The solution as a software entity
- The design steps or rules for constructing the solution
- The forces leading to the solution
- Evidence that the solution resolves forces
- The details that are allowed to vary and those that aren't
- One (at a minimum) actual instance of use (others suggest three)
- Evidence of generality across different instances
- Variants and subpatterns
- Other patterns that it relies on
- Other patterns that rely on it
- A relationship to other patterns with similar contexts, problems, or solutions

When to Use Design Patterns in Your Project

Because design patterns are a somewhat advanced topic, you might not want to delve into them until (1) you have access to an OO mentor/architect who is knowledgeable about implementing design patterns, and/or (2) time is allocated toward the end of the first release of the project—or sometime thereafter—to examine the need and implementation of design patterns. Attempting both to learn OOP and to design patterns can be an overwhelming process, so pace yourself. Meanwhile, the next two subsections provide you with examples of design patterns that you can use in your Visual Basic code.

The Singleton Pattern Example: An Overview

If you had any experience with Visual Basic 3.0 programming, you probably remember how difficult it was to allow users to start only one instance of your application. If you've been doing a little object-oriented programming, you might have come to the point where you need to make sure only one instance of a particular object is in memory. The Singleton design pattern is analogous to the first situation and is a solution to the second one.

The purpose of the Singleton pattern is to make sure that only one instance of an object is available to prospective client objects. The enforcement of one object instance can be important if that object is global within your application and even more so if that object is global to other applications within an enterprise or across several enterprises. An example of a Singleton object is a reporting object that resides on a server and is the broker for all requests for reporting services.

Learning How to Implement the Singleton Pattern in Visual Basic

In C++, you use the `Protected` keyword to help enforce the Singleton pattern policy. However, in Visual Basic, there is no obvious equivalent. The closest you can come to substituting the `Protected` keyword is to use the `Friend` and `Static` keywords. Class methods and properties declared with the `Friend` and `Static` keywords ensure that only classes within the enclosing component have access to these members. Nonetheless, in neither C++ or Visual Basic can you ensure that one and only one instance of a static object will ever be declared. A better idea might be to have your Singleton classes registered and tracked through a centralized Registry class. As Gamma, et al, suggest in *Design Patterns*, you could create a `SingletonRegistry` collection class with the following members:

```
Public Sub register(argObjName As String, argSingleton As Singleton)
'Add to some collection
End Sub

Public Property Get pSingleton()
'Here, you'd set pSingleton to some modular instance variable
End Property

Friend Static Function lookup(ByVal argObjName As String)
'Insert code to actually find the actual Singleton object being sought.
'The ByVal ensures that the name of the object in the argument argObjName
'is not modified. Return some meaningful error code or raise an event if
'object not found.
End Function
```

You can register the `Singleton` objects in the `Class_Initialize` event of each corresponding object's class. Assuming the Singleton class has been named `Singleton` and the `SingletonRegistry` class has been instantiated as `theSingletonRegistry`, the code in the Singleton's `Class_Initialize` event might look like this:

```
Private Sub Class_Initialize()
 theSingletonRegistry.register("Singleton", Me)
End Sub
```

Note

Remember that the `Me` keyword refers to the object representing the current instance of the `Singleton` class. Therefore, if you have a list of `Singleton` objects, named `Singleton1` through `Singleton10`, and the current instance refers to `Singleton7`, `Me` refers to `Singleton7`.

An Easy Example

An example of a Singleton in your Second Bank of Carrollton Bank Teller System might be the `Customer` class because your teller user (for simplicity's sake) can handle account transactions for only one customer at a time.

Going with the assumption that your `Customer` class needs to make sure that only one instance of it can be in memory, your Singleton class would look like Listing 3.1.

LISTING 3.1. THE SINGLETON `Customer` CLASS.

```
 1: VERSION 1.0 CLASS
 2: BEGIN
 3:    MultiUse = -1  'True
 4: END
 5: Attribute VB_Name = "Customer"
 6: Attribute VB_GlobalNameSpace = False
 7: Attribute VB_Creatable = True
 8: Attribute VB_PredeclaredId = False
 9: Attribute VB_Exposed = False
10: Attribute VB_Ext_KEY = "SavedWithClassBuilder" ,"Yes"
11: Attribute VB_Ext_KEY = "Top_Level" ,"Yes"
12: 'local variable(s) to hold property value(s)
13: 'Private mvarpSoleInstance As Customer  'local copy
14: Private mvarpSoleInstance As Object  'local copy
15:
16: Friend Property Set pSoleInstance(ByVal vData As Object)
17: 'used when assigning an Object to the property, on the left side
    ➥of a Set statement.
18: 'Syntax: Set x.pSoleInstance = Form1
19:     Set mvarpSoleInstance = vData
20: End Property
21:
22:
23: Friend Property Get pSoleInstance() As Object
24: 'used when retrieving value of a property, on the right side of
    ➥an assignment.
25: 'Syntax: Debug.Print X.pSoleInstance
26:     Set pSoleInstance = mvarpSoleInstance
27: End Property
28:
29:
30: Friend Static Function createSoleInstance() As Customer
31: Attribute createSoleInstance.VB_UserMemId = 0
32: If TypeName(mvarpSoleInstance) = "Customer" Then
33:         MsgBox "Only one instance allowed"
34:         Exit Function
35:     End If
```

▼

continues

```
36:
37:     Set mvarpSoleInstance = New Customer
38:     MsgBox "New Customer object created"
39: End Function
```

The property pSoleInstance was declared as Friend Static so that only those objects
within the project can access the Customer class instance. Notice the method
createSoleInstance. This is the key enforcer in your class. In it, you allow only one
instance of the Customer class via the Set...New syntax. Of course, more than one
instance of Customer can be created outside your class, which means that it must be
mutually agreed that the one instance created (in your case, theCustomer) will be the
only broker for creating instances of the Customer class. Nevertheless, you could have
designed this method as in Listing 3.2.

LISTING 3.2. THE MODIFIED createSoleInstance METHOD.

```
 1: Public Static Function createSoleInstance() As Customer
 2: Attribute createSoleInstance.VB_UserMemId = 0
 3:     Dim m_InstanceCount As Byte   'local copy
 4:     If m_InstanceCount = 1 Then
 5:         MsgBox "Only one instance allowed"
 6:         Exit Function
 7:     End If
 8:
 9:     Set mvarpSoleInstance = New Customer
10:     MsgBox "New Customer object created"
11:     m_InstanceCount = 1
12: End Function
```

In the createSoleInstance method in Listing 3.1, you used the TypeName method to test
whether your late-bound object is of the type Customer. When the class is first initialized, it is of the type Object. Therefore, the check for the TypeName will be False on the
first invocation of createSoleInstance. However, because it is the first time, the object
will be set to something other than Object, namely Customer. Thus, when a second
Set...New Customer is encountered, the TypeName test will be True, meaning that additional instances can't be allowed. In Listing 3.2, on the other hand, a static instance
counter is used to limit the instance count to one. Either way is an effective pattern for
▲ ensuring only one instance exists.

The Factory Pattern Example: An Overview

Factories provide a single interface for creating a particular object without your specifying their Visual Basic classes. One key benefit of this pattern is that it enables you to control groups of associated classes that your application creates at runtime. A related benefit is that a factory enables you the flexibility of decoupling a particular framework you use from the knowledge of classes the framework can't anticipate. This helps maintain consistency across your applications without requiring much effort.

> **Note**
>
> The runtime architecture of an application is more complex than the design-time architecture. This is because, among other things, many instances of classes interact at runtime.

3

Learning How to Implement the Factory Pattern in Visual Basic

Typically, you'll need only one instance of the concrete factory per application subsystem. The concrete factory object is responsible for implementing the interface of the abstract factory. Keep in mind that abstract classes don't give birth to (lead to instances of) real-world objects, but to concrete classes. Concrete classes are created as real-world objects. Finally, because Visual Basic doesn't support implementation inheritance, you need a mix of both interface inheritance and delegation to fully use this pattern.

An Easy Example

▲ REAL WORLD

In keeping with the banking theme of this book, let's say you've discovered that your bank client offers several account products to its customers. Such products include Personal Checking Plus and Personal Savings Plus. Operations such as opening a checking account, verifying check writing history, and so on, still apply and are part of the core of the application. On detailed analysis of the requirements, you discover that the main differences between these two products are as follows:

- Personal Savings Plus lets your money earn interest at 3% compounded monthly.
- Personal Checking Plus has overdraft protection.

Your client then tells you that if a customer doesn't want either of these products, he can still choose Basic Personal Savings and Basic Personal Checking accounts. Fortunately for you, your client has bankwide codes for each of these products, as detailed in

▼ Table 3.1.

▼ **TABLE 3.1.** BANK ACCOUNT CODES.

Product	Code
Basic Personal Savings	01
Basic Personal Checking	02
Personal Savings Plus	11
Personal Checking Plus	12

As the architect, you decide you want only one creator class with a factory method for any kind of bank product. You aptly name this class `AccountCreator` and decide to locate it on an account application server (I won't discuss second-tier servers here, for simplicity) to keep the client as thin as possible. (Note that *thin* means the client has only enough code to move information in and out of the user interface.) The product classes are `BasicPersonalChecking`, `BasicPersonalSavings`, `PersonalCheckingPlus`, and `PersonalSavingsPlus`. These products implement the `BankAccountProduct` interface class.

The `AccountCreator` interface class has the following members:

```
Public Function createAccount(ByRef argObject) As BankAccountProduct
Private Function createBasicPersonalChecking(argObject) As
➥BasicPersonalChecking
Private Function createBasicPersonalSavings(argObject) As
➥BasicPersonalSavings
Private Function createPersonalCheckingPlus(argObject) As
➥PersonalCheckingPlus
Private Function createPersonalSavingsPlus(argObject) As
➥PersonalSavingsPlus
Public Function getBankAccountCode()
Public Sub setBankAccountCode(argAccountCode As Byte)
```

The method `createAccount` is the factory method. A *factory method* creates objects of a particular class as if it were an object factory. Within it are invocations of private methods that are responsible for first making sure each one is able to create the requested bank product (known as a *precondition*). If so, the method creates the corresponding product by instantiating the appropriate object. The methods responsible for instantiating the proper bank product are `createBasicPersonalChecking`, `createBasicPersonalSavings`, `createPersonalCheckingPlus`, and `createPersonalSavingsPlus`. The methods `getBankAccountCode` and `setBankAccountCode` enable users of the `AccountCreator` object to get and set, respectively, the product code of the type of bank product the customer wants. These are also known respectively as *getters* and *setters* or, more formally, *accessors* and *mutators*.

▼ Refer to this chapter's code on the CD-ROM for more information.

The `BankAccountProduct` interface class has the following members:

```
Public Function getName()
Public Sub setName(argNewValue As String)
```

These getter and setter methods don't do anything because this is a pure interface class. Finally, each specialized product method invoked in the `createAccount` method uses the actual product classes such as `BasicPersonalChecking`, `BasicPersonalSavings`, `PersonalCheckingPlus`, and `PersonalSavingsPlus`. These classes implement the `BankAccountProduct` interface class; they have the interface's methods in common. In the `BankAccountProduct_setName` and `BankAccountProduct_getName` interface methods, a modular variable m_pName references the type name of the actual product class. This variable is set in the `Class_Initialize` event. Figure 3.5 shows a model of the classes that are active in the Factory pattern.

FIGURE 3.5.

The Factory pattern is helpful for controlling the instantiation of objects.

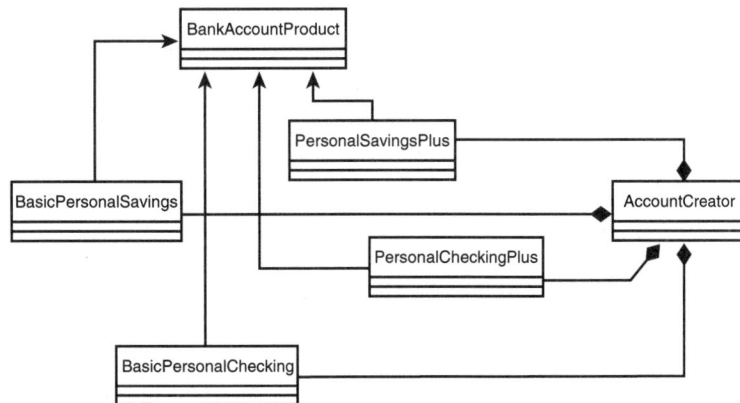

Tip

Keep in mind, though, that you can place code inside methods in pure interface classes. That way, if another class implements it and doesn't want to override a method but wants to use it instead, you call that method in the implementing class.

Say you have a `Parent` class that has a method `changeDiapers`. Then you have a `Mommy` class that implements `Parent` but also has a private method

▼

called `powderBaby`. However, in the `Parent` interface code part of the `Mommy` class, you could do the following (assuming the `Parent` class was instantiated as `theParent`):

```
Public Sub Parent_ChangeDiapers()
    theParent.ChangeDiapers
    powderBaby
End Sub
```

This way you still use the base behavior of the implemented method and add additional method calls to specialize the operation as well.

NEW TERM   A *modular variable* is a variable that has scope only within the module (class or general code) in which it is declared. This declaration, naturally, occurs in the General Declarations section.

▲   As mentioned earlier, the CD-ROM contains the code for this chapter. Feel free to load it in Visual Basic and run it.

Gearing Up for Code Implementation

Remember, as you move toward this new way of doing projects, the main complaint about the entire object-oriented development process is that it takes too long to move a project from inception to production. That's a fair criticism, given that many companies that first undertake the implementation of object technology generally fail because of lack of preparation, migrating poor development and project management habits to the new paradigm, and lack of experienced personnel. At the same time, those critics of object technology ignore the fact that most projects either end disastrously or achieve hardly any of their initial goals for numerous reasons. Your first OO project will be slow—there's no doubt about that. This is because you're forced to think about the proposed system from the point of view of the user. Also, planning for reuse is time-consuming, and the payback for reuse strategies is at least three years on a wide scale.

In traditional environments, the programmer placed himself or herself on the same pedestal as the user (sometimes higher!); the programmer's wants were considered as important as the user's. This often led to compromises in products that left the user dissatisfied. If the programmer was boisterous enough, the user was bullied into accepting the application and a month or two later abandoned its use. Because the programmer was typically not around to see this, he or she was left with the erroneous perception that the project was successful.

With true object-oriented development, the foundation of the system is constructed with only the user's needs in mind. Note the word *true* in the preceding sentence. Many newcomers to OOP introduce their previous traditions into the process. This "untrue" OO process leads to faulty use cases and, thus, foundations that have cracks everywhere. Only the end users and domain experts can provide the concrete for the foundation. It is your job to fashion and mold it into a stable, long-lasting slab. Just as with building a real house, laying a solid foundation will consume the bulk of the time it takes to develop the entire system. If you try to take shortcuts to produce a foundation in record time, your foundation will inevitably crack and, as with building contractors, you might be held liable for the damages. If you are an independent consultant, you'll want to take your time to properly develop the system's foundation.

After the foundation is nicely laid, the rest of the process will be quicker than you expect. Future projects that overlap with the first OO project will be that much faster because you'll be able to reuse code and documentation. With each successive project that has similar requirements, the project deadlines will be more easily met (with lots of time to spare). Time-to-market is thus minimal. Be patient! It might take nearly three years before you reach the point when a project benefits from full reuse (much shorter if you hire a consultant who has reusable class libraries and libraries of standard use cases). Because software is a company's capital asset, it would be wise to consider the three years, or fewer, as the initial investment period of the asset.

3

Summary

In this chapter, you gained a better understanding of the object-oriented design process. You became familiar with the Objectory design process introduced by Ivar Jacobson, the Object Modeling Technique by Jim Rumbaugh, and the Booch method by Grady Booch. You learned about the importance of traceability from one model and diagram to another, as well as the design-view class model.

You were introduced to two software development automation tools: Rational Rose/Visual Basic and Microsoft Visual Modeler. You learned some reasons you might want to use them, as well as the differences and similarities between them. You also learned how to break a proposed Visual Basic application into subsystem packages and how to name subsystem packages, classes, and objects.

Finally, you became familiar with an advanced issue in object-oriented design, namely, design patterns. Examples of the Singleton and Factory patterns were provided in the form of the `Customer` and `AccountCreator` classes.

Tomorrow you will round out the fundamental concepts of OOP with lots of sample code and explanations, using the Second Bank of Carrollton Bank Teller System example.

Q&A

Q What is design?

A Design is the process of elaborating an outline for one or more solutions to a given problem. Given information about the problem as documented in the artifacts of analysis, a design would embody the best solution for that problem.

Q Are the artifacts of design nonprogramming models?

A Yes. Although programming activities during construction are based on design models, the design models themselves aren't programming models. This distinction gives the flexibility to explore different solutions without prematurely committing lots of costly resources to any specific one.

Q Why is object-oriented programming a discovery-oriented process?

A The most fundamental reason lies in the complicated human requirements of computers. Humans expect computers to mimic not only complex human behavior but also even more complex human thinking.

Q What is a subsystem?

A An application component composed of one to many classes whose object instances interact with each other to carry out a common application behavior.

Workshop

The workshop includes quiz questions to help gauge your grasp of the material. Even if you feel that you totally understand the concepts presented here, you should work through the quiz anyway. The last section contains an exercise or two that you might work through to help reinforce your learning. You'll find the answers to the quiz in Appendix A, "Answers."

Quiz

1. How can executives and managers better facilitate the object-oriented design process?

2. What is at least one benefit of having clearly defined roles for project team members?

3. What are some advantages and disadvantages of creating and viewing design artifacts?

4. Who are the Three Amigos? Briefly explain their respective methodologies.

5. What is traceability? Why is it important?

6. Explain what a design pattern is and how it benefits software development practices in general.

Exercises

1. Assume you have the following use case from which you are expected to develop some system:

   Open an investment account.

   An investor requests the opening of an investment account. The investment specialist prompts the system to obtain the standard electronic application setup template from the database. The investment specialist asks the investor a series of relevant questions. On completion of the questions and after requesting and receiving identification from the investor, the investment specialist provides the necessary information to the system. Finally, the system processes the information.

   Based on this use case, one of your use-case specialists gives you, the architect, the following qualified list of candidate classes:

   > Investor
   >
   > Investment account
   >
   > Investment specialist
   >
   > System
   >
   > Standard electronic application setup template

   a. How would you model these classes and their associations? Using the verbs in the use case as clues, how would you model any methods?

   b. If a designer on your team discovers that an important collaborating class is missing, how would you ensure that this new discovery is used consistently throughout all models on your project?

   c. List some methods you would use to manage the overall design process. You might include a mixture of the methodologies of the Three Amigos.

3

DAY 4

Fundamental Object-Oriented Programming

Design is finally over, and you can now begin programming, right? Well, not quite. Design doesn't always end that nicely. In fact, you can expect to revisit design (in the capacity of designer and/or architect) as new discoveries are made during construction. The beginning and ending phases of an object-oriented project are similar to the rise and fall of empires. When Greece conquered Persia, the Persian Empire didn't immediately cease to exist. It faded away over time. The Greeks might have deposed the king and his top officials, but some Persian leadership persisted until Persia was assimilated (somewhat) into Greek life and culture. When the Romans later conquered Greece, the Greek Empire didn't immediately fall. It faded away. Similarly, the empire of Analysis doesn't immediately give way to the empire of Design, and the empire of Design doesn't immediately fall away under the conquest of the empire of Construction. As one phase rises in importance, the previous one begins to fade—and is sometimes briefly resurrected when there are new discoveries.

In the first three days, you learned about the concepts of object technology and received a primer on object-oriented programming. Today, you will take your learning a step further. You will learn how to construct actual Visual Basic code from the simple sequence diagrams you created on Day 2, "Fundamental Object-Oriented Analysis."

Explaining OOP's Role in Solution Development

The role of object-oriented programming is to provide you with a way to implement a particular design structure of collaborating class instances. This design structure is typically elaborated in a mix of class models, interaction diagrams such as sequence and collaboration diagrams, and state diagrams. Very little significant decision-making about the architecture of an application should occur while you're doing object-oriented programming. In fact, the more significant decisions that are made during the construction phase (synonymous with OOP) of development, the less sound the architecture. By *significant* is meant any decision that affects domain classes and key design patterns. There is some flexibility in making decisions about design patterns because these types of structures are not seen by the user (although great changes to them can affect the application's performance, which the user can complain about). Even domain classes are part of the user's vocabulary. What's more, they are the most valuable assets within the software that the customer (or even yourself as an entrepreneur) will want to reuse again and again. Thus, object-oriented programming should be for purely implementation purposes and not design, if possible.

Understanding Classes

After reading the first three chapters, you should have a good understanding of classes. Let's reinforce that knowledge and build on it with concrete programming examples. Just as a reminder, *classes* are clearly defined abstractions from complex conceptual entities discovered in the real world. Each class exhibits distinguishable characteristics, including attributes and behavior.

Visual Basic Classes

A Visual Basic class follows the same conventions of typical object-oriented classes, except that its internal implementation can't be inherited. A Visual Basic class can inherit the interface of another but is required to implement it. With Visual Basic classes, you have the flexibility of creating property methods in one of two ways: regular functions and subs, or built-in `Property Get` and `Let` methods (with an optional `Property Set` method for properties that reference objects). Regular `Function` methods enable clients of the class's instance to get a property value. A `Sub` method enables clients to set a property value. You were already exposed to these types of methods on Day 3, "Fundamental Object-Oriented Design," but for the sake of convenience, the following section illustrates each in simple examples.

Given a property `EmployeeName`, the following are viable options for property methods:

```
'A function
Public Function getEmployeeName() As String
End Function

'A sub
Public Sub setEmployeeName(argName As String)
End Function

Public Property Get EmployeeName() As String
End Property

Public Property Let EmployeeName(argNewValue As String)
End Property
```

If you want to use the `Set` property method, given an `Employee` object, you would have the following:

```
Public Property Set Employee(argObject As SomeClass)
End Property
```

There's not much difference between the property `Let` and `Set` methods, other than that the one is for non-object data and the other is for object references. This has been a source of confusion for many developers.

Understanding Three Key Concepts in Object-Oriented Programming

A good grasp of fundamental object-oriented concepts takes time. Nevertheless, there are three essential elements of object-oriented programming with which you should soon become well acquainted. They are

- Encapsulation
- Inheritance
- Polymorphism

Understanding Encapsulation

One of the most important pillars of object technology in achieving a solid separation of concerns is through encapsulation. In short, encapsulation is the separation of a class's interface from its internal, private implementation. Put in very real terms, you were created with a layer of skin over you to encapsulate your internal details, such as organs, veins, intestines, and so on. To use a more appetizing example, the information in the mail you receive is encapsulated from anyone's intimate knowledge (you hope) but yours. Sure, enough information is available on the external interface of the envelope (such as your name, address, city, state/province, and zip code) to route the envelope to you. However, the delivery person doesn't need to know what's inside the envelope in order to deliver it.

Classes, in general, must resemble the delivery person. No one class should be concerned with the internal details of another class. It should be concerned only with how to interact with a class's interface (like the information on the outside of an envelope). Encapsulation, then, contributes to the ease of an application's maintenance and evolution over time.

Encapsulation is often referred to as information hiding because of its goal of hiding internal information about the object and how it implements its class interface. Given that classes are abstractions, abstractions are only valid if they have achieved rock-solid encapsulation.

Let's quickly illustrate what this means. In Chapter 3, I discussed the following command button event:

```
cmdVerifyCheckAccountHistory_Click()
    theAccount.verifyCheckAccountHistory(SomeCustomerSSN)
End Sub
```

The command button, `cmdVerifyCheckAccountHistory`, is a member of the form object. No surprise there. However, because the form has knowledge of the object `theAccount`, the form subscribes to the `theAccount` object's `verifyCheckAccountHistory` method. That is, because the business activity of verifying checking account history is encapsulated in the `theAccount` object, the form was able to delegate the implementation of this operation to `theAccount`.

Understanding Inheritance

In general, Visual Basic doesn't support implementation inheritance, but it does enable you to use interface inheritance. *Interface inheritance* is the specializing of another class's interface for a particular context. Classes that implement the interface of another class share a unique relationship that can resemble a hierarchy or abstractions. In Booch semantics, each of such classes shares an "is a" relationship with the base class. For instance, a checking account is a type of bank account. Notice the use of the word *type*. A class's interface describes its type. For example, when you say CheckingAccount is a type of BankAccount, you are saying that the former inherits the interface of BankAccount. Therefore, if BankAccount has a public method deposit, CheckingAccount implements that same method in its own unique way, if necessary. In Visual Basic, this "is a" relationship would be realized as follows:

```
Class: CheckingAccount
Implements BankAccount 'In the General Declarations section of Checking
                       'Account
...
Private Sub BankAccount_deposit()
   'Insert code here...
...
End Sub

Class: BankAccount
Public Sub deposit()
...
End Sub
```

To get a better feel for inheritance in these classes, let's create them in Visual Basic. If you don't have it up and running, start it at this time with a new Standard project. Choose Add-Ins | Class Builder Utility from the menu. Simply create these classes by choosing File | New | Class from the menu for each. For the BankAccount class, be sure to insert a public function, deposit. To add a new method, select the BankAccount class in the Classes: browser, and select File | New | Method. You should see the Method Builder dialog box. Type in deposit and click the + button to add an argument, argAmount As Single. Click OK. Choose File | Update | Project and then File | Exit from the Class Builder menu. You now have two new class modules. Make the class module CheckingAccount the current module by clicking on it. Go to the General Declarations section, and type in the following:

```
Implements BankAccount
```

Check what you've typed in with Figure 4.1. The Implements keyword is how you tell Visual Basic that you want to inherit the interface of another class. Now click the (General) list box of the class module. You should see BankAccount listed just above the Class item. Choose BankAccount now. You should now see a Private Sub BankAccount_deposit (see Figure 4.2). You can enter any code you like. When you eventually run the project, all calls to the deposit method go to the implementation class (CheckingAccount, for this example).

FIGURE 4.1.

Showing how to specify the Implements *keyword.*

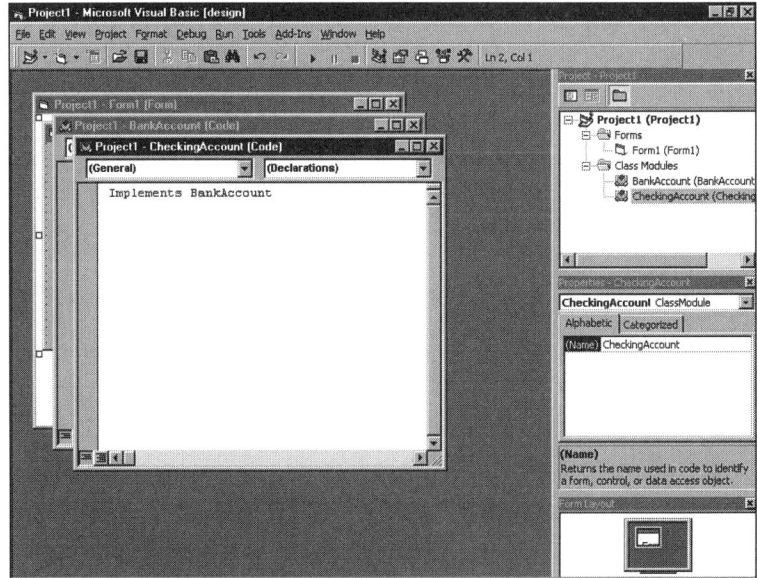

FIGURE 4.2.

Entering code in the deposit *method.*

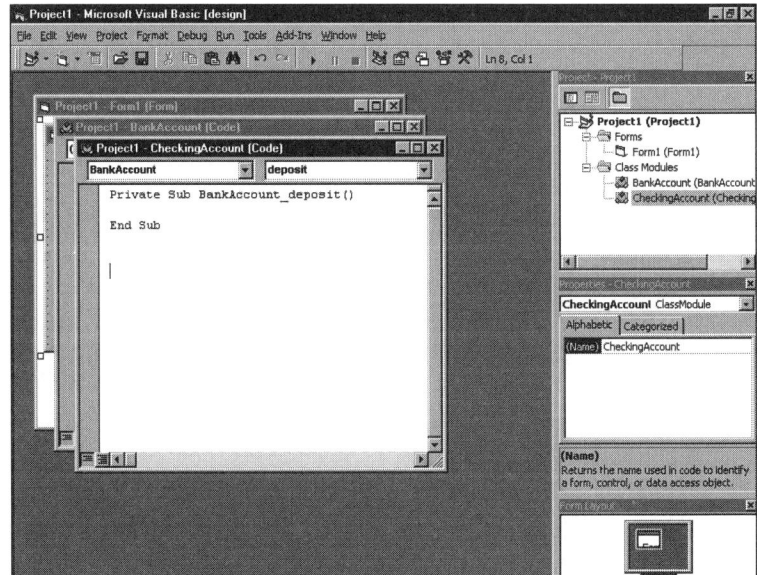

You're not finished yet. Implementing interfaces in Visual Basic can be clumsy. To make the preceding interface inheritance work, you'll need to include the following code in an initialization operation (such as Sub Main or some system initialization class):

```
Dim theCheckingAccount As New CheckingAccount
Dim theBankAccount As BankAccount
Set theBankAccount = theCheckingAccount
theBankAccount.deposit
```

What's the logic behind this? Although `BankAccount` might resemble an abstract class, it isn't one. It is a true interface class, meaning that although `BankAccount`'s interface to its clients remains the same, its implementation is delegated to the inheriting class `CheckingAccount`, a fact that is seamless to the client. This facilitates a plug-and-play mechanism whereby you can remove an implementing class and replace it with another that also implements the same interface. This other class could be, say, `SavingsAccount`. `SavingsAccount` would then specialize the `deposit` method, but the `BankAccount` interface class, which is broadly known by many classes, remains untouched. This means that you're spared the chore of having to go to every section of code that references the `BankAccount` object.

Understanding Polymorphism

Because Visual Basic supports interface inheritance, polymorphism is supported through the hierarchy of classes that implement a common interface. Polymorphism literally means *many forms*. In technical terms, polymorphism is realized when many classes implement a class's interface in special, unique ways.

Borrowing from your interface inheritance example, assume you have a `BankAccount` interface class and two implementation classes, `CheckingAccount` and `SavingsAccount`. Because `BankAccount` has a public method, `deposit`, both classes must implement it. Further, let's assume that `SavingsAccount` and `CheckingAccount` implement `deposit` as follows:

```
'SavingsAccount
Private Sub deposit(argAmount As Single)
    msgl_Balance = msgl_Balance + argAmount
End Sub

'CheckingAccount
Private Sub deposit(argAmount As Single)
    msgl_Balance = msgl_Balance + argAmount - Fee
End Sub
```

The following will use the first implementation:

```
Dim theSavingsAccount As New SavingsAccount
Dim theBankAccount As BankAccount
Set theBankAccount = theSavingsAccount
theBankAccount.deposit
```

whereas this will use the second implementation:

```
Dim theCheckingAccount As New CheckingAccount
Dim theBankAccount As BankAccount
Set theBankAccount = theCheckingAccount
theBankAccount.deposit
```

Thus, invoking `theBankAccount.deposit` with an implementation by `SavingsAccount`, an `argAmount` value of `100.00`, and a `msg1_Balance` of `0.00` would result in a new value for `msg1_Balance` of `100.00`. However, if you invoke `theBankAccount.deposit` with an implementation by `CheckingAccount` with the same `argAmount` value and a fee of `10.00`, `msg1_Balance` would equal `90.00`. The polymorphic effect is made manifest by the difference of `10.00` in the two different implementations of `BankAccount`.

Understanding Object Interface Communication

Object-to-object communication occurs through the interfaces of each object. In its most essential definition, an *interface* is the set of public methods that a class implements. For Visual Basic, a class interface also includes public properties. *Implementing an interface* means that an object supplies some expected behavior to its client. That expected behavior is made manifest in the form of some returned message, such as a value or object. In the course of supplying this expected behavior, an object can delegate some of its duties to other objects.

When a client object invokes the public method of another, is that method invocation an operation, or is the method itself an operation? There's much speculation on this issue in the object technology community. Nonetheless, an operation is more abstract than a method invocation and should not necessarily be seen as synonymous with the method itself. If a public method encapsulates all the code necessary to provide the expected behavior without the aid of private methods, the event of invoking that method triggers an operation. That is, the operation is a series of instructions. If the event of invoking the method results in other private methods in the object being invoked or even methods of other objects, the sum of the series of instructions implemented by all these methods is an operation.

REAL WORLD

To better understand how objects communicate, here's an example from the bank teller system under development. After elaborating the design of the application with your client at the Second Bank of Carrollton, you discovered the need for a Deposit class that acts as a controller and a BasicPersonalCheckingAccount class as a bank product class. These two objects, along with some prototypical lines of code, are represented in Listing 4.1.

LISTING 4.1. EXAMPLE OF INTEROBJECT COMMUNICATION IN THE SAMSONA BANK TELLER SYSTEM EXAMPLE.

```
 1: Object: theDeposit
 2:
 3: Methods:
 4: Public Function depositFunds(argAccountNumber As String,
    ⇒argAmount As Single)
 5:     'We'll use Call for the sake of simplicity.
 6:     Call theBasicPersonalCheckingAccount.adjustBalance(Me,
        ⇒argAccountNumber)
 7: End Function
 8:
 9: Sub Class_Initialize()
10:     msgl_Amount = 250.00
11:     ms_AccountNumber = "1002345"
12: End Sub
13:
14: Properties:
15: Amount
16:
17:
18: Object: theBasicPersonalCheckingAccount
19:
20: Methods:
21: Public Function adjustBalance(ByRef argObject, argAccountNumber
    ⇒As String)
22:     Dim LocalObject As Object
23:
24:     'If there's more than one account object in memory, a
        ⇒precondition
25:     'is that this object is the correct object. So check account
        ⇒number
26:     If argAccountNumber <> AccountNumber Then
27:         'Raise exceptions here...
28:         ...
29:         Exit Function
30:     End If
31:
```

continues

```
32:      'Delegate to private methods, where only one will be able to
33:      'process the message.
34:
35:      Set LocalObject = argObject
36:
37:      Call increaseFunds(LocalObject)
38:      Call decreaseFunds(LocalObject)
39:
40:      Set LocalObject = Nothing
41: End Function
42:
43: Private Function increaseBalance(ByRef argObject)
44:      'Make sure incoming object is of type Deposit
45:      If TypeName(argObject) <> "Deposit" Then
46:          Exit Function
47:      End If
48:
49: 'It's a Deposit object
50: CurrentBalance  = CurrentBalance + argObject.Amount
51:
52: End Function
53:
54: Private Function decreaseBalance(ByRef argObject)
55:      'Make sure incoming object is of type Withdrawal
56:      If TypeName(argObject) <> "Withdrawal" Then
57:          Exit Function
58:      End If
59:
60:      'It's a Withdrawal object
61:      CurrentBalance  = CurrentBalance - argObject.Amount
62: End Function
63:
64: Properties:
65: AccountNumber
66: CurrentBalance
```

Before explaining Listing 4.1, note several things. First, the theDeposit object doesn't have an AccountNumber property. Why? There's not any hard and fast rule, but to minimize the chance of violating encapsulation, the decision was made that theDeposit object be a controller of events between some user interface and the business domain object, theBasicPersonalCheckingAccount. Also note that theDeposit object has only one method and attribute (or property). This is intentional, to keep the example simple. In reality, your object's class will have at least two or three methods. Finally, check out

▼ the regular use of functions, as opposed to subs. Functions give you the flexibility of

▼ having returns as part of your postcondition behavior. Subs are used when postcondition processing isn't required, such as the simple setting of a property's value (although certain applications might even need to process the integrity of a built-in data type). Now back to the example.

Figure 4.3 illustrates the interaction between the bank teller, the `theDeposit` object, and `theBasicPersonalCheckingAccount` object. Using its `depositFunds` method as its operational starting point, the `theDeposit` object communicates with the `theBasicPersonalCheckingAccount` object via the latter object's `adjustBalance` method. The `adjustBalance` method accepts two arguments, the object reference of the client object (`theDeposit`, in this case) and the actual account number of the account to which the deposit is to be applied.

FIGURE 4.3.

A sequence diagram showing the interaction between the bank teller, the theDeposit *object, and the* theBasicPersonalCheckingAccount *object.*

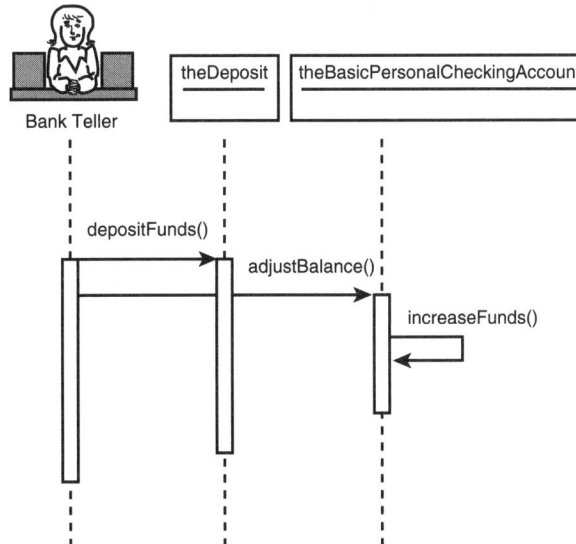

The `adjustBalance` method of the `theBasicPersonalCheckingAccount` object is interesting. At the top of the method body is a declaration of a local object variable called `LocalObject`. The purpose of this object variable is to localize the reference to the object represented by the argument `argObject`. The next few lines of code, included in the `If Then` statement, perform a precondition check to ensure that the object is the proper target for receiving the message. The qualifier is the `AccountNumber` value. If the account number passed in isn't equal to the account number of `theBasicPersonalCheckingAccount` object, an exception is raised and the operation is stopped. If the account number values

▼ are equal, the operation continues.

▼ The next four lines of code in the adjustBalance method are important. The LocalObject object variable is initialized to whatever object is represented by the argObject argument variable. Then LocalObject is passed to two private methods, increaseFunds and decreaseFunds, for special processing. Notice the seeming ambiguity of first increasing the funds and then decreasing the funds. On closer inspection, you'll find that there is no ambiguity at all. Only one method can handle the LocalObject message. Look at the bodies of these two private methods. As with the adjustBalance method, these two check to make sure that each can handle the incoming message. Because the LocalObject variable was set to the theDeposit object (via argObject), only increaseBalance can handle it, whereas decreaseBalance ignores it. Why do this? Because it avoids the unnecessary introduction of a complex If Then statement. That is, if you converted the following two lines of code

```
Call increaseFunds(LocalObject)
Call decreaseFunds(LocalObject)
```

to the following:

```
If TypeName(argObject) = "Deposit" Then

    'It's a Deposit object
    CurrentBalance  = CurrentBalance + argObject.Amount

ElseIf TypeName(argObject) = "Withdrawal" Then

    'It's a Withdrawal object
    CurrentBalance  = CurrentBalance - argObject.Amount

Else

    Exit Function

End If
```

it's harder to read—despite the two styles being functionally equivalent. Having such method calls avoids the clumsiness of complex If Then statements and makes it easier to maintain nicely encapsulated chunks of code. Finally, the two methods exhibit the behavior expected by the client: either to increment or decrement the CurrentBalance attribute by the value of the Amount property of the argObject object.

Tip

Having precondition checks is important in interobject communications. They ensure that the object is the proper recipient of a message. The idea of precondition checks is part of what's called *self-testing* objects. You will read more about this concept on Day 8, "Versioning and Debugging."

Defining Methods

Methods are nicely encapsulated series of code instructions that enable access to implemented behavior. Public methods enable external clients access to publicly known services, whereas private methods help public methods provide those services. In defining public methods, you'll need to review the specification for the expected class behavior, as documented in artifacts such as class diagrams and in interaction diagrams such as sequence diagrams and collaboration diagrams. In defining private methods, look for opportunities to break up numerous lines of code in public methods. For example, in the preceding paragraph, you saw two private methods that avoided the use of a potentially long and complex If Then statement body. Some private methods will already be defined in the design diagrams mentioned earlier.

Defining Accessors and Mutators

Defining accessors (get property values) and mutators (set property values) is simpler than defining regular methods. For every property (or attribute) a class has, you can create a getProperty method and a setProperty method. However, be careful. If you have a class that has nothing but accessors and mutators, you might potentially violate encapsulation because other classes might behaviorally use those methods in ways that could signal a lost method. That is, a method of a client object could have a method that manipulates the server object's property in a way that would make that method a candidate for the server object. For instance, referring to Listing 4.1, assume that the adjustBalance method of theBasicPersonalCheckingAccount object had been designed into the theDeposit object. Also assume that an accessor, getCurrentBalance, and a mutator, setCurrentBalance, are new methods for the theBasicPersonalCheckingAccount object. Now that the theDeposit object has the adjustBalance method, it would simply call getCurrentBalance of theBasicPersonalCheckingAccount object, increase it by the value of Amount, and call theBasicPersonalCheckingAccount.setCurrentBalance to assign the new value. In this case, having the accessor and mutator helps to violate encapsulation by having a foreign object manipulate the owning object's properties. In many cases, however, having accessors and mutators is okay for statistics and totaling or for listing values of a collection of the same type of objects for users to view.

Understanding Subsystems

By now, you have some familiarity with subsystems. Subsystems provide an opportunity to group classes together to carry out some major chunk of an application's behavior. The logical representation of a subsystem is called a *category*, although this sometimes leads to confusion between the two. The distinction between the two is a relic of C++ programming, with the separate header and implementation files that map to one logical class. For Visual Basic, a class interface and implementation are stored in one file, so there is no real distinction. Thus, a subsystem of five class files maps directly to a category of five classes. For simplicity, I'll use the term *subsystem*.

In technical terms, a subsystem is a physical group of class modules (*physical* meaning class files). A more robust meaning is that each class in the group plays a role in providing an expected behavioral response to a client of the subsystem.

Subsystems communicate with one another through public interface classes. Referring again to Listing 4.1, assume that you have a subsystem called `AccountManagement`. Both `theDeposit` and `theBasicPersonalCheckingAccount` are objects in it. The `theDeposit` object could easily be a public interface class because it played a similar role as user interface controller earlier. Any needs of a client subsystem to have the `AccountManagement` subsystem to handle deposits would be routed through `theDeposit`.

Identifying Technical Constraints of the Implementation Environment

Because Visual Basic still doesn't enable you to fully implement every pillar of object-oriented programming, there are some notions you'll need to keep in mind. Along with these notions, I'll discuss some solutions.

Visual Basic doesn't support implementation inheritance. This is a fancy sentence that means that the private members of class A cannot be inherited by class B. However, Visual Basic does support limited interface inheritance, which means that class B can inherit the public members of class A. I say *limited* because class B cannot inherit the public members that class A inherits from another class. The inheritance of public members in Visual Basic is done via the `Implements` keyword. This choice of wording might confuse some people. The keyword `Implements` doesn't imply implementation inheritance. It facilitates interface inheritance.

In any event, implementation inheritance can be replaced in most cases with delegation. Whole books have been written about delegation, but the idea, as explained briefly on Day 3, is that object A delegates some or all of its behavior to object B. The `Account` class used the `CheckingAccountHistoryInfo` class to verify a customer's checking account history. Hence, the `Account` class instance (`theAccount`) used the `CheckingAccountHistoryInfo` class instance (`theCheckingAccountHistoryInfo`) as follows:

```
Public Sub verifyCheckAccountHistory(SomeCustomerSSN)
    theCheckingAccountHistoryInfo.verify(SomeCustomerSSN)
End Sub
```

Delegation is synonymous with the "uses" relationship as defined in the Unified Modeling Language. That is, when one object delegates some or all of its responsibilities to another object, the former object is using that latter object.

Also, Visual Basic doesn't support the kind of polymorphism associated with inheritance lattices. In other words, if a superclass named `theSuperClass` has a method called `print`, and a subclass of `theSuperClass`, `theSubclass`, also has a specialized (or customized) method called `print`, and, in turn, a subclass of the `theSubclass` has a specialized method named `print`, the compiler would use the specialized method of the class instance being used for a given context (or section of code). With the absence of implementation inheritance and full interface inheritance, this kind of polymorphism is practically nonexistent. (Of course, a class's interface can be inherited one level down as if it were a pure virtual base class, but Visual Basic expects the public methods and properties to be implemented by the client class.)

Visual Basic supports the other kind of polymorphism, in which a collection of objects with one or more methods of the same name will have varying behaviors when iterated. That is, using the Samsona Bank Teller System example, suppose you have collection of history verification objects, `theCheckingAccountHistoryInfo` and `theCreditHistoryInfo`. As you saw in the previous chapter, each of these objects has a method called `verify`. Let's create a collection object called `HistoryVerifiers`. Here are the steps for creating such a collection object:

1. Start a new project in Visual Basic.
2. Create a class called `CheckingAccountHistoryInfo` and a class called `CreditHistoryInfo`. Using either Rational Rose/Visual Basic or Visual Modeler, you can generate them by choosing Tools | Code Generation Wizard from the menu of either application.

Background on Code Generation in Rational Rose and Visual Modeler

Automating the process of creating object-oriented programming code considerably reduces the normal risks associated with software development projects. Such risks include the obvious human error factor in coding, the risk of not properly transitioning from a model to the actual code base, the risk of not properly documenting code, and so on. Both Rational Rose/Visual Basic and Microsoft Visual Modeler offer automated code engineering and reverse code engineering to drastically reduce these risks. Because you used Rational Rose/Visual Basic for the use cases on Day 2, you should use Microsoft Visual Modeler in this chapter. Note that the processes of creating code from models and reverse engineering existing code are exactly the same in both products, so you will be able to use the following steps in either tool. If you own Visual Basic Professional or Enterprise, you can go to www.microsoft.com/vbasic, register in the Owners' Area as a licensed user, and download Visual Modeler for free. Otherwise, you need to go to www.rational.com and make arrangements to pay for Rational Rose/Visual Basic. If nothing else, you can still model your classes by hand.

Generating Code for the Samsona Bank Teller System Example

▼ REAL WORLD

After verifying the design models with peer architects at your company and with your client, you're ready for construction to begin. To keep things simple, your iteration plan only includes one iteration, meaning that all use cases must be implemented. You had anticipated the need for only one additional programmer, but after reviewing your design models, you make a better staff resource estimate that calls for two additional programmers, which your client agrees to. In reviewing the design models and project plans with your programmers, you advise them to refrain from activities that could lead to scope creep, such as making assumptions about requirements. If additional requirements are discovered, you advise your programmers to review them with you first.

For the application's architecture, you list the various components, mechanisms, and design patterns you plan to use. You expect to use any controls that ship with Visual Basic, plus the following subsystems:

Graphical User Interface Subsystem

Workgroup and User Security Subsystem

Internal Application Manager Subsystem

Business Rules Subsystem

Reporting and Printing Subsystem

File Operations Subsystem

Error-Processing and Exception-Handling Subsystem

Database Access Subsystem

▼ (Each subsystem will be covered in detail in subsequent chapters.) Your programmers are impressed with this separation of concerns and are eager to begin.

Caution

Make sure to have plenty of hardware capacity when simultaneously running both Visual Basic and Visual Modeler. I work with these tools on two PCs (PII-233 and P133), each with 32MB of RAM and 5GB of disk space (with the maximum recommended virtual memory setting). Otherwise, these tools could suffer serious performance degradation and crash your machine.

NEW TERM An *iteration plan* sets forth which use cases and/or features of the application will be implemented in each construction cycle.

With Visual Basic running, start Visual Modeler. Create the classes shown in Table 4.1, along with their corresponding properties and methods.

TABLE 4.1. CLASSES FOR THE SAMSONA BANK TELLER SYSTEM EXAMPLE.

Class	Properties	Methods
Customer	FirstName	establish
	LastName	verify
	MiddleName	
	Address	
	City	
	State	
	Zip	
	Country	
	Phone	
	DOB	
	SSN	
BankAccounts (Collection class)		
Account	Number	openAccount
	CurrBalance	closeAccount
	Status	withdraw
		deposit
		view
CreditHistoryInfo	CreditBureauID	verify
CheckAccountHistoryInfo	IsHistoryOK	verify

4

continues

▼ **TABLE 4.1.** CONTINUED

Class	Properties	Methods
Teller_Interface	None	closeAccount(argAcctNum As String)
		depositFunds(argAmount As Currency)
		openAccount(argSSN As String)
		queryCheckingHistory(argSSN As String)
		queryCreditHistory(argSSN As String)
		Private: verifyExistingAccount(Optional argSSN, Optional argAcctNum)
		withdrawFunds(argAmount As Currency)

Notice that BankAccounts is a collection class. You will implement this as a collection class in Visual Basic. You can manually put in the standard methods and properties that collections typically have, or you can automate the process of creating collection classes. To automate this process, first choose Tools | Class Builder Utility from the menu. If you've used Visual Basic before reading this chapter, you'll recognize the familiar Class Builder dialog. Choose File | New | Collection from the menu in the Class Builder dialog. You should see the Collection Builder dialog. By default, the name suggested for the new collection is Collection1. Change this to BankAccounts. Leave the Based On: drop-down list box alone because you are creating a new collection. In the Collection Of frame, choose New Class to trick the utility into letting you proceed (you won't need the class it creates). Click OK. Click File | Update project from the menu (Visual Basic needs to be running). Exit the Class Builder utility.

Note
If you encounter conflict problems with the existing BankAccounts class, delete it from the model, and re-create it as a collection class. Otherwise, add the typical collection properties and methods to the existing BankAccounts class in the model.

You will see the Reverse Engineering Wizard welcome dialog. Because you are creating the BankAccounts collection class first, using the Class Builder utility within Visual Modeler, you must reverse engineer it back into the current model. Thus, click the Next button. There's no need to select a component, so click the Next button again. The next step is to assign the new collection class to a Logical View Package. The standard packages are User, Business, and Data Services. User Services includes the class associated
▼ with graphical user interface processes. Business Services has those classes associated

▼   with real-world entities in the client's environment. The Data Services package houses the classes that facilitate the saving of precious business information from an application session to a persistent information repository, such as a database or a flat file. The BankAccounts collection class is a business domain class, so it belongs in the Business Services package. Drag it to the Business Services package folder now. Click the Next button. The wizard will now copy the collection class to your current model. Click the Finish button. Click the Close button. That's it.

Now let's generate the code. Choose Tools | Code Generation Wizard from the menu in Visual Modeler. The Code Generation Wizard dialog will appear. Click the Next button. In the current step, you're asked to select the classes in the model for which you want to generate code. Because by default all the classes are chosen for you, simply click the Next button. You are now asked to set the code generation properties of each class member (property or method). To keep things simple, just click the Next button. The current step asks you to set general code generation options, such as whether to include debug code, Err.Raise, and comments in code, as well as whether you want to generate new collection classes. By default, all these options are selected. Let's keep them. Click the Next button. The wizard now displays a list of your classes. Click the Finish button. The wizard generates the code for you. When it's finished, you'll see a summary of actions the wizard did during the process. When you're satisfied with what you see, click the Close button.

By now, you might be wondering where your newly generated code went. Don't worry. Switch to your current Visual Basic session. (If you didn't have Visual Basic running during the code generation process, Visual Modeler would have notified you that Visual Basic must be running in order to generate code.) You will see several cascaded code
▲   windows for each class created.

Putting the Finishing Touches on the Application

Although Visual Modeler is a smart tool, it's not smart enough to provide all the logic necessary to make your code work the way your client wants the system to work. If it were, you would probably be out of a job!

For your newly generated code to work, you'll have to re-examine the use cases to further determine what the user wants. This activity might prompt several more use-case iterations with the users to ensure that every requirement for the current release of the system is in place and that there are no discrepancies. It's far less costly in time and money to verify use cases before coding than afterwards, so be patient with this process.

The use cases will also guide you in developing the components of the graphical user interface because they generally tell you how the users will use the proposed system.

Your style of coding will no doubt differ from others, but the general goal is to keep your code style and syntax as simple and clear as possible. Never mind the individualistic signature and artistic flair too many developers hope to instill in their code. Traceability among all the artifacts of the development process, including the use cases and code, is important. This is particularly true for future evolutionary activities such as maintenance and software evolution.

Summary

In this chapter, you learned the essence of object-oriented programming in Visual Basic. In other words, you learned how to make classes communicate with each other to carry out a behavior or set of behaviors for a proposed system. You also became familiar with design models and learned the importance of not deviating from the system's architecture. You received some background on generating code in Rational Rose and Visual Modeler, as well as on identifying the known technical constraints of Visual Basic. After you generated some sample code, you had an idea of how to put the finishing touches on the application.

Q&A

Q What are the two ways in which you can create properties in Visual Basic?

A With regular functions and subs and with built-in `Property Get` and `Let` methods (with an optional `Property Set` method for properties that reference objects).

Q What is encapsulation?

A The separation of a class's interface from its internal, private implementation.

Q What is interface inheritance?

A The specializing of another class's interface for a particular context. Classes that implement the interface of another class share a unique relationship that can resemble a hierarchy or abstractions.

Q What is polymorphism?

A The realization of one class's interface through the classes that implement the interface of that class in special, unique ways.

Workshop

The workshop includes quiz questions to help gauge your grasp of the material. You'll find the answers to this quiz in Appendix A. Even if you feel that you totally understand the concepts presented here, you should work through the quiz anyway. The last section is an exercise or two that you might work through to help reinforce your learning.

Quiz

1. What is the role of OOP in solution development?
2. What is a long-term benefit of encapsulation?
3. How are the terms *type* and *interface* related?
4. How do you realize interface inheritance in Visual Basic?
5. What's the difference between collection and aggregate objects?
6. What are methods, accessors, and mutators?
7. What's the difference between a subsystem and a category?
8. What is a class diagram? a sequence diagram?

Exercises

1. Open a new Standard Visual Basic project. Use the Class Builder utility to create two classes with the following design specification:

```
Class: MedicalPatient

Methods:
Private Sub payBill
Public Function requestMedicalService

Attributes:
Name As String
ChargeCardType As String

Class: Physician
Methods:
Public Function renderService
Private Sub analyzeSymptoms()
Private Sub billPatient(argPatientObject As Object)

Properties:
Name As String
Certification As String
Degree As String
```

4

2. Using exercise 1, assume the Physician class is now responsible for scheduling regular visits. How would you modify both the MedicalPatient class and the Physician class so that the patient regularly visits the physician's offices and the physician schedules these visits?

3. Assume you have designed a user interface with a command button, cmdDepositFunds. How would you program the operation to deposit funds into a checking account? (Hint: Use Listing 4.1 for assistance.)

4. Create a class in Visual Basic called Tree that has a public method grow. Then create a class, OakTree, that implements the Tree class.

DAY 5

Class Interface
Inheritance in Visual Basic

Up to this point, you have learned about object-oriented programming in a general sense. From this day on, you will delve deeper into object-oriented programming, starting with interface inheritance.

Elaborating Classes at Design Time

Defining any Visual Basic class is one of the most difficult things you can do. A Visual Basic class is more than a convenient module that provides better localization of variables and functions. It represents a logical unit abstracted above mere code—a logically identified chunk of your application that is less coupled to other chunks of your application and plays a role in the application. Thus, you can have a class that controls the events between a form and the rest of the application, or you can have one or more data service classes that handle the exchange of information between the database and the rest of the application. For classes based on concepts from the user's domain, a Visual Basic class takes on even more meaning. For a bank, a meaningful Visual Basic class would be CheckingAccount. For a defense contractor, Government would be a meaningful Visual Basic class.

At design time, class definitions are static (as opposed to dynamic at runtime). During this time, you are defining and/or refining the uses of behavior between Visual Basic classes. Thus, the usage protocol between classes is your main concern. Included in this protocol is not only the precise invocation of methods but also the signature of the methods. This signature includes the ordering and types of arguments in a method's argument list. Considerable changes to class method signatures during construction (programming phase) can lead to extensive code rewrites and communication problems between classes and subsystems.

Sometimes you will find it necessary to convert semantic relationships between classes. For instance, you could have originally designed a CheckingAccount class to have an inheritance relationship to the BankAccount interface class. However, during construction, you found this relationship too awkward or performance costly. In this case, you could convert the relationship to delegation. Then BankAccount would have the common behavior and identity of all bank account products, and CheckingAccount would be given the delegated responsibility of behavior and identity that is particular to checking account products. Such architectural changes might trigger the need for a minor domain analysis to justify the new relationship.

> **Tip**
>
> When elaborating a class at design time, remember that you can't expect to correctly design the class's public methods and attributes the first time or even the second time. A good class interface takes time to develop and nurture. Class design is an iterative (cyclical) process.

When elaborating methods, you will fine-tune how each method operates. If a method contains too many lines of code (say, more than ten or twenty), you should definitely consider creating additional methods to offload some of the work. These additional methods are known as *helper* or *collaborating methods*. The idea is to keep class methods simple.

Preparing Visual Basic Objects for Runtime Behavior

At runtime, your classes come alive in the form of objects. One object collaborates with another to carry out some responsibility on behalf of a client. All this sounds wonderful, but in reality these object creatures you create consume resources that need to be accounted for while you're constructing the system.

> **Note** In most cases, memory issues are not your concern when performing analytic studies of a problem being solved. Only during design and construction of the solution are you concerned with performance-related resource issues.

The best way to manage your runtime object creatures is to implement tactics to reduce the amount of memory space your application needs. Do not neglect to declare the return type of a `Function` method, that is, if you have a method of the following form:

```
Public Function createAccount()
```

as opposed to the following form:

```
Public Function createAccount() As SomeBankProductType
```

then the `Function` method implicitly defaults to

```
Public Function createAccount() As Variant
```

Variants require more memory than other types because of the underlying mapping to specific types. Further, remember to reclaim any memory allocated to a particular object variable. For instance, say you have a class named `WireTransfer`. You then instantiate an object of this type as follows:

```
Set theWireTransfer = New WireTransfer
```

or as follows:

```
Dim theWireTransfer As New WireTransfer
```

To reclaim memory occupied by `theWireTransfer`—and as good programming practice—you should also include the following line of code when you're finished with this object:

```
Set theWireTransfer = Nothing
```

It's not easy to remember this important practice, and it takes time to form this habit.

Runtime constraints on object behavior also necessitate the practice of tracking and eliminating unused methods and attributes. If your Visual Basic class is becoming large with numerous methods, try restructuring your class by dividing it into other helper classes. This separation of concerns within large classes provides better memory efficiency because a smaller set of methods is housed in separate class modules. Visual Basic loads

5

class modules for serving objects into memory only when a client object invokes a method in the serving object's class module. Therefore, having a small set of logically related methods per class module means that the Visual Basic compiler only loads such modules into memory when one of those methods is invoked. A small set of methods would likely consist of three to five public methods and five to seven private methods. Do not overuse property methods; this can be an indicator of a poor design that might unnecessarily break encapsulation.

Finally, you should be aware of memory considerations in constructing components in Visual Basic. Because every in-process component has a chance of using the same memory location of other like components or executables, you must manipulate the component's base address to make it distinctive. This is important for distributed architectures in environments such as companies and university computer labs where multiple clients access a set of components on a given server. If this characterizes your situation, you need to rebase the component. See "Setting Base Addresses for In-Process Components" in Visual Basic's Books Online for more information.

NEW TERM   An *in-process component* is one that is realized in the form of a DLL or OCX file and runs in the address space of the client. ActiveX components can be designed as in-process.

Planning for Object Reuse Early in the Visual Basic Project

Planning for any form of reuse is very difficult and initially slows down your projects. However, one excellent benefit of object-oriented programming is that you can systematically take advantage of the work of predecessors. The best way to achieve reuse is through

- Well-defined class interfaces in which each interface has only a few, well-encapsulated public methods
- Elaboration of abstractions from unambiguous terms and concepts in the domain
- Uncomplicated class inheritance relationships or delegation
- Well-documented use cases that can be reused
- Commitment from fellow team members to practice good object-oriented programming

Planning reuse also requires the investigation of repetitive code patterns, among other project artifacts. For instance, if you notice that each of several methods you are using has code for loading information into a list box, you might need a commonly shared class responsible for loading information into a list box.

Pattern investigation does not have to be in code. The construction process itself can have repeatable patterns. Visual Basic enables you to benefit from such process patterns through the VBProject object, Visual Basic add-ins, and, generally speaking, the Extensibility Object Model.

Note | Read about the Extensibility Object Model in my book *Visual Basic 5 Development* (Sams Publishing, 1998).

The Difference Between Interface and Implementation Classes

In Visual Basic, any class that implements its own interface or the interface of another class is an *implementation class*. However, an *interface class* is a class whose sole responsibility is to enable its interface to be implemented by other classes. Borrowing from the Samsona Bank Teller System example, the CheckingAccount class is an interface class because its methods have to be implemented by (performed by) the BasicPersonalCheckingAccount class.

The distinction between interface and implementation classes is very important in component development. As part of Microsoft's overall design strategy, COM components implement at least one interface. This is not an option. Gradually, an interface can evolve, but the previous interface must still be supported, for the benefit of clients having no knowledge of the new interface.

Illustrating Example: Second Bank of Carrollton

For your Second Bank of Carrollton customer, for instance, say you created an interface class, ISavingsAccount, with the following public methods:

```
deposit()
withdraw()
calculateInterest()
```

Now your customer informs you that for new savings accounts, no withdrawals are allowed, only transfers to a checking account. On the surface, the answer seems simple: Eliminate the withdraw method—which you do that night. The next day you receive a call from some tellers who can't execute any savings withdrawal transactions for older savings account products. You have to go back and add that interface method, at a cost to both the Second Bank of Carrollton and your employer, Samsona Software.

Understanding How to Model and Design for Classes and Subsystems

You completed your initial set of interaction and class diagrams, started coding, and everything seemed to be smooth sailing. Then you ran into design flaws in some class interfaces that you did not anticipate while you were in the elaboration phase. What to do? Quite simply, you need to revisit those diagrams and pinpoint applicationwide ramifications of those flaws.

Designing and Modeling Classes

Although formal design might end as construction begins, you will still make some micro-level design decisions. For example, you have to refine a particular aggregation association between classes into either composition or containment. *Aggregation* represents a tightly or loosely coupled ownership relationship between an aggregate object and the objects it's aggregating. *Ownership* means that the aggregate object owns either the lifetime of an object (*composition*) or the exclusive use of services (*containment*) of an object. Aggregation is best defined by the distinction between composition and containment.

The composite object is responsible for creating and destroying the object of which it is composed. In some cases, the composite object specifies that another object be delegated such responsibility, as in the case of object factories and garbage collectors. In such cases, a factory must be tasked only with creating the object, and the garbage collector must be responsible only for destroying the object. If a factory or garbage collector uses these objects for any other reason, it could be argued that the factory and the garbage collector *contain* the object rather than create or destroy it.

Containment is similar to composition, except that the containing object is not responsible for the life of the contained object. An object can create another object for its exclusive use but can't pass the object to another for the other's use. This is the case with collections in which a containing object creates an object, populates it with data from a graphical user interface, and then passes that object to a collection. A collection object contains objects.

NEW TERM *Aggregation* is the tightly or loosely coupled ownership relationship between an aggregate object and the objects it's aggregating. *Composition* is the lifetime ownership of an object by an aggregate object. *Containment* is ownership of the exclusive use of an object by an aggregate object.

Illustrating Example: Second Bank of Carrollton

REAL WORLD ▼

Your client requires that the Samsona Bank Teller System dial up the Federal Reserve's online funds rate monitoring system every fifteen minutes to obtain the latest Fed Funds Rate. All bank products and internal bank holding accounts that depend on this rate must reflect it in calculating the interest rate for each type of interest-sensitive account. After completing the analysis and design for this requirement, you have the simplified account classes, as shown in Table 5.1.

TABLE 5.1. IMPORTANT APPLICATION CLASSES FOR THE SECOND BANK OF CARROLLTON.

Class	Attribute	Method
Savings	AccountNumber	calculateInterestRate()
	CurrentBalance	accrueInterest()
	InterestRate	deposit()
		withdraw()
InterestBearingChecking	AccountNumber	calculateInterestRate()
	CurrentBalance	accrueInterest()
	InterestRate	deposit()
		withdraw()
BankHolding	AccountNumber	calculateInterestRate()
	CurrentBalance	accrueInterest()
	InterestRate	deposit()
	TypeOfHolding	transfer()
		calculateTax()
FedFundsMonitor	PhoneNumber	calculateFundsRate()
	CurrentRate	getRate()
ObjectFactory	None	createSavings()
		createInterestBearingChecking()
		createBankHolding()
AccountCollection	None	addObject()
		removeObject()
		getObject()
		persistObjects()

▼ Listing 5.1 shows the declarations for each object.

▼ **LISTING 5.1.** OBJECT DECLARATIONS.

```
 1: In a general code module:
 2:
 3: Global theAccountCollection As New AccountCollection
 4: Global theObjectFactory As New ObjectFactory
 5: Global theFedFundsMonitor As FedFundsMonitor
 6:
 7: In ObjectFactory's General Declarations:
 8: Dim theBankHolding As BankHolding
 9: Dim theInterestBearingChecking As InterestBearingChecking
10: Dim theSavings As Savings
```

Figure 5.1 shows the sequence diagram for the course of events that determines the inter-action between these objects. Basically, interest is calculated and accrued for each type of account on a periodic basis. The object, theFedFundsMonitor, is responsible for pro-viding the current Fed Funds Rate.

FIGURE 5.1.

The sequence diagram illus-trating the inter-action between objects.

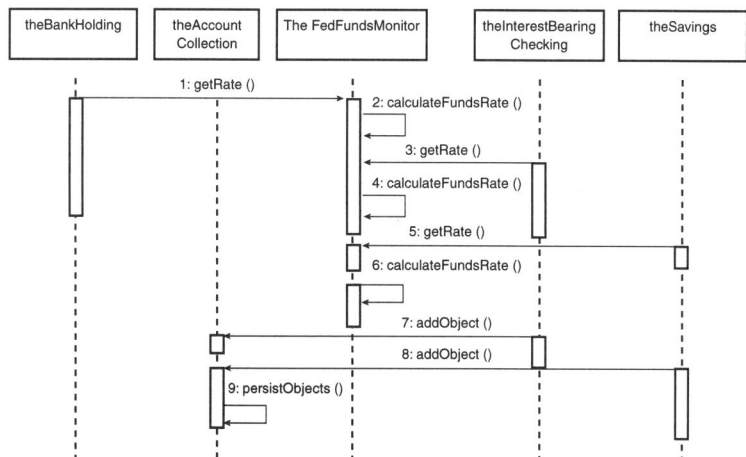

The object, theObjectFactory, initializes theInterestBearingChecking, theSavings, and theBankHolding. Note that although theObjectFactory creates these three objects, it is not responsible for their lifetimes. This means that theObjectFactory is not com-posed of these three objects.

Each of the objects theInterestBearingChecking, theSavings, and theBankHolding has lifetime responsibility for theFedFundsMonitor. Each is composed of instances of FedFundsMonitor.

Finally, when each of the three objects has destroyed its respective instances of
▼ FedFundsMonitor, each object adds itself (using the Me keyword) to

▼ theAccountCollection. The object theAccountCollection becomes a container of theInterestBearingChecking, theSavings, and theBankHolding.

Designing and Modeling Subsystems

As with classes, you might make some micro-level design decisions when programmatically grouping classes into subsystems. Some classes will be responsible for providing an externally visible interface to the services provided by the subsystem. Other classes will simply implement those services on behalf of the subsystem interface classes. There are two ways to construct subsystems: Expose several interface classes to external clients, or expose one interface class when the class is more of a broker. The former is more common with object repositories; the latter broker case is more common, in general, because it is really a design pattern. Table 5.2 contains some examples of these.

TABLE 5.2. SUBSYSTEM CLASSES.

Class	Attribute	Method
Savings	AccountNumber	calculateInterestRate()
	CurrentBalance	accrueInterest()
	InterestRate	deposit()
		withdraw()
InterestBearingChecking	AccountNumber	calculateInterestRate()
	CurrentBalance	accrueInterest()
	InterestRate	deposit()
		withdraw()
BankHolding	AccountNumber	calculateInterestRate()
	CurrentBalance	accrueInterest()
	InterestRate	deposit()
	TypeOfHolding	calculateTax()
		transfer(ByVal argAmount, ByVal argAccountNumber1, ByVal argAccountNumber2)

Programming broker classes is straightforward. It implies a delegation relationship between the broker class and the serving classes. Given a broker class BankHolding, the General Declarations section could include the following:

```
Private theInterestBearingChecking As New _ InterestBearingChecking
```

▼ `Private theSavings As New Savings`

▼   Further, let's examine the transfer() method:

```
transfer(ByVal argAmount, ByVal argAccountNumber1, _
    ByVal argAccountNumber2)
```

For simplicity's sake, ignore the types of each argument. argAmount is the amount of money to be transferred between accounts. Assume that argAccountNumber1 refers to an interest-bearing checking account and that argAccountNumber2 refers to a savings account. Assume that the object, theBankHolding, knows how to map each type of account to its corresponding methods and that a transfer is implemented as a withdrawal from the first account and a deposit to the second account. In code, a client object would view the transfer operation as follows:

```
'Declare theBankHolding object
Global theBankHolding As New BankHolding

. . .

'Place in some event or method
Dim acknowledgment As Integer
acknowledgment = theBankHolding.transfer(100, 2001, 3002)
```

Subsystems that expose public interface classes operate in a manner to provide a similar result but add more complexity. For instance, modifying your code, you have the following:

```
Public theInterestBearingChecking As New _ InterestBearingChecking

Public theSavings As New Savings

. . .

'Declare theBankHolding object
Global theBankHolding As New BankHolding



'Place in some event or method
Dim acknowledgment As Integer

acknowledgment = _
theBankHolding.theInterestBearingChecking.withdraw(100)

acknowledgment = _
theBankHolding.theSavings.deposit(100)
```

Notice that theInterestBearingChecking and theSavings are declared as Public with-
▼   in BankHolding. To use classes that act as interface agents for a subsystem, you must

▼ declare them Public. Keep in mind, also, that using this programming tactic introduces a level of complexity in that clients of the subsystem are exposed to more internal details than with the broker approach. This will add to the maintenance of the application as it evolves in the future. However, this approach is ideal for your object repositories in those situations in which clients will know about the interfaces anyway.

Finally, subsystems can be implemented as COM/DCOM or CORBA components. Components contain one to many objects that together provide a set of related services to the component's clients via interfaces. You can have components that interact with other components locally on the same machine or remotely on different machines. If you deploy components remotely, you are entering the realm of distributed computing, which is full of complexity.

> **Note** CORBA is an acronym for Common Object Request Broker Architecture. COM/DCOM stands for Component Object Model/Distributed Component Object Model.

Whether you're deploying components locally or remotely, every interface requires a separate, distinct interface ID. In the earlier example, given the following declarations:

```
Public theInterestBearingChecking As New _ InterestBearingChecking
```

```
Public theSavings As New Savings
```

both theInterestBearingChecking and theSavings would have to have published interface IDs. In COM/DCOM, each interface's version is given a globally unique identifier
▲ (GUID). The CORBA equivalent of GUID is the universally unique identifier (UUID).

5

COM has many interfaces beyond the scope of this book to describe. However, one COM interface must be noted. When implementing a COM component in Visual Basic, the interfaces inside implement COM's IUnknown interface. IUnknown's main responsibilities include runtime type checking and enforcement as well as interface reference counting. IUnknown publishes three methods—AddRef(), Release(), and QueryInterface()—that, together, make this interface class similar to the ObjectFactory sample class earlier. AddRef() is invoked when a class instance is created, and Release() is invoked to destroy the same class instance. QueryInterface() is seamlessly invoked to obtain a specific interface pointer using an interface pointer identifier. Although, as a Visual Basic developer, you won't have to worry about IUnknown, it's good to know what goes on under the hood as a starting point for investigating object reference flaws.

> **Note**
>
> You can learn more about creating and using ActiveX/COM/DCOM components in *Visual Basic 5 Development Unleashed* by Sams Publishing.

Revisiting the Unified Modeling Language (UML)

Since fall 1994, Grady Booch and James Rumbaugh, and later Ivar Jacobson, have led a group of professionals on a quest to unify the ways that object-oriented designers and programmers express the details of their proposed applications. Their quest was supported by the Object Management Group, which pursued a common modeling language. While developing this modeling language, the "Three Amigos" (as they're affectionately known) used this common notation development as a good excuse to also unify some methodology concepts. This section covers the simpler notions of the modeling language notation.

The Unified Modeling Language (UML) provides a common set of notational symbols to describe the architecture of a system, including use cases. Although some concepts embodied in the notation are a subject of interesting debate in the object technology community, UML 1.1 is gaining wide acceptance. A related notation, the Object Modeling Language, is also starting to gain some credible momentum; it is more an appendage to UML.

The UML supports the following important features:

- Object interaction modeling using sequence and collaboration diagrams
- Object and use-case state transition modeling
- Application partitioning using packages
- Class and component file organization

Sequence and collaboration diagrams express the communication of stimuli (or messages) between objects. Sequence diagrams show sequential steps of events, whereas collaboration diagrams express a fuller relationship between objects. Because objects and even use cases can change state, state diagrams help to explicitly describe these states. Packages enable you to divide an application into groups of logically related classes, thus helping to reduce complexity and allow for better allocation of development tasks. The component diagram provides you with a visual snapshot of the underlying file structure of classes and components.

Symbols

The UML supports many icons. For more detailed information on UML icons, please visit the Rational Web site at `www.rational.com`, or browse Microsoft Visual Modeler. Figure 5.2 shows the icons discussed in this section.

FIGURE 5.2.

Some UML icons.

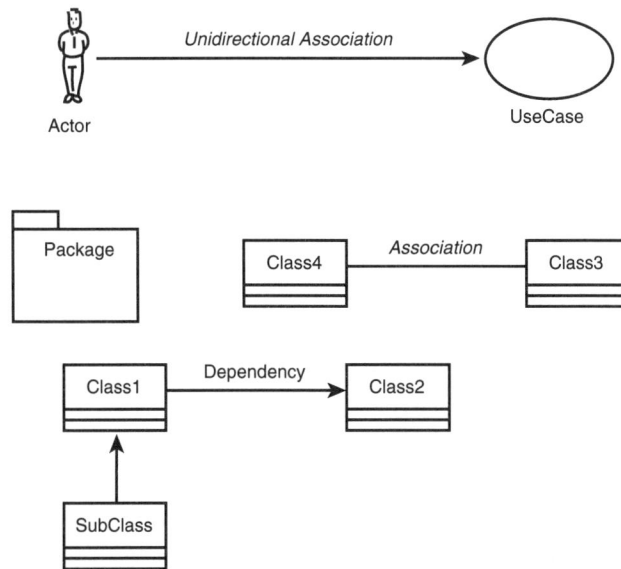

The Package icon (upper-left corner) represents a group of related classes and subpackages. The unidirectional association between the Actor and the UseCase (top) represents an association in which the Actor is providing stimulus to the UseCase, but no stimulus flows back to the Actor from the UseCase. The association between Class4 and Class3 is not as strict and can be interpreted as bidirectional (either class at the end of the association can provide stimulus to the other). The dependency relationship between Class1 and Class2 is the weakest coupling between two objects and specifies that not much is known about the relationship, other than that Class1 somehow depends on Class2. It's similar to a unidirectional association, except the latter implies this information about the class on the receiving end. Finally, the relationship between Class1 and SubClass is one of inheritance. This is the same icon you use for interface inheritance, with a stereotype of <<implements>>. A *stereotype* is an abstract characterization of a class.

The Importance of Not Deviating from the Architecture

An application's architecture is its skeletal system. Just as humans have a well-defined skeletal architecture, so do well-designed applications have well-defined architectures. This emphasis on application architecture is not only important in corporate development environments but also for personal projects. Having an architecture in place before the programming phase is like making rough drafts of a document before developing the final draft. When you're developing applications in the comfort of your home or office, it's nice to think through the logic of your program before expending time and energy on it. Remember those times when you quickly developed an application without architectural forethought, only to later forget how the lines of code work together? A documented architecture, complete with design models, helps preserve the thought processes in a common, easy-to-remember notation that serves as a snapshot of your mind at the time you designed the application.

Among the many factors that contribute to deviating from an architecture, three prominent ones include

- Lack of executive sponsorship of a project
- Inexperienced system architects
- Uncooperative users

Lack of Executive Sponsorship of a Project

One of the most difficult aspects of learning OOP is the discipline it takes for a programmer to adhere to the specifications of the application's predefined architecture. For those readers who must develop applications in a corporate environment, nothing is more frustrating than a team that isn't committed to a common architecture. There you are, sweating out the details of your object-oriented application, but another programmer on the team decides to ignore the design models and develop it his way! For object-oriented design models to have any real and effective meaning in the long run, an executive sponsor (someone in upper management) must ensure an environment for rewarding adherence to the architecture. This is important in the absence of healthy teamwork. Those who continue to ignore design models should be isolated from the object-oriented project. Lack of effective executive sponsorship can hamper the development of a robust, extensible, reusable system.

Inexperienced System Architects

Just as devastating as lack of executive sponsorship is inexperience among the ranks of the architects. The architect's chief duty is to develop and evolve the architecture of the proposed application. From the methods and properties of each class's interface to the communication channels between objects, the architect makes fundamental, far-reaching decisions about the very nature of the application. For large companies, such decisions can cost into the tens of millions. For small, independent software developers, a faulty architectural decision can mean hours of phone calls and emails from angry customers. Inexperienced architects tend to not understand the iterative, incremental nature of the object-oriented project. For this reason, experienced object technologists easily identify such individuals, but novices to OOP might not have this ability. The success of any object-oriented project depends on an architect's competence. If you develop software as a part-time commercial hobby, you should practice developing object-oriented software several times, using the concepts taught in this book, before selling the software publicly. This will reduce your customer service costs and give you more free time to enjoy life.

Proper executive sponsorship of a project increases the chance of finding and hiring the right technical architects and/or business analysts but cannot give a 100% assurance of this. Inexperienced technical leaders might not know how to adjust a given object-oriented methodology to the dynamics of user and executive behavior. This alone produces inadequate use cases (if any) and faulty system architectures. Other detracting factors include the inability to transition a project from one iteration to another, inability to give technical advisories to less experienced stakeholders in the project, and inability to manage the artifacts of the project. In essence, inexperience among the top echelon of a project's technical staff can have a devastating effect on the outcome of a project and its use cases.

Impatient Software Developers and Programmers

Let's assume you have reasonably proper executive sponsorship, knowledgeable project managers, and proactive user involvement in conveying use cases, so you're able to develop a sound architecture for the system. Because many Visual Basic programmers haven't embraced object-oriented programming, the odds of hiring impatient developers are good. Why is this important? Because many programmers feel that OOP minimizes individualistic efforts, a threat to programmer creativity. Many others feel that reading project artifacts and spending time following design models are useless activities. Of course, such sentiments couldn't be farther from the truth, but they persist.

Impatient developers have a tendency to take shortcuts, resorting to the spaghetti-style (disorganized) coding that is prevalent among many developers. User input is minimized to maximize programmer satisfaction. Such developers frown on anything resembling a use case, which means that the system's architecture will likely be faulty, to say the least.

Uncooperative Users

Always remember that the fundamental architecture of the proposed system starts in the mind of your intended user. This means that you must be very patient, sometimes very gentle, with your users in order to maximize the effectiveness of the requirements you receive. These requirements become the use cases by which you develop the proposed application. As with any business, you develop an application to solve a user's problem. A writer writes a book in hopes that others will read it. Likewise, you develop an application with the goal that others (or you) will use it.

Alas, as with any human interaction, you're not going to please everyone. Object technology represents a huge paradigm shift, not only for programmers but also for users. If some of your users disliked the periodic requirements inquiries and surveys in previous projects, they really won't like the many questions that crystallize during the normal iterations in an object-oriented project. Uncooperative users will often give you inadequate use cases, increasing the risk of your application's architecture being faulty. In such situations, you'll want surrogate users. *Surrogate users* are users who are usually not as knowledgeable as the real users but can provide enough information for you to come up with a reasonable architecture. Business analysts make excellent surrogate users. Commercial developers need to find new samplings of users from more diverse geographic, economic, and cultural backgrounds to maximize the effectiveness of their use cases.

In general, the more uncooperative your users are, the greater the risk of project failure. User nonparticipation in corporate environments is usually a symptom of political turmoil and/or lack of communication, but not always. If the users do not actively participate in the early architectural design of the system, you might as well update your resume. Not only will the system architecture be completely faulty, but also division and strife will develop among the project stakeholders, programmers will have to work around the clock in an attempt to find a miracle cure to help the project manager save face, and everyone will experience unnecessary stress. Users determine the system behavior, and without their participation, there is no architecture, and thus no scope, resulting in architecture deviation.

Summary

Let's face it. Visual Basic has come a long way. The third version brought component-based development to the mainstream in ways that other languages could only dream of. Version four improved on that, but version five has made not only object-oriented design easier but also customizing and automating the development environment itself. Nevertheless, Visual Basic still does not fully support object technology, in the more popular sense of that paradigm. Implementation inheritance is not in Visual Basic, though delegation can certainly compensate for this lack.

Simulating implementation inheritance in Visual Basic is not ideal. Some books and publications explain how to do some nice tricks with collections and classes to mimic implementation inheritance. However, attempting to make Visual Basic do what it was not designed to do can lead to performance issues and make the body of code difficult to read. Finally, because of the limitations in implementation inheritance, only a certain amount of polymorphism can be done in Visual Basic. However, interface inheritance and collections mitigate some of Visual Basic's shortcomings in this area.

In this chapter, you learned Visual Basic's support of class interface inheritance. A Visual Basic class is representative of a logical unit that is abstracted above mere code. A class interface is a contract with a client of that class that must be serviced. Building good interfaces is a fundamental part of reuse. Planning for any form of reuse is very difficult and will initially slow down a project. The distinction between interface and implementation classes is very important in component development. You learned that interfaces are what a component makes available to its clients. Tomorrow, you'll learn the basics of building and testing components. The two kinds of components you'll build are the Active DLL and the Active EXE, both of which are related.

Q&A

Q When are class definitions dynamic?

A At runtime, class definitions are most dynamic (for instance, going through iterative refinements). The process itself is dynamic, and the state of the class definition (including its relationships) reflects the results of that process. At runtime, the design time definitions do not change.

Q What's included in the signature of a method?

A The ordering and data types of arguments in the argument list.

Q What can happen if there are drastic changes to a class interface?

A Drastic changes to interfaces during construction can lead to extensive code rewrites and communication problems between classes and subsystems. Such architectural changes might trigger the need for a minor domain analysis to justify the new relationship.

Workshop

The workshop includes quiz questions to help gauge your grasp of the material. Even if you feel that you totally understand the concepts presented here, you should work through the quiz anyway. The last section contains an exercise or two that you might work through to help reinforce your learning. You'll find the answers to the quiz in Appendix A, "Answers."

Quiz

1. What are helper methods?
2. What is the best way to manage your runtime object creatures?

3. What's wrong with variants as return types?

4. What's a good way to help manage memory use?

5. What are the best ways to achieve reuse?

6. What is an implementation class?

7. What should you do when you discover design flaws in construction?

8. What is aggregation?

9. What responsibility does a composite object have?

10. Briefly explain containment.

Exercises

1. Open a new Standard Visual Basic project. Use the Class Builder utility to create the following interface class:

```
Class:
ITelevision

Methods:
Public Function turnOn()
Public Function turnOff()
Public Function incrementChannel()
Public Function decrementChannel()
Public Function displayMenu()

Attributes:
CurrentChannel As String
BrandName As String
ModelName As String
```

Now create a class that implements `ITelevision`.

2. Using exercise 1, try to discover new methods and properties to add to the interface. How would those changes affect the other class that already implemented that interface?

3. Review the code in Listing 5.1. List some ways you would improve the public methods and properties of the classes.

4. Review the following class:

Class:
```
Savings
```
Attributes:
```
AccountNumber
CurrentBalance
InterestRate
```

Methods:

```
calculateInterestRate()
accrueInterest()
deposit()
withdraw()
```

5. Now, consider a new requirement: You must allow all savings account products offered by the Second Bank of Carrollton to provide check writing services. How would you implement this new requirement?

DAY **6**

Building and Testing Components

In this chapter, you'll learn how to build simple ActiveX components and use a testing strategy for them. You'll learn from an example as well as by going through some workshop exercises. In detail, this chapter covers the following topics:

- Determining the need to build and implement ActiveX DLLs
- Building ActiveX DLLs and EXEs
- Test planning for ActiveX components
- The importance of use cases in test planning
- Incorporating object-oriented testing services into ActiveX components
- A sample test project: the Samsona Bank Teller System example

Determining the Need to Build and Implement ActiveX DLLs and EXEs

If you've developed software for a while now, you probably realize that you have reused some of your code over and over again. Structuring these lines of code into objects certainly helps with organizing your code in a logical way, but sometimes organizing code into objects is not enough. Often, you need to organize these objects into components, especially for large-enterprise and commercial software.

Components have grown in popularity over the years, thanks in large part to Microsoft's Visual Basic eXtensions (VBX), followed later by OCX technology—the predecessor of ActiveX. Other products contributing to the increasingly widespread use of components include Sun Microsystems' Java/JavaBeans, Visigenic's VisiBroker, and OMG's CORBA, which has been implemented by several vendors, including IONA.

Determining the need to build components takes time. Simply having a set of objects does not automatically mean those objects are good candidates for component building. Components require that the interaction between the objects be reusable, and reuse is not identifiable until those objects and their relationships are, in fact, used again. Therefore, you won't necessarily know when you're at a point to build a component until the time you use those objects and object interactions again. Until such time, you can begin learning and planning for the implementation of components.

Understanding the ActiveX DLL Project

An ActiveX dynamic link library is a component that at runtime exists in the same process as its client application. When a component runs in the same process as its client, the component is said to be an *in-process component*. The Professional and Enterprise versions of Visual Basic enable you to create DLLs. All the classes in an ActiveX DLL that implement the component's interface must be declared public so that clients of the DLL can access the DLL's services.

Visual Basic enables you to have several projects open simultaneously in the development environment when you are creating ActiveX DLL components. This means that you can simultaneously debug that component with an executable (EXE) project. Visual Basic also provides Automatic Quick Info and Data Tips to assist in your debugging efforts. You can even test your component in both design mode and run mode.

Each ActiveX DLL you create contains a type library.

Understanding the ActiveX EXE Project

An ActiveX executable (EXE) is a component that at runtime exists in a process different from its client application. When a component runs in a different process from its client, the component is said to be an *out-of-process component*. This means that a method in the client's process can't use a pointer to the component's address space. This is because memory addressing for the client process is different from the component's process. When the component needs a foreign reference, underlying ActiveX mechanisms resolve the out-of-process referencing by copying the data for the memory reference into the component's address space. The memory reference to the client's data is replaced with a memory reference to the copy that resides in the component's address space. Figure 6.1 illustrates this process-to-process mapping.

FIGURE 6.1.

ActiveX maps local in-process memory references to the component's out-of-process space.

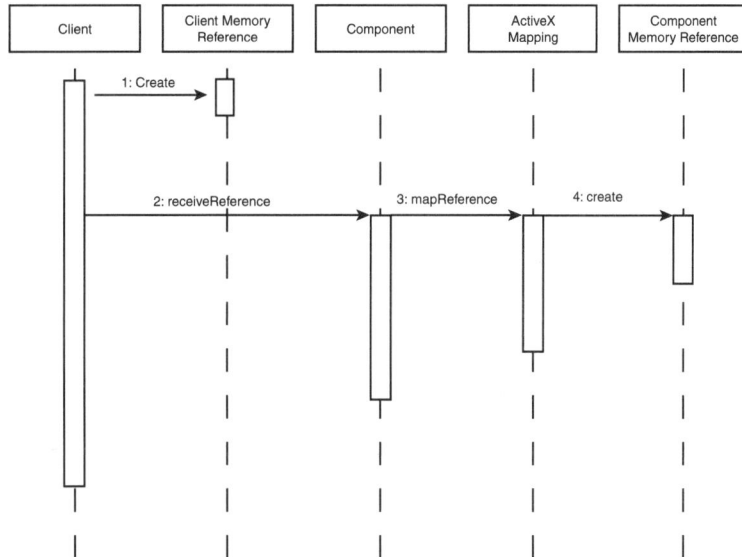

To recap, before you create any ActiveX component, you must have a solid idea of what you want the component to do. That is, you need to determine each component's roles and responsibilities. Although creating ActiveX components in Visual Basic is relatively easy, the process still involves extra steps that warrant wise use of your design time. Component reuse involves more than reusing the same component code; it also means not performing the same component creation steps over and over again, unnecessarily.

NEW TERM An *out-of-process component* runs in a process that is different from its client. That is, it runs in its own address space.

Building ActiveX DLLs and EXEs

In this section, you'll create an ActiveX DLL by using the code in Listing 4.1 (from Day 4, "Fundamental Object-Oriented Programming"). For your convenience, Listing 6.1 includes the code from Listing 4.1. Also included in the listing is a general code module with a Sub Main method. Normally, you would not need to include a Sub Main in an ActiveX DLL, unless you planned to initialize the component. In this case, you expect to initialize the component with the amount of the deposit and the account number.

> **Note**
>
> A general code module is also known as a *class utility* in Visual Modeler.

LISTING 6.1. THE CODE FOR CREATING AN ACTIVEX DLL FOR THE SECOND BANK OF CARROLLTON.

```
 1: Module: modMain
 2: Methods: Public Sub Main()
 3:
 4: Object: theDeposit
 5:
 6: Methods:
 7: Public Function depositFunds(argAccountNumber As String, argAmount As
    ➥Single)
 8:     'We'll use Call for the sake of simplicity.
 9:     Call theBasicPersonalCheckingAccount.adjustBalance(Me,
        ➥argAccountNumber)
10: End Function
11:
12: Properties:
13: Amount
14:
15:
16: Object: theBasicPersonalCheckingAccount
17:
18: Methods:
19: Public Function adjustBalance(ByRef argObject, argAccountNumber As
    ➥String)
20:     Dim LocalObject As Object
21:
22:     'If there's more than one account object in memory, a precondition
23:     'is that this object is the correct object. So check account
        ➥number
24:     If argAccountNumber <> AccountNumber Then
25:         'Raise exceptions here...
26:         ...
27:         Exit Function
```

```
28:     End If
29:
30:     'Delegate to private methods, where only one will be able to
        ➥process the
31:     'message.
32:
33:     Set LocalObject = argObject
34:
35: If returns Then
36:         adjustBalance = returns
37:         Exit Function
38:         Set LocalObject = Nothing
39:     End If
40:
41:     returns = decreaseBalance(LocalObject)
42:     If returns Then
43:         adjustBalance = returns
44:         Exit Function
45:         Set LocalObject = Nothing
46:     End If
47: End Function
48:
49: Private Function increaseBalance(argObject As Object)
50:     'Make sure incoming object is of type Deposit
51:     If TypeName(argObject) <> "Deposit" Then
52:         increaseBalance = False
53:         Exit Function
54:     End If
55:
56:     'It's a Deposit object
57:     CurrentBalance = CurrentBalance + argObject.Amount
58:     increaseBalance = True
59: End Function
60:
61: Private Function decreaseBalance(argObject As Object)
62:     'Make sure incoming object is of type Withdrawal
63:     If TypeName(argObject) <> "Withdrawal" Then
64:         decreaseBalance = False
65:         Exit Function
66:     End If
67:
68:     'It's a Withdrawal object
69:     CurrentBalance = CurrentBalance - argObject.Amount
70:     decreaseBalance = True
71: End Function
72:
73: Properties:
74: AccountNumber
75: CurrentBalance
```

6

To create the ActiveX DLL, open Visual Basic and create a new ActiveX DLL project. When you first open Visual Basic, you will see the New Project dialog box. Double-click the ActiveX DLL icon.

If you don't immediately see the New Project dialog box, choose File|New Project from the menu. Double-click the ActiveX DLL icon.

Notice the Project Browser to the right of the Visual Basic development environment. Modify the properties of Project1 to more meaningfully reflect your project. Using your mouse, right-click Project1 and choose Properties. Figure 6.2 shows the Project Properties dialog box that displays.

FIGURE 6.2.

The Project Properties dialog box, defaulted to the General index tab.

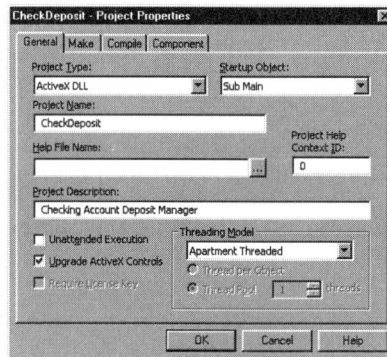

The Project Type (under the General index tab) is ActiveX DLL, so you need not modify this list box. The Startup Object should be Sub Main, so choose this option from the list box. For the Project Name, enter Check Deposit. For the Project Description, enter Checking Account Deposit Manager. Leave every other option as is.

Click the Make index tab (see Figure 6.3). The information in this container is very valuable for version management and protection of copyrights, if you plan to sell your component commercially. If you want your component's version to be automatically incremented every time you modify it, click the Auto Increment check box in the Version Number frame. If you have one or more icons associated with your component, use the Icon list box to select it. Finally, use the Type list box in the Version Information frame to enter information about the component and its physical file. When you select an item in this list box, use the Value text box to enter any relevant information. For example, if you select the Company Name item, enter the name of your company in Value. For any component development, especially commercial projects, it is highly advisable that you enter at least Company Name, File Description, Legal Copyright, Legal Trademarks, and

Product Name. For the sake of simplicity, ignore the command-line and conditional compilation arguments, as well as the Compile and Component tabs; use the default values. Click the OK button.

FIGURE 6.3.

The Make index tab of the Project Properties dialog box.

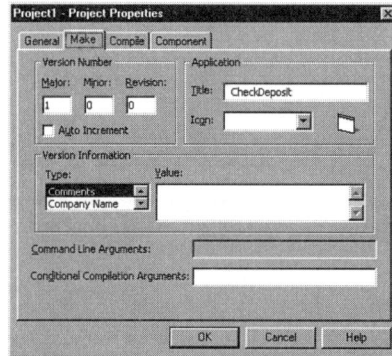

At this time, you should create two classes for the component project. Using what you've learned about adding classes to a Visual Basic project, add a class module for the class `Deposit` and the class `BasicPersonalCheckingAccount`, using the class specifications indicated in Listing 6.1. For the `Deposit` class, make the property `Amount` the default property if you use Class Builder (see Figure 6.4). When adding the `depositFunds` method, make sure it is the default method (see Figure 6.5). Having these defaults means that you don't have to explicitly type these class members in code—they are accessed by default.

FIGURE 6.4.

The default property for the `BasicPersonal-CheckingAccount` *class.*

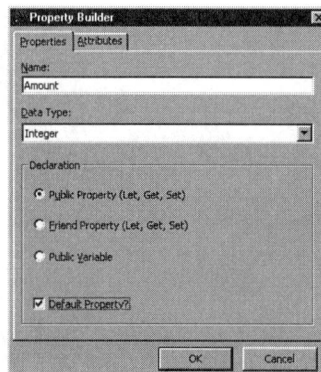

You now have one class in your component project. Figure 6.6 gives you an idea of what your project should now look like. Add the code from Listing 5.1 to your class modules.

FIGURE 6.5.

*The default
method for the*
`BasicPersonal-
CheckingAccount` *class.*

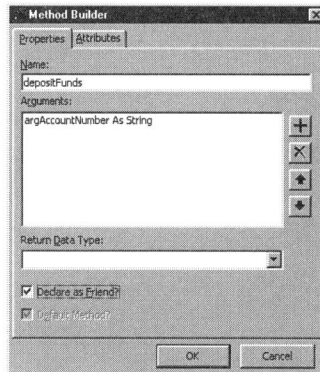

FIGURE 6.6.

*The CheckDeposit
project.*

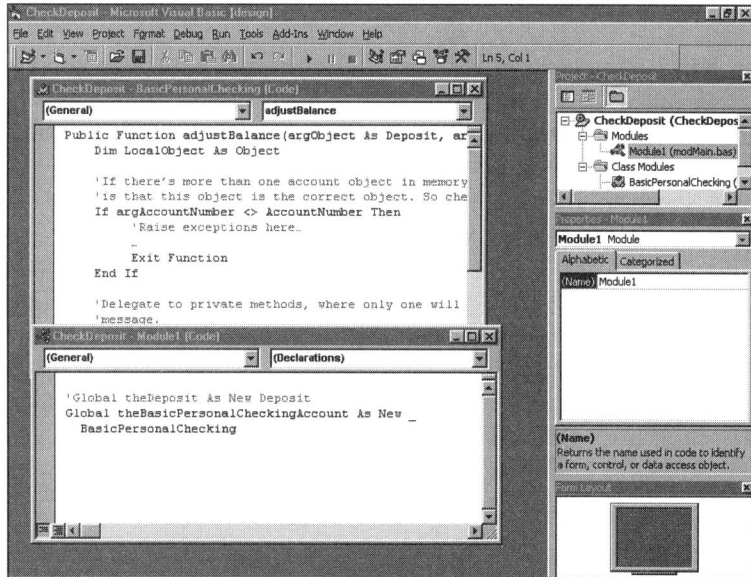

Your project needs a general code module. Choose Project|Add Module from the menu. You will see the Add Module dialog box (see Figure 6.7). Double-click the Module icon. In the Properties browser to the right, change the name of the module from Module1 to modMain. You need to add a `Sub Main` method, so choose Tools | Add Procedure from the menu. You will see the Add Procedure dialog box (see Figure 6.8). Enter `Main` and click OK. In the modMain's General Declarations section, enter the following declarations:

```
Global theBasicPersonalCheckingAccount As _
  CheckDeposit.BasicPersonalChecking
```

FIGURE 6.7.

The Add Module dialog box.

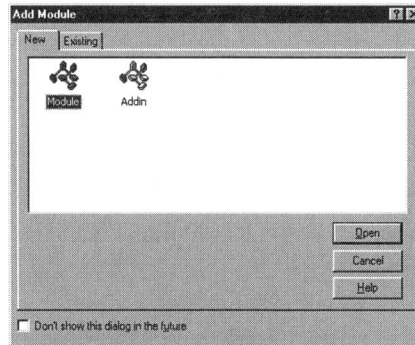

FIGURE 6.8.

The Add Procedure dialog box.

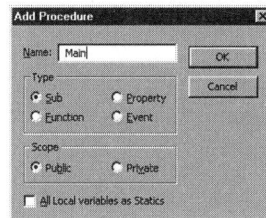

At this point, you need to add a test project to properly test the behavior of your component. You could conceivably create an ActiveX DLL without a test project, but it would be beneficial to read the next sections about testing components.

Test Planning for ActiveX Components

When you create an ActiveX component in Visual Basic, you have flexibility in testing it. That is, you can use debugging features such as Break in Class Module or Break on All Errors. Further, you can specify which errors to break by pressing Alt+F8. This combination enables you to skip to your error-handling mechanism when you've reached your desired error and/or raise that error for an external method (of the client object) to handle. Pressing Alt+F5 invokes your error-handling mechanism as well.

Testing any component requires a plan with clear goals. These goals reflect the type of application(s) in which the component is being deployed. Test planning for components takes into account that

- Components should be reusable.
- Components are loosely coupled with other components and applications.

Reusability and loose coupling are satisfied through a well-designed public interface or set of public interfaces. Testing the internal operations of a component requires the usual unit or class testing in which each private or friend method is sent expected arguments (given certain assumptions about the state of the system) to assess the outcome. The outcome can include return values and objects, as well as any anomalies associated with the method's operation. Testing the externally observable behavior of a component requires much the same pattern of effort, except there is much more at stake. With more advanced component systems, testing a facade for the component can also be involved.

NEW TERM   A *friend* method is accessible to other objects within the same component or application.

Drafting a Master Test Plan

In its simplest form, a master test plan summarizes the goal of the testing effort, the resources required to test the software, and the test cases to be examined. For simplicity, assume that

- The goal of the testing effort is to ensure that making a deposit works to the satisfaction of the Second Bank of Carrollton.
- Only one tester is required.
- There's only one test case.

The sole test case is discussed in the next section.

Drafting Test Cases

A test case is very similar to a use case in that it represents the value provided to the user by an application. When you use object-oriented methodologies, you base the content of the test case on a well-defined use case. Because each use case has one or more actors who perform it, a test case also has one or more actors on behalf of whom the tester is testing the software.

The use case for your component system is as follows:

Use Case: Deposit Funds into Basic Personal Checking Account

Description: A Bank Teller requests a given customer's basic personal checking account from the Samsona Bank Teller System by entering the customer's appropriate account number. When the account is presented to the Bank Teller, the Bank Teller enters the deposit amount. Finally, the Bank Teller requests that the Samsona Bank Teller System store the deposit transaction persistently.

Figure 6.9 shows the use-case diagram for this use case. Essentially, the test case has exactly the same verbiage and structure.

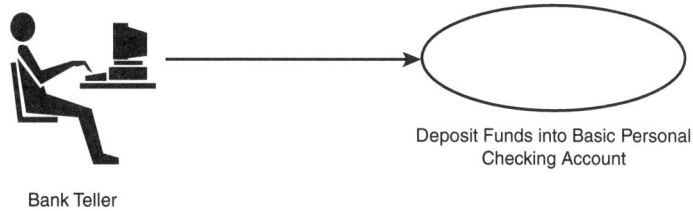

▼ **FIGURE 6.9.**

The use-case diagram for the use case Deposit Funds into Basic Personal Checking Account.

Bank Teller

Deposit Funds into Basic Personal Checking Account

Drafting Test Scripts

Recall that a use case is implemented in one or more scenarios. Each scenario represents an instance of the use case, given a set of conditions and assumptions. A scenario is realized in the form of a sequence diagram or scenario script. Remember, a set of scenarios for a use case typically consists of a normal path accompanied by one or more abnormal paths.

In much the same way, a well-written test script is the realization of a test case, given a set of conditions and assumptions. Thus, a test script is equivalent to a use-case scenario and can be realized in the form of a sequence diagram or scenario script as well. Figure 6.10 illustrates the sequence diagram for the normal path of your sole use case.

FIGURE 6.10.

The sequence diagram for the use case Deposit Funds into Basic Personal Checking Account.

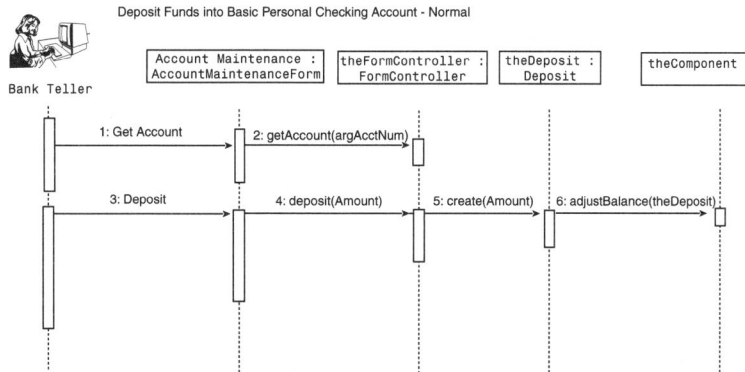

Deposit Funds into Basic Personal Checking Account - Normal

Bank Teller | Account Maintenance : AccountMaintenanceForm | theFormController : FormController | theDeposit : Deposit | theComponent

1: Get Account
2: getAccount(argAcctNum)
3: Deposit
4: deposit(Amount)
5: create(Amount)
6: adjustBalance(theDeposit)

6

For the abnormal paths of a use case, you can use either a sequence diagram or a scenario script for each path. An abnormal path is equivalent to an exception. That is, an *abnormal path* is any deviation from the normal path of a use case. Most abnormalities are not complex, so a scenario script would be sufficient. For your example, you will create a scenario script to document the scenario in which the account number on the deposit is wrong:

▼   *Abnormal Path: The Account Number on the Deposit Is Wrong.*

1. The Bank Teller requests that the Samsona Bank Teller System store the deposit transaction persistently.

2. The Samsona Bank Teller System validates the deposit information and finds the account number is wrong.

3. The Samsona Bank Teller System notifies the Bank Teller of the error.

Here, the scenario has been simplified to the interaction between the Bank Teller and the Samsona Bank Teller System. With more advanced scripts, you can include the actual names of forms and objects participating in the scenario. This scenario script, and the sequence diagrams, can be migrated to test scripts as follows:

Test Script #1: Deposit Funds into Basic Personal Checking Account—Normal

1. A Bank Teller requests a given customer's basic personal checking account from the Samsona Bank Teller System by entering the customer's appropriate account number.

2. When the account is presented to the Bank Teller, the Bank Teller enters the deposit amount.

3. The Bank Teller requests that the Samsona Bank Teller System store the deposit transaction persistently.

Test Script #2: The Account Number on the Deposit Is Wrong.

1. The Bank Teller requests that the Samsona Bank Teller System store the deposit transaction persistently.

2. The Samsona Bank Teller System validates the deposit information and finds the account number is wrong.

▲   3. The Samsona Bank Teller System notifies the Bank Teller of the error.

Note

As mentioned earlier, use cases provide the basis for test cases, and in fact, both are equivalent. Use cases, then, make test planning much easier for the test team, which is especially important for components. Given that many testers are not expert at the relatively new ActiveX component technology, use cases for component systems help take much (if not all) of the guess-work out of formulating test cases.

Incorporating Object-Oriented Testing Services into ActiveX Components

As you progress in your knowledge of developing object-oriented components, you might find it necessary to incorporate test classes in your components for unit testing the component before deploying it. Thus, for every method called in your component, you could have one or more lines of code that invoke a method on the test class to record the values of incoming arguments, errors encountered within the method being tested, and the value of returns. In the lessons for Day 8, "Versioning and Debugging," Day 14, "The Internal Application Manager Subsystem," and Day 18, "The Error-Processing and Exception-Handling Subsystem," you will learn more about structuring objects to incorporate self-testing logic within subsystems of classes and an entire application itself.

A Sample Test Project: The Samsona Bank Teller System Example

◄ REAL WORLD

Now you will set up the project so that you can test your component. The name of the test project is TestCheckDeposit. To add a test project to the project group, do the following:

1. Choose File | Add Project from the menu. This opens the Add Project dialog box. Double-click the Standard EXE icon. This action creates a project group.

Note
> Refrain from choosing File | Open Project or File | New Project. Doing so will close your ActiveX DLL project.

2. In the Properties Browser, rename the test project (now Project1) `TestCheckDeposit`.

3. In the Project Browser, right-click on TestCheckDeposit. Choose Set as Start Up from the pop-up menu. TestCheckDeposit is now the startup project for the project group. This step is necessary in order to test the ActiveX DLL.

4. From the menu, choose Project References. This opens the References— TestCheckDeposit dialog box. Figure 6.11 shows this dialog box. Click the check box for CheckDeposit and then click OK.

▼

6

Note

If CheckDeposit isn't in the References list, click Cancel; then go back to the Project Browser. Make TestCheckDeposit active by clicking on it. Now you can resume step 4.

FIGURE 6.11.

The References—TestCheck Deposit dialog box.

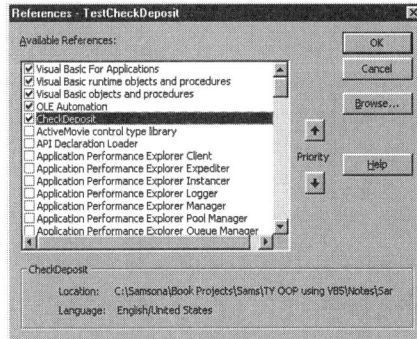

5. Choose View | Object Browser from the menu. The Object Browser dialog box displays, as shown in Figure 6.12. In the Project/Library list box near the upper-left corner, select CheckDeposit. In the Classes list below, you will see the classes that belong to this component. This list not only lets you review the members of the component but also confirms that your component is recognized by Visual Basic. Click the Close button in the upper-right corner when you finish viewing the member classes.

FIGURE 6.12.

The Object Browser dialog box.

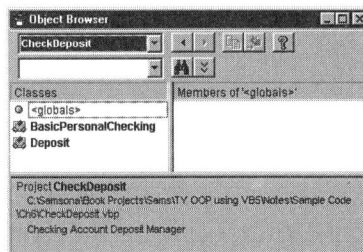

6. Save TestCheckDeposit and the project group (CheckDepositGroup) by choosing File | Save Project Group from the menu. Save the form as AcountMaintForm instead of Form1. Save the project group as CheckDepositGroup instead of Group1. In the Properties Browser, rename the form (now Form1) frmAccountMaintForm. (If you prefer, you could name the form frmAccountMaint.)

To round out your testing project, incorporate the logic from your test/scenario scripts into your form. Based on an examination of Test Scripts #1 and #2, you know you need the members listed in Table 6.1 for your form.

TABLE 6.1. SETTING UP THE FORM `frmAccountMaintForm`.

Member	Name
Form Caption	Basic Personal Checking
Label (Account Number)	`lblAccountMaintForm(0)`
Label (Deposit Amount)	`lblAccountMaintForm(1)`
Label (Error Message)	`lblAccountMaintForm(2)`
TextBox	`txtAccountNumber`
TextBox	`txtDepositAmount`
CommandButton	`cmdStore`
CommandButton	`cmdDone`

For the Error Message label (`lblAccountMaintForm(2)`), set its BorderStyle to 1 — Fixed Single. Your form will now look like Figure 6.13.

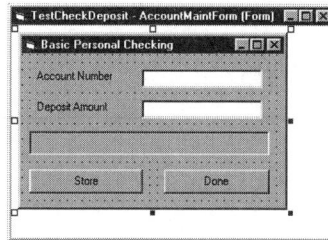

FIGURE 6.13.

The frm-AccountMaint-Form *form.*

You don't want the `BasicPersonalChecking` class communicating directly with the `frmAccountMaintForm` form. Therefore, add a class named `FormController` to control the flow of events from the form to the component. Add methods to the class that resembles Listing 6.2. In the form, enter the following declaration in General Declarations:

```
Private theFormController As New FormController
```

LISTING 6.2. THE `FormController` CLASS METHODS AND DECLARATIONS.

```
1: Private theForm As Form
2:
3: Public Sub setForm(argForm As Form)
```

continues

```
 4:     Set theForm = argForm
 5: End Sub
 6:
 7: Public Sub depositFunds(argAmount As Single, _
 8: argAccountNumber As String)
 9:     Dim returns, sAccountNumber As String
10:
11:     Set theDeposit = New Deposit
12:     sAccountNumber = argAccountNumber
13:
14:     theDeposit.Amount = argAmount
15:
16:     returns = theBasicPersonalCheckingAccount.adjustBalance( _
17:     theDeposit, sAccountNumber)
18:
19:     If returns Then
20:         theForm.lblAccountMaintForm(2).Caption = "Complete"
21:     End If
22:
23:     sAccountNumber = ""
24:     Set theDeposit = Nothing
25: End Sub
26:
27: 'Include the following event handler:
28: Private Sub theBasicPersonalCheckingAccount_
    ➥OnWrongAccountNumber(argMsg As String)
29:     theForm.lblAccountMaintForm(2).Caption = argMsg
30: End Sub
```

The command button cmdStore should have the following code in its Click event:

```
Private Sub cmdStore_Click()
    theFormController.setform Me
    theFormController.depositFunds _
        txtDepositAmount, txtAccountNumber
End Sub
```

The command button cmdDone should have the following code:

```
Private Sub cmdDone_Click()
    Set theFormController = Nothing
    Unload Me
End Sub
```

You are now ready to test drive your component. First, make sure the code for

▼ adjustBalance in the BasicPersonalChecking class resembles Listing 6.3.

▼ **LISTING 6.3.** THE adjustBalance METHOD WITH A RAISED EVENT.

```
 1: Public Function adjustBalance(argObject As Deposit,
    ⮡argAccountNumber As String) As Boolean
 2:     Dim LocalObject As Object, returns As Boolean
 3:
 4:     'If there's more than one account object in memory, a precondition
 5:     'is that this object is the correct object. So check account
        ⮡number
 6:     If argAccountNumber <> AccountNumber Then
 7:          'Raise exceptions here...
 8:          Dim sMsg As String
 9:          sMsg = "Wrong account number, Please retry."
10:          RaiseEvent OnWrongAccountNumber(sMsg)
11:          Set LocalObject = Nothing
12:          Exit Function
13:     End If
14:
15:     'Delegate to private methods, where only one will be able to
        ⮡process the message.
16:
17:     Set LocalObject = argObject
18:
19:     returns = increaseBalance(LocalObject)
20:     If returns Then
21:          adjustBalance = returns
22:          Set LocalObject = Nothing
23:     Exit Function
24:     End If
25:
26:     returns = decreaseBalance(LocalObject)
27:     If returns Then
28:          adjustBalance = returns
29:          Exit Function
30:          Set LocalObject = Nothing
31: End If
32: End Function
```

Notice the use of RaiseEvent OnWrongAccountNumber. Raising events is simple. To add
an event, make sure that the BasicPersonalChecking class is the current module. Choose
Tools | Add Procedure. You'll see the Add Procedure dialog box. Remember this dialog
box from earlier? Enter OnWrongAccountNumber for the name of the event; then click the
Event option button in the Type frame. Click OK. Visual Basic automatically adds a declaration for the event in the General Declarations of the BasicPersonalChecking class.
Now enter the following line of code in the same location, as illustrated in Listing 6.3:

```
Dim sMsg As String
sMsg = "Wrong account number, Please retry."
RaiseEvent OnWrongAccountNumber(sMsg)
```

6

▼ In the General Declarations section, be sure the declaration looks like the following:

```
Public Event OnWrongAccountNumber(argMsg As String)
```

In the class `FormController`, enter the following declaration:

```
Private WithEvents theBasicPersonalCheckingAccount As _
CheckDeposit.BasicPersonalChecking
```

While in the same form, click the object list and select `theBasicPersonalChecking Account`. You should see the `theBasicPersonalCheckingAccount_OnWrongAccount Number` event in the method/event list. In this event, enter the following code:

```
theForm.lblAccountMaintForm(2).Caption = argMsg
```

Make the `Initialize` event look like the following:

```
Private Sub Class_Initialize()
    mvarAccountNumber = "002"
End Sub
```

Make sure the TestCheckDeposit project is the startup (default) project.

The value `"002"` is a dummy account number to test both the normal and abnormal paths of your use case. You can now run the application to test the normal path. Press F5. When your test form displays, enter `"002"` for the account number and `500` for the deposit amount. Click Store. When the component has finished processing the deposit request, the error message label will display `Complete`. To test the abnormal path, enter an account number different from `"002"`. You will see the error message `Wrong account number, Please retry`.

Finally, building the ActiveX component is easy. Simply choose File|Make CheckDeposit.dll from the menu. Your new component is registered with the operating system. To create an ActiveX EXE, start a new ActiveX EXE project and import the CheckDeposit files and projects to the new project and choose File|Make
▲ CheckDeposit.exe from the menu.

Summary

This chapter teaches you how to plan, create, and test an ActiveX component. You learned the importance of use cases in test planning and of incorporating object-oriented testing services into ActiveX components. You then followed the sample test project for the Samsona Bank Teller System. Finally, you learned how to raise events in your component to trap business rule violations in the form of abnormal use case paths. In tomorrow's lesson, you will learn how to effectively use third-party controls in your applications.

Q&A

Q **True or False: Determining the need to build components is a quick and easy process.**

A False

Q **What is an ActiveX dynamic link library?**

A An ActiveX dynamic link library is a component that at runtime exists in the same process as its client application.

Q **What is an in-process component?**

A A component that runs in the same process as its client.

Q **What is an out-of-process component?**

A A component that runs in a process remote from its client.

Q **What do you need to know about an ActiveX component before creating it?**

A You need to determine the component's roles and responsibilities.

Workshop

The workshop includes quiz questions to help gauge your grasp of the material. You'll find the answers to this quiz in Appendix A, "Answers." Even if you feel that you understand the concepts presented here, you should work through the quiz. The last section contains exercises that help reinforce your learning.

Quiz

1. What is another name for a general code module?
2. What is the value of the Make index tab in the Project Properties dialog box?
3. What is required when testing a component?
4. What is a master test plan?
5. What is the importance of a test script?

Exercises

1. Modify the TestCheckDeposit project to display the current balance of the account after each deposit.
2. Modify the TestCheckDeposit project to enable the bank teller to perform withdrawal transactions.
3. Given the code in this project, how would you extend the `BasicPersonalChecking` class to enable the bank teller to void a deposit transaction?

6

DAY **7**

Incorporating Third-Party Components

In this lesson, you will learn about

- Deciding to use third-party controls in a Visual Basic project
- Documenting use cases for using third-party controls
- Gray box versus black box controls: The MicroHelp problem
- Designing class and object models with third-party controls
- Industry discussions on the use of third-party controls

Deciding to Use Third-Party Controls in a Visual Basic Project

If you're like most Visual Basic developers, on more than one occasion you've needed to incorporate a third-party control in your application. Projects with tight deadlines but complex code implementation requirements usually trigger such a need. No doubt you have been relieved to find a tool that solved some or all of your problems, or you have been disappointed when you couldn't find one. Often, when you found a control, it failed you in some way. The third-party tool market, though imperfect, has matured over the years. Today, probably not even a handful of low-level programming problems haven't been encapsulated in some control on the market.

It's widely known in the software development community that with Visual Basic, Microsoft single-handedly brought the third-party control industry to the forefront of the mass market. Specifically, the Visual Basic Extensions (VBX) control market brought the buying and selling of third-party controls to a level of reality that was unprecedented. Whenever you read about the history of third-party controls and components in programming magazines and books or hear about it in seminars, you typically discover that VBX controls were at the beginning of it all. Therefore, when it comes to making decisions about acquiring and implementing third-party controls, Visual Basic developers, in general, have the most experience.

There are advantages and disadvantages in deciding to acquire third-party controls. The advantages are decreased development time (and therefore reduced development costs) and reuse over many projects. Buying a third-party control is like buying "canned" labor; that is, the third-party vendor has put its labor force's time and energy into that control so that you don't have to put your time and energy into reproducing the same code. What's more, you can reuse that canned time and energy over many projects, thus gaining increased returns on investment over time. However, there are the disadvantages.

With the proliferation of VBX, OCX, and now ActiveX controls over the years, Visual Basic developers have experienced a wide range of negative side effects. Many controls were poorly documented, rendering the controls almost useless. Other controls were awkward or required too many function calls and declarations, making development and maintenance tasks almost as painful as developing the code yourself. Some vendor technical support staffs were overwhelmed with calls and emails so that it was difficult to reach them for help. As if that were not bad enough, some vendors took the money and ran after releasing a first version, leaving you to wonder whether they were under investigation by a television news magazine or the government. More than a few vendors went bankrupt.

Because the disadvantages became so rampant in the third-party control market, many individual programmers and organizations sought better ways of incorporating these still useful controls. Some of the ways include the following:

- Creating the component committee
- Formulating an evaluation and selection criteria
- Pricing components versus in-house component development

Creating the Component Committee

The task of software development is already a tremendous one. Adding to that the task of choosing effective and appropriate third-party controls makes it even more difficult. When a Visual Basic developer, typically pressed for meeting deadlines, has to evaluate third-party controls, that developer's evaluation will not likely be thorough. It can take days or weeks for developers to evaluate, test, and implement one or more third-party controls. There's a need, then, for a separate committee (either in-house or an independent external organization) composed of one or more developers and testing experts who can dedicate exclusive time to evaluating third-party controls.

Evaluating a control by committee doesn't end at the control itself. The committee can test the documentation for accuracy. It can also evaluate the vendor's response to technical support and general questions about the control. Finally, the committee can test the control by creating test applications that incorporate the control. To be even more thorough, the committee can have the quality assurance and testing team test the application to make sure the component can handle a full production environment. A thorough committee might even investigate the financial soundness and commercial health of the third-party vendor when it has decided on a control but is unsure whether the company might be around long. If this latter approach is taken, the committee would look at whether the vendor is constantly in debt, no matter how large or small.

For these reasons, it is generally not wise to have project developers evaluate third-party controls while they are also faced with pressing deadlines. If you're involved in a small project in which the financial and productivity stakes of the application aren't great, having a committee might be overkill. However, if you're developing commercial applications for sale on the market or for organizations for whom the application's success or failure can mean millions of dollars either way, it is well worth it to thoroughly investigate the third-party vendor. This is especially important if the control is difficult to replace in the case of failure.

Formulating an Evaluation and Selection Criteria

Regardless of whether you evaluate a control yourself or use a committee, there are some factors to consider in making a decision to use a third-party control. Briefly, you need to ask questions such as these:

- How long has the vendor been in business? This question is important only when the stakes on your project are high and the control might not be easily replaced. Many fine vendors on the market are just starting out, so don't necessarily rule them out if the controls they sell can be easily replaced in the case of failure.

7

- How easy is it to use the control? Let's face it, some controls are so complex that you become frustrated and develop the code yourself. Some controls seek to do so much that they overwhelm the developer with confusion. Plus, the more complex the control, the more reliant on it you can become, meaning that that vendor can have a virtual monopoly over your business. This has been the case with, for instance, MicroHelp, maker of the famous (or infamous) third-party controls for earlier versions of Visual Basic. These are discussed in a later section.

- How much does the control cost relative to developing the code yourself? Some controls have become so cost-effective and productivity-effective that either developers buy them without the need of evaluating them or Microsoft licenses them for inclusion in Visual Basic. FarPoint's Spread control and the True Grid control, respectively, are notable examples of both scenarios.

- Can you reuse this control to obtain a fair return on investment? Any wise organization, for-profit or nonprofit, always seeks benefits that exceed the initial cost of a product or service. For organizations and individuals developing software, the same standard applies to third-party controls. In acquiring a control, you don't buy it for use on only one project. You want to be able to use it over and over again. Many controls fit this criteria. Some, however, are so specialized that they aren't reused. For individual developers, this is not always an issue. However, for organizations with recurring software development needs, realizing a return on investment for every cash expenditure is (or should be) a high priority.

- Is the control well documented? Believe it or not, some controls are shipped with little or no documentation. They come with a readme file with general comments, but that's it. A control that has no documentation is a control that hasn't been completely developed. Avoid controls with little or no documentation.

- How responsive is technical support? Out of fairness, even the best vendors are overwhelmed these days with technical support questions (including this author). To keep the controls as inexpensive as possible, some vendors have to avoid hiring technical support staff. Larger organizations charge a fee for incidents because the costs for technical support have increased over the past few years (around the same time that Microsoft helped promulgate the third-party control market to unheard of heights in the industry). Be prepared to pay for incidents. On the other hand, the vendors should at least post commonly asked questions (and their answers) on a Web page or in newsletters if they are overwhelmed. Larger, more established vendors should have some form of technical support staff—if not in-house, then external subcontractors.

- Will the vendor be around to provide technical support? Fly-by-night vendors have proven costly for organizations that use their controls. A way to reduce the dependence on a particular vendor is to seek out competitors and have a backup in case of vendor failure. Check the vendor's financial health if information is available and the risks warrant it. Because you're using object-oriented programming techniques, create facades or wrappers around the control, even if it is the kind of control that you place on a form; you can always pass a well-developed control by reference to form controllers for further processing. If the control doesn't have a nicely exposed interface so that you can pass it to controllers, avoid it.

Pricing Components Versus In-House Component Development

As mentioned earlier, organizations and individuals seek a return on investment in acquiring third-party controls and components. If you're developing state-of-the-art applications at home that will make you millions of dollars, it's possible you're not going to worry about costs. However, organizations want a return on investment. They look at industry magazine reviews for any mention of potential man-hour savings. They review the average number of hours it took to develop (or try to develop) similar code in-house. In more wary organizations, they might check out the competition to see whether their peers have effectively implemented such controls at a reasonable cost.

In his book *Software Reuse*, Ivar Jacobson—the pioneer of use cases—mentions some ways that organizations can assess the cost and return on investment of software components to be reused. For organizations to achieve reusability with third-party controls as a way to obtain a return on investment, organizations must pay up-front costs to

- Assess the applications with which to achieve reuse.
- Properly define the application's architecture so that the component has a role to play within it.
- Reorganize, when necessary, the domain that will use the application so as to optimize the usefulness of the application and the components in it.
- Make sure all project teams are aware of (and trained in) the control or component being evaluated or implemented so that all opportunities for reuse are available.

Figure 7.1 shows a graph that Jacobson uses to explain the cost factor in return on investment. The figure has been specifically adapted to the case of third-party controls and components. Keep in mind that, as Jacobson mentions, it will typically cost you much more money to develop a control or component in-house for reusability than to create it for one-time use on a particular project. Buying well-designed third-party controls can mitigate these costs, but they must be reused several times to achieve a desired return on investment.

7

FIGURE 7.1.

The benefit of reusability versus time.

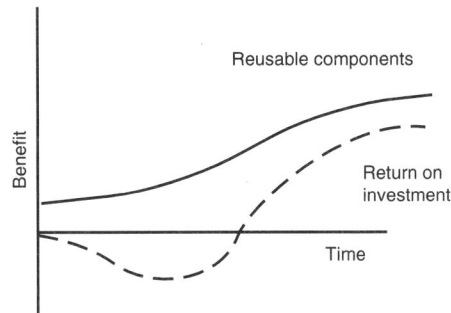

> **Note**
>
> Incorporating third-party controls and components early on involves cost and little reuse. Plan on little benefit over the first few months and possibly the first year or two. In time, reuse of the control will increase the return on investment substantially—also, incrementally, as increased technology, competition, and upgrades of the controls reduce the increase of returns on investment.

Documenting Use Cases and Scenarios for Using Third-Party Controls

As mentioned earlier, you have to define architecture for your application that includes a role to be fulfilled by any third-party control you plan to acquire and implement. Use cases will imply major subsystems within your application. Scenarios, with their corresponding sequence diagrams, will describe the roles that need to be performed by certain subsystems in the application. Assuming for a moment that you don't hire an evaluation committee, you need to evaluate and specify the role the control is to perform by

- Accepting proposals from in-house developers
- Accepting proposals from third-party vendors directly
- Measuring use cases against proposals

Accepting Proposals from In-House Developers

Although typically pressed for time, you or your development staff will be the best initial point of contact when it comes to acquiring a third-party control. Generally, a developer will have used a control in the past to solve a similar problem being undertaken by the current project. Thus, that developer should create a brief proposal listing the pros and cons of using that control and describing how it helped solve the problem. This proposal need not be formal or any longer than one page.

Accepting Proposals from Third-Party Vendors Directly

Third-party vendors, ever the capitalistic entrepreneurs, will gladly furnish you with testimonials, white papers, and magazine articles touting their products. Given this, you should use your best common sense when evaluating the role to be played by a control based on the proposals of third-party vendors alone. In the case of less known vendors offering a unique control that you need but can't find anywhere else, you must rely solely on the vendors documents and your thorough evaluation.

Measuring Use Cases Against Proposals

When you have all your proposals and related literature in hand, you should compare them against what role your use cases and interaction diagrams (sequence and collaboration) require. If the control doesn't have a well-defined role in your application, your investment in it is little more than a gamble. In fact, it might be a sign that the investment is based on successful marketing rather than need. Comparing the proposals against the use cases and scenarios is important because some of your developers might have a heavy bias for a particular control. This isn't necessarily bad, but the control must be justified objectively.

Gray Box Versus Black Box Controls: The MicroHelp Problem

Earlier in this lesson, I discussed the real risk that some vendors either take your money and run or simply go out of business through bankruptcy or declining market share. Of all the vendor failures in the history of third-party controls, none have been more infamous than MicroHelp.

For those Visual Basic developers who don't remember MicroHelp, it was one of the more successful third-party vendors riding the wave of the rising third-party control market. Visual Basic developers came to rely on MicroHelp for valuable components to use in their applications. MicroHelp was the darling of the industry.

For some unusually bizarre reasons, the third-party component operations of MicroHelp collapsed in 1996. MicroHelp stopped supporting its Visual Basic products. Developers and organizations scrambled for answers, and their technical support concerns went unanswered by the vendor. The third-party control market came under closer scrutiny by some organizations who were already weary of placing their trust—and sometimes their companies—in the hands of third-party vendors. Some reports said that one of the heads of MicroHelp cashed out of the company to pursue personal or religious activities.

7

Whatever the reason, a well-publicized battle between the outgoing heads of MicroHelp and the buyer, Luckman Interactive, Inc., as well as heavy Wall Street and Canadian investment firms, resulted in not only the demise of the MicroHelp Visual Basic product line but also a black eye on the entire third-party market. Thankfully, Microsoft and better established Visual Basic control vendors rallied to assure developers and organizations that third-party controls, in general, are still sound investments.

If you or your organization still use (or are just stuck with) MicroHelp controls and don't know where to turn for technical support, there is still some hope for you. For better or worse, the companies that were brave enough to assume control of MicroHelp's products might not be responsive enough to your questions because they don't have quite the financial backing that MicroHelp once enjoyed. Nevertheless, try to contact the following companies for further assistance:

Company: BeCubed Software

Product: OLETools and VBTools

Web site: http://www.becubed.com

Email: sales@becubed.com and tech@becubed.com

Company: The Mandelbrot Set

Product: Code Complete, Code Analyst, Splash Wizard, and AutoCoder

Web site: http://www.TheMandelbrotSet.com

Company: Luckman Interactive

Product: VBViewer

Web site: http://www.luckman.com

Note: The company most likely is not providing support for this product (this author didn't see any reference to it on its Web site).

Company: EllTech Development, Inc.

Product: Compression Plus, Fax Plus, Encryption X-ponents/Encrpyt-It Plus, Communications Library

Web site: http://www.elltechdev.com

Company: VideoSoft

Product: Game+Multimedia/VSDirectX, SpellPro/VSSpell

Web site: http://www.videosoft.com

Note: This company makes many other fine Visual Basic components, so support issues should be better than average.

Company: MicroDexterity, Inc.

Product: Muscle32/Stamina

Web site: http://www.microdexterity.com

Email: sales@mdxi.com or support@mdxi.com

Red Flags to Look for with Black Box Components

Gray box controls are those controls where you have knowledge of the interfaces of public classes within a component. With gray box controls, you have some inkling as to which classes and subsystems in the control are responsible for certain behavior. *Black box controls*, on the other hand, don't give you any clues as to how the component processes your method calls. You know only the external interface. This has its benefit and drawback.

The Benefit of Choosing Gray Box Components

The benefit is that you don't have to worry about the internal complexities of the control. This is acceptable for a well-designed control. Just plug it into your code, and you're ready to deploy the application to your users.

The Risk of Selecting Black Box Components

The drawback is that when things go wrong, you won't know which part of the control is at fault so that you can plan to replace it. Because the risk of vendor failure is real, blind dependence on a third-party control can be unhealthy.

Designing Class Models with Third-Party Controls

After you've assigned your third-party controls to roles in your object interaction diagrams (such as sequence or collaboration diagrams), you incorporate them by role name in your class model. Ideally, the control should perform the role of an object implementing an interface class. It is important to use only the role name because at some point you might find it necessary to replace the control with a comparable but improved one. Therefore, you want to encapsulate your interaction diagrams and class models from such changes by assigning adequate role names to your controls.

For instance, assume you're using Crystal Reports for your reporting. Now compare Figure 7.2 with Figure 7.3. In Figure 7.2, step 5, openReport, is implemented by an

7

object named `CrystalReports` without an interface class or some facade to encapsulate potential changes or failures in the control. As a result of directly modeling calls to Crystal Reports, function calls have to match exactly what Crystal Reports requires. However, suppose that later the project requires the use of ActiveX communications with Access 97 or beyond. The sequence diagram in Figure 7.2 would have to be changed, as well as every other diagram that used Crystal Reports. What's more, every place in the Visual Basic code where Crystal Reports is referenced would also have to be changed. In the end, this costs you and the organization more money than necessary because you could have wrapped the calls to Crystal Reports behind an object that implements the `IReporting` interface class.

FIGURE 7.2.

The wrong way to implement third-party controls such as Crystal Reports in your sequence diagrams.

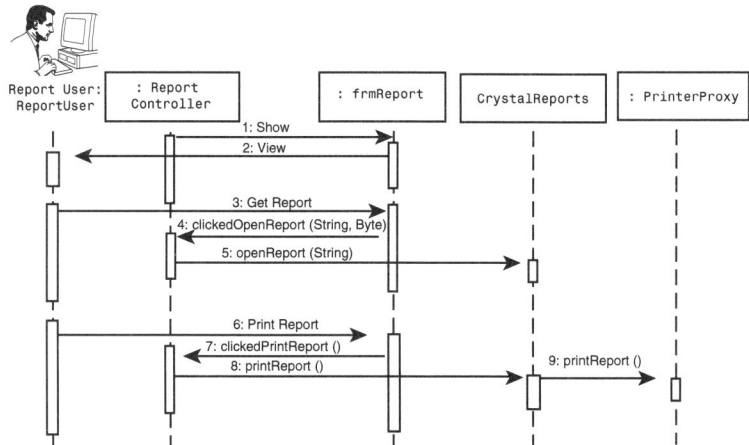

FIGURE 7.3.

The right way to implement third-party controls such as Crystal Reports in your sequence diagrams.

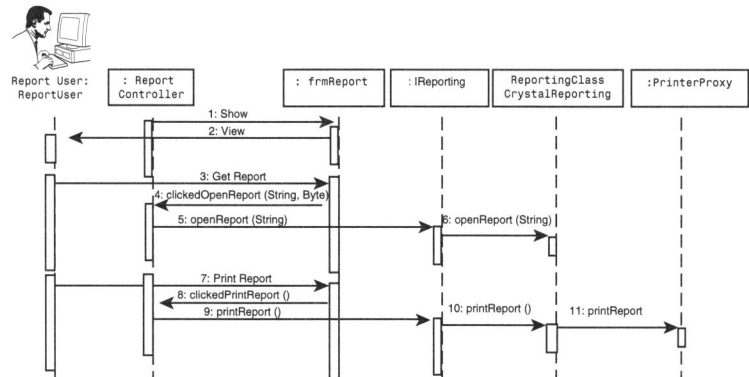

Figure 7.3 shows a proper way to encapsulate your application from potential changes or failures in a particular third-party control. In the figure, all application requests for reporting services are routed through the instance of the `IReporting` interface class. The encapsulation doesn't stop there. The `IReporting` instance then calls the facade class for the third-party control Crystal Reports, named `CrystalReporting`. This same design pattern can also be applied to your use of the MS Comm control (`IComm` could be an interface class), the various grid controls (`IGrid`), and so on.

The Industry Relies on the Use of Third-Party Controls

For computer software companies in the computer industry, a popular product or group of products results in not only dramatically increased revenues but also in telephone calls and emails for technical support. Some of these customer contacts are requests for enhancements to the product or full extensions. Microsoft and many other companies have come to appreciate the value added to their products by third-party vendors.

In the early 1980s, Hewlett Packard market share in the industry was enhanced by the third-party vendors (software and hardware) whose products supplemented its HP3000 product. In 1984, Eugene Volokh of VESOFT Company listed some factors that make third-party vendors able to grow with original equipment manufacturers (OEMs, such as Microsoft, Hewlett Packard, IBM, and so on). In paraphrasing, the list includes

- *Reverse economy of scale*. Third-party vendors are able to respond more quickly to market forces (such as customer demand for changes) than the original equipment manufacturer. For instance, because there was a need for a grid control more powerful than Microsoft Grid, third-party vendors responded with True Grid and Spread VBX. When True Grid became the favorite of Visual Basic developers, Microsoft licensed it to be shipped with the language product.

- *You can't please everybody*. Third-party vendors are able to meet niche market demands to which OEMs can't afford to respond. This might have been the reason that Crystal Reports took off early in the history of Visual Basic VBX controls.

- *OEM quality versus third-party vendor low price*. OEMs seek to compete with third-party vendors on the basis of reliability and quality, not price. Of course, this strategy can backfire, as was the case with Apple Computer in the 1980s. At the same time, a customer is willing to pay a premium if the company, OEM, or third-party vendor, is available for technical support.

7

In general, third-party vendors and supportive OEMs such as Microsoft have enjoyed a relatively tranquil relationship. The economic practice of software sales has gradually evolved to the point where the return on investment for OEMs and third-party vendors mutually benefits both parties. Visual Basic will lead the way toward improving this economic marriage of convenience between OEMs and third-party vendors, which should benefit the productivity of Visual Basic development customers for many years to come.

Summary

Today you learned about the process of deciding whether to use third-party controls in a Visual Basic project. This chapter discusses how to document use cases for using third-party controls and how to design class and object models with third-party controls. You also learned about gray box controls versus black box controls. In closing, the chapter describes how the computer industry relies on third-party controls.

Tomorrow, you will learn concepts in version control, debugging, and using object-oriented approaches to traditional complex conditional branching such as `If Then` branching.

Q&A

Q What company single-handedly brought the third-party control industry to the forefront of the mass market?

A Microsoft.

Q True or False: One way to improve the choice of third-party control is to formulate an evaluation and selection criteria?

A True.

Q What is a disadvantage of letting a busy developer evaluate one or more third-party controls?

A It can take days or weeks for developers to evaluate, test, and implement one or more third-party controls. When a Visual Basic developer, typically pressed for meeting deadlines, has to evaluate third-party controls, his or her evaluation will not likely be thorough.

Q What are possible sources of information in determining the cost of buying a third-party control versus developing similar code yourself?

A Look at industry magazine reviews for any mention of potential man-hour savings. Review the average number of hours it took to develop (or try to develop) similar code in-house. Check out the competition to see whether their peers have effectively implemented such controls at a reasonable cost.

Q What advice should you or your organization keep in mind when acquiring third-party controls and components for reusability?

A Keep in mind that, as Jacobson mentions, it will typically cost you much more money to develop a control or component in-house for reusability than to create it for one-time use on a particular project. Buying well-designed third-party controls can mitigate these costs, but they must be reused several times to achieve a desired return on investment.

Q What artifact should a developer present to his or her project manager regarding a third-party control to be used?

A A developer should create a brief proposal that lists the pros and cons of using that control and describes how it helped solve the problem. This proposal need not be formal or any longer than one page.

Q True or False: When you have all your proposals and related literature in hand, you should compare them against the general descriptions of user requirements when making the decision to purchase a third-party control.

A False. You should compare them against what role your use cases and interaction diagrams (sequence and collaboration) require.

Workshop

The workshop includes quiz questions to help gauge your grasp of the material. You'll find the answers to this quiz in Appendix A, "Answers." Even if you feel that you understand the concepts presented here, you should work through the quiz. The last section contains an exercise to help reinforce your learning.

Quiz

1. What advantages and disadvantages must you consider when deciding whether to acquire third-party controls?

2. What are better ways of incorporating controls that are still useful?

3. Describe one or more benefits of having a separate committee evaluate third-party controls for use in an enterprise?

4. What questions should you ask in evaluating third-party controls?

5. For what purposes must organizations pay up-front costs in seeking return on investment through component reusability?

7

6. What is a strategy for incorporating third-party controls over a period of time?

7. What strategies might you use in evaluating third-party controls if you don't have an evaluation committee?

Exercise

Using Figures 7.2 and 7.3 as examples, draw a sequence diagram that shows a right way to implement your favorite third-party control and another that shows the wrong way.

WEEK 1

In Review

The lessons for Week 1 got you started in object-oriented programming concepts in Visual Basic. You learned important concepts in object-oriented analysis, design, and programming, as well as class inheritance and building ActiveX components.

The purpose of the first lesson is to give you a primer on object-oriented programming that is generally universal. You read a survey of fundamental concepts in object-oriented programming that provided the foundation for the subsequent lessons in the book. You learned that a *class* is a design-time template that determines the behavior of objects based on it and that Visual Basic allows you to perform OOP using the class module and the Class Builder utility.

Day 2, "Fundamental Object-Oriented Analysis," presented you with the essentials of performing object-oriented analysis. You learned how to discover important entities or abstractions in your user requirements and other sources in your domain. You also learned how to implement user requirements as use cases. Moreover, you learned that the three primary roles usually involved in the use case identification process are the requirements gatherer, the object-oriented analyst, and the architect. You saw that the requirements gatherer would typically interrogate end users, business managers (or domain experts), and project managers in order to draft both a problem statement and optionally an initial requirements model. The object-oriented analyst then carefully examines the requirements model to understand the requirements and elaborate on the requirements model, to assess the implications of each requirement, and to remove inconsistencies and requirements that have been discovered to no longer be valid. Object-oriented architects work with analysts and designers to ensure that project team members are able to trace the names of business objects between the list of requirements, analysis models, and design models. Architects sometimes perform the roles of both the analyst and designer; otherwise, the architect is a mediator and final decision-maker with regard to the system architecture. With the advent of the software reuse structure of the business organization, these roles will become more specialized (partitioned into smaller roles).

You then learned that the problem statement is used to capture, in plain English, how the user sees the system helping her complete her business processes. From this problem statement, the analyst and architect identify and list meaningful nouns and verbs, which helps the technicians identify potential actors, classes, class behavior, and use cases. After a list of these objects is drafted, the superfluous or vague items are discarded in favor of those with stronger meaning to the current problem domain (or business context). The main artifacts of the analysis process are the problem statement, the use case model, and an analysis class model.

On Day 3, "Fundamental Object-Oriented Design," you learned the fundamentals of object-oriented design. This includes the creation of class diagrams that reflect the Visual Basic class modules you discovered you need, as well as interaction diagrams that show how these classes interact to carry out user requirements.

In the first three lessons, you learned about the concepts of object technology and received a primer on object-oriented programming. On Day 4, "Fundamental Object-Oriented Programming," you took your learning a step farther. You learned how to construct actual Visual Basic code from the simple sequence diagrams you created in previous lessons. You received some background on generating code in Rational Rose and Visual Modeler, as well as identifying the known technical constraints of Visual Basic. After you generated some sample code, you got an idea of how to put the finishing touches on the application.

Day 5, "Class Interface Inheritance in Visual Basic," covers class interface inheritance, in which one class implements the interface (public methods and properties) of another class. Specifically, you learned that a Visual Basic class is representative of a logical unit that is abstracted above mere code. A *class interface* is a contract with a client of that class that must be serviced. Building good interfaces is a fundamental part of reuse, but planning for any form of reuse is very difficult and initially will slow down a project. The distinction between interface and implementation classes is very important in component development. You learned that interfaces are what a component makes available to its clients.

At the end of the week, you learned how to build simple ActiveX components. You also implemented a testing strategy for such components. You learned the importance of use cases in test planning as well as incorporating object-oriented testing services into ActiveX components. You learned from an example as well as by going through some workshop exercises. Then you wrapped up the week by looking at incorporating components developed by third parties.

WEEK 2

At a Glance

In Week 2, you learn how to build objects that test themselves. That is, you create objects that have methods that test their own preconditions, including making sure that the data or class type of an incoming parameter is of the type expected. Next you delve deeply into the process of breaking up a proposed application into subsystems, including components. You learn how to identify and use design patterns for subsystems and their interactions.

Toward the middle of the week, you learn the art of refining use cases as application and subsystem architecture blueprints. You learn about revisiting use cases in your environment, the problem statement, and the use case model. You also learn specifically how to incorporate in the design models new discoveries in the way the end user uses your VB application.

Later in the week, you learn more about the subsystems making up the real-world example. You study the basics of the Graphical User Interface Subsystem, learning how to use the modeling techniques for GUIs and understanding the encapsulation of data presentation into a separate class. Then you implement a Graphical User Interface Subsystem by placing the core logic you generally insert in forms into classes that control the interaction between the forms and the rest of the application.

Toward the end of the week, the Workgroup and User Security Subsystem is presented to you. This critical subsystem shows how to implement related security issues, including a class for encrypting the password. Then you wrap up the week by learning the concept of the Internal Application Manager as a mechanism for managing the states an application goes through during a typical session.

DAY 8

Versioning and Debugging

In this chapter, you'll learn how to build objects that test themselves. That is, you'll create objects that have methods that test their own preconditions, including making sure that the data or class type of an incoming parameter is of the type expected. This lesson also presents advice on how to debug your classes, as well as version control tips for classes and subsystems of classes using Visual SourceSafe. In detail, the topics in this chapter include the following:

- Understanding the theory behind the self-testing object
- Designing business logic constraint checking into VB classes
- Verifying business logic services: Is the development approach effective?
- Inserting debug identifiers for VB classes
- Using Visual Modeler to add debugging footprints
- Logging testing activities
- Understanding the need for logging class test results
- Recording test logs

- Saving and displaying test logs
- Using source code control with emphasis on SourceSafe
- Using Visual SourceSafe
- Local directory structuring
- The Samsona Bank Teller System Example

Understanding the Theory Behind the Self-Testing Object

Testing and quality assurance are important activities for any object-oriented programming project. Gone are the days when ignoring these aspects of effective development was basically accepted. Today's technology is far more complex and demanding than previous technological paradigms, meaning that serious flaws and potentially critical mishaps must be addressed at every level of an application's design.

Self-testing involves creating tests during the design phase that you then build into classes. During class or unit testing, you or a peer developer invokes these methods, noting preconditions, invariants, and postconditions. During application testing, a tester will indirectly invoke these methods, upon which the test class will store the results of the test for its responsibilities in a log file or display the results on the screen.

Testers will need to test not only the application, but the user documentation and design model logic as well. This means that testers will face increasing pressure to ensure quality at as many checkpoints and milestones in a project as possible. Of course, as a crack programmer and designer, you can do your part to make sure that your class testing (unit testing) efforts are effective. Thus, classes and subsystems of packages will need to be designed and programmed to test themselves—that is, test their own publicly visible behavior.

Before you build in the testing features that your Visual Basic classes and subsystems need, you should be familiar with testing activities in general. With a heightened sense of appreciation for the testing process, your implementation of self-testing facilities should be of increased quality.

As a programmer, you have been involved in code and design inspections, code reviews, or code and design walkthroughs. Inspections give a chance for your peers and architects to review your code and design models, praise the good parts, and offer constructive criticism of any discovered flaws.

8

For distributed applications you may deploy using Microsoft's DCOM or OMG's CORBA, a test engineer will verify the quality of that system on each of its target platforms. A thorough distributed portability test will also check the behavior of Visual Basic or the ActiveX component on each remote system, and may also check interactions between the application and the remote system at the machine level.

Further, distributed systems require integration testing. If the remote system is object-oriented, integration testing will assess the quality of the communication between both systems' object interfaces. If the remote system is not object-oriented, the integration test will concentrate on the communication between the object interface of your application (as represented by the public object) and the non-object-oriented interface of the remote system. With integration testing, the test engineer is testing the interaction between your application and the remote system actor. (Recall that any external system with which your application interacts is also known as an *actor* to your system.)

In Day 6, "Building and Testing Components," you were introduced to test cases. Testers need to create test cases based on use cases you or a team member creates. An instance of a test case is a test script. For complex systems involving thousands of users and dozens of external system actors, you can expect hundreds (in some cases, thousands) of test scripts. Test scripts can be extremely technically detailed, incorporating tests for automatically generated reports, access violations of an object by several competing client objects, database concurrency/multiple user access, software and hardware fault tolerance constraints, and so forth.

Testing also includes graphical user interface testing. Ergonomics and human factors in engineering may come into play if your system is to be used by dozens or hundreds of users who must sit in front of your application practically all day performing use cases against it. It is important to design your GUIs not only with visual appeal, but also with self-testing mechanisms so that simple errors like date formats and currency values are trapped before the business service tier or server is activated for more complex processing. There's nothing more annoying than entering lots of key business data, submitting it for business processing, and having it rejected some time later for an invalid date value.

With iterative and incremental development, you'll want to regression-test your application for each increment. Self-testing methods in your objects help minimize the effort involved in regression testing by allowing the tester to concentrate more on business rule violations and less on data type violations. During regression testing, expect the tester to give you valuable input for improvement of your code, design models, and use cases.

If you develop Visual Basic applications for commercial sales, or are in a politically charged corporate climate where getting early user feedback is critical, you will probably have a beta test engineer on your project. Beta testing is a way of validating your application against user expectations before making a major commitment to deploying it on a large scale. Beta testing is also a good way of seeing the effectiveness of your self-testing methods against the way demanding users treat your application.

In general, self-testing objects are the best ways to localize errors of any sort in your application. Tests that fail can be better traced to classes and methods because the responsibilities of methods are highlighted by self-testing policies. Finally, having self-testing methods in your objects identifies you as a conscientious supporter of testing, something that will endear you to your testers during your project's testing cycles.

As indicated, checking preconditions and postconditions upon invoking a method is an important part of localizing errors. Building these mechanisms into your Visual Basic classes includes

- Using argument data type checking
- Using return data type checking

Using Argument Data Type Checking

The task of implementing type checking for arguments of Visual Basic types seems pretty simple, you might think. Simply specify the data type of the argument in the argument list, and let Visual Basic handle the rest. This strategy might work for incoming parameters of the same data type as expected by the respective argument, but what about parameters of type Variant? You must prepare for type mismatch errors with respect to the Variant data type and any other user-defined object types. Let's look at some examples.

Suppose you have a class with a method as follows:

```
Public Sub testMethod(ByVal argString As String)
    MsgBox argString
End Sub
```

Further, suppose this class has another method as follows:

```
Public Sub tryThis()
    Dim vTestData As Variant
    vTestData = "www.samsona.com"
    testMethod vTestData
End Sub
```

Notice that the method, testMethod, expects incoming parameters to be of the String data type. However, you passed in a Variant (vTestData) that stores a String value. Happily, the method tryThis accepts this parameter as a valid argument. However, let's change the type of argString from String to Integer:

```
Public Sub testMethod(ByVal argInteger As Integer)
    MsgBox argString
End Sub
```

The method, testMethod, still executes but displays the wrong data (in this case, it displays the error number of the "Type Mismatch" error). You need to build in the ability to prevent further execution of the method when such an error occurs. Thus, you would need to modify testMethod as follows:

```
Public Sub testMethod(ByVal argVariant As Variant)
    Dim iInteger As Integer
    If VarType(argVariant) = vbInteger Then
        iInteger = argVariant
        MsgBox iInteger
    End If
End Sub
```

Note that this method assumes that you want the flexibility of having an argument of any Visual Basic data type. The variable iInteger is set to the value of argument argVariant if argVariant is internally stored as an Integer. In addition, if argVariant is internally an Integer, the value of iInteger is displayed in a message box. It's good practice to use a local variable instead of the actual argument for internal method implementation code. In any case, if you try to pass in any value that is not an Integer, the testMethod method will ignore the request. If the value is an Integer, this method will be able to process the request.

This pattern of type checking does not apply only to intrinsic data types such as Integer and String. You can use the pattern for Object data types, whether Visual Basic or your own. In the preceding example, you'd simply replace Integer with some interface or implementation object of your choosing, such as the following:

```
Public Sub testMethod(ByVal argObject As Object)
    Dim theBasicPersonalChecking As BasicPersonalChecking
    If TypeName(argObject) = "BasicPersonalChecking" Then
        Set theBasicPersonalChecking = argObject
        MsgBox theBasicPersonalChecking.AccountNumber
    End If
End Sub
```

You could allow Visual Basic to enforce the argument object type by replacing the generic type Object with theBasicPersonalChecking; however, if you need the flexibility of accepting any type of object (for processing by more than one internal private method), you need to do the type checking yourself.

Using Return Data Type Checking

Related to type checking for method arguments is type checking for returned values and objects. The idea here is to make sure that the type of the variable or object returned is of the expected type. Listing 8.1 shows an example of return type testing using the previous example code as the basis.

LISTING 8.1. CLASS: TestClass.

```
 1: Public Function testReturns(ByVal argInteger As Variant) _
 2: As TestClass
 3:     Dim anotherTestClass As TestClass
 4:     On Error GoTo errtestReturns
 5:
 6:     If argInteger < 32767 Then
 7:         Set anotherTestClass = New TestClass
 8:         anotherTestClass.SomeInteger = argInteger + 100
 9:         Set testReturns = anotherTestClass
10:     End If
11:     Exit Function
12: errtestReturns:
13:     Dim sMethodName As String
14:     sMethodName = "testReturns"
15:     theErrorHandler.processVBTypeError Err, Me, sMethodName
16:     sMethodName = ""
17: End Function
18:
19: Module: modMain
20:
21: Public Sub main()
22:     'theTestClass.tryThis
23:
24:     Dim localClass As Object
25:     'Dim SomeArgument As Integer 'For positive Type-Check Test
26:     Dim SomeArgument As String 'For negative Type-Check Test
27:
28:     SomeArgument = 11 'Positive Type-Check Test
29:     'SomeArgument = "string" 'Negative Type-Check Test
30:
31:     Set localClass = theTestClass.testReturns(SomeArgument)
32:
33:     If TypeName(localClass) <> "Nothing" Then
34:         If TypeOf localClass Is TestClass Then
35:             MsgBox localClass.SomeInteger
36:         End If
37:     End If
38: End Sub
```

Notice Sub main(), starting at line 21. For the sake of convenience, there are two declarations and uses of the same variable, SomeArgument (see line 29). One use is for positive testing (the operation and return you expect) and negative testing (what you don't expect). The modMain module is the surrogate client, whereas TestClass is the server. The type of the return variable, localClass, is the same as the server class, TestClass. Thus, from modMain's viewpoint, there are two objects of the same class, including theTestClass.

8

If you create a `TestClass` class module and a `modMain` module with the methods in Listing 8.1, and you run the example as is, `SomeArgument` will lead to a successful pass of program execution. The correct type will be returned. However, if you comment the `Integer` version of `SomeArgument` and uncomment the `String` version, the return type will not be passed back, meaning that `localTestClass` will never be initialized with the return object. However, even in this potentially embarrassing situation, the elegant return-type checking mechanism ensures that non-`Integer` arguments will not lead to an unexpected object being returned.

NEW TERM   *Positive testing* is a testing activity that seeks a desirable result given a request for service. *Negative testing*, on the other hand, is a testing activity that seeks an undesirable result given a request for service.

Designing Business Logic Constraint Checking into VB Classes

Business rule logic encompasses any preconditions and postconditions that are specific to a given business. Thus, in the Second Bank of Carrollton example, a rule could be that any checking account must be a valid bank product, of which Basic Personal Checking is one. Or the bank might require that all new savings accounts must be opened with a minimum of $100.00. Day 15, "The Business Rules Subsystem," goes into greater detail about business rules. Here you are only interested in looking at a method that has such a constraint built into it. The next section shows a simple example of a business rule logic that you can check.

The Samsona Bank Teller System Example

REAL WORLD   The branch manager of Second Bank of Carrollton just remembered two important business rules that she forgot to mention. The application you're building for her needs to capture, in the case of deposit transactions, whether cash or a check is being deposited. If the transaction involves cash, the bank must enforce federal law for deposits of $10,000 or more. This means that the application must check for this limit for every cash deposit transaction. If the transaction involves a check, the date the funds are available is by default ten business days (unless the teller comes across a situation that requires overriding of this rule—let's ignore this complexity for this example).

Let's use the classes from the ActiveX component project developed on Day 6.

Listing 8.2 shows the enhanced `Deposit` class. Notice the three new properties, `FundsAvailabilityDate` (line 52), `DepositType` (line 65), and `TransactionDate` (line 40). `FundsAvailabilityDate` is set to ten business days from the day the check deposit was made (lines 17 and 18). `DepositType` captures from the Bank Teller user interface controller class whether the transaction is by cash or by check. `TransactionDate` captures the date the transaction was made, which would be the current date (at least, for this example).

Now notice the new methods: `enforceFundsAvailability` (starting at line 13) and `enforceCashDepositLimit` (starting at line 29). The `enforceFundsAvailability` method sets the date the funds will be available by setting the `FundsAvailabilityDate` property. The `enforceCashDepositLimit` method enforces the federal bank regulations regarding cash deposits. The check for these rules and the type of deposit is done immediately upon entering the methods. If the precondition is true, each method will process the rule according to bank or legal specifications. Only one method will be able to process the incoming `Deposit` object. That's because the deposit transaction can only be of one type, either cash or check. To help you with a deposit type identifier, you have an `Enum` named `eDepositType`.

LISTING 8.2. THE Deposit CLASS.

```
 1: Private mvarAmount As Single 'local copy
 2: 'local variable(s) to hold property value(s)
 3: Private mvarDepositType As Byte 'local copy
 4: 'local variable(s) to hold property value(s)
 5: Private mvarFundsAvailabilityDate As Date 'local copy
 6: Private mvarTransactionDate As Date 'local copy
 7:
 8: Public Enum eDepositType
 9:     Cash
10:     Check
11: End Enum
12:
13: Public Function enforceFundsAvailability(argDeposit _
14: As Deposit) As Boolean
15:     If DepositType = eDepositType.check Then
16:         TransactionDate = Date
17:         FundsAvailabilityDate = DateAdd("d", 10, _
18:             TransactionDate)
19:
20:         MsgBox "Funds won't be available until " & _
21:             CStr(FundsAvailabilityDate)
22:
23:         enforceFundsAvailability = True
24:         Exit Function
25:     End If
26:     enforceFundsAvailability = False
27: End Function
28:
```

```
29: Public Function enforceCashDepositLimit(argDeposit As Deposit) As
    ➥Boolean
30:     If argDeposit.DepositType = eDepositType.Cash Then
31:         If argDeposit.Amount > 10000 Then
32:             'Could raise event at this point...
33:             MsgBox "Cash amount not allowed per federal law"
34:         Exit Function
35:     End If
36:     enforceCashDepositLimit = False
37:     End If
38: End Function
39:
40: Public Property Get TransactionDate() As Date
41: 'used when retrieving value of a property, on the right side of an
    ➥assignment.
42: 'Syntax: Debug.Print X.TransactionDate
43:     TransactionDate = mvarTransactionDate
44: End Property
45:
46: Public Property Let TransactionDate(ByVal vData As Date)
47: 'used when assigning a value to the property, on the left side of an
    ➥assignment.
48: 'Syntax: X.TransactionDate = 5
49:     mvarTransactionDate = vData
50: End Property
51:
52: Public Property Let FundsAvailabilityDate(ByVal vData As Date)
53: 'used when assigning a value to the property, on the left side of an
    ➥assignment.
54: 'Syntax: X.FundsAvailabilityDate = 5
55:     mvarFundsAvailabilityDate = vData
56: End Property
57:
58:
59: Public Property Get FundsAvailabilityDate() As Date
60: 'used when retrieving value of a property, on the right side of an
    ➥assignment.
61: 'Syntax: Debug.Print X.FundsAvailabilityDate
62:     FundsAvailabilityDate = mvarFundsAvailabilityDate
63: End Property
64:
65: Public Property Let DepositType(ByVal vData As Byte)
66: 'used when assigning a value to the property, on the left side of an
    ➥assignment.
67: 'Syntax: X.DepositType = 5
68:     mvarDepositType = vData
69: End Property
70:
71:
```

continues

LISTING 8.2. CONTINUED

```
 72: Public Property Get DepositType() As Byte
 73: 'used when retrieving value of a property, on the right side of an
     ➥assignment.
 74: 'Syntax: Debug.Print X.DepositType
 75:
 76: 'Purpose: To determine if cash or check
 77: 'being deposited. If Cash, must enforce
 78: 'federal law for deposits of $10000 or more.
 79: 'If check, FundsAvailabilityDate is set to
 80: 'ten business days from today.
 81:     DepositType = mvarDepositType
 82: End Property
 83:
 84:
 85: Friend Sub depositFunds(argAccountNumber As String)
 86:     'You'll use Call for the sake of simplicity.
 87:     Call theBasicPersonalCheckingAccount.adjustBalance(Me,
     ➥argAccountNumber)
 88: End Sub
 89:
 90: Public Property Let Amount(ByVal vData As Single)
 91: 'used when assigning a value to the property, on the left side of an
     ➥assignment.
 92: 'Syntax: X.Amount = 5
 93:     mvarAmount = vData
 94: End Property
 95:
 96:
 97: Public Property Get Amount() As Single
 98: 'used when retrieving value of a property, on the right side of an
     ➥assignment.
 99: 'Syntax: Debug.Print X.Amount
100:     Amount = mvarAmount
101: End Property
```

Listing 8.3 shows the `BasicPersonalChecking` class. The method `increaseBalance`, which is called by the `adjustBalance` public interface method, provides specific behavior implementation for deposit transactions. It invokes the `enforceCashDepositLimit` method of the `localDeposit` object. If this method processes successfully according to its policy enforcement goal, there's no need to invoke the object's other method, `enforceFundsAvailability`. However, if `enforceCashDepositLimit` was not able to handle the message, `enforceFundsAvailability` is indeed invoked. Note that you don't need the test for `booReturns` because `enforceFundsAvailability` will check the deposit type anyway. Thus, you could modify the two method calls as follows:

```
booReturns = _ localDeposit.enforceCashDepositLimit(localDeposit)
booReturns = _ localDeposit.enforceFundsAvailability(localDeposit)
```

LISTING 8.3. THE `BasicPersonalChecking` CLASS.

```
 1: Private mvarClassDebugID As Variant 'local copy
 2: 'Implements BankAccountProduct
 3: Private m_pAccountType As String
 4: Private mb_ProductID As Byte
 5: 'local variable(s) to hold property value(s)
 6: Private mvarAccountNumber As String 'local copy
 7: Private mvarCurrentBalance As Single 'local copy
 8:
 9: Public Event OnWrongAccountNumber(argMsg As String)
10: Public Property Let CurrentBalance(ByVal vData As Single)
11: 'used when assigning a value to the property, on the left side of an
    ➥assignment.
12: 'Syntax: X.CurrentBalance = 5
13:     mvarCurrentBalance = vData
14: End Property
15:
16:
17: Public Property Get CurrentBalance() As Single
18: 'used when retrieving value of a property, on the right side of an
    ➥assignment.
19: 'Syntax: Debug.Print X.CurrentBalance
20:     CurrentBalance = mvarCurrentBalance
21: End Property
22:
23:
24: Public Property Let AccountNumber(ByVal vData As String)
25: 'used when assigning a value to the property, on the left side of an
    ➥assignment.
26: 'Syntax: X.AccountNumber = 5
27:     mvarAccountNumber = vData
28: End Property
29:
30:
31: Public Property Get AccountNumber() As String
32: 'used when retrieving value of a property, on the right side of an
    ➥assignment.
33: 'Syntax: Debug.Print X.AccountNumber
34:     AccountNumber = mvarAccountNumber
35: End Property
36:
37:
```

continues

LISTING 8.3. CONTINUED

```
38: Private Function decreaseBalance(argObject As Object)
39:     'Make sure incoming object is of type Withdrawal
40:     If TypeName(argObject) <> "Withdrawal" Then
41:         decreaseBalance = False
42:         Exit Function
43:     End If
44:
45:     'It's a Withdrawal object
46:     CurrentBalance = CurrentBalance - argObject.Amount
47:     decreaseBalance = True
48: End Function
49:
50: Private Function increaseBalance(argObject As Object)
51:     Dim localDeposit As Deposit, booReturns As Boolean
52:     'Make sure incoming object is of type Deposit
53:     If TypeName(argObject) <> "Deposit" Then
54:         increaseBalance = False
55:         Exit Function
56:     End If
57:
58:     'It's a Deposit object
59:     Set localDeposit = argObject
60:
61:     'Test for Cash or Check deposits
62:     booReturns = _ localDeposit.enforceCashDepositLimit(localDeposit)
63:     If Not booReturns Then
64:         booReturns = _
            ➥localDeposit.enforceFundsAvailability(localDeposit)
65:     End If
66:
67:     CurrentBalance = CurrentBalance + argObject.Amount
68:     increaseBalance = True
69: End Function
70:
71:
72: Public Function adjustBalance(argObject As Deposit, argAccountNumber
    ➥As String) As Boolean
73:     Dim LocalObject As Object, returns As Boolean
74:
75:     'If there's more than one account object in memory, a
        ➥precondition
76:     'is that this object is the correct object. So check account
        ➥number
77:     If argAccountNumber <> AccountNumber Then
78:         'Raise exceptions here...
79:         Dim sMsg As String
80:         sMsg = "Wrong account number, Please retry."
81:         RaiseEvent OnWrongAccountNumber(sMsg)
```

8

```
82:              'Set LocalObject = Nothing
83:              Exit Function
84:          End If
85:
86:          'Delegate to private methods, where only one will be able to
             ➥process the message.
87:
88:          Set LocalObject = argObject
89:
90:          returns = increaseBalance(LocalObject)
91:          If returns Then
92:              adjustBalance = returns
93:              Exit Function
94:              Set LocalObject = Nothing
95:          End If
96:
97:          returns = decreaseBalance(LocalObject)
98:          If returns Then
99:              adjustBalance = returns
100:             Exit Function
101:             Set LocalObject = Nothing
102:         End If
103:
104: End Function
105:
106:
107: Public Sub getAccountType()
108: End Sub
109:
110: Public Property Get ClassDebugID() As Variant
111: 'used when retrieving value of a property, on the right side of an
     ➥assignment.
112: 'Syntax: Debug.Print X.ClassDebugID
113:     If IsObject(mvarClassDebugID) Then
114:         Set ClassDebugID = mvarClassDebugID
115:     Else
116:         ClassDebugID = mvarClassDebugID
117:     End If
118: End Property
119:
120:
121: Private Property Get BankAccountProduct_ClassDebugID() As Variant
122:     Const E_NOTIMPL = &H80004001
123:
124: End Property
125:
126: Private Function BankAccountProduct_getAccountType() As String
127:     BankAccountProduct_getAccountType = m_pAccountType
128:
```

continues

LISTING 8.3. CONTINUED

```
129: End Function
130:
131:
132: Private Function BankAccountProduct_getProductID() As Byte
133:     BankAccountProduct_getProductID = mb_ProductID
134:
135: End Function
136:
137: Private Sub BankAccountProduct_setProductID(argMsgID As Byte)
138:     mb_ProductID = argMsgID
139: End Sub
140:
141:
142: Private Sub Class_Initialize()
143:     'm_pAccountType = TypeName(Me)
144:     'mb_ProductID = BankProducts.BasicPersonalChecking
145:     mvarAccountNumber = "002"
146: End Sub
147:
148: Private Sub Class_Terminate()
149:     m_pAccountType = ""
150:     mb_ProductID = 0
151: End Sub
```

VERIFYING BUSINESS LOGIC SERVICES: IS THE DEVELOPMENT APPROACH EFFECTIVE?

Developing business applications is quite complex because many business rules tend to be somewhat confusing or vague at times. This is specifically true for companies where business processes are very dynamic, sometimes volatile. This volatility reflects the fluidity of market forces—supply and demand. The development approach best suited for such dynamic changes is object-oriented programming, coupled with object-oriented analysis and design. That way, you can develop effective business policy enforcement classes that are able to more fully test preconditions and postconditions by encapsulated behavior.

VALIDATING BUSINESS LOGIC SERVICES: IS THE SYSTEM DEVELOPED CORRECTLY FOR BUSINESS LOGIC?

The answer to this question depends on how your client company, or you as an entrepreneur, views the success of your project. The best measure for correctness of development is in reusability and quality. Reusability can't be determined effectively until you use your classes in another application. Reusability and quality are enhanced by self-testing objects where methods test object and data types upon entry and exit of such methods, as well as how invariants, such as local variables in methods, are used.

Inserting Debug Identifiers for VB Classes

8

You can use Class Builder or Visual Modeler to insert debugging identifiers in your Visual Basic classes. This is extremely helpful for debugging runtime errors. Listing 8.3, in fact, includes debugging identifiers and debugging code.

As long as you're in debug mode, all of the debugging code inserted by Class Builder, Visual Modeler, or yourself is active. You activate debug mode by entering the following code in the General Declarations section of the desired class:

```
'set this to 0 to disable debug code in this class
#Const DebugMode = 1
```

You deactivate debug mode as follows:

```
#Const DebugMode = 0
```

If DebugMode = 1, any code in the following code body is active:

```
#If DebugMode Then
    'Your debug mode code here...

#End If
```

If DebugMode = 1, such code is not active, meaning that the code won't show up in your project executable or ActiveX component.

Every class that you want to be tracked for debugging will have a private property, mlClassDebugID, associated with the public property ClassDebugID. This identifier, a purely runtime creature, is assigned a value in the class's Initialize event and is used to help identify the class for global debugging. In General Declarations of the class, the following code is inserted by Class Builder or Visual Modeler:

```
#If DebugMode Then
    'local variable to hold the serialized class ID that
    'was created in Class_Initialize
    '##ModelId=349AE9A00316
    Private mlClassDebugID As Long
#End If

#If DebugMode Then
    '##ModelId=349AE9A30398
    Public Property Get ClassDebugID()
        'if you are in debug mode, surface this property that consumers
        ➡can query
        ClassDebugID = mlClassDebugID
    End Property
#End If
```

The `Class_Initialize` event, then, would have the following code structure:

```
Private Sub Class_Initialize()
    #If DebugMode Then
        'get the next available class ID, and print out
        'that the class was created successfully
        mlClassDebugID = GetNextClassDebugID()
        Debug.Print "'" & TypeName(Me) & "' instance " & _ mlClassDebugID
        ➡& " created"
    #End If

    'Your code here...

End Sub
```

The debugging function, `GetNextClassDebugID()`, assigns the next available class debug ID number to the current class instance. The `GetNextClassDebugID()` function resides in the global `ModClassIDGenerator` module. The function is as follows:

```
Function GetNextClassDebugID() As Long
    'class ID generator
    Static lClassDebugID As Long
    lClassDebugID = lClassDebugID + 1
    GetNextClassDebugID = lClassDebugID
End Function
```

The `Class_Terminate` event has a similar structure:

```
Private Sub Class_Terminate()
    'the class is being destroyed
    #If DebugMode Then
        Debug.Print "'" & TypeName(Me) & "' instance " & _
        ➡CStr(mlClassDebugID) & " is terminating"
    #End If
End Sub
```

The `Debug.Print` line prints the object's type (class) name and debug identifier to the debug console window at runtime. To have To have Class Builder insert debugging code in your classes, choose Add-Ins | Class Builder Utility from the menu. In Class Builder, choose View | Options. You should see the Class Builder Options dialog box, as illustrated in Figure 8.1. Click the check box for Include Debug Code in Initialize and Terminate Events.

FIGURE 8.1.

Use the Class Builder Options dialog box to insert debug code into your applications.

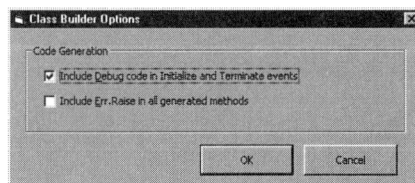

8

Note   For more information on debugging in Visual Basic, check out the Visual Basic Book Online.

Using Visual Modeler to Add Debugging Footprints

Adding debugging footprints (or lines of code) in your Visual Basic projects is similar to the debugging insertions provided by Class Builder, but requires that you have a model with at least one class in it.

To try out the debug code insertion feature, open Visual Modeler. Right-click on the Logical View folder in the package browser to the left, and choose New Class from the pop-up menu. Visual Modeler inserts a new class icon in the browser with a default name of NewClass. Leave the name as is. Now choose Tools | Code Generation Wizard from the menu. Click the Next button three times. You should see the Code Generation Wizard - General Options dialog box, as illustrated in Figure 8.2. Notice in the Code Generation Options frame that the check boxes Include Debug Code and Include Err.Raise in All Generated Methods are already checked. If you're going to use your own error handling classes, you should uncheck the second check box. With Visual Basic up and running, click the Finish button. Browse the NewClass class in your project.

FIGURE 8.2.

Use the Code Generation Wizard – General Options dialog box to insert debug code in your applications.

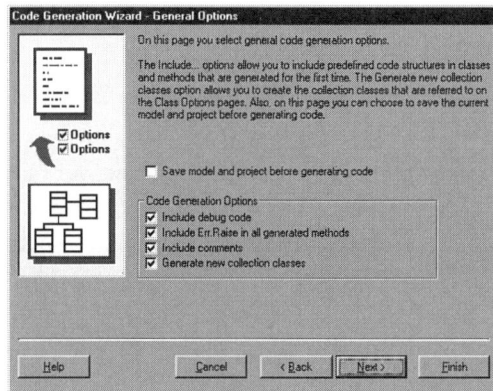

> **Note**
>
> If you own a copy of the Professional or Enterprise editions of Visual Basic, you can get a free copy of Visual Modeler at www.microsoft.com/vbasic in the Owners' Area. Have the registration number of your copy of Visual Basic handy.

LOGGING TESTING ACTIVITIES

For some applications, you may find it helpful to log runtime errors in a text file or even a database such as Access. In such cases, it's faster to use text files located in log directory located on the client or server machine.

Understanding the Need for Logging Class Test Results

Logging class test results helps in two ways. First, the test/quality assurance team can use the results to compare with the team's test script results. Second, the tasks of current and future maintenance programmers will be made much less tedious because they can easily pinpoint class methods that are in error. For corporate developers, this speeds up the process of resolving user complaints. For entrepreneurial and commercial developers, customer satisfaction will be greatly improved, giving you an edge on your competition.

Recording Test Logs

Remember the testReturns method of the TestClass earlier? Recall the error handling code:

```
Public Function testReturns(ByVal argInteger As Variant) _
As TestClass
    Dim anotherTestClass As TestClass
    On Error GoTo errtestReturns
    . . .
Exit Function
errtestReturns:
    Dim sMethodName As String
    sMethodName = "testReturns"
    theErrorHandler.processVBTypeError Err, Me, sMethodName
    sMethodName = ""
End Function
```

The theErrorHandler object has a form, as illustrated in Figure 8.3.

FIGURE 8.3.

The frmTest *form is used for recording and displaying class errors.*

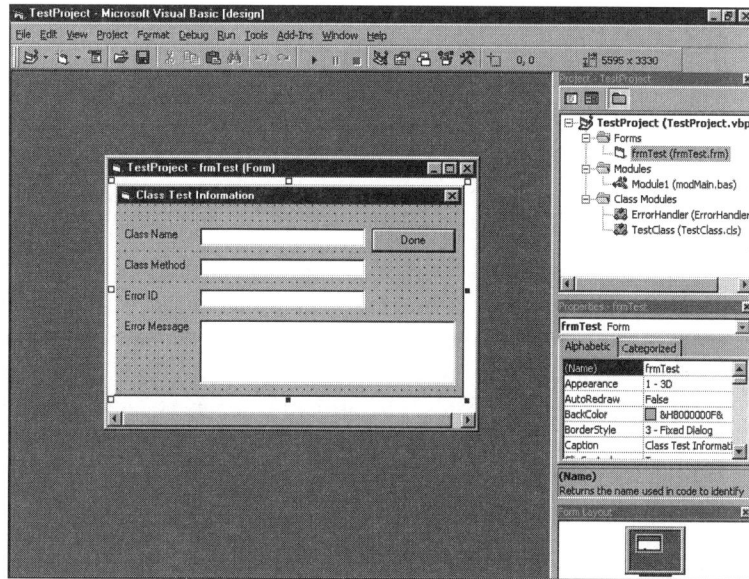

Saving and Displaying Test Logs

Using either a file or database, you would capture each of the text box values using the label captions as fields (or columns). The frmTest form is used for displaying class errors. Use your favorite persistence code (database or file) for storing errors. You can use a Rich Text Box to which to assign the values of each text box and save the file using the Rich Text Box's SaveFile method, as follows:

```
frmTest!SomeRichTextBox.Text = "Class Name: " & _
    txtTest(0).Text & ";Class Method: " & txtTest(1).Text . . .
frmTest!SomeRichTextBox.SaveFile App.Path & "\" & _ SomeFilename, rtfText
```

To use this approach, you'd have to have a Rich Text Box control on the frmTest form.

Using Source Code Control with Emphasis on SourceSafe

If you've developed software for any length of time, you have come to realize the absolute importance of version control software. One of the important benefits of version control software is that it helps you organize and track the latest version of your software, as well as its revision history. For a team of two or more developers, version control software serves as a shared repository of subsystem classes and components that can be checked out and checked in by one person at a time.

A small development team may have a version control server for several clients. Keep in mind that not all projects should use only one version control server. Larger, more complex projects may require multiple version control servers, one server per subsystem. Why such a configuration? Because development projects that design and implement applications with more than one major subsystem or component require a parallel development effort. Parallel development gives developers the flexibility of having an individual, encapsulated workspace in which to develop the subsystem.

No two subsystems or components will be developed equally by their respective owners. Some subsystems will be more complex than others, or one owner may be a bit slower than another. It would be a mistake to force the faster subsystem team to wait for the other. With a version control strategy that supports parallel development, teams that depend on another team's subsystem or component can work with a mocked-up facade until the first stable version of the team's deliverable is made available. These dependent teams can then incorporate subsequent updates as necessary and when available. All teams must offer up a stable first version of their subsystems or components that collectively would constitute the project's baseline.

NEW TERM   A reasonably stable version of the application in development upon which each subsystem or component development team can build is a *baseline*.

> **Tip**
>
> For more in-depth treatment of parallel development strategies, browse to an article by noted object technologist/OMT creator Jim Rumbaugh at `http://www.rational.com/support/techpapers/omt/joop9509.html`.

Microsoft's Visual SourceSafe, which ships with the Professional and Enterprise Editions of Visual Basic, is a version control software system that can support serial and parallel development strategies. Some Visual Basic projects you've been on probably only implemented a serial development strategy, where your deliverable was absolutely dependent on that of another team. Thus, you probably had only one SourceSafe server, with everyone having full access to everyone else's subprojects. Setting up a parallel development strategy requires a little more effort, but is not difficult. You'll explore that strategy in the next section.

Using Visual SourceSafe

If you have your Visual Basic CD-ROM and have not installed SourceSafe, do so now. Follow the instructions. Install both the administrative server and client units. Once you've completed the installation, log in to the server and set yourself up as a user using your name.

Now run the client. Create a new project by choosing File | Create Project from the menu. You should see the Create Project dialog box, as illustrated in Figure 8.4. Enter `Samsona Bank Teller System` and click OK. Click on the new SourceSafe project and create a subproject (using the same steps) called Second Bank of Carrollton. This hierarchy is important in environments where an application might be reused for more than one in-house client/user group or commercial mass-market customer.

8

FIGURE 8.4.

The Create Project dialog box.

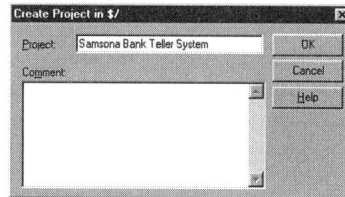

An object-oriented, iterative, and incremental development project requires a master SourceSafe project that is structured per increment, per iteration, with folders that reflect the various subsystems, components, use-case models, and documentation. For the Second Bank of Carrollton project folder, create subprojects named First Iteration, Second Iteration, Third Iteration, and Fourth Iteration. These correspond to the four use cases identified in Day 2: Open an Account, Close an Account, Deposit New Funds, and Withdraw Funds.

Label each iteration by the name of the use case as well. To label each Iteration subproject, select the iteration project folder and choose File | Label from the menu. Figure 8.5 shows the Label dialog box with an entry for Open an Account. Each iteration, when complete, becomes an executable release, whether implemented as a standard executable or ActiveX component.

FIGURE 8.5.

Creating a label for the First Iteration.

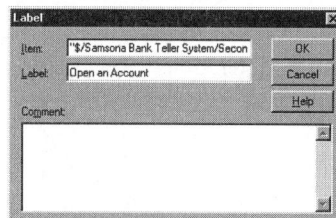

For each iteration, you need increments to help you move step by step to complete the iteration. Ideally, each increment is represented as a use-case scenario implemented in a sequence diagram. Thus, create an increment project per iteration, commenting each increment project according to the name of each sequence diagram in Table 2.2. Label each increment project as Increment1, Increment2, and so on. Figure 8.6 should help you get started. It shows the first increment in the First Iteration.

FIGURE **8.6.**

Increment1 of the First Iteration.

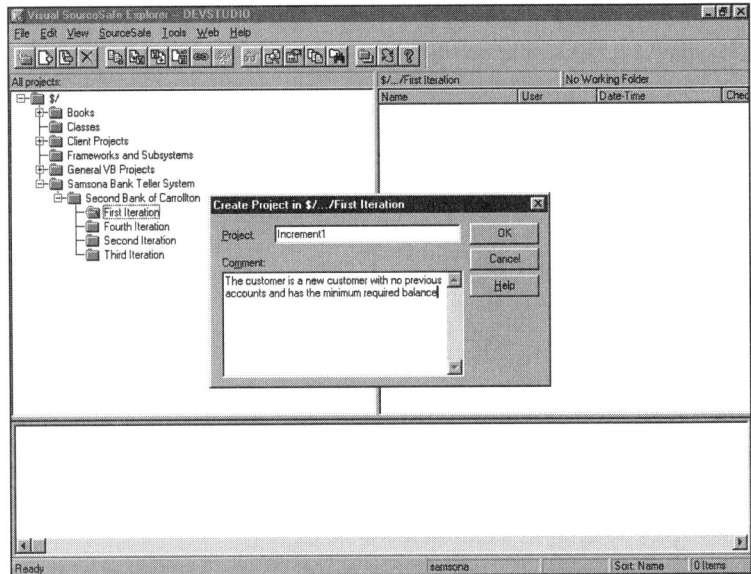

When your master SourceSafe project structure for the Samsona Bank Teller System is finished, it should resemble Figure 8.7 (except for the author's other projects). For each increment, you will probably have more than one subsystem and/or component to implement each increment (sequence diagram). In upcoming lessons, you will not only learn about designing and coding subsystems, but you will place them in SourceSafe and set rights to them so that only the owners of those subsystems or components have access to them while under development. After each increment is complete, you then make the subsystems and components in them available for others. Evolving subsystems and components may span several increments and iterations.

FIGURE 8.7.

The master SourceSafe project structure for the Samsona Bank Teller System.

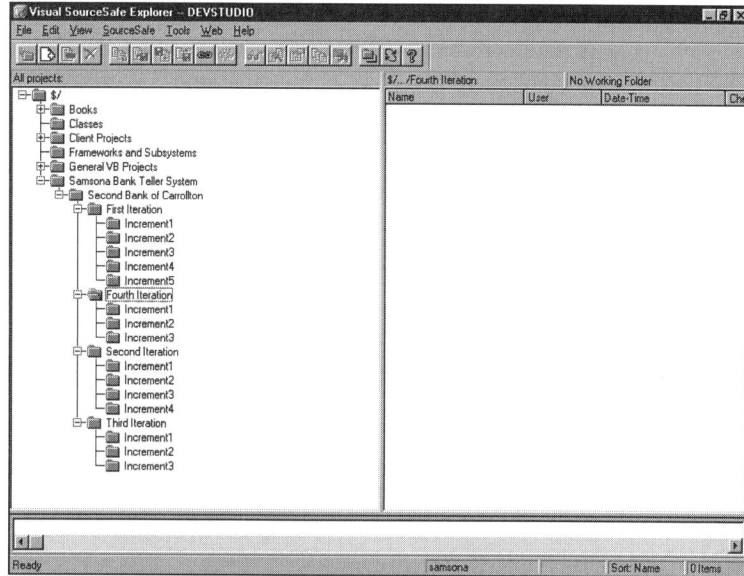

In order to encourage parallel development, you can set permissions per folder in the SourceSafe Administrative server. Run the SourceSafe Admin system. Choose Tools | Rights by Projects from the menu. Figure 8.8 shows what the Project Rights dialog box looks like. You should notice that your name is the only user other than Guest per project. You can assign Read, Change, Add, and Delete/Destroy access to each project. However, non-owners should not have any of these rights; when your deliverables are available, non-owners can have Read access rights only. Non-owners need not have Add, Change, or Delete access.

FIGURE 8.8.

Use this dialog box to facilitate parallel iterative development.

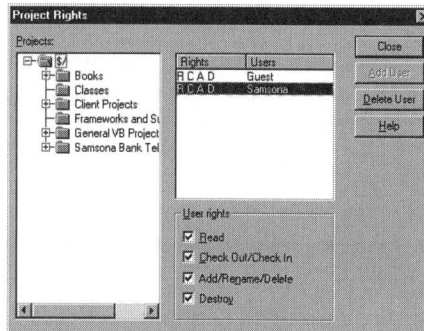

Finally, you can cloak projects to aid in parallel development. To *cloak* a project means that you're not interested in a particular project. Thus, cloaking such a project means that its files are not copied to your local file structure. For instance, if you check out or get a copy of the master project and its subprojects, each subproject that is cloaked will not be copied to your hard disk. This is especially helpful for cloaking projects you don't own as a developer; you don't know what state a foreign subproject is in, so there's no need to access the files in it.

To cloak a project, first create a subproject called Subsystem1 under the Increment1 subproject of the First Iteration project. Select the Subsystem1 subproject by clicking on it. Choose File | Properties from the menu. Click the This Project Is Cloaked for Me check box to cloak a project you don't own (see Figure 8.9). Click the Close button. Notice that the Subsystem1 project folder icon is now dimmed.

FIGURE 8.9.

Click the This Project Is Cloaked for Me check box to cloak a project you don't own.

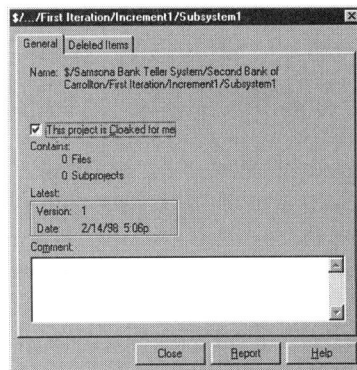

Local Directory Structuring

Every project you create in SourceSafe, or at least every project that you own as a developer on a team, will need a corresponding working directory on your hard disk. In general, you can create any local working folder on your hard disk as you deem necessary. However, a good rule of thumb is to name your local folder with the same name as the corresponding project folder in SourceSafe.

Nonetheless, you don't have to have the exact same hierarchy unless you have a SourceSafe server dedicated to your individual subsystem or component projects. You only need to create corresponding local folders for each SourceSafe project folder you own. For instance, because you cloaked the Subsystem1 folder earlier, you would not need to create a local folder named Subsystem1.

8

To set a local working directory on your hard disk, click on each SourceSafe project folder you own, and choose File | Set Working Folder from the SourceSafe menu. Figure 8.10 shows the Set Working Folder dialog box you should now see. Enter the name of the folder using the SourceSafe project folder name. If it doesn't exist, click the Create Folder button. If you need to create a folder on a remote machine, click the Network button to map a network drive.

FIGURE 8.10.

The Set Working Folder dialog box.

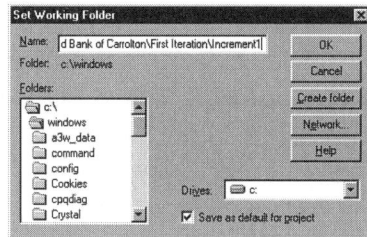

Summary

In this chapter, you learned the basics of building objects that test the preconditions and postconditions for which they are responsible. Also presented in this lesson were the fundamentals of creating debugging code for your classes, as well as version control tips for components and subsystems of classes using Visual SourceSafe. Tomorrow, you'll learn fundamental concepts that help you effectively break down an application into smaller parts called subsystems.

Q&A

Q What is involved in self-testing objects?

A Self-testing involves creating tests during the design phase that you then build into classes.

Q At a minimum, what artifacts will testers need to test?

A Testers will need to test the application you develop, the user documentation, and the design model logic as well.

Q What kind of testing is necessary for distributed systems?

A Distributed systems require integration testing.

Q What is good practice with regard to using arguments in an argument locally?

A It's good practice to use a local variable instead of the actual argument for internal method implementation code.

Q What is business rule logic?

A Business rule logic encompasses any preconditions and postconditions that are specific to a given business.

Workshop

The workshop includes quiz questions to help gauge your grasp of the material. You'll find the answers to this quiz in Appendix A, "Answers." Even if you feel that you totally understand the concepts presented here, you should work through the quiz anyway. The last section includes exercises for you to work through to help reinforce your learning.

Quiz

1. What testing activities should you, as an object-oriented Visual Basic developer, know?

2. What's the importance of code inspections?

3. What two method responsibilities are examples, respectively, of precondition and postcondition processing?

4. When is it necessary to check the data type of an argument?

5. Why is the development of business applications complex?

6. What features in Microsoft Visual SourceSafe support parallel iterative development?

Exercises

1. In SourceSafe, create a project under the Samsona Bank Teller System project for the following:

   Bank Transaction Policy

   Bank Personnel Policy

   Bank Regulation Policy

2. Review the following code from the `TestClass` class:

```
Public Sub testMethod(ByVal argString As String)
    MsgBox argString
End Sub
```

   Modify the `testMethod` code so that the method does not accept `argString` parameters whose first character is alphabetic.

3. Using the `testMethod` code in exercise 2, convert the method into a function that returns a boolean value of True upon successfully fulfilling its responsibility.

4. Using the results of exercise 3, create a client class that invokes the `testMethod` method. Check the type of the return in the client method.

5. Review the following inline error handling code from the `testReturns` method of the `TestClass` class:

```
errtestReturns:
    Dim sMethodName As String
    sMethodName = "testReturns"
    theErrorHandler.processVBTypeError Err, Me, sMethodName
    sMethodName = ""
```

Create a class called `ErrorHandler` that implements the indicated behavior and stores the error information. (Hint: The `processVBTypeError` method should process the `Err` object by its property values, capture the type name of the class indicated by the `Me` keyword, and capture the name of the method, displaying this information in a form and saving it to a file.)

DAY 9

Breaking Up an Application into Subsystems

In earlier lessons, you learned how to create classes and make those classes come alive at runtime in your applications. You also were exposed to the idea of subsystems and tightly encapsulated subsystems known as components. On Day 3, "Fundamental Object-Oriented Design," you learned about the design of subsystems. Day 6, "Building and Testing Components," introduced you to the implementation of a subsystem into an ActiveX component. Today, you will delve deeply into the process of breaking up a proposed application into subsystems, including components. The topics discussed include

- Looking at the subsystem-based model of application development, including the object structure of a complete subsystem, the object interaction structure of a subsystem, and encapsulation for subsystems
- Identifying and using design patterns for subsystems and their interactions

- Defining and naming the design pattern
- Describing how to apply the design pattern
- Describing the solution provided by the design pattern
- Listing the consequences of using the design pattern
- Using and reusing design patterns for subsystems, including analyzing and designing subsystem interfaces
- Brief case studies of real-world behaviors of applications

Examples from the Samsona Bank Teller System are included to round out your learning experience.

The Subsystem-Based Model of Application Development

The easiest and fastest way to develop any application is to enter many lines of code in any form or module without regard to tiers, subsystems, or components. Although this approach provides timeliness, it typically doesn't provide quality, maintainability, or reusability. Over the past fifty years of software development, the industry has learned that modularity, encapsulation, abstraction, and reusability are some of the most important attributes of effective, high-quality, low-cost (in the long term) software. Grouping objects into subsystems and components goes a long way toward achieving such goals and is part of the underlying concepts in the latest version of Visual Basic.

You can view a subsystem as a partition of the application. The current Business Extension to the Unified Modeling Language (UML) equates a subsystem to an *object system*. This partition can be loosely interpreted as tiers, although not all subsystems fit nicely into the typical three-tier model.

The Object Structure of a Complete Subsystem

By now, you have an idea that a subsystem is a subset of the objects in an application that perform some behavior, but what exactly does that mean? What are the requirements of such a subsystem or component? In other words, how do you determine and design the interactions among the objects in a subsystem to provide a given set of behaviors that clients of that subsystem expect?

NEW TERM   According to the Business Extension of the UML, an *object system* is a top-level subsystem in an object model. An object system contains organization units, classes (workers, work units, and entities), and relationships.

A subsystem-based application model, whether based on Microsoft's three-tiered Service model or a more specialized type of model, should reflect the concept that each subsystem must

- Have well-defined interface classes acting as ambassadors, facades, or mediators
- Encapsulate any platform-specific or legacy-specific dependencies from its core services
- Ensure type-safety either in the form of self-testing objects or delegating type-checking to the Visual Basic compiler
- Permit the easy addition and deletion of classes at design time and objects at run-time without endangering its own object interaction structure
- Have an interface that is easy to review by developer-users to plan for use
- Be efficient in terms of memory and other resources

All of these factors encourage reuse of subsystems and components. Ideally, you should be able to use and reuse a subsystem as is, without being unreasonably burdened with services not being properly fulfilled by it.

Note It's not always easy to create a perfect subsystem during the first Visual Basic project, so there's no need to worry about perfection too early.

Moreover, you could ideally have a subsystem made up entirely of interface classes so that that subsystem serves as a type template for more concrete subsystems that implement this abstract subsystem. This means that every interface class in the subsystem would need to be public. Exercise 1 in the Workshop at the end of this lesson walks you through the detailed steps for creating and implementing an abstract subsystem in the form of an ActiveX component.

To create an abstract component, follow these general steps:

1. Open a new Visual Basic ActiveX DLL or EXE project.
2. Create one or more classes, each with public methods and/or properties but no code. Typically, these interface classes should meaningfully represent the goal and nature of the component, such as Bank Transaction Policy Enforcement.
3. Choose Project Properties from the menu and give the project a name that reflects the component's goal. You might use the term *Abstract* in both the project name and description.
4. Save the project with a filename prefixed with the word *Abstract*.

5. Using the guidelines from Day 6, proceed to create your ActiveX component by choosing File | Make from the menu.

To create a concrete component that implements the interface classes in your abstract component, follow these steps:

1. Open a new ActiveX project.

2. Choose Project References from the menu to add the abstract component you created to your new project.

3. Add one or more classes to your project. If you design one class to implement every interface in the abstract component, you only need to add one class.

4. In the General Declarations section of each class you just added, enter `Implements <abstract component>.<name of abstract interface>`, where `<abstract component>` is the abstract component you created earlier, and `<name of abstract interface>` is the name of the interface class in your abstract component you wish to implement. If your class will implement more than one interface, then you will need to repeat this step for each one.

5. Implement each interface method for each interface object in each class's object list. That is, add some code to each interface method. Debug your code thoroughly.

6. In the `NewBasicPersonalChecking` class's object list, look for the `AbstractCheckingProduct` interface object. If you're able to see it, then you've successfully created an abstract component. Move the code from the class methods to the interface methods of the `AbstractCheckingProduct` interface object.

7. Using the guidelines from Day 6, proceed to create your ActiveX component by choosing File | Make from the menu.

To create subsystems in a quality fashion, it is also important to control the versions of subsystems. As mentioned on Day 8, "Versioning and Debugging," a good way to manage the versions of a subsystem in SourceSafe for relatively large projects is to allocate an independent source project to it, inaccessible to external, nonowner users.

The Object Interaction Structure of a Subsystem

The meaningful substance of subsystems is represented by the interactions between objects contained within them. The object interactions are realized based on the kinds of objects in the subsystems. Based on the Objectory Process Extension of the UML, such object kinds for a subsystem might include

- Entity
- Control
- Boundary

An *entity* class is one that is passive with respect to interactions with clients of the subsystem. An entity class instance, then, doesn't originate these interactions on its own. It receives transactions, typically from a controller class; applies business or domain rules; and then requests that the resulting information be persisted. Because of the importance of entity objects to a company or project, they participate in more than one operation. For business applications, an entity class can be equivalent to a business domain class.

A *control* class controls interactions between objects in the subsystem. Typically, a control class implements behavior that is specific to one subsystem operation (equivalent to a use case). An object of this kind lives only as long as the service request's life cycle. The life cycle of a control object typically doesn't extend beyond that of the fulfillment of a given subsystem operation in which it participates. Control classes, also called controller classes, are very helpful for controlling flows of information between forms and business classes. You use them anywhere you deem necessary, especially when internal application transactions are complex enough to warrant having a class responsible for controlling them.

NEW TERM A *subsystem operation* is similar to a use case, except that the client of the subsystem is another subsystem, component, or class within the application. ActiveX EXE components are treated like external system actors, meaning that operations on them are actually use cases.

A *boundary* class is one that lies on the periphery of a subsystem, but is contained within that subsystem. The responsibility of a boundary class is to interact with clients or external system actors outside the subsystem and all the kinds of objects within the subsystem. The relationship between a boundary class and its subsystem is similar to the relationship between a user interface and an application. In fact, a user interface realized as a form is a boundary object itself. Other examples of boundary classes include classes that interact with application programmer interfaces (APIs); external database object mechanisms such as RDO and ADO; and classes that communicate with peripheral devices such as printers, modems, storage devices, scanners, and so on. They are called boundary, then, because logically they act as the gatekeepers between the application and the outside environment.

NEW TERM An *entity class* is passive with respect to interactions with clients of the subsystem. A *control class* controls the interactions between objects in the subsystem. A *boundary class* lies on the periphery of a subsystem, but is contained within that subsystem.

Encapsulation for Subsystems

Rules for encapsulation that apply to classes also apply to subsystems in the large. Subsystem encapsulation is protected by one or more boundary classes, whose responsibility it is collectively to fulfill the contract of the subsystem to its clients.

On Day 6, you simplified the ActiveX component so that the `BasicPersonalChecking` class performed the role of the boundary and entity class. (No control class was needed because the gap between the subsystem boundary and the entity objects was nonexistent.) As a boundary class, the `BasicPersonalChecking` class interacted with its client (`FormController`). As an entity class, it also supplied a service based upon the client's request for operation. For my simple example, this was acceptable, but for more complex projects, it usually is necessary to keep entity classes pure of subsystem implementation details that are better handled by boundary and control classes.

Identifying and Using Design Patterns

One of the most useful attributes of well-defined subsystems and components is that they can be reused. Subsystems can themselves implement one or more design patterns, with the usual case being one or two patterns. To identify and implement design patterns for subsystems and components, you use the same rules as for applications.

Defining the Design Pattern

Defining a design pattern includes determining the problem to be solved by the pattern and the subsystem service it will help fulfill. (Recall the factory example of Day 3.) A bank teller application would have a partition dedicated to providing access to specific bank products, so the `AccountCreator` class and each of the bank product classes constitute an application subsystem. You could have created an ActiveX component from the `AccountCreator` Factory pattern implemented in this project.

Naming the Design Pattern

The rules for naming a design pattern are the same as for an application. Of course, the name should be relevant to the subsystem or component in which it is to be implemented. A design pattern seeks to solve a design problem that the subsystem needs solved. Simple, clear design pattern names help to increase the vocabulary of the developers on your project and in your enterprise; they also help you avoid duplication of code across several subsystems and components you own.

Reuse of subsystems starts with your not duplicating a design solution and often leads to encapsulation of a subsystem into a component. Help others use your pattern by describing the scenarios for which the pattern applies. When possible, detail the participating objects and their interactions. Most importantly, explain what motivated you to come up with the pattern in the first place.

Applying the Design Pattern

For any subsystem, you should only apply design patterns when you've discovered a recurring problem that needs a reusable solution. The design pattern itself should be abstract so that you can implement it easily in more than one subsystem or component, which might experience the same problem in different ways. For instance, revisiting the factory example from Day 3, the AccountCreator factory class, when abstracted, can be used for different families of bank products, including checking accounts, savings accounts, capital investment accounts, personal loan accounts, commercial loan products, and so on.

Describing the Solution

A good design pattern should be described in basic terms so that there's a general reference to a family of related problems. In a subsystem, there's a way that the objects work together to solve a problem through fulfilling a service based upon an operation the subsystem implements for a client. On Day 3, you called the Factory design pattern's class AccountCreator. This name leaves room to solve the problem of creating accounts for the various families of bank products. Thus, you should view a design pattern as a template that describes a problem, provides a solution, and lists the consequences that result from implementing the solution both at a business level and at a technical (for example, memory requirements) level.

Listing the Consequences

As mentioned in the preceding section, providing a design solution to a problem leads to certain consequences. At a business level, the consequence is that some valuable service is fulfilled effectively, such as the creation of a bank product or the implementation of a telecommunications switch. At a technical level, the implementation of a design pattern can lead to increased resource consumption. However, the trade-off here is that you get better organized code that is easily reusable and can be evolved over time as the customer's needs change.

How to Use and Reuse Design Patterns for Subsystems

The chief benefit of using design patterns is to reduce all implementation dependencies between subsystems and components. Subsystem interface classes provide this independence. Again, the `AccountCreator` class on Day 3 provided reasonable independence between the user-interface subsystem and the bank account product subsystem. The key concept here is to avoid making client classes and subsystems that invoke operations on implementation classes. Instead, try to use the services of interface classes.

Analyzing and Designing Subsystem Interfaces

Analysis for interface classes involves elaborating a business abstraction or concept often. This usually means analyzing use cases for key concepts, but also includes (but is not limited to) assessing the following:

- Application performance requirements
- Interactions with external and remote applications, servers, and components
- User-interface requirements
- Real-time, embedded system requirements (as you can now use Visual Basic to create Windows CE applications)

> **Note**
>
> The expression *key concept* should be understood to represent those business processes or entities that seem important to the user. A key concept is often repeated by the user during the interview. If you miss a key concept early in the process of creating the use cases, you'll definitely hear about it from the user during user acceptance testing.

You should design a subsystem interface in the form of interface classes. For instance, if you have to design an application to, among other things, communicate with a SQL Server relational database, you might design a class called `IDatabase` whose responsibility it is to allow flexible communications with it using remote data objects (RDOs), active data objects (ADOs/OleDB), data access objects (DAOs), or open database connectivity (ODBC) (Direct or API). Database subsystems are covered on Day 19, "The Database Access Subsystem."

In general, `IDatabase` may have an important public method that looks like this:

```
Public Function openConnection(argConnectionString As _ String) As Boolean

End Function
```

If you are using DAO, an implementation class, `DaoDatabase`, might look like this:

```
'General Declarations
Implements IDatabase

Public Function IDatabase_openConnection(argConnectionString As _ String)
As Boolean

    Dim returns

    . . .

    returns = _

    SomeDAOVariable.OpenConnection(argConnectionString)

End Function
```

Real-World Case Studies

If you've developed applications for any length of time, whether commercially or onsite at a company, you probably have come across problems you've solved before—problems that encompass entire applications or individual subsystems and components. By far one of the most popular kinds of applications developed in the world today is the order entry system.

When a bank customer opens an account, she is essentially ordering a bank product. The order entry specialist is the bank teller. The bank may have corporate operations that handle behind-the-scenes details for fulfilling the bank product order such as FDIC compliance, verification of the customer's checking and credit histories, placing requests for new checks and checkbooks, cross-marketing for other bank products the customer might be interested in given her income and assets, and so on.

In the telecommunications industry, a major service provider and owner of network elements and services typically orders switches, terminals, tandem nodes, end office nodes, and subscriptions to external networks. To fulfill a telecommunication order, one or more back office workgroups are tasked with work requests to configure signaling, routing, and trunking information to prepare a place in the network for the new network element or service.

In software sales, the customer would order software either in a store or online via the Web. For non-online orders, the software retailer or manufacturer would then process the order, sending work requests to shrink-wrap operations, billing, and for large orders, quality assurance specialists and attorneys. After the bundling, billing, legal, and quality checks are complete, the shipping team ships the product. In the case of an online order, the Web site server combines all of these tasks unto itself, requesting demographic and legal/licensing information from the customer.

An order entry system typically exhibits behaviors related to the following:

- Capturing an order for some product or service
- Enforcing rules related to the product or service being ordered
- Submitting subsequent auxiliary order fulfillment requests to back office workers/workgroups

Advanced order processing systems would incorporate a subsystem for tracking order fulfillment progress for each worker/workgroup. Because the work of each worker will not be done at the same speed, tracking becomes quite complex in terms of the overall fulfillment of the order. That is, each work request associated with a given order is like a fulfillment thread. If the customer cancels the order, all fulfillment threads must be closed. In this case, some threads may be complete, which means that whatever work was done will need to be rolled back. Finally, order processing is not complete until the last work request is fulfilled.

Generally speaking, you can break up an order entry and processing application into the following subsystems:

```
OrderEntryCapture
ProductRuleEnforcement
WorkRequestSubmission
WorkRequestTracking
```

Figure 9.1 shows a Visual Modeler class diagram of the control classes of these subsystems. Figure 9.2 shows the component view of these subsystems. (The component view is helpful when you plan to implement your subsystems as components.) The dashed arrow between the components symbolizes the dependency relationship. It is a semantically weak notation that lets you know that the component on the originating side of the arrow needs some operation to be performed by the receiver-side component. The OrderEntryCapture component is dependent on WorkRequestSubmission to approve the order and submit it to the workers/workgroups through the WorkRequestTracking component. For the approval operation, WorkRequestSubmission is dependent on ProductRuleEnforcement.

FIGURE 9.1.

Subsystem control classes for an order processing application.

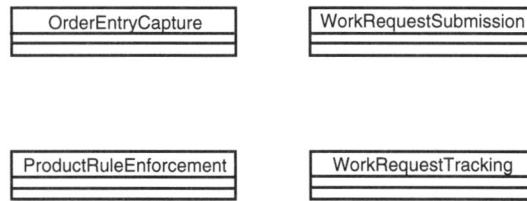

FIGURE 9.2.

Subsystems implemented as components.

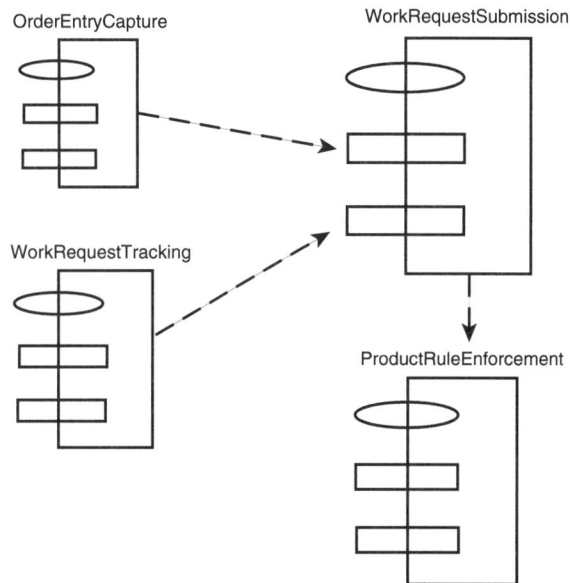

Candidate Subsystems for the Samsona Bank Teller System Example

REAL WORLD

Your client, the Second Bank of Carrollton, is quite pleased with the progress you're making with the bank teller system. You've shown her and her staff prototypes at the expected milestone dates, even though the code behind the scenes was ugly in many places. You and your staff developers told yourselves that you'd organize the code later when the design models stabilize.

Well, that time has come. Adding code increment by increment to the application has become more and more complex and disorganized. At the same time, your team of designers has elaborated the interaction and class diagrams to a point that accurate low-level details are stable enough to be implemented in Visual Basic code. As the chief architect, you also realize that some of the modifications in the application's architectural

▼ design will require modification to the content of the use cases and user guides. The use-case modification is necessitated by new discoveries about gaps in business process steps. (The use-case modifications are discussed on Day 10, "Refining Use Cases as Application and Subsystem Architecture Blueprints." What's important here is that you want to capture the new subsystem structures of the application.)

After conducting an architectural assessment with your designers, you and your staff have realized the subsystems described in Table 9.1.

TABLE 9.1. THE SUBSYSTEMS OF THE SAMSONA BANK TELLER SYSTEM.

Subsystem	Responsibility
BankTransactionPolicy	Enforces bank rules governing account deposits by check and cash, openings and closures, balance inquiries
CustomerService	Enforces bank and government policy regarding dispute resolution and product inquiries
BankPersonnelPolicy	Enforces the various levels of access each teller has to certain application features
GraphicalUserInterface	Contains the forms and control objects
WorkgroupAndSecurity	Contains objects that represent workgroups and users; also contains login procedure
InternalApplicationManager	Initializes and terminates global classes and logs application activities
ReportingAndPrinting	Builds reports and prints them on the default printer
FileOperations	Opens and closes files using regular file commands and the Rich Text Box
ErrorProcessing	Processes errors and exceptions raised in code
Persistence	Opens and closes database access connections, recordsets, and SQL string builds for relational databases

The BankTransactionPolicy, CustomerService, and BankPersonnelPolicy subsystems are collectively the business rule subsystem of the Samsona Bank Teller System. This implies that a subsystem itself can be made up of subsystems and components. Based on your assessment, you decide to implement these subsystems as ActiveX EXE components. Figure 9.3 shows the class diagram of these subsystems. Figure 9.4 shows the
▼ component diagram for the three business policy components.

FIGURE 9.3.

Subsystems for Samsona Bank Teller System.

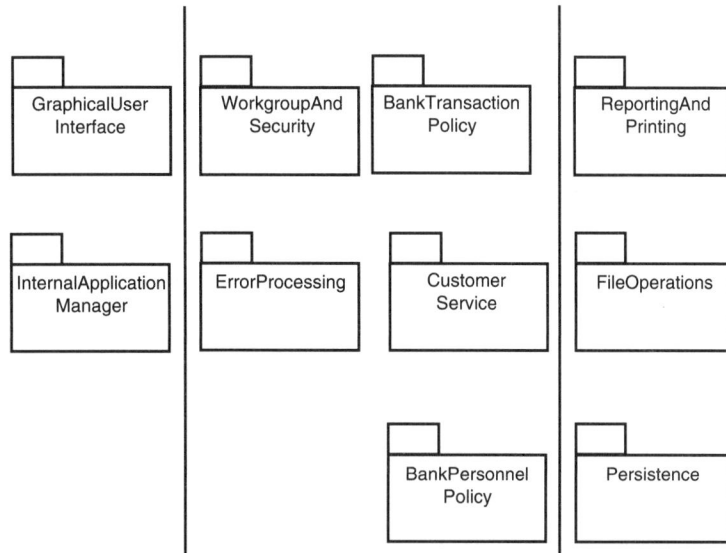

9

FIGURE 9.4.

Components for Samsona Bank Teller System.

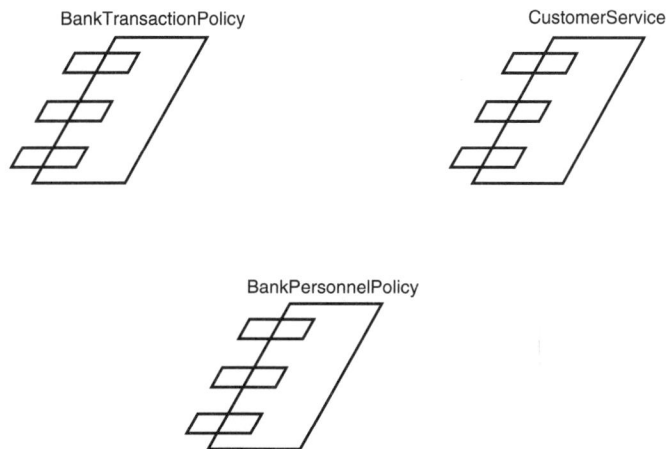

Summary

This lesson presents the concept of organizing an application into subsystems and components. You looked at the subsystem-based model of application development, including the object structure of a complete subsystem, the object interaction structure of a subsystem, and encapsulation for your subsystems. You also identified and used design patterns for subsystems and their interactions. You learned about naming a design pattern, describing how to apply the design pattern, and detailing the solution provided by the design pattern. You learned how to use and reuse design patterns for subsystems, including analyzing and designing subsystem interfaces. A brief set of case studies of real-world behaviors of applications are followed by examples from the Samsona Bank Teller System. Tomorrow's lesson teaches you how to refine your use cases so that they are in better shape for subsequent design and programming tasks.

Q&A

Q What's a problem with quickly coding an application without organization?

A Such a development process usually neglects quality, maintainability, and reusability.

Q What are some important attributes of effective, low-cost software?

A Modularity, encapsulation, abstraction, and reusability.

Q What's a synonym for the UML Business Extension expression *object system*?

A Subsystem.

Q What questions should you ask in designing a good object structure of a subsystem?

A What are the requirements of such a subsystem or component? In other words, how can you determine and design the interactions among the objects in a subsystem to provide a given set of behaviors that clients of that subsystem expect?

Q What is the meaningful substance of subsystems?

A The meaningful substance of subsystems is represented by the interactions between objects contained within them.

Q What are the three kinds of classes in the Object Process Extension to the UML?

A Entity, control, and boundary.

Q What is the responsibility of boundary classes with respect to subsystems?

A They have the responsibility of collectively fulfilling the contract of the subsystem to its clients.

Q What is the responsibility of control classes in subsystems?

A They fill the gap between the subsystem boundary and the entity objects.

Q What's the goal of a design pattern?

A A design pattern seeks to solve a design problem that the subsystem needs solved. It also helps you to avoid duplication of code across several subsystems and components you own.

Q How can you help other developers use your design patterns in their subsystems?

A By describing the scenarios for which the pattern applies. When possible, detail the participating objects and their interactions. Most importantly, explain what motivated you to come up with the pattern in the first place. The design pattern itself should be abstract so that you can implement it easily in more than one subsystem or component that experiences the same problem in different ways.

Q What is a negative consequence of using a design pattern?

A At a technical level, the implementation of a design pattern can lead to increased resource consumption. However, the trade-off here is that you get better organized code that is easily reusable and can be evolved over time as the customer's needs change.

Workshop

The workshop includes quiz questions to help gauge your grasp of the material. You'll find the answers to this quiz in Appendix A, "Answers." Even if you feel that you totally understand the concepts presented here, you should work through the quiz anyway. The last section contains exercises for you to work through to help reinforce your learning.

Quiz

1. What fundamental concepts should a subsystem-based application model reflect?
2. What is a helpful prefix you should use for the name of an abstract component?
3. How can you decrease the dependency between two subsystems?
4. What is involved in analyzing and designing a subsystem interface?
5. What is one of the most popular kinds of applications? What typical behaviors does it exhibit?

Exercises

1. Using the ActiveX component built on Day 6, "Building and Testing Components," create an abstract component that has a class, `AbstractCheckingProduct`, with the same methods and properties as the `BasicPersonalChecking` class. Hint: Follow these steps:

    1. Open a new Visual Basic ActiveX DLL project. Create a class called `NewBasicPersonalChecking`.

2. Add the `BasicPersonalChecking` class to your project. Choose File | Save As from the menu to rename the actual filename of the class to `AbstractCheckingProduct`.

3. Cut and paste the code of each `AbstractCheckingProduct` method into the interface methods in the `NewBasicPersonalChecking` class.

4. Save the project as `AbstractInterface`. Remove the `NewBasicPersonalChecking` class from the project so that you can use it later in a separate sample project.

5. Using the guidelines from Day 6, create the `AbstractInterface` DLL.

6. Open a new Standard EXE project.

7. Add the `NewBasicPersonalChecking` class to the new project.

8. Choose Project References from the menu to add the `AbstractInterface.DLL` file to your project.

9. In the `NewBasicPersonalChecking` class's General Declarations section, enter `Implements AbstractInterface.AbstractCheckingProduct`.

10. In the `NewBasicPersonalChecking` class's object list, look for the `AbstractCheckingProduct` interface object. If you're able to see it, then you've successfully created an abstract component. Move the code from the class methods to the interface methods of the `AbstractCheckingProduct` interface object.

2. Using the list of subsystems for the Samsona Bank Teller System, create additional subsystems that you might find helpful for your own bank. Use Visual Modeler or a pencil and paper to create a class diagram and component diagram.

3. Create a simple order entry application in Visual Basic for a hypothetical video rental store using a subsystem named `OrderEntryCapture`. Add a form named `frmOrderEntry`. Add a class named `VideoRental`, which represents an order. Add a class called `FormController` to control the interactions between the form and the `VideoRental` order class. The use case for such an application is as follows:

A customer presents a video to the cashier along with a rental identification card. The cashier enters the customer's ID from the card, the name and ID of the video, and the amount of the video. (Assume that the customer is not a new customer.) The cashier submits the rental order for processing. The application verifies that the customer exists, that the customer has no delinquent rentals, and that the credit card associated with the ID on the rental card is current. If this information is acceptable, the order is approved and the customer is allowed to rent the video.

DAY **10**

Refining Use Cases as Application and Subsystem Architecture Blueprints

This chapter expands on what you learned on Day 2, "Fundamental Object-Oriented Analysis," about use cases and domain analysis, in general. In particular, you'll learn about revisiting use cases in your evironment, the problem statement, and the use-case model. This chapter also shows you how to refine user requirements into a better use-case model, as well as the art of working with end users, business analysts, executives, and project managers. You'll also learn how to incorporate new discoveries in the way the end user uses your Visual Basic application in the design models. Other topics covered include

- Preserving the artifacts of use-case analysis and development, in general
- Assessing terminology and traceability, including domain-specific terminology for the Samsona Bank Teller example and related traceability issues involved in refining use cases

Revisiting Use Cases in Your Environment

For many newcomers to object-oriented programming, the cyclical and sometimes chaotic nature of object technology—and projects that implement such technology—can be frustrating. The expression *iterative incremental development* sounds appealing and has become a popular catch phrase in the software development industry. However, when you do iterative incremental development, the process is often frustrating and sometimes seemingly stuck in analysis paralysis or design demise. Some describe the iterative incremental development experience as resembling the movie *Groundhog Day* (the movie's star Bill Murray keeps waking up on the same day, having the same nightmarish experiences).

After you've practiced the iterative development approach often enough, it's really not that bad. In fact, iterative development isn't exclusively object-oriented; it's just that object technology has capitalized on the best practices of preceding development methods. The most experienced developers who don't use object technology have done some form of iterative development. What we've learned in the last half century of software development is that new discoveries about the problems we are trying to solve will occur throughout the entire life cycle of a project. If the discovery is important enough, you must resolve it with analysis and design activities before implementing the new requirement. Therefore, revisiting use cases should become natural to you as you develop your Visual Basic applications.

Project managers who are more comfortable with other methodologies shun any notions of making and resolving key discoveries too often. In such cases, you should seek an approach that comes across as controlled, in which discoveries are resolved according to a prioritization plan. A project that looks chaotic (which is characteristic of any software development project) will typically involve managers in technical minutiae more than is necessary and healthy. Before revisiting any use case, then, you should have some kind of iteration plan in place.

NEW TERM   An *iteration plan* captures the project activities you and your team members must perform, as well as delivery of the artifacts that result from these activities.

Although you can certainly create an iteration plan at any time during your project, you should definitely have one a few weeks before you begin actual code construction. This is because an iteration plan can be pegged with scheduled dates for deliverables from analysts, designers, programmers, and testers. However, these dates, as well as the iterations in the iteration plan, aren't going to be reasonably well-known until you're in the middle of designing the low-level details of the solution your application represents. Therefore, attempting to force an iteration plan to be static before any detail design activities are in place produces a plan full of guesswork. Such a plan shouldn't be completely relied on as a static representation of what's going to happen in a project and when deliverables will be made.

Efforts to prematurely create a static iteration plan often (but not necessarily) result in frustration and low morale. Nonetheless, you can still have a partial iteration plan in place to cover your analysis and design activities. Just keep in mind that it will be extremely dynamic; its volatility will be based on the numerous discoveries you're bound to make that will change its structure.

Depending on the object-oriented development process you choose, your iteration plan can be structured in one of two ways: one or more increments per iteration or one or more iterations per increment. If you choose the Objectory Process (the official Unified Modeling Language [UML] process), analysis, design, and construction can be decomposed into iterations, with one or more increments per iteration.

NEW TERM The UML defines an *iteration* as a complete development loop resulting in a release (internal or external) of an executable product, a subset of the final product under development, which grows incrementally from iteration to iteration to become the final system.

During each iteration, don't be surprised if you go through analysis, design, construction, testing, and deployment. An iteration can lead to an executable release of your application to one or more groups or market segments of users. Some of these phases, or process components, will require different levels of treatment, depending on monetary and political factors.

REAL WORLD An iteration plan can be used as the basis for your package structure in Visual Modeler, Rational Rose for Visual Basic, or your pencil-and-paper model. It can also be the basis for your SourceSafe project structure. The iteration plan for the Samsona Bank Teller System example, depicted in Table 10.1, resembles its SourceSafe project structure and can also be the basis for your package structure in Visual Modeler.

TABLE 10.1. A SAMPLE ITERATION PLAN FOR THE SAMSONA BANK TELLER SYSTEM. THE ASTERISK (*) REPRESENTS NEW DISCOVERIES THAT YOU AND YOUR CLIENT, THE SECOND BANK OF CARROLLTON, AGREE SHOULD BE IN THE REVISED USE-CASE MODEL.

Iteration	Increment
1. Open an Account	1.0. The customer is a new customer with no previous accounts and has the minimum required balance.
	2.0. The customer has an existing account that is active.
	3.0. The customer has an existing account that is inactive.

continues

▼ **TABLE 10.1.** CONTINUED

Iteration	Increment
	4.0. The customer is new but doesn't have the minimum required balance.
	5.0. The customer is a new customer with no previous accounts but wishes to deposit more than $10,000 in cash.
	*6.0. The customer is a new customer but has a negative checking account history.
2. Close an Account	1.0. An active account exists, and the customer is authorized to close it.
	2.0. The account being closed is inactive.
	3.0. The customer isn't authorized to close the account.
	4.0. The customer is authorized to close the account, but either the account is deficient or the customer owes money to the bank.
	*5.0. The account number entered by the bank teller is incorrect.
3. Deposit New Funds	1.0. An active account exists, and the customer is authorized to deposit money in it.
	2.0. The customer isn't authorized to deposit money in the account.
	3.0. The amount being deposited exceeds $10,000 in cash.
	*4.0. The deposit is in the form of a check.
	*5.0. The account has been frozen by the government.
4. Withdraw Funds	1.0. An active account exists, and the customer is authorized to withdraw money from it.
	2.0. The customer isn't authorized to withdraw money from the account.
	3.0. The teller tries, at the customer's request, to withdraw more money than is available.
	*4.0. The account has been frozen by the government.

The Problem Statement

Based on the your new discoveries, your client (the Second Bank of Carrollton) agrees to ▼ the updated problem statement in the subsequent paragraphs.

▼ The Second Bank of Carrollton needs a system that enables its bank tellers and authorized bank personnel to open an account (such as a checking or savings account), close an account, deposit funds into the account, and withdraw funds from the account. The account products currently available to customers are listed in Table 10.2.

TABLE 10.2. THE ACCOUNT PRODUCTS OFFERED BY THE SECOND BANK OF CARROLLTON.

Product	Product Code
Basic Personal Savings	01
Basic Personal Checking	02
Personal Savings Plus	11
Personal Checking Plus	12

10

A full description of the problem statement follows:

1. Open an Account

   A new or existing customer can open an account. If the customer is a new customer with no previous accounts and has the minimum required balance, he is free to apply for an account. The bank teller must be able to capture the customer's demographic information, such as full name, address, birth date, Social Security number, home and business phone numbers, amount of initial deposit, and desired bank product(s). When this information is captured, the bank teller submits it for electronic approval (business rule validation) by the application. During this process, the application connects to the checking account history system (CAHS) to obtain information relevant to the customer. The application also checks for existing accounts, type of transaction (cash or check) as entered by the bank teller, and type of new account. When approved, the application notifies the bank teller that the account is open (active).

   If, during the electronic approval process, the application finds that the customer has an existing, active account, the application notifies the bank teller, reminding her to notify the customer that the new account will be part of the family of accounts under the customer's Social Security number. The account is then opened.

   If the customer has an existing account that is inactive, the bank teller is notified. *The application cancels the transaction.*

   If the customer is new but doesn't have the minimum required balance as entered by the bank teller, the application notifies the bank teller, and the transaction is
▼ canceled.

▼   If the customer is a new customer with no previous accounts and wishes to deposit more than $10,000 in cash as entered by the bank teller, *the application notifies the bank teller that the amount exceeds the federally mandated limit regarding such cash transactions. The application then presents to the bank teller the required cash transaction form online, transferring the information from the application. When the bank teller completes reviewing the form, the bank teller indicates to the application that the form is correct. The form is printed out for the customer's signature*, and the account is opened.

If the customer is a new customer and has a negative checking account history, the application notifies the bank teller. The application cancels the transaction.

2. Close an Account

At customer request, the bank teller indicates to the application that she wants to close an account. The bank teller enters the account number of the account. The application prompts the teller to ask the customer for his driver's license and Social Security number to verify that the customer is authentic. After the bank teller indicates to the application that the customer is authentic, the application prints out the account number, customer information, and current balance. The balance is then zeroed out, the master bank transaction repository is updated, and the account closed.

If the account being closed is inactive, the application notifies the bank teller. The application cancels the transaction.

If the bank teller indicates to the application that the customer is not authorized to close the account, the application cancels the transaction.

If the customer is authorized to close the account, but the account is deficient, or the customer owes money to the bank, and the account being closed is the last or only one the customer had, the application notifies the bank teller. In the case when there's enough money in the account, the bank teller has the option of performing the use case Withdraw Funds on behalf of the bank in the amount of the debt owed.

If the account number entered by the bank teller is incorrect, the application informs the bank teller. The correctness of the account number is determined in one of two ways:

1. The account number entered by the bank teller is compared with all account numbers in the bank account repository.

2. The second, fourth, and ninth digits in the ten-digit account number must always add up to 24 (to reduce the risk of errors due to keying more than one key simultaneously or other typos).

▼

▼   3. Deposit New Funds

The bank teller indicates to the application that she wants to deposit funds to a certain account. *The application prompts the teller for the account number. When the teller provides the account number, the application verifies that the account is still active and prompts the teller to verify that the customer is authorized to deposit funds to the account. If so, the application displays details about the account, including the customer's full name, Social Security number, account status, and account balance. The teller then enters the amount of the deposit. The application persists the deposit transaction to the account repository.*

If the customer is not authorized to deposit money in the account, the application notifies the teller. *The application cancels the transaction.*

If the amount being deposited exceeds $10,000 in cash, *the application notifies the bank teller that the amount exceeds the federally mandated limit regarding such cash transactions. The application then presents to the bank teller the required cash transaction form online, transferring the information from the application. When the bank teller completes reviewing the form, the bank teller indicates to the application that the form is correct. The form is printed out for the customer's signature.*

If the deposit is in the form of a check, the teller notifies the application. The application validates the policy for the deposit and informs the teller to notify the customer that the funds won't be available for ten business days. After the teller enters the amount of the deposit, the application applies the deposit to the account in a temporary balance separate from the regular balance, until the funds' availability date has been reached. *The application persists the deposit transaction to the account repository.*

If the application discovers that the account has been frozen by the government, the application notifies the teller. The application cancels the transaction.

4. Withdraw Funds

The bank teller indicates to the application that she wants to withdraw funds from a certain account. *The application prompts the teller for the account number. When the teller provides the account number, the application verifies that the account is still active and prompts the teller to verify that the customer is authorized to deposit funds to the account. If so, the application displays details about the account, including the customer's full name, Social Security number, account status, and account balance. The teller then enters the amount of the withdrawal. The application persists the deposit transaction to the account repository.*

10

▼   If the customer is not authorized to withdraw money from the account, *the application notifies the teller. The application cancels the transaction.*

If the teller, at the customer's request, tries to withdraw more money than is available, the application notifies the teller. *The application cancels the transaction.*

If the application discovers that the account has been frozen by the government, the application notifies the teller. The application cancels the transaction.

Notice the italicized sentences. These sentences represent reusable behavior. Hooray! You're midway through the development process and already you've identified some
▲   reusable artifacts.

The Use-Case Model

The use-case model is the backbone of a project. All the artifacts in the object-oriented project are dependent on it in one way or another. Described another way, a use-case model is realized by the design model, meaning that solutions are represented in artifacts such as a class diagram, sequence diagram, collaboration diagram, state transition diagram, and activity diagram. The use-case model is eventually implemented in the implementation model, an example of which is your program code. Finally, the use-case model is verified against quality assurance constraints in the test model. The test model is represented by a master test plan, its test cases, and test scripts. You can even argue that a use-case model is important beyond the deployment of your application because it can be reused by business process designers and in other software development efforts.

Revisiting use cases helps to continually verify that the system is still on track to fulfill the requirements or user expectations of the Visual Basic application. This revisitation also helps to ensure that the use case model remains robust and easily extensible as discoveries are made about the problem and solution. Always keep in mind that the importance of updating the content of the use cases is that the use case model not only defines the application's behavior but also provides a basis for the development process of your project itself.

Although the use-case model must be understandable and acceptable to the users, it must also be a technically valid basis for the application in the eyes of the developers. Updating the use cases becomes important when gaps in business processes related to the application are discovered.

Refining User Requirements into a Better Use-Case Model

Requirements for the application you're going to develop will change. You can plan on it. New requirements that you discover can be incorporated into the existing iteration or scheduled into a future iteration, according to your business or safety priorities. In any case, always keep in mind that the organizations for which you're developing the application will change processes. Therefore, you must create dynamic models of existing processes, making sure your model remains flexible for change.

The purpose of your business process model can be to model either the existing processes or the desired business processes. Modeling existing processes is called *reverse engineering*. This is to be distinguished from reverse engineering code, however, although the patterns are similar. Modeling the desired process is called *forward engineering*.

10

NEW TERM   *Reverse engineering* is an activity that involves modeling the current business processes.

NEW TERM   *Forward engineering* is an activity that involves modeling the desired or proposed business processes.

Working with End Users

It's easy to take for granted the meaningfulness of modeling existing processes. Some developers have even been tempted to misinterpret as frivolous those users who customize their business processes in strange ways. However, the fact remains that business processes typically change. That is, they evolve as new business needs, dictated by market forces, are discovered. Unlike object-oriented projects, real-world business processes tend to come into existence in a chaotic, unplanned way. As a developer, you have to accept this as normal, no matter how crazy the processes seem. Creating and elaborating a reverse-engineered business process model requires the help of your users. After this model is in place and able to be extended as processes change, you are better equipped to understand the problem you're trying to solve with Visual Basic.

Working with Business Analysts

Sometimes, trying to understand the problem you're solving through business process models can be overwhelming if you're also tasked with developing the solution in a short amount of time. In these situations, it's best to seek the help of one or more business analysts or business process designers. Management needs to give these individuals a mandate to reverse engineer the current set of business processes in your users' domain. The business engineering process itself can often be time-consuming, and not every analyst will be knowledgeable about object-oriented business process modeling methods. You might need to assist them in understanding how to capture meaningful models of the business processes your application will affect. The important thing is that if you effectively involve your users in the development of the solution, they will appreciate it when you improve their otherwise tedious tasks.

Involving users in the refining of your use cases and sequence diagrams goes a long way toward filling in gaps in business activities you've modeled. Users can also help to validate your assumptions about how your Visual Basic application will solve their problems. At the end of each iteration, you should plan on user review and testing.

Working with Executives

Executives and upper-level managers are a skeptical bunch. Given the notoriety of many unsuccessful software development projects, this skepticism is probably justified. Typically, your executive sponsor will request from you, as the architect, or your project manager, periodic updates that answer the following questions:

- Given the current state and cost of the project, how long will the project take, and what's the estimated project cost? What's the opportunity cost of not continuing with this project?

- What meaningful objectives have the project achieved? What goals remain to be achieved, and will the achievement of those objectives lead to some increase in the effectiveness of business processes?

- If you measure the complexity of the project by the number of classes developed so far, how many classes will it take to deliver a solution?

While redesigning business processes, you should begin to see light at the end of the tunnel. That is, you should be able to visualize the potentially positive effect your application will have on the users in the domain. However, don't become lost in your dreams. In redesigning business processes, you have to continually wear the hat of an abstractionist, looking for key concepts hidden deep within the processes.

Finally, the development work you're doing has implications for the bottom line—increased revenues or reduced cost. Executives want their investment in your skills to deliver a solution that means increased profits. The term for this in financial circles is *return on investment* (ROI). However, the funny thing about this financial expectation is that some executives analyze the ROI for only a single project. A real return on investment should be measured across several software development projects. Executives should be looking for how a component, developed in project A, can be effectively reused in succeeding projects B, C, D, E, and so on. Reuse of components is like having a part of a project that pays for itself over and over again. You've probably heard the expression "the gift that keeps on giving." Because reusable objects and components provide a lasting return on investment, they should be valued across many projects, not just one. The labor of a skilled developer (such as you) can be encapsulated in a reusable component and implemented repeatedly, providing diminishing costs. This line of thinking should be the basis of your discussion with curious managers and executives, should you ever be summoned to speak to them about the progress of your project.

Working with Project Managers

Managers and executives have to be assured that any refinement of use cases isn't wasteful. Be prepared to give pep talks to management about how important it is to allow the proper resolution of discoveries in business processes. In fact, you could argue that the modifications in business processes could lead to cost savings, increased revenues, or both; they could possibly be implemented before the application is complete.

Many concerns of executives are also the concerns of project managers, but at a finer level of detail. Questions you can explicitly or implicitly expect from your project managers about the state of the project itself include

- How much has Component A cost to develop? How long will it take to develop the other components and subsystems?

- What goals are you trying to achieve for each iteration and increment? What's the state of each use case, and how will each use case improve its corresponding business process?

- How has the complexity of the domain affected the morale of the project team?

- If the project is behind schedule, how can you improve the process? If improvement involves hiring more resources, what will be their responsibilities?"

If the enlightened project manager is new to object-oriented programming, she might also ask, "How can we structure the project in order to effectively run it?"

New Discoveries in How the End User Uses the Visual Basic Application

Because interactions between project teams and users are often less than amiable, developers' assumptions about user expectations tend to replace natural discoveries of business processes. Planning iterations and increments localizes this occurring hostility to one increment instead of the entire development process. Actively including user input to validate your discoveries increases the chance of success for your Visual Basic application.

Discoveries should diminish in time and will often affect the architecture of your system at some point. Assessing the state of your Visual Basic project with regard to discovery resolution is an important activity that should be periodically performed. Factors to take into consideration for state assessment include

- The number of interface and implementation classes
- The number of classes that implement the interface classes
- The number of public methods per class
- Coupling between objects

The number of interface and implementation classes indicates how well focused your project is. You typically have more implementation classes than interface classes, though a class can implement more than one interface. It is perhaps better to plan your applications to have subsystems and components that implement more than one interface. Nevertheless, given a reasonably complex application, if your project tends to have no interface classes, that's a red flag indicating the application architecture is lacking.

The number of public methods per class indicates how well the architecture of the application is evolving. It is certainly okay to have classes that have nothing but public methods. However, most of your classes should typically have private methods. More complex classes should have a handful of public methods but possibly 15 or 20 private methods and more. If your complex classes require more than 20 public and private methods, though, you should consider dividing the classes into smaller classes. In so doing, make sure there's minimal coupling between the classes.

Coupling between objects helps ensure proper encapsulation. Objects with well-defined classes will not duplicate the behavior of dissimilar objects at runtime. Ways of determining well-defined classes include the following:

- Determining, in your own opinion, whether the classes have evolved properly. Of course, with this approach, you might be biased in favor of your creation. Therefore, in cases when your opinion is the only one available, it's good to spend some time away from a subsystem or component and to work on another. Some time later (perhaps a week), revisit the subsystem. If you can still follow the behavior and logic of the classes in it, they're probably okay.

- Conducting peer reviews. Having peers, especially expert object-oriented developers, review your class structures is very effective.

- Conducting user reviews. If your users can identify your domain classes, including properties and methods, your classes are typically in good shape. For commercial application developers, for proprietary reasons, you probably can't show your users your actual core domain classes, so you have to rely on beta tests of both the application and the user guides to indirectly verify the goodness of your classes. However, with your user guides, you can describe your domain classes as key concepts and possibly query your users whether these key concepts are well-defined.

- Having other project members and project teams use your classes. Reuse over time is the single best way of determining whether your classes are well designed.

If you're heading up a team of developers, try not to be too hard on yourself if any of these project state factors are negative. Problems will occur and mistakes will happen. Use the results of the assessment, instead, to encourage better development habits and to come up with a strategy for correcting any problems.

Documenting the Expected Response of the System

10

Refining your use cases throughout the life of your project is important for the system's accuracy in responding to user stimuli. Use cases give life to otherwise static requirements typical of many projects.

Not all use cases should have the same priorities. That means that when a deadline is fast approaching and you need to cut back on revisiting some use cases, you should try to revisit the core use cases. Core use cases are the ones that you want in your first (and, if necessary, second) iteration. If you can't meaningfully revisit most of your core use cases, your project is in jeopardy of being rejected by users during user acceptance testing.

Use cases also have implications for performance. The implementation of a use case in code must conform to performance expectations. Therefore, performance requirements need to be reassessed and tracked in a separate but linked file.

Preserving the Artifacts of Use-Case Analysis and Development in General

As you iterate through the development of your application, you will have to refine your artifacts. Such artifacts include

- User requirements, which are realized in a use-case model (and associated performance requirements)
- Interaction diagrams such as sequence and collaboration diagrams
- State and activity diagrams
- Class diagrams

- The component diagram, which visually documents your ActiveX components
- The deployment diagram, which visually documents where your ActiveX EXE, Active documents, Active Server Pages, and other out-of-process components reside
- Program code
- User and developer guides
- The iteration/project plan, which will evolve in structure like all your other artifacts

Evolving your project artifacts will involve every project stakeholder, including yourself and your team (if applicable), project manager, domain experts and key users, and sometimes executives. At certain points during the earlier part of your project, you will revisit at least 80% of your artifacts at varying degrees of treatment. Again, this number will decrease as your project stabilizes. If you don't often revisit a substantial number of artifacts, the return on investment for your project will diminish, as will the usefulness of your application in the eyes of your users. Of course, you don't want to revisit your artifacts for the sake of doing so or to try to know everything about your users' domain in the first few iterations. Revisit artifacts only when you make significant discoveries about either the domain or the artifacts themselves while evolving them. For an application in which you expect to have fewer then 100 classes, for instance, you might have a dozen or so user meetings (half a dozen beta tests) that will each prompt anywhere from a handful to several dozen or more discoveries.

Preserving your artifacts involves knowing enough about your application's purpose to properly manage and evolve the artifacts. A measurement of the preservation of your artifacts can be given by assessing your current knowledge of your use cases. A use case should have many scenarios in the forms of sequence diagrams. If, after elaborating your use cases, you have only one sequence diagram per use case, something is wrong. You can have many sequence diagrams, but look for opportunities to share diagrams between use cases.

Finally, as your project evolves, you shouldn't have several hundred use cases. Typically, applications require no more than a few dozen use cases. If you keep in mind that a use case is a meaningful course of events that a user goes through in performing some business process, you should be fine in elaborating your use cases. A well-structured prototype can do wonders in helping you refine your use cases.

Assessing Terminology and Traceability

In refining the artifacts of your projects, you must be careful about being able to trace key concepts between the artifacts. Although some of your classes will not appear in your use cases, it is very likely that the core subsystems and components in your application will be traceable from your use cases through your Visual Basic code. Avoiding putting business validation logic in your forms ensures that you can effectively trace terminology. Having business logic embedded in your forms means that some key concepts haven't been properly identified; you and your team will not be able to trace user requirements properly. Even for personal individual projects, it is very wise to separate key core application logic from the form. Often, you and most developers will create a Visual Basic application one month, leave it for a while, and then return to it much later, only to find you don't quite remember what the code means. Having a clean separation of concerns between the forms—which are part of the graphical user presentation—and the core architecture of the application goes a long way toward creating a well-preserved, reusable application. Developing such an application maximizes traceability of key user terminology.

10

Domain-Specific Terminology for the Samsona Bank Teller Example

▼ **REAL WORLD**

Your client at the Second Bank of Carrollton has come to realize that you will often make discoveries related to domain terminology as you elaborate your use cases and other artifacts. With each discovery, you have to validate it with the branch manager and key bank tellers. As part of the Elaboration phase, you now need to elaborate the use cases you have. Your problem statement was revised earlier in this chapter to reflect new discoveries as needed. The repeated descriptions in the problem statement calls for a sharing of common events among use cases. To structure your use-case model to reflect this sharing, you typically show a uses relationship between use cases. You can also use the extends relationship, but this is less common and a little more advanced, so ignore

▼ the extends relationship. Figure 10.1 shows the latest use-case model.

▼ FIGURE **10.1.**

*The latest
version of the
Samsona Bank
Teller System
use-case model.*

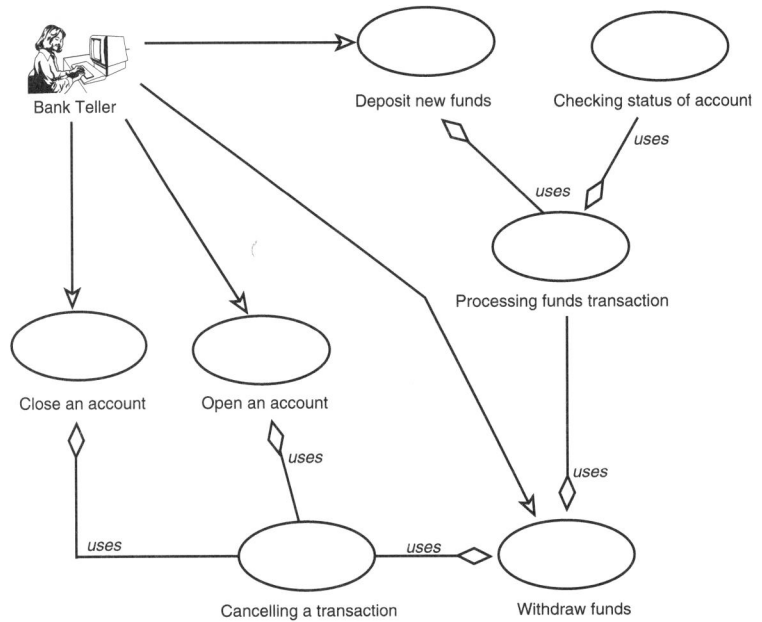

Depicting the extends relationship between use cases is similar to depicting the relationship between an interface class and an implementation class. When one use case extends
another, you can say that that use case implements the stated behavior of the use case in
a specialized way.

For a bank, say you have a use case Open a Checking Account. Now, the bank has a use
case for opening a special bank account product, Open a Basic Personal Checking
Account. If the Open a Checking Account use case represents the basic stated behavior of
all checking account use cases, the use case Open a Basic Personal Checking Account
implements the former one but is specialized for the Basic Personal Checking product. As
you can see, this form of use case relationship can become complicated and is, therefore,
unpopular with newcomers to object technology.

The content of each of your use cases now is as follows:

Open an Account

A new or existing customer can open an account. If the customer is a new customer
with no previous accounts and has the minimum required balance, he's free to apply
for an account. The bank teller must be able to capture the customer's demographic
information, such as full name, address, birth date, Social Security number, home and

▼ business phone numbers, amount of initial deposit, and desired bank product(s). When this information is captured, the bank teller submits it for electronic approval (business rule validation) by the application. During this process, the application will connect to the checking account history system (CAHS) to obtain information relevant to the customer. The application also checks for existing accounts, type of transaction (cash or check) as entered by the bank teller, and type of new account. When approved, the application notifies the bank teller that the account is open (active). Perform use case Processing Funds Transaction for the initial deposit.

If, during the electronic approval process, the application finds that the customer has an existing, active account, the application notifies the bank teller, reminding her to notify the customer that the new account will be part of the family of accounts under the customer's Social Security number. The account is then opened.

If the customer has an existing account that is inactive, the bank teller is notified. Perform use case Canceling a Transaction.

If the customer is new and doesn't have the minimum required balance as entered by the bank teller, the application notifies the bank teller, and the transaction is canceled.

If the customer is a new customer and has a negative checking account history, the application notifies the bank teller. Perform use case Canceling a Transaction.

Deposit New Funds

The bank teller indicates to the application that she wants to deposit funds to a certain account. Perform the use case Processing Funds Transaction. The account is increased by the amount of the deposit.

Withdraw Funds

The bank teller indicates to the application that she wants to withdraw funds from a certain account. Perform the use case Processing Funds Transaction. The account is decreased by the amount of the withdrawal.

If the teller tries, at the customer's request, to withdraw more money than is available, the application notifies the teller. Perform the use case Canceling a Transaction.

Close an Account

At customer request, the bank teller indicates to the application that she wants to close an account. The bank teller enters the account number of the account. The application prompts the teller to ask the customer for his driver's license and Social Security number to verify that the customer is authentic. After the bank teller indicates to
▼ the application that the customer is authentic, the application prints out the account

▼ number, customer information, and the current balance. The balance is then zeroed out, the master bank transaction repository is updated, and the account is closed.

If the account being closed is inactive, the application notifies the bank teller. Perform the use case Canceling a Transaction.

If the bank teller indicates to the application that the customer is not authorized to close the account, perform the use case Canceling a Transaction.

If the customer is authorized to close the account, but the account is deficient, or the customer owes money to the bank, and the account being closed is the last or only one the customer has, the application notifies the bank teller. In the case where there's enough money in the account, the bank teller has the option of performing the use case Withdraw Funds on behalf of the bank in the amount of the debt owed.

If the account number entered by the bank teller is incorrect, the application informs the bank teller. The correctness of the account number is determined in one of two ways:

1. The account number entered by the bank teller is compared with all account numbers in the bank account repository.

2. The second, fourth, and ninth digits in the ten-digit account number must always add up to 24 (to reduce the risk of errors due to keying more than one key simultaneously or other typos).

Processing Funds Transaction

The application prompts the teller for the account number. After the teller provides the account number, the application verifies that the account is still active and prompts the teller to verify that the customer is authorized to deposit to or withdraw funds from the account. If so, the application displays details about the account, including the customer's full name, Social Security number, account status, and account balance. The teller enters the amount of the transaction and applies it. The application persists the transaction to the account repository.

If the customer isn't authorized to deposit money in or withdraw money from the account, the application notifies the teller. Perform the use case Canceling a Transaction.

If the amount being deposited exceeds $10,000 in cash, the application notifies the bank teller that the amount exceeds the federally mandated limit regarding such cash transactions. The application then presents to the bank teller the required cash deposit record form online, transferring the information from the application. When the bank teller has completed reviewing the form, the bank teller indicates to the application

▼ that the form is correct. The form is printed out for the customer's signature.

▼ If the deposit is in the form of a check, the teller notifies the application. The application validates the policy for the deposit and informs the teller to notify the customer that the funds won't be available for ten business days. After the teller enters the amount of the deposit, the application applies the deposit to the account in a temporary balance separate from the regular balance until the funds' availability date has been reached. The application persists the deposit transaction to the account repository.

If the application discovers that the account has been frozen by the government, the application notifies the teller. Perform the use case Canceling a Transaction.

Checking Status of Account

If the application discovers that the account has been frozen by the government, the application notifies the teller.

Recall that on Day 2, the following terms were identified in the original set of use cases:

Teller

Samsona Bank Teller System

Process

Bank accounts

Account

Funds

After re-evaluating the revised use cases and related requirements, you came up with an expanded list of candidate abstractions and reduced them to these stronger candidate classes and subsystems:

```
FundsTransactionProcessor <<Subsystem Controller>>

DepositFunds <<Controller>>

WithdrawFunds <<Controller>>

OpenAccount <<Controller>>

CloseAccount <<Controller>>

StatusChecker <<Controller>>

CustomerRequest

Transaction

GovernmentRegulator <<Subsystem Controller>>

CashDepositRecord
```

▼   `Printer`

10

▼   Report

    ReportBuilder

    BankTransactionRepository

    CustomerManagement <<Subsystem Controller>>

    Customer

    CustomerAuthorization

    AccountNumberProcessor <<Subsystem Controller>>

    AccountNumberComparison

▲   CheckDigits

Assessing Traceability upon Refining Use Cases

After you examine the list of strong candidate classes in the preceding section, you will
probably recognize the classnames as derived from the use cases, for the most part. Keep
in mind that not all your classes will be listed in the use cases. However, if they aren't
listed, they should definitely be associated in some way with the classes that are.
Therefore, every time you refine your use cases, ask yourself two questions:

- Are each of these classes covered in the description of the use cases?
- If not, are they used by the classes in the use cases, or do they themselves use the
  classes in them?

Not all your classes have to be directly associated with the classes that participate in the
use cases. They can be associated with classes that are, in turn, associated with classes in
the use cases. In auditing your use cases, then, make sure there is a noticeable chain of
association, such that the chain leads back to the use-case model. This will help you
ensure that the user requirements are being properly addressed by the architecture of
your Visual Basic application.

Summary

This chapter builds on what you know about use cases and domain analysis, in general,
from Day 2. In particular, you learned about revisiting use cases in your evironment as
well as updating the problem statement and the use-case model. This chapter shows you
the art of working with end users, business analysts, executives, and project managers.
You learned how to incorporate new discoveries about the way end users expect to use
your Visual Basic application into the design models. Moreover, you gained insight into
preserving the artifacts of use-case analysis and development in general. Finally, you

learned about assessing terminology and traceability, including domain-specific terminology for the Samsona Bank Teller example, and related traceability issues involved in refining use cases. Tomorrow, you'll learn the fundamental concepts necessary to implement a Graphical User Interface Subsystem. The lesson for Day 12, "Graphical User Interface Subsystems: An Example," continues the presentation of the GUI subsystem, giving you actual implementation advice and code.

Q&A

Q **True or False: The most experienced developers who don't use object technology have done some form of iterative development.**

A True

Q **What should you do when you make a discovery about the domain while in the middle of any project phase?**

A If the discovery is important enough, you must resolve it with analysis and design activities before implementing the new requirement.

Q **What is an iteration plan?**

A An iteration plan captures the project activities you and your team members must perform, as well as delivery of the artifacts that result from these activities.

Q **What is a negative side effect of prematurely creating a static iteration plan?**

A Creating a static iteration plan prematurely often (but not necessarily) results in frustration and low morale.

Q **How important are use cases?**

A The use-case model is the backbone of a project. All the artifacts in the object-oriented project are dependent on it in one way or another.

Q **Briefly, what is reverse engineering and forward engineering?**

A Modeling existing user processes is reverse engineering. Modeling the desired model is forward engineering.

Q **What can you do if you're overwhelmed with business process discoveries?**

A It's best to seek the help of one or more business analysts or business process designers.

Q **What is a factor that helps to increase the chances of success for your project?**

A Actively including user input to validate your discoveries.

Q **What is a red flag that indicates the application architecture is lacking?**

A When your project tends to have no interface classes.

10

Q What are some important ways to determine whether you have well-defined classes?

A Some ways include

- Determining whether the classes have evolved properly in your own opinion. Of course, with this approach, you can be biased in favor of your creation. Therefore, in cases when your opinion is the only one available, it's good to spend some time away from a subsystem or component and work on another. Some time later (perhaps a week later), revisit the subsystem. If you can still follow the behavior and logic of the classes in it, they're probably okay.

- Conducting peer reviews. Having peers, especially expert object-oriented developers, review your class structures is very effective.

- Conducting user reviews. If your users can identify your domain classes, including properties and methods, your classes are typically in good shape. For commercial application developers, for proprietary reasons, you probably can't show your users your actual core domain classes, so you have to rely on beta tests of both the application and the user guides to indirectly verify the goodness of your classes. However, with your use guides, you can describe your domain classes as key concepts and possibly query your users whether these key concepts are well-defined.

- Having other project members and project teams use your classes. Reuse over time is the single best way of determining whether your classes are well designed.

Workshop

The workshop includes quiz questions to help gauge your grasp of the material. You'll find the answers to this quiz in Appendix A, "Answers." Even if you feel that you understand the concepts presented here, you should work through the quiz. The last section is an exercise to help reinforce your learning.

Quiz

1. What are two ways you can structure an iteration plan?
2. What are the benefits of revisiting your use cases?
3. Why is it important to involve your users in the refining of your use cases?
4. Explain the financial implications of elaborating business processes while developing your applications.

5. What four factors should you take into account when assessing the state of your development efforts?

Exercise

Update the iteration plan to reflect the latest use cases as documented in the section "Domain-Specific Terminology for the Samsona Bank Teller Example." (Hint: Each use case can have its own increment.)

10

DAY **11**

The Graphical User Interface Subsystem: A Primer

This chapter presents you with an overview of the objects and forms that make up a vibrant Graphical User Interface Subsystem. In particular, you will learn

- The purpose of the Graphical User Interface (GUI) Subsystem
- Using the modeling techniques for GUIs
- Encapsulating data presentation into a separate class
- Describing the classes in the subsystem, particularly the methods, arguments and preconditions, and returns and postconditions
- Describing the properties, data types, accessor behavior, mutator behavior, and event classes; designing GUIs; ergonomics; and internationalization with resource files

An Overview of the Graphical User Interface Subsystem

In general, designing graphical user interfaces is more a function of ergonomics and human factors research than object-oriented programming. The most important goal of designing any user interface is to provide a simple metaphor for helping the users articulate their work needs. Like any well-structured software, graphical user interfaces require constant improvements in user-friendliness and accessibility throughout the life of the project.

Understanding the Fundamental Concepts Underlying the Subsystem

As with object-oriented development, developing user interfaces requires analysis or assessment of the human interaction with the application, as depicted in the use cases, as well as design and implementation. It is a mistake to assume that user interfaces can be mocked up quickly. Developing user interfaces involves using the most effective controls, placing the controls on the form in a manner that optimizes user productivity, and planning for human factors such as eye strain, carpal tunnel syndrome, and other hazards associated with long-term use of computer applications.

Besides having a user interface that is truly user-friendly, you should also include some mechanism for handling the flow of information into and out of a form. Creating such a mechanism or subsystem can be complex at times, but it helps to decouple the form from the actual business class. Such decoupling maximizes the chance of your classes and forms being reused by promoting independence among these objects.

Mapping Use-Case Actor Stimuli to GUI Navigation

As mentioned earlier, developing a good graphical user interface requires that you at least review your use cases. Use cases show the interaction between human actors and the application under development. Recall that each use case contains one to many scenarios, each of which contain one to many steps. A step could be described as clicking a mouse or pressing the Enter key. In other words, your use-case scenarios are the artifacts that provide the foundation for building your graphical user interfaces. Constant user feedback helps keep your foundation accurate.

Practical Guidelines for Implementing the Graphical User Interface

- Expect to consume at least a third of your project schedule in designing the forms and making them reasonably usable. Poorly designed GUI forms reduce the productivity of the users because they have to compensate for the GUI design flaws. This compensation for flaws also reduces the chances of the software being reusable, because your form controllers might have flawed public methods that control the flow of events in the forms.

- Properly place the data entry controls in the order that users expect. You can find clues about this order by interviewing your users and/or analyzing artifacts from the domain from which the users will input the data. This includes paper documents that are the source of the data being entered.

- At every opportunity, be sure to set the tab stop values of each of the form objects. For grids and spreadsheets, be sure to allow the user to tab to the next logical column in the row. When necessary, design your GUI form to automatically tab to the next logical data entry item. Enforcing these issues alone can boost productivity by 25–30%.

Note

> Of course, autotabbing can cause a slight delay when the user realizes he or she made a mistake in the preceding field. Predicting which fields have a higher probability of errors is difficult. You and your users must weigh the benefits of autotabbing against the potential problem.

- Labels should be captioned clearly so that the user doesn't have to guess what a data entry field means. For grids and spreadsheets, make the column and row headings equally informative. Stay away from acronyms.

- Make sure the user doesn't have to scroll a form full of too many controls. This is especially important for critical business tasks that are time-sensitive. Instead of forms that are scrollable, use wizards—either the Wizard Manager or a customized wizard. If users have to input large amounts of records that represent pure data entry apart from interviewing their customers, try to use grids for such data entry. Default to the first logical field on the form when the form loads.

11

- If your users normally enter standard units of measurement such as miles (mi.), kilometers (km), and so on, or other standards such as Street (St.) or Road (Rd.), Mr. or Mrs. or Ms., and megahertz (MHz), try to accommodate them by autopopulating them, structuring them into masks, or providing a drop-down list of these options. Do the same for date and time units.

- Make calculate fields read-only. To give the user a visual clue, make the background color different from the other fields. Labels are good for read-only fields. You can do the same for fields that contain default data to indicate to the user that this field contains a default data item. When all data entry transactions are complete, make sure your Graphical User Interface Subsystem confirms all items entered on one or more forms. If accepted by the user, continue to the next process. If not, return to the form. If the form was in the process of being unloaded, set `Cancel = True` in the form's `Query_Unload` event.

These practical guidelines, full of advice, should help you understand many issues involved in designing a form or set of forms. Many developers think GUIs are easy and shouldn't take long. However, making a form usable can take considerable time, more so for complex projects.

Using the Modeling Techniques for GUIs

Traditionally, the development of graphical user interfaces has been reserved for pure artistic talent. Indeed, creativity is important when designing a user interface. Modeling a user interface requires more technical treatment, however.

Let's model a simple user interface. Figure 11.1 shows a generic user interface mechanism for controlling the flow of information into and out of a form. You will use the code from Day 6, "Building and Testing Components." In that chapter, you had a form, `frmAccountMaintForm`, that was controlled by the `FormController` class instance, `theFormController`. The code for this interaction is shown in Listing 11.1. The `FormController` class interacted with the `BasicPersonalChecking` class instance, `theBasicPersonalCheckingAccount`, through the latter's `adjustBalance` method (see Listing 11.2).

FIGURE 11.1.

A generic user interface mechanism for controlling the flow of information into and out of a form.

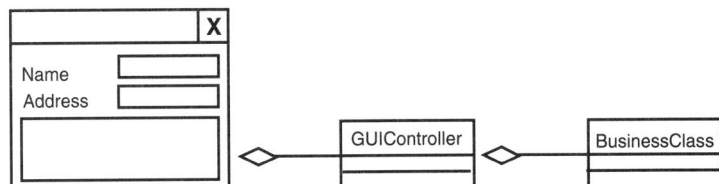

Figure 11.2 shows the relationships between the form frmAccountMaintForm, the FormController class, and the BasicPersonalChecking class. Between the frmAccountMaintForm form and the FormController class is an association described as *control stimuli*. This means that every user interaction with the form that requires information from the related business classes will be controlled through the FormController class. The open diamond means, for instance, that the form is requesting services from the FormController class. This is also called *navigation*.

FIGURE 11.2.

The relationships between the form frmAccountMaintForm, *the* FormController *class, and the* BasicPersonalChecking *class.*

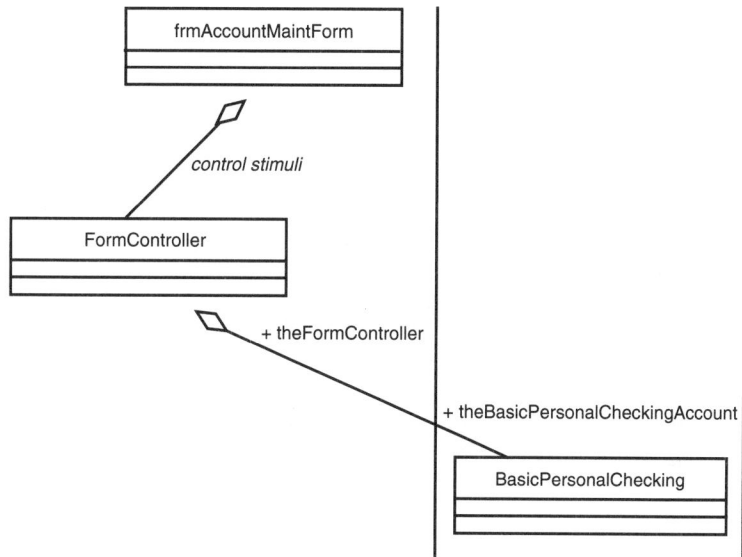

LISTING 11.1. frmAccountMaintForm's cmdStore_Click EVENT.

```
1: Private Sub cmdStore_Click()
2:     theFormController.setform Me
3:     theFormController.depositFunds _
4:         txtDepositAmount, txtAccountNumber
5: End Sub
```

LISTING 11.2. THE `BasicPersonalChecking`'s `adjustBalance` METHOD.

```
 1: Public Function adjustBalance(argObject As Deposit,
➥argAccountNumber As String) As Boolean
 2:      Dim LocalObject As Object, returns As Boolean
 3:
 4:      'If there's more than one account object in memory, a precondition
 5:      'is that this object is the correct object. So check account
         ➥number
 6:      If argAccountNumber <> AccountNumber Then
 7:           'Raise exceptions here...
 8:          Dim sMsg As String
 9:          sMsg = "Wrong account number, Please retry."
10:          RaiseEvent OnWrongAccountNumber(sMsg)
11:          'Set LocalObject = Nothing
12:          Exit Function
13:      End If
14:
15:      'Delegate to private methods, where only one will be able to
16:      'process the message.
17:
18:      Set LocalObject = argObject
19:
20:      returns = increaseBalance(LocalObject)
21:      If returns Then
22:          adjustBalance = returns
23:          Exit Function
24:          Set LocalObject = Nothing
25:      End If
26:
27:      returns = decreaseBalance(LocalObject)
28:      If returns Then
29:          adjustBalance = returns
30:          Exit Function
31:          Set LocalObject = Nothing
32:      End If
33:
34: End Function
```

NEW TERM *Navigation* is the act of a client object requesting services from a serving object.

Figure 11.3 illustrates the `frmAccountMaintForm` form. As you can see, it's simple. A use case that is realized by this form could be called Make a Deposit. A simple normal scenario could be named Deposit Funds to a Particular Active Account by Account Number. The steps for this scenario might be

1. Enter account number.

2. Enter amount of deposit.

3. Persist the transaction by clicking the Store button.

4. Complete the transaction by clicking the Done button.

FIGURE 11.3.

The actual
`frmAccountMaintForm`
form, as seen in
Visual Basic.

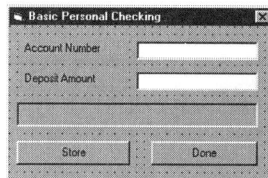

Ideally, you might try to create such scenario scripts so that you have a guideline for the behavior and features of each form. This practice of scripting your forms also encourages reuse of forms by not only other team members but also other teams.

Understanding the Encapsulation of Data Presentation into a Separate Class

Attempting to map fields on a form to properties in a class can be tedious. The most pressing concern is to avoid breaking the rule of encapsulation. That is, in theory, the only object that should access the values of a business or domain class is the class itself. Any other class that needs such information is probably not properly designed.

The Graphical User Interface Subsystem Object Model

You can use the diagram in Figure 11.1 to design the mechanism for effectively modeling the interactions between forms and business classes. Because the form is, in a sense, a class, you can model it as a class in your model. Indeed, a form can have methods, attributes, and events just like classes. In the specification for your form class in Visual Modeler, make sure to mention that the class represents a form. Figure 11.4 gives you an example of the specification window for the `frmAccountMaintForm` form.

FIGURE 11.4.

The specification window for the frmAccountMaintForm *form.*

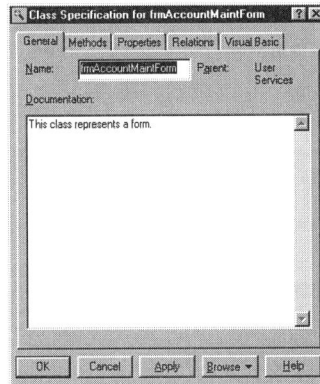

The Graphical User Interface Subsystem Class Hierarchy Model

Classes that control the interaction between forms and business/domain classes can be members of complex class hierarchies that show interface inheritance and delegation. You incorporate interface inheritance by assessing the various kinds of behavior that forms exhibit redundantly. For instance, if all your forms have Add, Modify, and Delete buttons that behave similarly, you could have an interface class, IInfoMaintenance, that provides a common interface for this type of behavior. The IInfoMaintenance class would have the following methods:

```
Public Sub clickedAddBtn()
Public Sub clickedModifyBtn()
Public Sub clickedDeleteBtn()
```

The IInfoMaintenance class would need to be declared globally for some subsystems, as follows:

```
Global theIInfoMaintenance As New IInfoMaintenance
```

For GUI subsystems implemented as ActiveX components, you would declare the interface object variable as MultiUse. MultiUse enables client applications to create objects from the class. That is, you can create many instances of this interface class. However, you need only one instance of such an interface class, so a public declaration is suitable.

In some cases, an interface class for form controllers is not enough. You can have behavior for each Add, Modify, and Delete button that is common across many forms. Certainly, you wouldn't want to repeat the same code in each of these forms, although

Visual Basic does have features for rubber-stamping common code. Instead, it is better to delegate common behavior in form objects to classes. Therefore, `IInfoMaintenance` becomes `InfoMaintenance`. Its methods might look like Listing 11.3.

LISTING 11.3. SOME METHODS FOR `InfoMaintenance`.

```
 1: Public Sub clickedAddBtn(ByRef argObject, argString As String)
 2:    If TypeOf argObject Is TextBox Then
 3:       argObject.Text = argObject.Text & argString
 4:    End If
 5:    If TypeOf argObject Is Label Then
 6:       argObject.Caption = argObject.Caption & argString
 7:    End If
 8:    If TypeOf argObject Is ListBox Then
 9:       argObject.AddItem argObject.List(argObject.ListIndex)_ argString
10:    End If
11:    If TypeOf argObject Is ComboBox Then
12:       argObject.AddItem argObject.List(argObject.ListIndex)_ argString
13:    End If
14: End Sub
15:
16: Public Sub clickedModifyBtn(argObject As Object, argString As String)
17:    If TypeOf argObject Is TextBox Then
18:       argObject.Text = argString
19:    End If
20:    If TypeOf argObject Is Label Then
21:       argObject.Caption = argString
22:    End If
23: End Sub
24:
25: Public Sub clickedDeleteBtn(argObject As Object)
26: If TypeOf argObject Is TextBox Then
27:       argObject.Text = ""
28:    End If
29:    If TypeOf argObject Is Label Then
30:       argObject.Caption = ""
31:    End If
32:    If TypeOf argObject Is ListBox Then
33:       argObject.RemoveItem argObject.ListIndex
34:    End If
35:    If TypeOf argObject Is ComboBox Then
36:       argObject.RemoveItem argObject.ListIndex
37:    End If
38: End Sub
```

11

> **Tip**
>
> You can use the `CodeModule` object to add, modify, or delete code associated with a particular class or form. For more information, see your Books Online in Visual Basic.

Notice that you could have combined the `If Then` code for both `ListBox` and `ComboxBox` objects as follows:

```
If TypeOf argObject Is ListBox or TypeOf argObject _
Is ComboBox Then
    argObject.AddItem argObject.List(argObject.ListIndex)_ argString
End If

If TypeOf argObject Is ListBox Or TypeOf argObject _
Is ComboBox Then
    argObject.RemoveItem argObject.ListIndex
End If
```

Feel free to choose either option.

Describing the Classes in the Subsystem

The kinds of forms and objects that participate in a Graphical User Interface Subsystem can vary widely. In the preceding section, you were introduced to the `IInfoMaintenance` and `InfoMaintenance` classes. You could also have a class that handles common behavior for buttons that close a form, that perform cancellations or undo operations, and so on. A good name for such a class might be `FormOperations`.

Describing the Methods

The `FormOperations` class might have the following methods:

```
Public Sub clickedOKBtn()
Public Sub clickedCancelBtn()
Public Sub clickedUndoBtn()
Public Sub clickedDoneBtn()
Public Sub clickedSaveBtn()
```

Assume the `FormOperations` class has an instance named `theFormOperations`. Also assume you have a form, `frmForm`, with a command button, `cmdDone`. The `frmForm` form might invoke `clickedDoneBtn`, as follows:

```
Public Sub cmdDone_Click()
  theFormOperations.clickedDoneBtn Me
End Sub
```

The Me keyword refers to frmForm. In the clickedDoneBtn method, the code would be

```
Public Sub clickedDoneBtn(argForm As Form)
    Unload argForm
    Set argForm = Nothing
End Sub
```

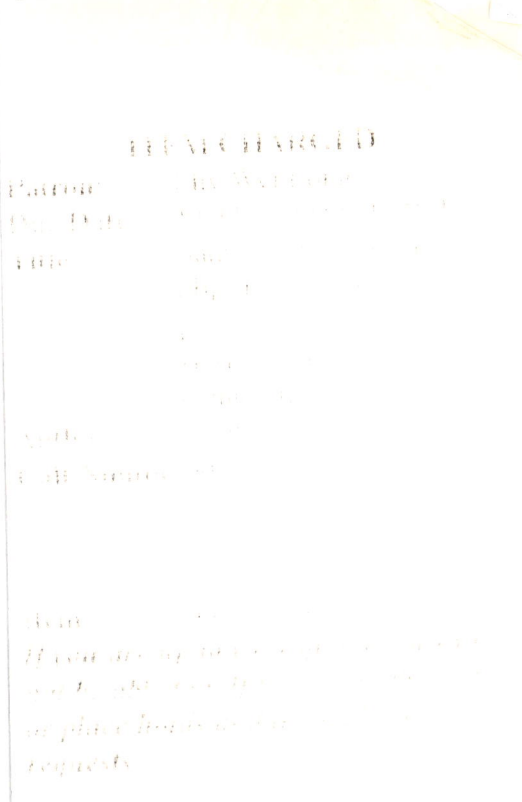

aren't as straightforward. Standard pro-
hical user interface policy in place at
ving such a policy, even in an infor-
the GUI subsystem organized and

(cmdOK) in much the same way as
se in your environment, invoke the

cel button typically stops the
he Undo button reverses the entry
transaction is committed. Some-
s nothing or is used to hide or
is because it doesn't specifically
ore appropriate for small forms that
ess is underway that can be can-
ly called the Cancel button should

nstance, theTransaction, your
ng:

```
    Set frmProgress = Nothing
End Sub
```

The frmProgress object is a standard form for showing the progress of a transaction. It can have a ProgressBar control on it.

Tip

Often in today's programming environment, the Cancel button means either *close the form* or *undo a transaction*. With object-oriented programming, you need a clean separation of concerns. You can achieve this separation with two distinct buttons, Close and Undo Transaction. If you notice, you can clearly tell what a Close button does, as opposed to an Undo Transaction button. However, Cancel is too ambiguous.

Tip

> If given the choice, you should probably choose the cmdDone naming conven-
> tion. The word *OK*, which is not a verb, is sometimes ambiguous because it
> doesn't indicate a business process being complete. The word *Done* is a verb,
> and it definitely clues the user to the completion of a task. In general, com-
> mand buttons should have names in verb form indicating some action or
> event.

The undo operation would be similar to that of the Cancel button, except it is appropriate
for most forms. That is, everywhere a user can enter information and submit that information in a transaction for processing, you should have an Undo button. An undo operation requires

- Cancellation of a transaction
- Repopulation of previous data into display controls such as text boxes, labels,
  combo and list boxes, and grids

For the transaction cancellation, invoke the clickedCancelBtn method. For the restoring
of displayed information, you need some mechanism for keeping the previous data without ruining the encapsulation of the business/domain classes from which the information
came. The Memento design pattern is good for this.

A Memento class has two methods, getState and setState. These methods are used to
save (set) the state of a business class before new data is entered by the user and to
restore (get) that state in the event the user cancels the transaction. The business class
instance creates the Memento—typically in a createMemento() method—and passes it to
a Caretaker object. In the case of forms, the Caretaker is the form's controller. For
your purposes, the controller is named FormController.

To be a proper caretaker, FormController needs two methods, clickedModifyBtn() and
clickedUndoBtn(), and a property, theBusinessMemento. Listing 11.4 shows the two
methods.

LISTING 11.4. THE clickedModifyBtn AND clickedUndoBtn METHODS CARRY OUT THE
UNDO RESPONSIBILITIES OF FormController ON BEHALF OF ITS FORM.

```
1: Public Sub clickedModifyBtn()
2:     Set theBusinessMemento = theBusiness.createMemento
3:     theBusiness.MyName = "Samsona Software"
4:     theForm.Text1 = theBusiness.MyName
5: End Sub
6:
```

```
 7: Public Sub clickedUndoBtn()
 8:     theBusiness.setMemento theBusinessMemento
 9:     theForm.Text1 = theBusiness.MyName
10: End Sub
```

The object, theBusinessMemento, is a property of FormController created using Class Builder. Class Builder takes care of the details of creating properties by automatically inserting the get, let, and, if necessary, set statements and the modular declaration of the private object variable. That private declaration is

```
Private mvartheBusinessMemento As BusinessMemento
```

The class BusinessMemento represents a Memento object for a hypothetical business class named Business. The createMemento method of theBusiness creates a BusinessMemento object that holds the state of theBusiness using a private array of values. Each of these array items represents the values of each property of theBusiness. The Business class will be discussed shortly. The form object, called theForm, represents the privately declared reference to the sample form, frmTest. For the sake of convenience, it is probably advisable to design your form controllers to actually own a reference to the form it controls. For typical startup forms, use Sub Main to invoke a method to display the form, as follows:

```
Public Sub Main()
    theFormController.showForm
End Sub
```

The showForm method looks like Listing 11.5. Here, the MyName property of theBusiness object is initialized to the name of the author. The object, theForm, is then initialized to the actual form, the Text1 control on the form is initialized to the MyName property of theBusiness, and then the form is displayed.

LISTING 11.5. THE showForm METHOD OF theFormController.

```
1: Public Sub showForm()
2:     theBusiness.MyName = "John Conley"
3:     Set theForm = New frmTest
4:
5:     theForm.Text1 = theBusiness.MyName
6:     theForm.Show
7: End Sub
```

The method, `clickedModifyBtn`, invokes `theBusiness.createMemento` before the modify transaction even begins. The `clickedModifyBtn` method is invoked by the Modify button (code named `cmdModify`) on the form. The method invocation looks like the following:

```
Private Sub cmdModify_Click()
    theFormController.clickedModifyBtn
End Sub
```

The global declarations for `theBusiness` and `theFormController` objects are in the General Declarations of the sample code module, `modMain`, as follows:

```
Global theBusiness As New Business
Global theFormController As New FormController
```

After the Memento is created, you allow the user to make modifications. When the user decides that he or she doesn't want to keep the changes, `theForm` invokes the `clickedUndoBtn` method.

The `clickedUndoBtn` method invokes the `setMemento` method of `theBusiness`, passing it back the object, `theBusinessMemento`, created by `theBusiness.createMemento`. The `setMemento` method of `theBusiness` returns `theBusiness` back to its previous state. This is important to do before setting `theForm.Text1` to the `MyName` property of `theBusiness`.

The object, `theBusiness`, has two methods that are important for undo operations: `createMemento()` and `setMemento()`. Listing 11.6 shows the code for the two methods.

LISTING 11.6. THE `createMemento` AND `setMemento` METHODS.

```
 1: Public Function createMemento() As BusinessMemento
 2:     arrMemento = Array(theBusiness.MyName)
 3:     Set theBusinessMemento = New BusinessMemento
 4:     theBusinessMemento.setState arrMemento
 5:     Set createMemento = theBusinessMemento
 6: End Function
 7:
 8: Public Sub setMemento(argMemento As BusinessMemento)
 9:     Dim PreviousState
10:     PreviousState = argMemento.getState
11:     MyName = PreviousState(eMemento.bMyName)
12:     PreviousState = ""
13: End Sub
14:
15: 'Declarations
16: 'local variable(s) to hold property value(s)
17: Private mvarMyName As String 'local copy
18:
19: Private arrMemento
20:
```

```
21: Private theBusinessMemento As BusinessMemento
22: Private Enum eMemento
23:     bMyName = 0
24: End Enum
```

In the `createMemento` method, the array, `arrMemento`, is created. This array can hold as many items as there are properties in the class. Here, the `Array` statement is used to create the array, but you can create your array by using the regular `Dim` statement. The object `theBusinessMemento` is then instantiated, and its `setState` method is invoked, whereupon the array `arrMemento` is passed as an argument. Finally, a reference to `theBusinessMemento` is passed back to `theFormController` (or any client, for that matter, because more than one form controller can request a Memento).

When the user stimulates an undo operation, `theFormController` invokes the `setMemento` method, passing in the reference to `theBusinessMemento` it received from invoking the `createMemento` method. A local variable, `PreviousState`, is created to hold the reference to the state array returned when invoking the `getState` method of the Memento. In this simple example, there's only one property for `theBusiness`. The private enum `eMemento`, then, has only one enumerator, `bMyName`, which is set to zero. The property `MyName` is restored to the value referenced in `PreviousState(eMemento.bMyName)`, which in your example is `"John Conley"`.

In `theForm` (which represents `frmTest`), the call to trigger the undo operation looks like the following:

```
Private Sub cmdUndo_Click()
    theFormController.clickedUndoBtn
End Sub
```

> **Tip**
>
> The enumerator `bMyName` is prefixed with the letter *b*. This is purely arbitrary in order to differentiate it from the actual property name. If you don't differentiate the enumerator from the actual property name, Visual Basic will return an error because it considers two or more declarations of the same name in the same module ambiguous.

The method `clickedSaveBtn` involves triggering the operation to persist information to some file or database. The general name for any form of persistence is *information repository*. In the `FormController` class, the method would be declared as

```
Public Sub clickedSaveBtn()
```

As with the undo/Memento operations, the client form invokes this method on the `FormController` class instance. However, because the operations for saving information involve file operations and database operations, further details on implementation are addressed on Day 17, "The File Operations Subsystem," and Day 19, "The Database Access Subsystem."

Arguments and Preconditions

Some arguments listed earlier require special attention. In Listing 11.3, the method `clickedAddBtn` has the following arguments:

```
ByRef argObject
argString As String
```

Because the type of `argObject` is not known, the method had to test it. That is, the precondition for this method is that the object referenced by `argObject` has to be either a `TextBox`, `Label`, `ListBox`, or `ComboBox`. A type failure of any of these preconditions means that the method can't process the event/stimulus. The `argString` argument in this example didn't have an associated precondition. The `clickedModifyBtn` and `clickedDeleteBtn` methods follow the same general pattern.

In Listing 11.6, you came across several additional arguments. Look at the `createMemento` method. The object, `theBusinessMemento`, has a method, `setState`, that accepts an argument that represents an array of property values (`arrMemento`). No preconditions applied for this argument, although the method is not meaningful unless there are values in the `Memento` array.

In the `setMemento` method, you find an argument, `argMemento`, that is of type `BusinessMemento`. Here, you've enlisted the help of the Visual Basic compiler in making sure the argument is, indeed, of the expected type.

Returns and Postconditions

For the most part, the returns and postconditions were straightforward. In Listing 11.4, you read the following line of code:

```
Set theBusinessMemento = theBusiness.createMemento
```

The `createMemento` method returns an object of type, `BusinessMemento`. This means that as a postcondition, `theBusinessMemento` had to be declared as the expected type.

The other postcondition was that the state of `theBusiness` object would change, which necessitated the need to create a Memento to memorize the previous state.

Describing the Properties

The object, `theBusiness`, has a simple property, `MyName`, for example only. The object, `theBusinessMemento`, has an important state property that holds the `Memento` array, `arrMemento`, for `theBusiness` object. The object, `theFormController`, has an object property, `theBusinessMemento`, which is a reference to the `Memento` object created by `theBusiness` object.

Designing GUIs

In designing graphical user interfaces, it is important to incorporate only as many controls as your user needs on any given form. Forms should load as quickly as possible. String values should originate in resource files when possible. The next two sections briefly examine these issues.

Ergonomics

Users of your software want to work as quickly and safely as possible. You provide speed through shortcut keys and controls that are logically arranged in order, based on how users complete their tasks. Therefore, in certain countries such as the United States, and in European nations, that read information from left to right, you would place a Done button somewhere near the bottom-right corner of the form. In countries in the Middle East, you would probably place the Done button at the bottom left.

Moreover, you should name your controls according to the names of the properties of important business/domain classes. This will help you in mapping displayed data to key business class instances. Colors need to be soft for normal tasks and bright for warnings or important messages that require the user's utmost attention. Text boxes should have black text with a white background color. Images displayed should not be so large that they slow down the loading and displaying of forms. Finally, controls on the form should be placed with enough space between them to soothe the eyes.

Internationalization with Resource Files and the Registry

With the Internet making geopolitical borders seemingly disappear, Visual Basic programmers are finding it necessary to cater their software to users of other countries. This catering of software for multinational users is generally known as either *internationalization* or *localization*. Resource files are very fitting for catering to multination users, particularly if you develop software for sale on the Internet, where users reside in every country in the world.

11

> Although I only discuss how to use a resource file class to load text values into labels, it is interesting to briefly note how internationalization is supported. In the Professional and Enterprise editions of Visual Basic, internationalization is fundamentally supported in the LocaleID (LCID) of the standard executable and ActiveX controls you create.
>
> When you create an ActiveX control, that control is associated with a `UserControl` object. This object has an object reference to an `AmbientProperties` object. A set of ambient properties helps to interface your control to the application in which it is used. This `AmbientProperties` object, in turn, has a `LocaleID` property that you check to find out the country in which the application is being operated. Knowing this information helps you internationalize your software. For more information on `LocaleID`, refer to the "Localizing Controls" article in Visual Basic Books Online.

You can create a resource file with any word processor and the resource compiler found under the \Tools subdirectory in your Visual Basic root directory or the Visual Basic CD-ROM. For your purposes, use the form in your Memento example. Listing 11.7 shows the specifications for the form you can use to create the form. Figure 11.3 shows what the actual form looks like.

LISTING 11.7. THE SPECIFICATIONS FOR THE FORM `frmAccountMaintForm`.

```
 1: VERSION 5.00
 2: Begin VB.Form frmTest
 3:    Caption        =   "Modify Name"
 4:    ClientHeight   =   3195
 5:    ClientLeft     =   60
 6:    ClientTop      =   345
 7:    ClientWidth    =   4680
 8:    LinkTopic      =   "Form1"
 9:    ScaleHeight    =   3195
10:    ScaleWidth     =   4680
11:    StartUpPosition =  3   'Windows Default
12:    Begin VB.CommandButton cmdUndo
13:       Caption     =   "Undo"
14:       Height      =   375
15:       Left        =   2760
16:       TabIndex    =   3
17:       Top         =   2280
18:       Width       =   1455
19:    End
20:    Begin VB.TextBox Text2
21:       Height      =   285
22:       Left        =   1440
23:       TabIndex    =   2
24:       Text        =   "Text2"
```

```
25:        Top            =    1200
26:        Width          =    2055
27:     End
28:     Begin VB.TextBox Text1
29:        Height         =    285
30:        Left           =    1440
31:        TabIndex       =    1
32:        Text           =    "Text1"
33:        Top            =    600
34:        Width          =    2055
35:     End
36:     Begin VB.CommandButton cmdModify
37:        Caption        =    "Modify Name"
38:        Height         =    375
39:        Left           =    960
40:        TabIndex       =    0
41:        Top            =    2280
42:        Width          =    1455
43:     End
44: End
45: Attribute VB_Name = "frmTest"
46: Attribute VB_GlobalNameSpace = False
47: Attribute VB_Creatable = False
48: Attribute VB_PredeclaredId = True
49: Attribute VB_Exposed = False
50:
51: Private Sub Command1_Click()
52:     theFormController.setupUndo
53:     theBusiness.MyName = "Samsona"
54: End Sub
55:
56: Private Sub cmdModify_Click()
57:     theFormController.clickedModifyBtn
58: End Sub
59:
60: Private Sub cmdUndo_Click()
61:     theFormController.clickedUndoBtn
62: End Sub
```

11

A resource file contains definitions for the resources your application uses. The most common resources are

- String
- Bitmap
- Data, in the form of a byte array
- Icon

Every item for a resource in your resource definition file has an associated index value. The value 1 is reserved for your application's icon. The DOS-based resource compiler compiles the RC file into a RES file. For the sake of simplicity, consider adding only string text to the label controls.

To keep your example simple, add two labels to the left of the two text boxes. Keep the default name, Label1, and let them both be in the same control array. Now create the simple resource file that will contain only the captions for the two labels. Using Notepad or WordPad, enter the following in the blank text document:

```
#define sNAME 2
#define sURL 3

STRINGTABLE DISCARDABLE
BEGIN
   sNAME, "Samsona Software"
   sURL,  "http://www.samsona.com"
END
```

The #define statement is a compiler directive that defines constants and variables to be used. STRINGTABLE DISCARDABLE means that the table of string values can be discarded from memory when no longer in use. Save the file as memento.rc. At an MS-DOS command prompt, enter the following:

```
RC /r /fo memento.res memento.rc
```

If you have the Memento project files in a folder that is different from the Visual Basic folder, specify the full path name of the resource definition file.

Add the resource file to the Visual Basic project. Choose Project | Add File from the Visual Basic menu. You will see the Add File dialog box. Browse to the folder that contains the resource file, memento.res. Choose the file and click OK.

Create a class called, fittingly, ResourceFile. Add the following methods to the ResourceFile class:

```
Public Function loadString(argIndex As Integer)
Public Function loadPicture(argIndex As Integer, argFormat As Byte)
Public Function loadIcon(argIndex As Integer)
Public Function loadData(argIndex As Integer, argFormat As Byte)
```

Though you're going to use loadString only, it's good to go ahead and add the other methods supported for resource file operations. In the loadString method, include the following code:

```
Public Function loadString(argIndex As Integer)
    Dim locaIndex As Integer
    locaIndex = argIndex
    loadString = LoadResString(locaIndex)
    locaIndex = 0
End Function
```

Make the following declarations in the FormController class:

```
Private theResourceFile As ResourceFile

Private Enum eResourceIds
    bName = 0
    bURL
End Enum
```

Modify the setForm method of the FormController class as follows:

```
Public Sub showForm()
    theBusiness.MyName = "John Conley"
    Set theForm = New frmTest

    'Instantiate the resource file class
    Set theResourceFile = New ResourceFile
    theForm.Label1(0).Caption = _
        theResourceFile.loadString(eResourceIds.bName)
    theForm.Label1(1).Caption = _
        theResourceFile.loadString(eResourceIds.bURL)
    theForm.Text1 = theBusiness.MyName
    theForm.Show
End Sub
```

That's it. If everything went okay, you have now successfully created a resource file class. Coincidentally, this ResourceFile class is part of the general File Operations Subsystem discussed on Day 17.

Summary

This chapter covers many essential tactics for designing and implementing objects in the Graphical User Interface Subsystem. You learned modeling techniques for GUIs, the encapsulation of data presentation into a separate class and the classes in the subsystem. Finally, you became familiar with some ideas behind ergonomics and the internationalization with resource files. Tomorrow, you learn how to implement the Graphical User Interface Subsystem.

Q&A

Q True or False: Designing graphical user interfaces is more a function of ergonomics and human factors research than object-oriented programming.

A True.

Q What is the benefit of creating a graphical user interface mechanism or subsystem?

A Creating such a mechanism or subsystem helps to decouple the form from the actual business class, which maximizes the chance of reuse of your classes and forms by promoting independence among these objects.

Q What artifact from your project is useful in creating the foundation for your GUI functionality?

A Developing a good graphical user interface requires that you, at least, review your use cases.

Q What class of objects controls the interaction between a form and a business class?

A A form controller class such as `FormController`.

Q What's the name of the class whose responsibility is to encapsulate the common functionality of buttons on a form?

A `FormOperations`.

Workshop

The workshop includes quiz questions to help gauge your grasp of the material. You will find the answers to this quiz in Appendix A, "Answers." Even if you feel that you understand the concepts presented here, you should work through the quiz. The last section contains exercises to help reinforce your learning.

Quiz

1. What are some benefits of scenario scripts?

2. What design pattern is useful for implementing the undo operations for an Undo button?

3. What are some negative aspects of naming buttons *OK* and *Cancel*?

4. What are the main requirements of an undo operation?

Exercises

1. Open a new project in Visual Basic. Create a form with two labels and two text boxes that correspond to the CompanyName and CompanyAddress properties of a Company class you create. Create a form controller class that controls the flow of information between the form and the Company business class.

2. Using the project in exercise 1, implement an Undo button and its underlying undo operations. Use the Memento example for assistance.

11

DAY 12

The Graphical User Interface Subsystem: An Example

Day 11, "The Graphical User Interface Subsystem: A Primer," lays the foundation for understanding how to implement the Graphical User Interface Subsystem. This chapter goes into more detail, continuing with the Samsona Bank Teller System example. In particular, you will learn

- Practical guidelines for implementing the graphical user interface (GUI)
- Designing the Visual Basic form with a corresponding class
- Designing control interaction through forms
- Using the Facade design pattern
- Incorporating into the Samsona Bank Teller System example

Review of the Practical Guidelines for Implementing the Graphical User Interface

Your client, the Second Bank of Carrollton, has repeatedly emphasized the importance of, as the branch manager puts it, "easy-to-use windows and shortcut keys." The branch manager has stressed, "We don't want our bank customers waiting too long to open a new account or to engage in any bank transaction." She expects her tellers to be in front of the computer more than 70% of the time. Prolonged use of the older legacy system has produced complaints of eye soreness and headaches due to the monochrome dumb terminal and of stiffness in fingers and joints from excessive keystrokes. She hopes that mouse clicks and, if possible, wizards will greatly minimize the keystrokes and the need to look at the monitor for lengthy periods.

You had a hunch that the graphical user interface usability requirements might be a moderate effort, and you were correct. To be safe, you review the practical guidelines you learned on Day 11:

- Expect to consume at least a third of your project schedule designing the forms and making them reasonably usable.
- Properly place the data entry controls in the order that users expect.
- At every opportunity, be sure to set the tab stop values of each form object.
- Labels should be captioned clearly so that the user doesn't have to guess what a data entry field means.
- Make sure the user doesn't have to scroll a form full of too many controls.
- If your users normally enter standard units of measurement such as miles (mi.), kilometers (km.), and so on, or other standards such as Street (St.) or Road (Rd.), Mr. or Mrs. or Ms., and megahertz (MHz), try to accommodate them by auto-populating them, structuring them into masks, or providing a drop-down list of these options.
- Make calculate fields read-only.

Designing the Visual Basic Form with a Corresponding Class

After talking with the branch manager, you're ready to design the forms you need for the application. You remember that the fundamental requirements for the forms are reflected in the use cases. The list of use cases you examine are as follows:

- Deposit New Funds
- Open an Account
- Withdraw Funds
- Close an Account
- Canceling a Transaction
- Processing Funds Transaction

Assessing the exact forms to design is usually difficult for most Visual Basic applications you develop. It is common to have one form per use case. However, some use cases are used by others. This means that if Use Case A has a Form A and uses Use Case B, assuming Use Case B has a Form B, there would need to be a command button on Form A whose controller invokes a method on the controller of Form B in order to show Form B.

Every application has an implied use of the system for starting up the system and shutting it down. Although you can certainly have formal use cases for these business tasks, scenario scripts are acceptable. Ignore the script for shutting down the application for the Bank example. The scenario script for starting the application is as follows:

1. From the desktop, choose the application icon.
2. Initialize global object variables.
3. Display the main form.

Notice step 3. When you document your use cases, you will seldom mention any kind of main form, just business processes. Nevertheless, as is the case with all GUI applications, the user wants all major business processes supported in the application to be instantly accessible when the application starts. For the Bank example, your startup form will be an MDI form. Given this, you come up with the set of forms in Table 12.1.

12

TABLE 12.1. THE INITIAL SET OF FORMS FOR THE SAMSONA BANK TELLER SYSTEM.

Form Name	Caption
frmDeposit	Deposit New Funds
frmOpenAccount	Open an Account
frmWithdraw	Withdraw Funds
frmCloseAccount	Close an Account
frmCancelTransaction	Cancel a Transaction
frmCheckAccountStatus	Check Status of Account
frmMDI	Samsona Bank Teller System

Except for the MDI form, frmMDI, and the forms frmCancelTransaction and frmCheckAccountStatus, each of these forms has the Done and Undo buttons. The forms frmCancelTransaction and frmCheckAccountStatus have only a Done button.

frmCancelTransaction has the field List of Transactions. frmCheckAccountStatus has the field Combo List of Accounts by Account Number (user selects one) and the field Status.

The MDI form, frmMDI, has a menu that will also invoke the methods of every controller class. Every controller's showForm() method must have a corresponding menu item because use cases in a GUI-based system are executed through each form. Because you later discover that the MDI form can access several controllers, you create a class, MDIController.

You probably noticed that the use case Processing Funds Transaction doesn't have any forms associated with it. This is intentional because this use case requires special attention. This use case is triggered by changes in the state of a transaction. For instance, when the teller enters all the required information for opening an account, the teller clicks a Done or Submit button. This stimulus triggers a change in state of the account-opening transaction, from something like New to In Process. Let's reexamine the use-case description.

> The application prompts the teller for the account number. When the teller provides the account number, the application verifies that the account is still active and prompts the teller to verify that the customer is authorized to deposit to or withdraw funds from the account. If so, the application displays details about the account, including the customer's full name, Social Security number, account status, and account balance. The teller enters the amount of the transaction and applies it. The application persists the transaction to the account repository.

> If the customer isn't authorized to deposit money in or withdraw money from the account, the application notifies the teller. Perform the use case Canceling a Transaction.

> If the amount being deposited exceeds $10,000 in cash, the application notifies the bank teller that the amount exceeds the federally mandated limit regarding such cash transactions. The application then presents to the bank teller the required cash deposit record form online, transferring the information from the application. When the bank teller completes reviewing the form, the bank teller indicates to the application that the form is correct. The form is printed out for the customer's signature.

> If the deposit is in the form of a check, the teller notifies the application. The application validates the policy for the deposit and informs the teller to notify the customer

that the funds won't be available for 10 business days. After the teller enters the amount of the deposit, the application applies the deposit to the account in a temporary balance separate from the regular balance, until the funds' availability date has been reached. The application persists the deposit transaction to the account repository.

If the application discovers that the account has been frozen by the government, the application notifies the teller. Perform the use case Canceling a Transaction.

To determine the forms needed for this use case, look for clues about displaying information to the user or prompting the user for some information. Also, you might find clues that suggest that the user needs to be updated with the current state of processing. (Fortunately, you covered this requirement with frmCheckAccountStatus.)

The first paragraph is a generic description of transactions that are processed. Because depositing and withdrawing funds have similar tasks, they were encapsulated generically in this use case. This is further justification for the frmMDI form. In the second sentence, you read that "the application. . . *prompts* the teller to verify that the customer is authorized to deposit to or withdraw funds from the account." Aha! This requirement isn't incorporated into our list of forms. The application must prompt the user about something. If you study this enough, you see that this is basically a message box. Given a controller class for this use case, TransactionProcessor, you need the following method:

displayAuthMessage()

This is short for *display authorization message to teller, reminding him or her to make sure the user has valid identification*. Use the Visual Basic MsgBox command to display the incoming message.

Reading further, if the customer is authorized to make a transaction, "The application displays details about the account, including the customer's full name, Social Security number, account status, and account balance." Now you need an Account Detail form. The code name of this form is frmAccountDetail. The fields on this form include

- First Name (lblAccountDetail(0), txtAccountDetail(0))
- Last Name (lblAccountDetail(1), txtAccountDetail(1))
- Social Security Number (lblAccountDetail(2), txtAccountDetail(2))
- Account Status (lblAccountDetail(3), txtAccountDetail(3))
- Account Balance (lblAccountDetail(4), txtAccountDetail(4))

To keep this example simple, ignore other customer attributes such as address, phone number, and those with which you're probably already familiar. Next, you read that "if the customer isn't authorized to deposit money in or withdraw money from the account, the application *notifies* the teller." Because this notification follows a similar pattern to the one encapsulated in the method, `displayAuthMessage`, use the same method with the following modification:

```
displayAuthMessage(argMessage As String)
```

where `argMessage` is the text of the message you want to display. The two possible values for this argument, then, are

1. Make sure the user has valid identification, and match the name and Social Security number against the same information in the account detail.

2. The customer isn't authorized to make this transaction. Canceling transaction.

The next paragraph deals with a cash deposit exceeding the $10,000 limit. When this transaction state is achieved, the application must display a message, `Cash deposit is over $10,000. Please fill out the Cash Deposit Record.` Reuse `displayAuthMessage` but rename it to `displayMessage` to accommodate this kind of message display. When the user clicks the Done button on the message box, the application needs to display the online Cash Deposit Record form, `frmCashDepositRecord`. Although you don't have the fields of this form in the use case, you recall that your user said the form has to include the information in the Account Detail form as well as the bank's ABA (American Bankers Association) number, which is 999099990.

In the next paragraph, the application is required to prompt the teller to inform the customer that for check deposits, the funds won't be available for 10 business days. The message for the `displayMessage` method is

> Notify customer that the check(s) deposited require 10 business days before funds are available.

Finally, in the last paragraph, the application is required to notify the teller if the account being accessed has been frozen by the government. The message for the `displayMessage` method is

> Notify the customer that the account has been frozen by the government.

To discover the other forms you need, you should analyze the remaining use cases and other artifacts that might indicate the need for specific forms. A list of the remaining forms needed for the Samsona Bank Teller System is as follows:

```
frmMaintainBankProducts
frmMaintainCustomer
frmMaintainAccount
frmMaintainUsers
frmMaintainWorkgroups
```

Table 12.2 shows the fields (each of which requires a text box and a label) and buttons for each of these forms.

TABLE 12.2. FORMS NEEDED FOR THE SAMSONA BANK TELLER SYSTEM.

Form	Field	Button
frmMaintainBankProducts	Product Name	Done
	Combo List of Product Types (Checking, Savings, Investment, Credit)	Add New Product
	Product ID Number	Modify
		Delete
		List of Existing Products
frmMaintainCustomer	First Name	Done
	Last Name	Add New Customer
	Social Security Number	Modify
	Customer Status	Delete
frmMaintainAccount	ID Number	Done
	Status	Get List
	Balance	Add New Account
	Product Number	Modify
	Customer Number	Delete
	List of Existing Accounts (when requested)	
frmMaintainUsers	First Name	Done
	Last Name	Add New User
	ID Number	Modify
	User Status	Delete
	Phone Number	

continues

12

TABLE 12.2. CONTINUED

Form	Field	Button
frmMaintainUsers (cont.)	Grid of Assigned Workgroups (ID, Name, Description, Department Number, Manager, Assigned Role (if any))	
	List of workgroups from which to choose a workgroup	
	List of roles from which to choose a role	
frmMaintainWorkgroups	Workgroup Name	Done
	ID Number	New Workgroup
	Workgroup Status	New Role
	Department Number	Modify Workgroup
	Manager	Modify Role
	List of Users	Delete Workgroup
	List of Roles	Delete Role
	List of Users Assigned to Role	Assign User to Role
	List of Workgroups	Unassign User to Role
	Role Name (for new roles, or to modify existing role names)	

The events of each of the GUI controls on each form will have corresponding methods in their respective controllers. For standard events based on clicking a text, grid, list, or label control, FormOperations will handle processing them. Examples include maximum length of text (default to 255 characters for some controls), date formatting, and so on. However, if clicking a text, grid, list, or label control requires processing that is not standard, such as autopopulating a list of bank products, the form's controller needs to have a meaningful method to handle this responsibility. If you're imaginative, you might even create helper classes for your controllers so that these controllers don't grow too large.

Designing Control Interaction per Form

The controller objects for each form are as follows:

```
DepositFunds
OpenAccount
WithdrawFunds
CloseAccount
CancelTransaction
CheckAccountStatus
MDIController
TransactionProcessor
MaintainBankProducts
MaintainCustomer
MaintainAccount
MaintainUsers
MaintainWorkgroups
```

As of this point, the `TransactionProcessor` controller has responsibility for more than one form. Those forms include

```
frmCashDepositRecord
frmAccountDetail
```

Because the number of forms and controller classes is increasing, you should create two new packages in the Visual Modeler model. To create packages, find the User Services package in the package browser in Visual Modeler. Right-click on the package's corresponding folder and choose New Package from the popup menu. Name one package `Forms` and the other `Controllers`.

Figure 12.1 shows the forms that are in the Samsona Bank Teller System. Figure 12.2 shows the controllers for the forms. To keep the example as simple as possible, ignore the forms that have very similar functionality, such as `frmDeposit` and `frmWithdraw`. You could use one form for these processes, but that requires additional logic for differentiating the type of transaction (which can be determined by the `TransactionType` property of the respective business classes).

12

FIGURE 12.1.

A class model representation of the forms.

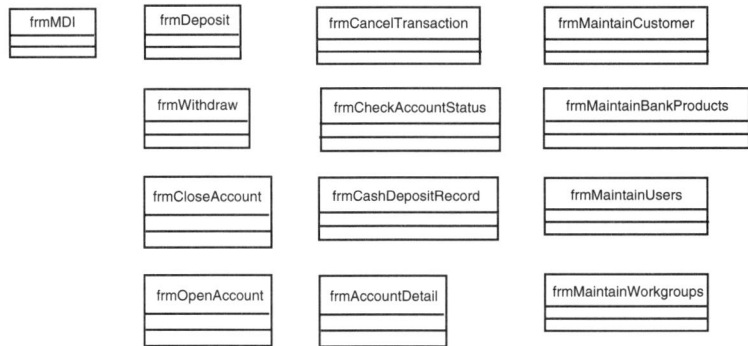

FIGURE 12.2.

A class model representation of the controllers.

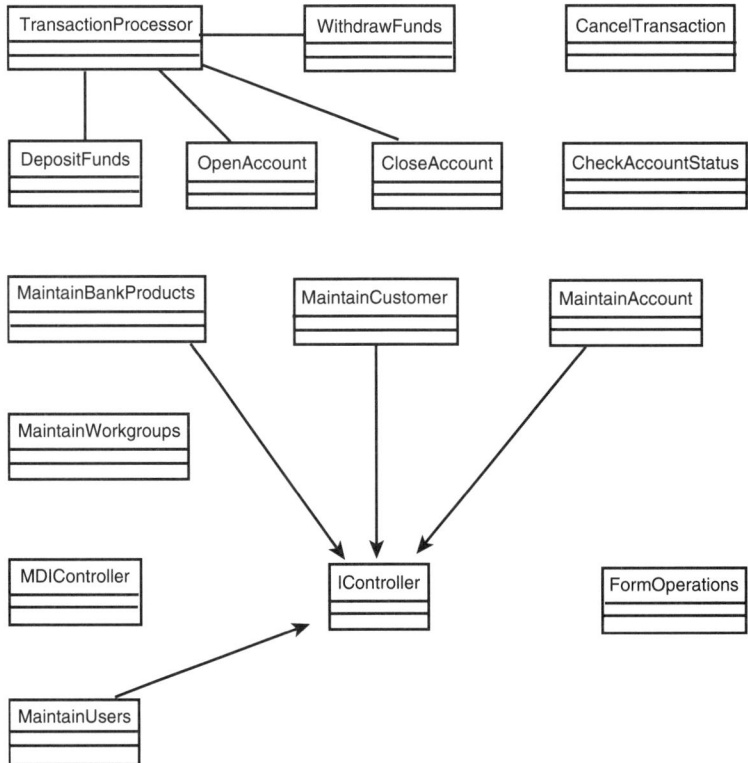

Table 12.3 shows the methods you should now have per controller class.

TABLE 12.3. FORM CONTROLLER CLASSES AND THEIR RESPECTIVE METHODS.

Classname	Methods
DepositFunds	showForm()
	clickedDoneButton()
	clickedUndoButton()
OpenAccount	showForm()
	clickedDoneButton()
	clickedUndoButton()
WithdrawFunds	showForm()
	clickedDoneButton()
	clickedUndoButton()
CloseAccount	showForm()
	clickedDoneButton()
	clickedUndoButton()
CancelTransaction	showForm()
	clickedDoneButton()
CheckAccountStatus	showForm()
	clickedDoneButton()
TransactionProcessor	showForm()
	clickedDoneButton()
	clickedUndoButton()
	getTransactionList()
	getAccountList()
	getCashDepositRecord()
MDIController	AllControllers(n).showForm
	(where n is the current form's controller)
MaintainBankProducts	showForm()
	clickedDoneButton()
	clickedUndoButton()
	clickedDoneButton()
	clickedNewButton()
	clickedModifyButton()
	clickedDeleteButton()
	getProductList()

continues

12

TABLE 12.3. CONTINUED

Classname	Methods
MaintainCustomer	showForm()
	clickedDoneButton()
	clickedDoneButton()
	clickedNewButton()
	clickedModifyButton()
	clickedDeleteButton
MaintainAccount	showForm()
	clickedDoneButton()
	clickedUndoButton()
	clickedDoneButton()
	clickedNewButton()
	clickedModifyButton()
	clickedDeleteButton
	getAccountList()
MaintainUsers	showForm()
	clickedDoneButton()
	clickedDoneButton()
	clickedNewButton()
	clickedModifyButton()
	clickedDeleteButton
	assignToRole()
	assignToWorkgroup()
MaintainWorkgroups	showForm()
	clickedDoneButton()
	clickedDoneButton()
	clickedNewWorkgroupButton()
	clickedModifyWorkgroupButton()
	clickedDeleteWorkgroupButton
	clickedNewRoleButton()
	clickedModifyRoleButton()
	clickedDeleteRoleButton
	getUserList()
	getRoleList()

The code for the methods in Table 12.1 is on the CD-ROM. The interface class, `IController`, abstracts the common methods that many of the controllers implement.

Using the Facade Design Pattern

The Facade design pattern comes from the book *Design Patterns* by Gamma, et. al. This pattern provides a mechanism for better organizing the interfaces between one subsystem and another.

Overview

Facades are just what the name implies. They are like faces between subsystems. To be exact, these faces are interfaces. As you create the Graphical User Interface Subsystem, you need to decouple it from the other subsystems with which it interacts. For the Graphical User Interface Subsystem, controller classes perform this role well. As you should remember, *controller classes* control the flow of events between forms and business/domain classes. Sometimes, the flow of events can originate from more than one form per controller. Such is the case with `TransactionProcessor`. Let's examine this controller in more detail with respect to its role as a complex facade.

Learning How to Implement in Visual Basic

Implementing the Facade design pattern is easy. There's a good chance you, or a developer you know, already use classes in Visual Basic in a facade manner. Essentially, wherever you have two interface classes representing two subsystems that intercommunicate, you can decouple these interface classes by inserting a facade between them.

An Easy Example

In the Bank example, the `TransactionProcessor` controller is a facade between both the `frmCashDepositRecord` and `frmAccountDetail` forms and their respective objects, `CashDepositRecord` and `AccountDetail`.

Figure: Class Model

Figure 12.3 shows the class model involving the `TransactionProcessor` and the Graphical User Interface and Business Rules Subsystems between which it serves as a facade.

12

FIGURE 12.3.

An example of a facade.

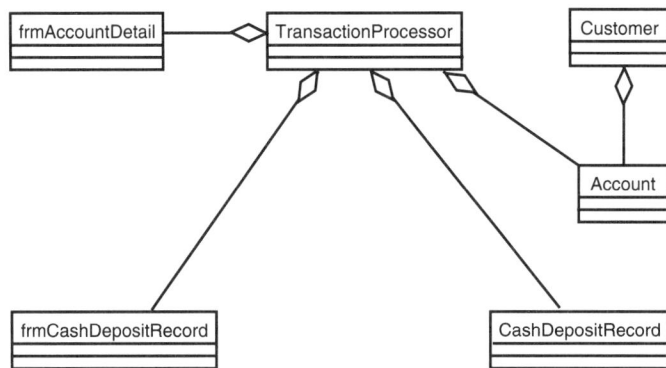

The Customer, Account, and CashDepositRecord classes are part of the Business Rules Subsystem. The two forms are part of the Graphical User Interface Subsystem. TransactionProcessor, then, is not only a controller for the two forms but also, effectively, a facade between the Graphical User Interface Subsystem and the Business Rules Subsystem.

Incorporating into the Samsona Bank Teller System Example

Now that you have completed your controller classes and GUI requirements, you can create the subsystem. You simply need to create the forms in the Visual Basic development environment and generate the code for the controllers in Visual Modeler. The generated code is nothing more than empty classes, methods, and properties. The code listing in the next section shows the code for the Samsona Bank Teller System that includes only the forms and form controllers.

As for the forms, use the described fields and buttons in this chapter to create them. The forms listed in the subsequent text will give you an idea of mapping the use cases in the continuing Bank example into the visual presentation that your user sees. The complete list of forms is as follows:

frmDeposit (Figure 12.4)
frmOpenAccount (Figure 12.5)
frmWithdraw (Figure 12.6)
frmCloseAccount (Figure 12.7)
frmCancelTransaction (Figure 12.8)
frmCheckAccountStatus (Figure 12.9)
frmMDI (Figure 12.10)
▼ frmAccountDetail (Figure 12.11)

▼   frmCashDepositRecord (Figure 12.12)
    frmMaintainBankProducts (Figure 12.13)
    frmMaintainCustomer (Figure 12.14)
    frmMaintainAccount (Figure 12.15)
    frmMaintainUsers (Figure 12.16)
    frmMaintainWorkgroups (Figure 12.17)

Figures 12.4 through 12.17 illustrate the forms you need.

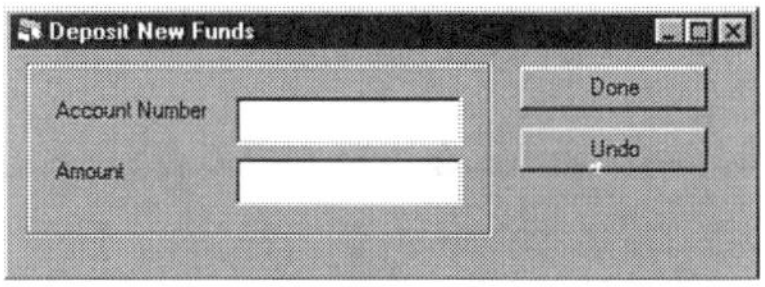

FIGURE 12.4.

The frmDeposit *form.*

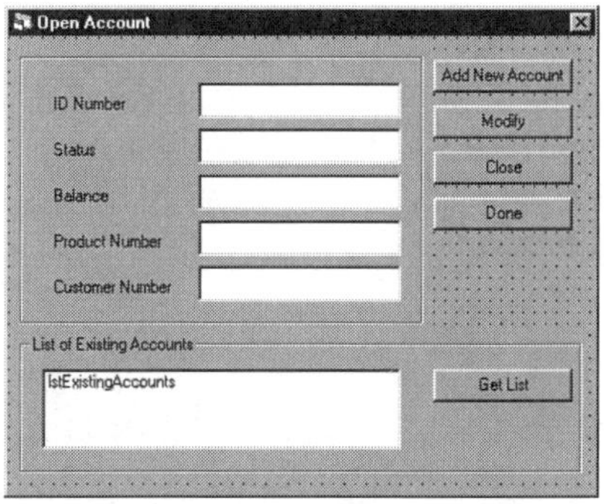

FIGURE 12.5.

The frmOpenAccount *form.*

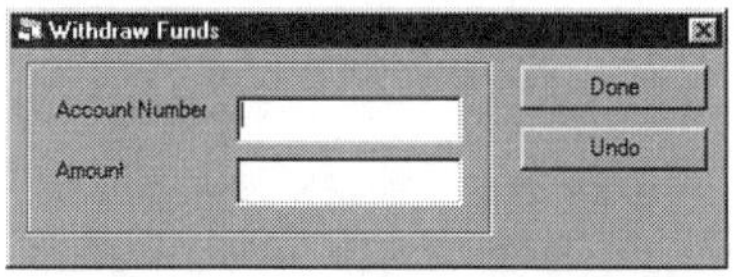

FIGURE 12.6.

The frmWithdraw *form.*

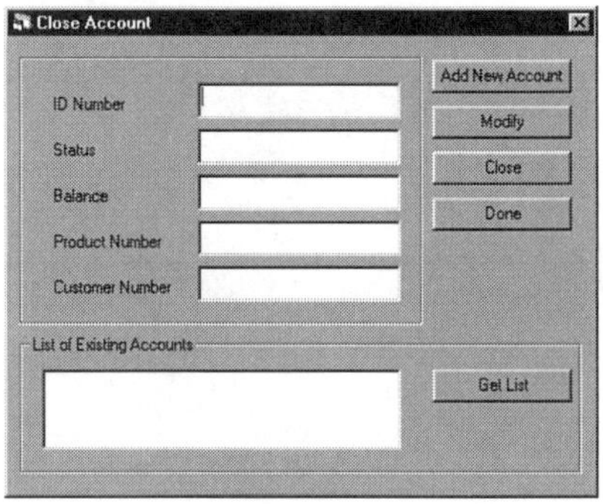

12

FIGURE 12.7.

The frmCloseAccount *form.*

▼

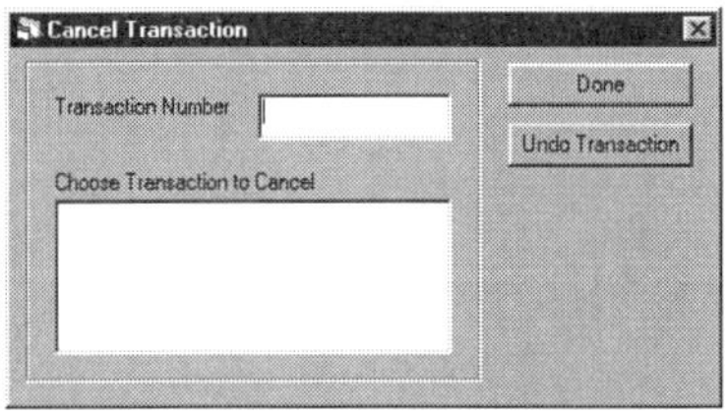

▼ FIGURE **12.8.**

The frmCancel-
Transaction
form.

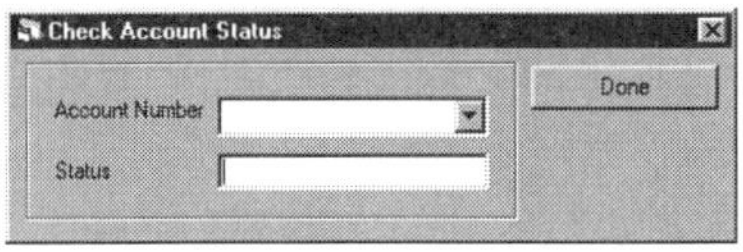

FIGURE **12.9.**

The
frmCheckAccount-
Status form.

FIGURE **12.10.**

The frmMDI form.

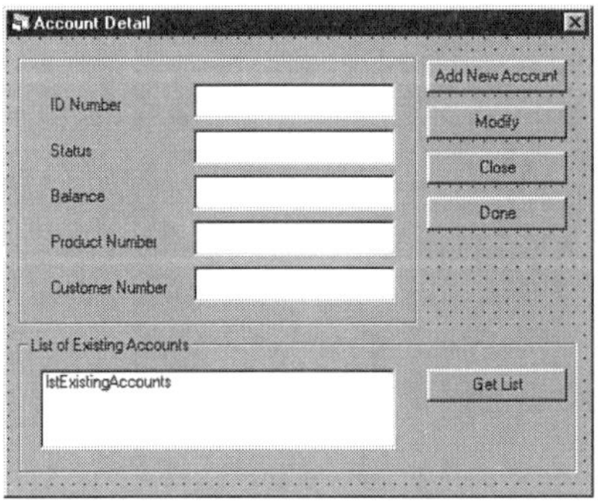

FIGURE **12.11.**

The frmAccount-
Detail form.

▼

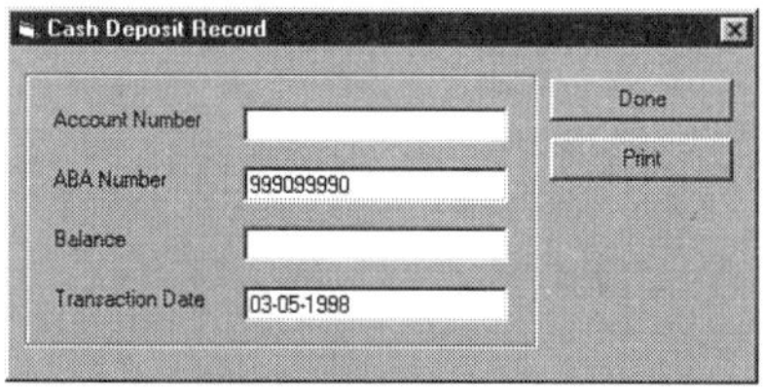

FIGURE 12.12.

The frmCash-DepositRecord *form.*

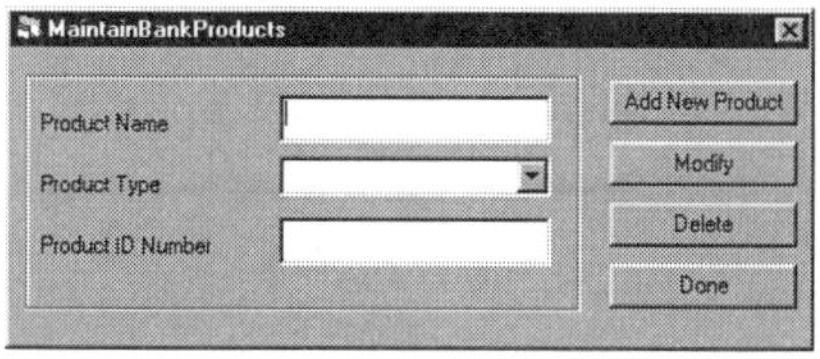

FIGURE 12.13.

The frm-MaintainBank-Products *form.*

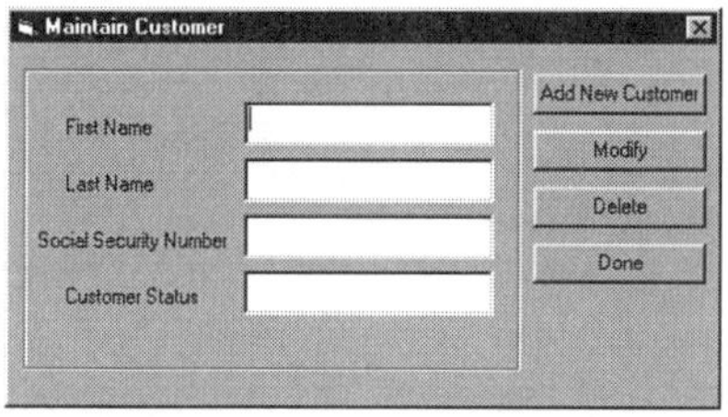

FIGURE 12.14.

The frm-Maintain-Customer *form.*

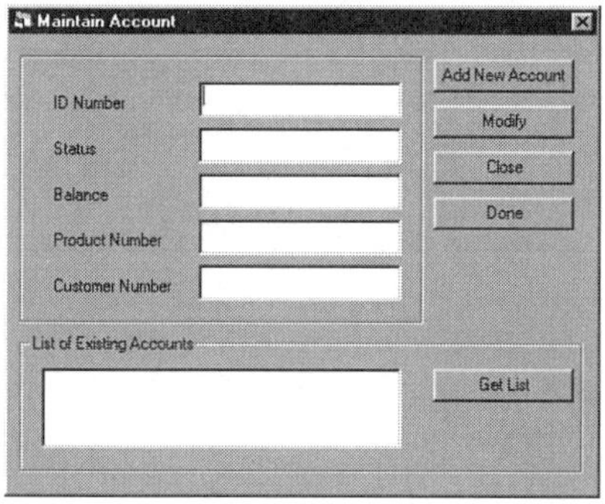

FIGURE 12.15.

The frm-Maintain-Account *form.*

12

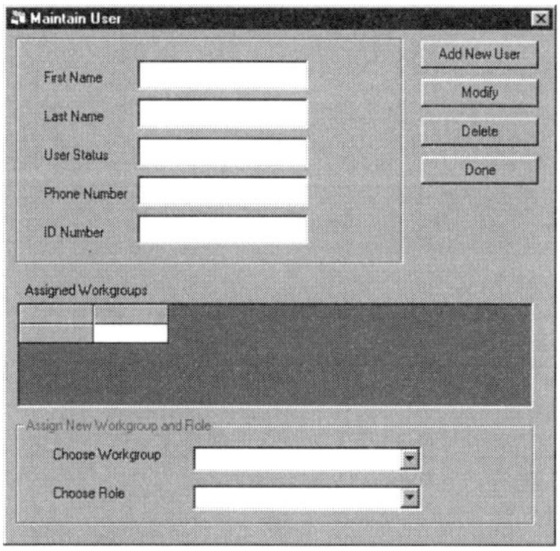

▼ **FIGURE 12.16.**

The frm-
MaintainUsers
form.

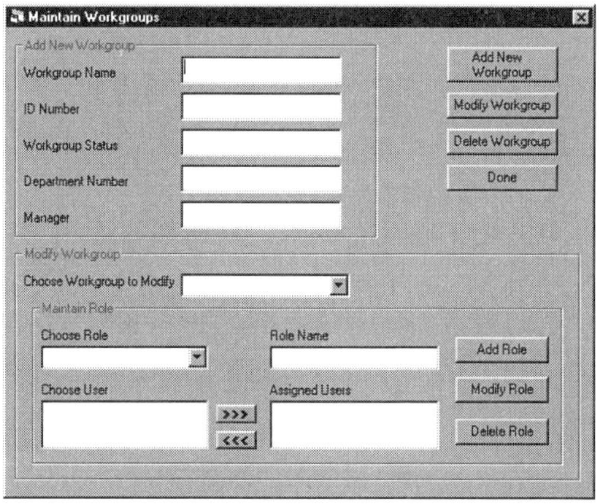

FIGURE 12.17.

The frm-
MaintainWork-
groups *form.*

The menu for frmMDI can be implemented as a menu array. However, you can implement
the menu in any way that suits your environment. Use the following items:

Account

Open New Account

View Account

Check Status

Make Deposit

▼   Make Withdrawal

▼   Save

Close Account

End

Customer

Setup

Check Status

View

Tools

Maintain Bank Products

Maintain Users

Maintain Workgroups

Create Cash Deposit Record

Report

View Online

Print Account Detail

Print Customer Detail

Printer Setup

Because you are working with only the Graphical User Interface Subsystem, each menu item will contain only calls to show forms via each form's controller. In the subsequent chapters, you'll incorporate more subsystems that give additional functionality to our
▲   sample application. Finally, add a `StatusBar` control to `frmMDI`.

Summary

This chapter provides you with the practical fundamentals necessary to create an effective Graphical User Interface Subsystem. In particular, you learned some guidelines for implementing the graphical user interface. You also learned how to design the Visual Basic form with a corresponding controller class, including treatment of the interaction between the two objects. You became familiar with the Facade design pattern, which is a role that can be played by both the form and the controller class. Finally, you received detailed directions for incorporating the Graphical User Interface Subsystem into the Samsona Bank Teller System Example. The remaining chapters add functionality to the application, one subsystem at a time, given that the Graphical User Interface Subsystem is already in place. The code for this chapter is lengthy; you can obtain a copy of it from the CD-ROM.

For tomorrow's lesson, you learn about the first in a series of subsystems, the important Workgroup and User Security Subsystem. You will discover how to implement some security features and sample code for encrypting passwords and how to make your application architecture reflect the roles and workgroups in your users' domain.

Q&A

Q How much time can you reasonably expect to spend designing the Graphical User Interface Subsystem?

A Expect to consume at least a third of your project schedule designing forms and making them reasonably usable.

Q How should data entry controls be placed on a form?

A Place the data entry controls in the order that users expect. You can obtain clues about this order from interviewing your users and/or analyzing artifacts from the domain from which the user will input the data. This includes paper documents that are the source of the data being entered.

Q What is a potential problem with autotabbing from field to field?

A Autotabbing can cause a slight delay if the user realizes he or she made a mistake in the preceding field.

Q What is a possible solution to having a scrollable form full of controls?

A Instead of forms that are scrollable, use wizards—either the Wizard Manager or a customized wizard. If users have to input large amounts of records that represent pure data entry apart from interviewing their customers, try to use grids for such data entry.

Q What kinds of information can be autopopulated after the user enters data in a field?

A If your users normally enter standard units of measurement such as miles (mi.), kilometers (km.), and so on, or other standards such as Street (St.) or Road (Rd.), Mr. or Mrs. or Ms., and megahertz (MHz), try to accommodate them by either autopopulating them, structuring them into masks, or providing a drop-down list of these options. Do the same for date and time units.

Q **What is one of the most important sources of information in the creation of the Graphical User Interface Subsystem?**

A Use cases. Remember that the fundamental requirements for the forms are reflected in the use cases.

Q **What is the benefit of a FormOperations class?**

A It processes standard events based on clicking a text, grid, list, or label control.

Workshop

The workshop includes quiz questions to help gauge your grasp of the material. You'll find the answers to this quiz in Appendix A, "Answers." Even if you feel that you understand the concepts presented here, you should work through the quiz. The last section contains exercises to help reinforce your learning.

Quiz

1. Describe one way you can design the form to automatically tab to the next data entry field?

2. How should you treat calculated fields with regard to user data entry?

3. What's the best way to document the steps necessary to start up an application?

4. What is the relationship between a GUI control event and a controller class method?

5. What is a way to break up a large controller class?

6. What two packages should you create in Visual Modeler to help you separate forms from controller classes?

7. What's the purpose of the Facade pattern?

8. Can a controller class be responsible for more than one form?

9. How does one form display another form?

Exercises

1. Create a method in each controller class to center the forms for which they are responsible.

2. Create a class that each controller class calls in order to center the form(s) it owns. (Hint: Create a centerForm for this class. Invoke the class's centerForm method from each controller class's Initialize event.)

3. Create a controller class for the frmCashDepositRecord form. This requires that you modify the TransactionProcessor controller class.

12

DAY 13

The Workgroup and User Security Subsystem

This chapter presents you with an overview of the Workgroup and User Security Subsystem. In particular, you'll learn about the following topics:

- The purpose of this subsystem
- Security issues for Internet and desktop applications
- The classes in the subsystem, as well as their methods, properties, arguments, and returns
- Practical guidelines for implementing the Workgroup and User Security Subsystem
- How to incorporate the subsystem into the Samsona Bank Teller System example
- The subsystem code listings for the Samsona Bank Teller System example

Overview of the Workgroup and User Security Subsystem

If you develop software for business, whether on site at your client companies or as a commercial firm, your application needs to address logging in users and the enforcement of varying access rights based on their job functions. In addition, due to the proliferation of family-unfriendly organizations and individuals on the Internet, parents expect the software you develop for them to allow them to restrict certain sites from their curious children. This, too, requires that you enforce a level of access for the parents that is different from the children. The Workgroup and User Security Subsystem helps you design and implement your application's security needs. Figure 13.1 shows a typical model for this subsystem.

FIGURE 13.1.

The Workgroup and User Security model.

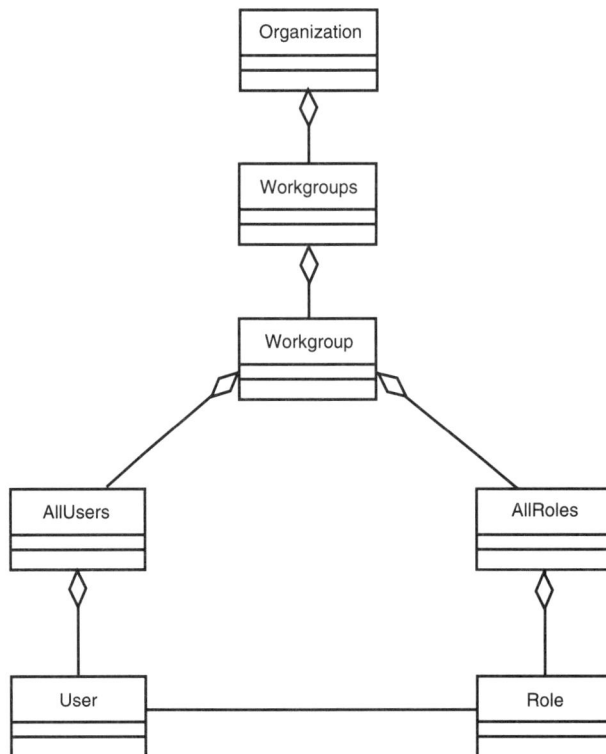

Planning for security encompasses several areas of potential weaknesses. One such weakness is where buggy software at the server site inadvertently permits external hackers to issue sensitive commands to server applications. Such unauthorized access can ultimately destroy the server, which can cost a company not only lost productivity, but potentially millions of dollars in publicly available trade secrets. Individual users can lose privacy in the form of exposed credit card numbers, Social Security numbers, and bank account numbers not only on the Internet, but in any company that processes sensitive financial information about millions of people.

Other security concerns include the interception of very sensitive information from the user's machine to the server machine, configuration information leaking from the server that a hacker could use to break into and possibly mimic the host, unauthorized access to business Web pages where the hacker could edit them, and unauthorized access to personal Web pages that could be as libelous as having your phone number written on the wall of a public bathroom. It is definitely worthwhile to hire capable, competent network administrators who are experienced in setting up Internet and intranet site servers. It is also advisable to encrypt passwords and other vital information that passes along an organization's network.

One reason that may lend itself to the need for tedious Internet security planning is the fact that the Internet Protocol, commonly referred to as *IP*, is an open, nonproprietary, Internet-working protocol. All those words simply mean that when something goes wrong with IP security, there is no one company to blame (so you can't blame big software companies like Oracle or Microsoft). Of course, the Transmission Control Protocol (TCP) supplements IP by providing end-to-end reliability over a full-duplex connection.

You should be aware of two areas of network security. *Transmission security* centers on the flow of data across a network. You implement this kind of security at various network access points, such as encoded transmission devices and modems that are password-protected. *Access security* tries to control user access to a server's software, hardware, and system services. You filter access control at three layers of the OSI reference model: application, network, and data link. Test the system for security leaks and educate users on the importance of maintaining security before going into production with it. Again, make it a habit to truly encrypt passwords after users enter them into your application.

NEW TERM *Transmission security* is the level of protection given to the flow of data across a network.

NEW TERM *Access security* is the level of control of user access to a server's software, hardware, and system services.

13

Understanding the Purpose of This Subsystem

The Workgroup and Security Subsystem enforces the security of your application and makes sure that users are only able to do the business tasks they are supposed to do. The `Security` classes manage security with an encryption algorithm based on the masterful SHA-1 encryption algorithm based on the National Institute of Standards and Technology and implemented in VB5 by Ken Miller. The code is modified here to be encapsulated in objects for better maintainability and reusability.

> **Note**
>
> For more information on the National Institute of Standards and Technology, visit its Web site at `http://www.nist.gov`. Ken Miller's code was presented in the February 1998 issue of the *Visual Basic Programmer's Journal*.

The topic of workgroup design and administration is quite complex and has filled several books and dozens of papers. In this chapter, you learn the basics of workgroup structure and simple workflow concepts, complete with classes that correspond to the Second Bank of Carrollton example.

> You might avoid staying up all night trying to figure out a 100% foolproof algorithm for solving all of the world's corporate network security concerns. As long as humans remain imperfect, we can't totally rid the Internet world of every virus problem for every computer system. Numerous cookbooks are uploaded to the Web on a regular basis that teach people how to put together a devastating, "undetectable" virus. Just as there are not perfect antivirus solutions, there are not perfect viruses, as well. Viruses are versatile, and their authors know how to plant them on any programmable machine. Computers that have applications that can interact with and even modify other applications are vulnerable to viruses. These viruses can easily spread between different users' applications. As you've probably already guessed, no computer is safe. That's the reality.

You should keep users' access to server system programs by implementing *access controls*. Using such controls at every access checkpoint helps to confine virus opportunities to the time window of user authorization. Keep in mind, though, that the broader the access control implementation, the higher the cost of that security policy. Antivirus software helps somewhat but is not always successful, nor is it nearly mathematically perfect.

NEW TERM *Access control* is an object whose responsibility it is to secure any access checkpoint, such as the client application, the request for remote data from a database server, request for services from remote server objects, and so on.

Most viruses are harmless in that they only display social messages or, at most, crash your computer system. Harmful viruses are those that delete files or stay resident and eventually render your machine useless unless you reformat your hard disk.

Like human viruses, computer viruses spread as you and I use our computers regularly. Viruses that are time-sensitive are sometimes easy to circumvent: simply reset your computer's clock. Of course, if you don't know the virus is resident, you're unlucky. That's what makes viruses potentially devastating for companies. What can you do about this? At the risk of sounding pessimistic, not much. As long as human nature remains unpredictable, expect viruses to live on in cyberspace. Nonetheless, although it's difficult to prevent every virus or security violation, you can help prevent potential hackers from grabbing passwords. This subsystem has an encryption algorithm for ciphering a password.

Understanding Security Issues for Internet Applications

As mentioned earlier, if you develop software for families, your application will need to keep their young children from accessing certain Web sites that might be harmful to them. Of course, developing applications to keep track of young children doesn't compare to developing an application for a large organization where security violations can cost millions of dollars.

For instance, if you fail to track how long a user is not actively interacting with your application, the session may be vulnerable to unauthorized passersby if the user is in fact away from his or her desk. A session unchecked can also leave the intranet environment vulnerable to spying applications that might continuously poll for unattended sessions. For Web-based applications, using a method for checking unattended sessions can help to prevent such snooping. You could create a class called `SessionAuditor`. It would have a method, `trackNonUse`, that uses a `Variant` argument, `argMessage`, to allow for polymorphic calls. For a Web application, the method implementation would look like the following:

13

```
Public Sub trackNonUse(argMessage As Variant)
    Static bAuditActivated As Boolean, lElapsedTime As Long
    Const TIME_TO_CLOSE_SESSION = 900000 '15 mins
    bAuditActivated = False
    Do
        lElapsedTime = lElapsedTime + 1
        If lElapsedTime = TIME_TO_CLOSE_SESSION Then
            bAuditActivated = True
        End If
    Loop Until bAuditActivated = True
    'Insert code here to shut down session

    lElapsedTime = 0
End Sub
```

The variable bAuditActivated is a boolean flag that represents the change in state from an attended application to an unattended application. It is set to False so that, when you invoke it from a text box's change event or any mouse event, it is reset; that is, the occurrence of one of these events means that the application is not unattended. The constant TIME_TO_CLOSE_SESSION holds the maximum amount of time (in milliseconds) before the closing of a session. You could use this same method for desktop applications as well (although a Timer control might be better).

In addition, companies expect your applications, if deployed on the Web, to have some security mechanisms built in them to

- Allow only paying customers into restricted areas on the site geared for premium content
- Allow only employees of the company to access the Web site remotely
- Completely disallow general, unrestricted access

Understanding Security Issues for Desktop Applications

When an application is to be deployed on several desktops, security concerns are less drastic than with the Internet, but are nonetheless important. Keep in mind that security threats do not necessarily come from subtle viruses that may hide in your system. Hackers have the ability to launch offensive attacks against Web-based applications such as your browser or email system. One Australian company, which custom designs email systems, had the misfortune of having a security fix for its email system reverse engineered by hackers. The hackers used the information in the code to strengthen their hack attacks.

As with Web applications, unattended application sessions are also a potential security problem for desktop applications. For these desktop applications, you would enforce unattended session policies by, among other ways, using the `Timer` control in conjunction with placing code in the events associated with text box changes and mouse clicks. As with the Web application, you could implement the same class, `SessionAuditor`.

Sabotage is also a problem. Disgruntled employees will exploit weaknesses and errors in your application to get revenge on a boss or for some slight they experienced. Further, forcing users to use a system that is either flawed or, for reasons unknown to you, undesirable, only exaggerates the problem. In a paper titled "A Case of Sabotage," by Peter Bickford, from Human Interface, the author captures the sentiment of some users of workgroup-oriented, corporate applications as follows:

> Even if you assign every user in your company a login ID and tell them they're absolutely required to use the system, you're unlikely to get the results you want if users aren't also convinced of the benefit (to *them*) of following your directives. At best, you'll end up with users who do only the minimum required of them and never use the full capabilities of the system. Worse, they may use passive resistance to thwart the system: "Well, gee, I keep *meaning* to enter my project information, but I've been too busy with more important things." Some users may even engage in acts of outright sabotage, such as padding the figures they enter in the system or deliberately blocking out all the free space in their workgroup calendar to prevent others from scheduling their time.

You can minimize security threats posed by sabotage by, at a minimum, including users in the design of the architecture of the system, and in particular the behavior of the various workgroups. Without effective executive sponsorship, however, such efforts may be difficult.

Concepts of Workgroups and Workflow

Workflow automation involves the coordination of often complex business processes. The simplest business processes that you may automate with Visual Basic may require much flexibility as your clients' infrastructure changes dynamically, requiring an adaptation to changing conditions. Whether you're developing a Visual Basic application for a large enterprise on site at the company or as a commercial operation that markets and sells software systems, the modeling of any workgroup architecture with workflows is never an easy task. In the most sophisticated multinational corporations, workflow architects and administrators have to concern themselves with issues involving the following:

- Parallel routing of tasks between workgroups (and roles within those workgroups)
- Evolving workgroup structures

13

- Tasks that are queued per workgroup and role
- Rolling back problem processes and tasks
- Email and messaging facilities such as the Internet/intranet or Messaging Application Programming Interface (MAPI)
- Assigning users to roles and workgroups
- Tracking the costs and time delays associated with each task, totaled per role and workgroup
- The order sequence for when one workgroup is dependent on another for the overall product to be delivered
- How many workflow servers to have in operation at any given time in case one server goes down (threatening the workflow between workgroups)

Structuring workgroups and designing the flow of work between them involves lots of business rules and triggering events (which are conveniently supported in Visual Basic classes). In this lesson, I won't cover lots of business rules because a separate lesson, Day 15, "The Business Rules Subsystem," deals with business rules. Here, you simply want to capture the basic mechanics of the interactions between workgroups and roles.

Each use case has a sequence of events associated with it. These sequences of events are, in effect, tasks. If you think about it, everything you do at work for which your employer is really paying you is in essence a part of a bigger workflow. Imagine for a moment that you've just been hired by an investment firm. The bank would have a process called Acclimate New Employee that has a sequence of events associated.

The investment firm uses a mix of manual and automated processes to process you in as a new employee. The hiring manager triggers the New Employee on Board event that routes forms related to 401(k) and other benefits to the Human Resources workgroup. In parallel (parallel routing), a message is sent to the Security workgroup so that an employee badge can be made for you upon your passing a background check. Also in parallel, the Information Services and Computer Security workgroup receives a form from the hiring manager with your personal information so that you can get authenticated to the proper computers and have an email account. By now, you probably get the picture. The general steps involved in a typical task within a workflow include the following:

- Choose and start an associated task, which can include starting a software application.
- Implement the work for that task, which can include creating one or more records or documents.
- Delegate the work to the proper role or workgroup.

Delegating work should be automated as you may perform the same task or process often. Each repetition typically involves the same downstream role or workgroup, and it is thus wise to optimize workflows accordingly. However, in the real world, such repetitions occur often because many companies are not working at optimal workflow. This means you have to make adjustments with regards to how to automate the delegation of work. Microsoft Exchange and Lotus Notes are good groupware applications that ease (though not by much) the delegating of work between workgroups.

A workgroup can often be equivalent to a department or business group within an organization, but this is not always necessarily true. A role sometimes is associated with a particular user. However, because the structure of companies changes often, it is generally wise not to tightly couple a workgroup with a traditional department or a role with a user. Workgroups in a workgroup model are not typically hierarchical, though they certainly can encapsulate rules associated with a traditional hierarchy. Roles can be performed by more than one user, and a user can perform more than one role. Any application you design that incorporates any of the concepts of workflow needs the ability to route each task to a specific role instead of an individual user/employee. This separation of concerns between a role and user mitigates the likely risk of a user changing job functions, thus encapsulating your application from such attrition issues.

One of the most important but understated functions of a good workflow solution is the ability to handle exceptions, which are rampant in every organization. When evaluating workflow automation solutions, most users underestimate the complexity of even the simplest business processes and the importance of exception handling.

Explaining all of the complexities of workflow automation and modeling every kind of workgroup structure is beyond the scope of this book. However, the following sections give you some insights into concepts such as

- Workflow Routing
- Workgroup Management
- Task Management

13

Workflow Routing

As suggested in the section "Concepts of Workgroups and Workflow" many, if not most, business processes and tasks are not performed serially. That is, they are not often performed one at a time where one process or task must follow another. Many processes and tasks occur in parallel, with some being done serially as needed. The routing of workflow follows this general pattern.

Parallel and Serial Work Routing

The completion of a sequence of events in a use case typically occurs in parallel with the completion of other independent use cases in order to reduce the cycle time it takes to deliver an end product to some beneficiary. In the case of a bank, that beneficiary is usually the customer. With parallel routing, you don't want to design every organization process or task to be unnecessarily dependent on another.

For instance, among the set of use cases for the Second Bank of Carrollton, a bank teller could perform the use cases Deposit New Funds and Withdraw Funds on behalf of a customer in any order because the performance of one is not dependent on the performance of the other. In the case of the use case Open a New Account, two tasks are involved that can and should occur in parallel: *(a)* verifying the customer's previous checking account histories at all banks and *(b)* verifying if the customer has other accounts with the bank.

 Whether your client wants to design serial or parallel routing of work, you might consider an architecture that allows the client the flexibility of choosing either or both. If the routing is serial, the navigation from one process or task to another is similar to navigating records in a recordset. Consider a single process with three tasks, for instance. This process is the responsibility of one workgroup. Further, assume that the process is fully automated and that messaging between roles in the workgroup are taken care of by some class, WorkMessenger, that hides all the details of sending messages once a task is completed. For your purposes, it will be an empty class that only displays a message box with the message Work has arrived. In Visual Basic, you could design and implement a simplified set of classes as listed in Table 13.1.

TABLE 13.1. Sample classes for WorkMessenger.

Class/Module Name	Notable Member	Description
modWorkflow		A global module that contains declarations used by the classes in the Workgroup and User Security Subsystem.
	eProcess	An Enum that identifies a particular instance of a process in the AllProcesses collection.
	eRole	An Enum that identifies a particular instance of a role in the AllRoles collection.
	eTasks	An Enum that represents the tasks necessary to complete the process.
SomeWorkgroup Proxy		A workgroup class.

Class/Module Name	Notable Member	Description
	startProcess()	A method that delegates the starting of a process to a specific instance of a `Process` object. By simply allocating memory for the `Process` class instance, the process is started.
	endProcess()	A method that delegates the ending of a process to a specific instance of a process object. By simply deallocating memory for the `Process` class instance, the process is ended.
	isProcessComplete	A boolean property that checks to see if a process has completed or not (reads `ProcessState` property of the `SomeProcess` class).
	AllRoles	A property that is a collection of roles.
	AllProcesses	A property that is a collection of processes.
	CurrProcess	A property that represents the current process object.
	CurrRole	A property that represents the current role object.
WorkMessenger		A class that routes work from one workgroup or role to another.
	sendMessage(argMsg)	A simple method that sends a message, `argMsg`, by email to the user assigned to a role that's responsible for the next task in the process's sequence of tasks.
Process		A controller class that represents a process. It is owned by the `SomeWorkgroupProxy` class.
	startProcess()	A method that starts a process. Invoked in `Class_Initialize`.
	endProcess()	A method that ends a process. Invoked in `Class_Terminate`.
	ProcessID	A `String` property that represents the ID of the process.
	ProcessState	A `Byte` property that indicates the state of the process.

continues

13

TABLE 13.1. CONTINUED

Class/Module Name	Notable Member	Description
	CurrTaskID	A String property that represents the ID of the current task. Typically, each task would own some object that represents the unit of work to the user, such as a Visual Basic form or MS Word document.
	startTask()	A method that delegates the actual presentation of the work to the proper role.
	endTask()	A method that delegates the actual ending of the presentation of the work to the proper role. This is a request to roll back a task.
	isCurrTaskComplete	A boolean property that indicates whether a task is complete or not. (You could also get the same information by checking the CurrTaskID property value to see if it changed. However, having an "is" property explicitly set is easier to maintain in code.)
WorkerRole		A type of controller class that is responsible for displaying the unit of work to the role. A role is created only after the user has successfully logged in and each authorized role has been checked.
	arrTaskName	A String array that contains the name of each task performed by the role.
	showTask()	Shows the form for either Form1 or Form2. Uses CurTaskID to get the right form.
	RoleID	A String property that represents the ID of the role.
	AllForms	A private collection of forms the role presents to the user.
ManagerRole		See description for WorkerRole.
	arrTaskName	A String array that contains the name of each task performed by the role.
	showTask()	Shows Form3.
	RoleID	A String property that represents the ID of the role.
	AllForms	A private collection of forms the role presents to the user.

The class `SomeWorkgroupProxy` is the workgroup class for the example. However, notice the suffix `Proxy`. I use this suffix because the actual workgroup component that manages and enforces rules related to a workgroup will typically be housed on a workgroup server. Nonetheless, for simpler systems, you could have these workgroup proxy objects on every client machine at a small client site. Taken together, they would represent a virtual workgroup server without the need for a dedicated, centralized, physical server. Of course, this means that you have to have some map (such as a component diagram) that reminds you of the location and responsibilities of each workgroup proxy.

For a role class, some of the same members are similar to those of other form controllers. Each role class could implement a `showTask()` method that presents the task to the user based on the value of the `CurrTaskID` of the `Process` object. For example, a role could display a Visual Basic form that is particular to a specific role performed by a user. Given this coupling between a role and the form for which a role is responsible, you could add code to disable/enable or to change the visibility of controls on common forms that do not apply to other roles. This makes maintaining the code to control the accessibility of GUI controls much easier. In the example, the `WorkerRole` class will have a collection of forms, indexed by the value of `CurrTaskID` of the `Process` object and the `Enum`, `eTasks`. The `ManagerRole` class does not need such a collection, but for consistency sake, let's incorporate one.

On each form will undoubtedly be GUI controls that, upon interaction with the user, trigger some meaningful event that needs further processing. The most common event you're likely to process is a control's click event. Thus, each form controller tends to have a method, `clickedControl()`, that is an abstract type of method that processes each specialized GUI control click event.

For each form you also would want to display some caption that represents the task being performed by the user. The string array `arrTaskName` would hold the name of each task performed by the role. You'll use the `eTasks` `Enum` to identify each item in the array. Listing 13.1 shows the three `Enum`s in the module, `modWorkflow`.

For the `TaskName` property of Role1, the values are `Do Task1` and `Do Task2`. There are three empty forms, which simply represent the three tasks. Each has a command button named `cmdDone` and captioned `Done`. The startup object for the project is `Sub Main`, which is in the module, `modMain`. Due to the length of the code, you can find it on the CD as part of the Second Bank of Carrollton application.

By no means is the list of classes in Table 13.1 exhaustive of the typically complex workgroup/workflow system. However, you can certainly use it as a starting point for developing such a system. If your environment is not complex at all, you can use these

13

classes with only minor modifications to fit your situation. Just make sure to keep the classes pretty independent of each other by promoting good class interface design.

Dynamic Routing

If you plan to build a sophisticated workflow system, you might implement dynamic routing capabilities in your application. Dynamic routing gives the user the flexibility of adjusting the flow of work based on volatile business events. Changing business conditions at runtime can create the need for adaptability based on constraints your application's administrative users provide. These constraints would be entered through a Visual Basic form and then persisted in a database.

Ad Hoc Routing

Configuring a system for dynamic routing requires that all possible business process changes are known in advance. However, there are some processes that cannot be determined, especially in terms of who the recipient of a given task might be. It is very possible that the task owner is known only when an instance of the process object is in memory during a user session. Programming for ad hoc specification of a recipient may be done with much flexibility. For example, the name of the recipient may be typed in the form at a previous step, or read from a database.

Workgroup Management

Workgroup management involves administering groups of users based on a goal the group must achieve. A goal typically is realized by the completion of one or more tasks in a business process. In particular, workgroup management is concerned with the makeup of dynamic groups, the process owners in those groups, the order in which roles are performed by users, and costing issues related to processes.

Dynamic Workgroups

Your application can give the user the ability to define a workgroup at runtime. This is helpful for those workgroups that neither you or your users knew about as you designed your application. Your user creates the workgroup by

   Providing a name on a form

   Adding users and roles to the workgroup by choosing them from list boxes

   Persisting this information in the database

Your application then notifies the new users of this workgroup.

Process Owners

Your administrative users will need the ability to associate one or more process owners to a workgroup. A process owner has the sole responsibility of modifying a process. Providing more than one process owner allows your users' managers the ability to have surrogate process owners in case one of them is sick, out of town for meetings, or on vacation.

Ordered Sequence of Roles in Workgroups

Some processes require that several roles be ordered in sequence in order to create a finished product. Your application should let the user define such a sequence. In this strategy, the sequence is as follows:

1. A time-sensitive task is assigned to the first user of the first role in the workgroup.

2. If the user is not able to do the task by the task's deadline, your application automatically routes the task to the next user with the same role.

The ordered sequence should be defined in the database. That way, your application simply looks up the sequence and applies the routing based on the information it receives. You can do the same thing for weighted workgroups, where the ordered sequence is dependent on which role and user has the greatest weight (a percentage value that represents relative importance).

Process Costing

Your application should give the process owner the ability to determine the cost of a given process. This helps the process owner assess the process benefits against its actual cost.

Task Management

Task management is concerned with the assignment of tasks to roles and users behind the roles. In administering this assignment, task management tracks the buildup of tasks in queues, rolling back tasks, and times when tasks are completed.

13

Task Queues

Some process owners need the ability to queue their tasks at the workgroup level. That is, instead of immediately routing tasks to an individual, tasks are routed to a workgroup queue. This way, users receive a task once they're free to work on it. Having this capability is beneficial for those environments where more than one user implements a role.

Rollback

Your application needs to be able to roll back a task or flow of work when business conditions require this. This is quite similar to implementing an Undo mechanism for tasks. Rolling back a task can be quite complicated and requires particular attention to details in your sequence diagrams and quite a bit of analysis with users, especially process owners.

Task Completion Times

Process owners and/or application administrators sometimes need to specify the completion time for each task, and possibly each step within a task, in the process. You might design the application to allow the completion time to be fixed, or allowed to vary depending on the weight of the task, the product, the customer, and so on.

The Workgroup and User Security Subsystem Object Model

The Branch Manager of your client, the Second Bank of Carrollton, calls you to see how things are going with the application. You tell her you're at the point where you're modeling the bank's workgroup and security requirements and thus need her help in verifying any related concerns. She assures you that the workgroup model is very simple as not much work flows from one workgroup to another. After speaking with her database administrator, she gives you the following additional specifications:

1. "Although I'll sign off on cash deposit record forms for cash deposits in excess of $10,000, I want each record stored in the `Regulations` database in the `tblCash_Deposit_Records` table. Each record has a field, `WasSigned`, that must be assigned a value: `True` if the customer, the teller, and myself have signed, or `False` if otherwise. Most of the time, all three signatures are there. But sometimes, I'm not available, so I sign them at some point before the end of the day. Thus, I want a report automatically printed by 3 p.m. daily listing just the account number and the value of the `WasSigned` field. My printer ID is `\bank01\brmgr`. Every week, our regional bank compliance officers audit us to make sure the cash deposit records are signed."

2. "Be sure that, for every new account, the DOS-based check account history system is called so that the teller doesn't have to leave the session in the new application to start another. The DOS-based system is very important to our workflow."

▼ After some additional exchange between you and your client, you realize that the current requirements call for two workgroups:

- Account Transactions
- Account Administration

The Account Transactions workgroup is primarily responsible for processing deposit and withdrawal transactions. The roles in this workgroup include

- Bank Teller
- Regular Account Manager

The Account Administration workgroup is responsible for opening accounts, modifying customer and account characteristics, and closing accounts. Because the workers in this workgroup tend to be very experienced personnel, there are only two roles in this workgroup:

- Regular Account Manager
- Investment Account Manager

The Branch Manager, unlike managers in other banks, does not want the roles in one workgroup to perform the tasks of a role in the other. Also, she wants password protection.

Figure 13.2 shows the sequence of events that occurs in establishing a work session on behalf of a user.

▲ The bank branch manager wants the password to be encrypted as it travels across the network. She also wants the password stored in the database to be encrypted as well.

Modeling the Workgroup and User Security Subsystem Classes

Modeling the classes in this type of subsystem is seldom easy. In fact, one of the more difficult tasks for the designer and developer is implementing a suitable login mechanism and tracking the various roles a user is likely to perform. To create a proper, truly secure login mechanism, your more sophisticated users expect you to encrypt the password— not just trust a text box's password character display alone. Your customers don't want the actual text of the password stored in the database; they want the encrypted text value. If you develop a login mechanism for an Internet application tasked with keeping parents' children from certain features on the Web, the parents would expect that the more curious children aren't able to peep into the database and get the passwords. They, too, would need encryption. The classes for an application's security policy have also been modeled and included in the sample code for this lesson.

13

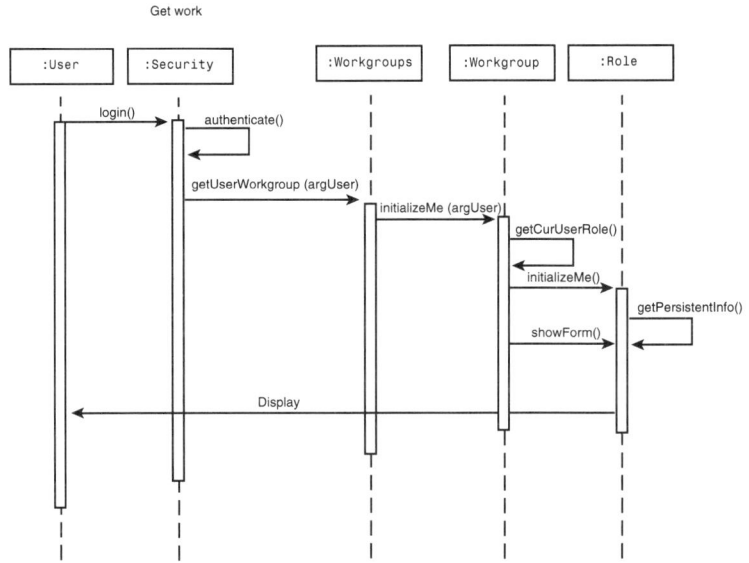

FIGURE 13.2.

The sequence of events that occurs in establishing a work session on behalf of a user.

The Hierarchy Model

Figure 13.3 shows the typical classes you might implement as part of this subsystem. The AllUsers class is not used in the Second Bank of Carrollton example. However, for large, complex applications where components are distributed across many workgroup and enterprise servers, don't be surprised if you need to implement a large AllUsers collection to keep track of logged-in users.

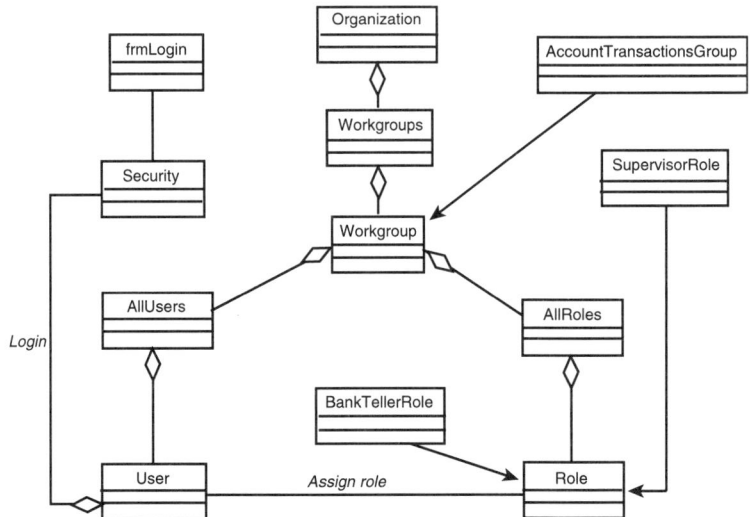

FIGURE 13.3.

A typical class model for the Workgroup and User Security Subsystem.

Describing the Classes in the Subsystem

The form, frmLogin, captures the user's ID and password. Security enforces the security policy of the enterprise at the application level. The classes Role, AllRoles, and SupervisorRole implement behavior relative to a particular role or set of roles. The class AllRoles is owned by the Workgroup, which keeps track of which user can implement which roles and which tasks belong to which role. Workgroup and Workgroups are classes that track the workgroups that exist in the application domain. Workgroups is a collection of workgroup objects.

Process tracks the sequence of tasks that must be implemented to produce the workgroup's meaningful product. This class also knows which task is the current task and communicates with the Workgroup class to know which role is the current role. AllProcesses is a collection of Process objects and is necessary for environments where the number of processes supported by a given workgroup will expand some time in the future. As a good policy for developing commercial- and industrial-grade object-oriented applications, always include such a collection.

The User and CSession classes track the user as well as information about the current user session, such as login and logoff times. You could expand this functionality to track every transaction of the user, which is useful for security audit and technical support purposes. Here, the capital "C" in CSession means controller. The CSession class owns the SHA1Encryption class, which is responsible for encrypting the password.

The class AccountTransactionsGroup is the workgroup class implemented in the Second Bank of Carrollton example. It has two roles, BankTellerRole and ManagerRole.

Describing the Methods

The collection classes AllProcesses and AllRoles each have an Add method. The purpose of this method is to add a Process and Role object, respectively, to each collection. Each collection's Remove method removes each object from each collection.

The controller class, CSession, controls events and state changes with respect to a logged-in session. It also controls the form, frmLogin. The class has the following methods:

- authenticate
- clickedLogin
- showForm

The method authenticate is responsible for the login process. It works in conjunction with the showForm method to display the login form to the user.

13

Each Role object has a showTask method that shows the GUI representation of the task to the user. For Visual Basic applications, the task will probably be presented as a form primarily, or an Office document or flat file attachment secondarily.

The Process object has the following methods:

- startProcess
- endProcess
- startTask
- endTask

The startProcess method is responsible for taking care of the initialization process that pertains to the process it represents. The endProcess method does the opposite, implementing the rules necessary to end a process successfully. The methods startTask and endTask have a similar relationship, except they apply to a task instead of an entire process. That is, whereas a process can require multiple forms to result in its end product, a task only has one form.

The SHA1Encryption class has a single public method, encrypt. It is responsible for accepting a password as an argument and encrypting it, returning the encrypted password value to the client. It uses several private methods for the actual encryption algorithm.

The class Workgroup has the following methods:

- startProcess
- endProcess
- determineRoles

The methods startProcess and endProcess are pretty self-explanatory. They trigger the starting and stopping of processes in the AllProcess collection. What makes these methods different from the ones in the Process class is that the former delegates the actual starting and stopping of each process to the objects themselves as they know best the details of their responsibilities. The determineRoles method involves accessing the role IDs of the roles the user can perform in this workgroup lookup roles by user ID.

Data Types

The collection classes AllProcesses and AllRoles each have the following properties:

- Count
- Item

Use the `Count` property to retrieve the number of elements in the collection. The `Item` property is used to reference the desired element in the collection. To use it, you treat it as you do any function, passing in the key value of the object you want.

The more special property of the `CSession` class is the `isLoggedIn` property. This simply is a boolean indicator to test whether the user successfully logged in to the system. It's particularly useful when initializing all classes and forms that depend on the user having successfully logged into the application.

Every `Role` class has a property for every form and the IDs of the role it represents. The `AllForms` property contains every form that the role uses in implementing its tasks. The `RoleID` property is the identifier of the underlying role and is meaningful to the customer.

The `Process` class has the following properties:

- `CurrTaskID`
- `isCurrTaskComplete`
- `ProcessID`
- `ProcessState`

The `CurrTaskID` property holds the task identifier of the current task being performed by the role's user (also known as a role instance). The `isCurrTaskComplete` property is a boolean indicator that lets the `Workgroup` object know whether the current task is complete. The `ProcessID` and `ProcessState` properties are the identifiers and current state of the process, respectively. `ProcessState` could have just as easily been named `ProcessStatus`.

Finally, the very important class, the `Workgroup`, has the following properties:

- `AllProcesses`
- `AllRoles`
- `CurrProcess`
- `isProcessComplete`

13

The `AllProcesses` and `AllRoles` properties holds references to the collection of `Process` and `Role` objects, respectively, owned by the `Workgroup`. These properties make it easy to track processes and worker roles from the time the user logs in until the user logs off and terminates the application. The `CurrProcess` property holds a reference to the current `Process` object that implements the current process. The `isProcessComplete` property is a boolean indicator that lets the `Workgroup` object know whether a process has been completed. The process is complete when the corresponding `Process` object is set to Nothing and is not in memory. Knowing this information makes it easier to move from one process to another, whether the next process is owned by the workgroup or not.

Incorporating the Subsystem into the Samsona Bank Teller System Example

▼ REAL WORLD

Implementing the class for this subsystem requires some work, but you assure your client at the Second Bank of Carrollton that it's no problem. You brief your developers on the steps necessary to complete this transformation. You instruct the developers to do the following:

1. Add the CSession, AccountTransactionsGroup, BankTellerRole, and RegularAccountManagerRole classes and the other class in Figure 13.3 to the project. Add the methods and properties mentioned earlier.

2. Add two modules, modMain and modWorkflow.

3. Move the declarations for the following controller classes to the BankTellerRole class: CancelTransaction, CheckAccountStatus, DepositFunds, WithdrawFunds. This is done so that the corresponding forms are represented as tasks owned by the BankTellerRole class. This, in turn, makes it more convenient to localize changes and impacts associated with these forms to the proper role.

4. Move the declarations for the following controller classes to the RegularAccountManagerRole class: CancelTransaction, CheckAccountStatus, CloseAccount, DepositFunds, OpenAccount, WithdrawFunds.

5. Add the following forms to the AllForms collection property of BankTellerRole: frmDeposit, frmWithdraw, frmCashDepositRecord, frmCancelTransaction, frmCheckAccountStatus.

6. Add the following forms to the AllForms collection property of RegularAccountManagerRole: frmDeposit, frmWithdraw, frmCashDepositRecord, frmCancelTransaction, frmCheckAccountStatus, frmOpenAccount.

7. In the MDI form, frmMDI, create a menu with items that reflect the names of the forms in steps 5 and 6. Have only one main menu item, Processes. Have two submenu items, Bank Teller and Regular Account Manager. For the Bank Teller menu, have submenus that have names that closely match the names of respective forms in step 5. Do likewise for the Regular Account Manager menu with respect to step 6.

▼

▼ In the module, `modWorkflow`, your developers need the following declarations:

```
Enum eProcess
    DoProcess1
End Enum

Enum eRole
    WorkerRole = 1
    ManagerRole
End Enum

Enum eTasks
    Task1 = 1
    Task2
    Task3
    Task4
    Task5
    Task6
End Enum

Global theAccountTransactionsGroup As _ AccountTransactionsGroup
Global theAccountAdministrationGroup As _ AccountAdministrationGroup
```

When doing steps five and six, you explain to the developers that they should define module-level variables in each `Role` class and initialize them in their respective `Class_Initialize` events. The code would look as follows:

```
For BankTellerRole:
Private mvarAllForms As New Collection 'local copy

mvarAllForms.Add frmDeposit, CStr(eTasks.Task1)
mvarAllForms.Add frmWithdraw, CStr(eTasks.Task2)
mvarAllForms.Add frmCashDepositRecord, CStr(eTasks.Task3)
mvarAllForms.Add frmCancelTransaction, CStr(eTasks.Task4)
mvarAllForms.Add frmCheckAccountStatus, CStr(eTasks.Task5)

For RegularAccountManagerRole:
Private mvarAllForms As New Collection 'local copy

mvarAllForms.Add frmDeposit, CStr(eTasks.Task1)
mvarAllForms.Add frmWithdraw, CStr(eTasks.Task2)
mvarAllForms.Add frmCashDepositRecord, CStr(eTasks.Task3)
mvarAllForms.Add frmCancelTransaction, CStr(eTasks.Task4)
mvarAllForms.Add frmCheckAccountStatus, CStr(eTasks.Task5)
mvarAllForms.Add frmOpenAccount, CStr(eTasks.Task6)
```

▼

13

▼

Note	The code is too lengthy to list here. You can find a copy of the code for this lesson on the CD.
	Feel free to simply open up the code associated with this chapter that's on the CD-ROM (\Ch13). Use it when going over the steps mentioned earlier.

▲

Summary

This lesson presented you with an overview of the Workgroup and User Security Subsystem. In particular, you learned about the purpose of this subsystem and the subsystem's classes, as well as their methods, properties, arguments, and returns. This chapter covers security issues for Internet and desktop applications and discusses practical guidelines for implementing the Workgroup and User Security Subsystem. Finally, you learned how to incorporate the subsystem into the Samsona Bank Teller System example.

Q&A

Q What is transmission security?

A *Transmission security* is the flow of data across a network.

Q What is one way to secure information that flows from your application to another point in the network?

A By encrypting vital information such as passwords, you secure the information flowing across the network.

Q What's the purpose of the Workgroup and User Security Subsystem?

A The Workgroup and User Security Subsystem enforces the security of your application and makes sure that users are only able to do the business tasks they are supposed to do.

Q What is one of the most important but understated functions of a good workflow solution?

A One of the most important but understated functions of a good workflow solution is the ability to handle exceptions, which are rampant in every organization.

Q What is the benefit of dynamic routing?

A Dynamic routing gives the user the flexibility of adjusting the flow of work based on volatile business events. Changing business conditions at runtime can create the need for adaptability based on constraints your application's administrative user provide. These constraints would be entered through a Visual Basic form and then persisted in a database.

Q **What are task queues?**

A Task queues are lists of tasks that need to be completed as part of a process. Some process owners need the ability to queue their tasks at the workgroup level. That is, instead of immediately routing tasks to an individual, tasks are routed to a workgroup queue. This way, users receive a task once they're free to work on it. Having this capability is beneficial for those environments where more than one user implements a role.

Workshop

The workshop includes quiz questions to help gauge your grasp of the material. You'll find the answers to this quiz in Appendix A, "Answers." Even if you feel that you totally understand the concepts presented here, you should work through the quiz anyway. The last section includes exercises for you to work through to help reinforce your learning.

Quiz

1. What security features should you implement in your commercial or industrial applications?

2. What are some factors to look for with regard to application sabotage?

3. What are the general steps involved in a typical task?

4. Why is it generally wise not to tightly couple a workgroup with a traditional department or a role with a user?

5. Briefly explain the order sequence of roles in a workgroup.

Exercises

1. Using the code provided on the CD, design and implement a `InvestmentAccountManager` role class.

2. In a series of steps, explain how you would consolidate the use of common forms between the `BankTellerRole` and `RegularAccountManager` role classes. Try to implement this strategy into the example code.

3. Implement code in each role class that displays the start and stop times for each task in a message box.

13

DAY 14

The Internal Application Manager Subsystem

This chapter presents you with an overview of the Internal Application Manager Subsystem. In particular, you learn how to

- Understand the purpose of this subsystem
- Understand application state issues for Internet and desktop applications
- Manage application settings and user preferences
- Use the Windows 95 Registry and VB5
- Use the older INI file
- Manage logging of user interactions with the application
- Manage logging errors and exceptions
- Manage logging memory allocations/deallocations
- Use the classes in the subsystem, as well as their methods, properties, arguments, and returns
- Understand practical guidelines for implementing the Internal Application Manager Subsystem
- Incorporate the subsystem into the Samsona Bank Teller System example

An Overview of the Internal Application Manager Subsystem

Developing applications for any purpose requires some ongoing understanding of how they behave at runtime in different environments. In particular, your application needs to record important transactions that occur between the user and the application. In implementing object-oriented programming, you need three objects to manage this transaction logging. Figure 14.1 shows the objects that participate in logging the transactions of the users.

FIGURE 14.1.

*The essential objects
needed for the Internal
Application Manager
Subsystem.*

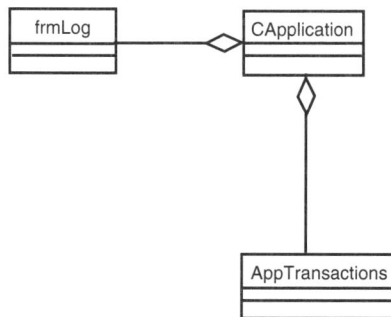

Understanding the Purpose of This Subsystem

The Internal Application Manager Subsystem is responsible for initializing the entire application, tracking every user transaction, and terminating the application. In previous chapters, you used the module, modMain, as the starting point for initializing the application. However, a more elegant, object-oriented approach is to encapsulate the declaration of global object variables in the application controller class, CApplication. Within CApplication, you don't declare each object variable as Global, but as Public. This is because Visual Basic doesn't allow you to declare global variables within classes. Only code modules can hold global declarations. Nonetheless, object-oriented programming requires a minimal use of global variables, specifically those that aren't object variables.

The biggest benefit of this subsystem lies in two areas:

- Security
- Troubleshooting and Customer Support

The benefit of this subsystem to security is evident in the information contained in the log. Every add, update, delete, and read operation aimed at the database can be logged properly in a hidden file or straight to a database. Every login attempt can also be recorded. For security-sensitive environments such as financial institutions, top-secret military and private-sector organizations, and even Internet-wary parents with children at home, this application transaction logging mechanism is essential.

If you're an active or a would-be entrepreneur, or a commercial software establishment, implementing this subsystem adds to the benefits of using classes with regard to troubleshooting and customer support. How many times have you had trouble understanding what your customers and/or users are trying to explain about application errors or functionality problems? Some developers have spent hours, even days, trying to negotiate an understanding of a problem with users. With an application transaction logging subsystem in place, you can record transactions that you have estimated will likely cause problems ahead of time. That way, when a user calls you with a problem, you can simply ask the user to click a menu item named Customer Support and ask him to either read the contents of the text box or print and fax/mail the file contents to you. For the advanced developer, you can design the menu item to email the file to you when the user encounters a problem repeatedly and call him before he calls you (well, it was a nice thought, anyway).

Understanding State Issues for Internet Applications

If you deploy your application on the Internet, you need to track state changes with regard to HTML pages, Active Server Pages, and ActiveX components as they are routed in and out of your Web server. The classes in this subsystem reside on the Web server in a subsystem ActiveX component, waiting for each transaction as they come in. The logging information is then persisted in a file or database table.

Understanding State Issues for Desktop Applications

Tracking desktop applications follows a similar pattern. If you deploy your application on a desktop, you need to track state changes with regard to forms, classes, components, and Active Documents. The classes in this subsystem can be encapsulated in an ActiveX DLL or EXE, waiting for each transaction as they come in. The logging information is then persisted in a file or database table.

Managing Application Settings and User Preferences

14

Earlier, you read some benefits of implementing this subsystem including customer support and security. In some cases, your application might require that some user preferences be recorded and remembered the next time the user uses the application. For such

requirements, the controller class CApplication enforces these preferences in conjunction with the Graphical User Interface subsystem. You can record these preferences to a
database, a regular file, an INI (initialization) file, or the Registry.

Using the Windows 95 Registry and Visual Basic

If you plan to use the Registry to record user preferences and possibly application transaction information, you need a class for this. In Visual Basic, you create a facade class
called RegistryFacade. Recall that a facade class is one that is literally a facade for
encapsulating function calls, particularly those associated with legacy systems or APIs.
In this context, the class RegistryFacade encapsulates the calls to the Registry functions
that Visual Basic supports. Listing 14.1 shows the code in this class that you might
implement.

LISTING 14.1. THE CODE LISTING FOR THE CLASS RegistryFacade.

```
 1: VERSION 1.0 CLASS
 2: BEGIN
 3:   MultiUse = 0    'False
 4: END
 5: Attribute VB_Name = "RegistryFacade"
 6: Attribute VB_GlobalNameSpace = False
 7: Attribute VB_Creatable = True
 8: Attribute VB_PredeclaredId = False
 9: Attribute VB_Exposed = False
10:
11: 'Used as default for getRegSetting method
12: 'if no argument values are passed in. Populated
13: 'in saveRegSetting method
14: Private m_pLastAppName As String
15: Private m_pLastSection As String
16: Private m_pLastKey As String, m_pCurrentKey As String
17: Private m_returns
18:
19:
20: Public Function saveRegSetting(argAppName As String, _
21: argSection As String, argKey As String, argSetting)
22:     'Populate module-level variables as default for
23:     'getRegSetting method
24:     Dim returns
25:     m_pLastAppName = argAppName
26:     m_pLastSection = argSection
27:     m_pLastKey = argKey
28:     SaveSetting AppName:=argAppName, section:=argSection, _
29:             Key:=argKey, setting:=argSetting
30:
31: End Function
32:
```

```
33: Public Function getRegSetting(argAppName As String, _
34: argSection As String, argKey As String, Optional argDefault)
35:     On Error GoTo getRegSettingErr
36:     m_returns = Switch(argAppName = "", True, argSection = "", True)
37:     If m_returns Then
38:         'You need values
39:         MsgBox "Please enter both the Application Name and the
          ➥Section"
40:         Exit Function
41:     End If
42:     If IsMissing(argDefault) Then
43:         m_pCurrentKey = GetSetting(AppName:=argAppName,
➥section:=argSection, _
44:                         Key:=argKey)
45:     Else
46:         m_pCurrentKey = GetSetting(AppName:=argAppName,
➥section:=argSection, _
47:                         Key:=argKey, Default:=argDefault)
48:     End If
49:
50:     If argAppName <> "" And argSection <> "" And argKey <> "" Then
51:         'Send defaults from last save
52:         If Not IsMissing(argDefault) Then
53:             m_pCurrentKey = GetSetting(AppName:=m_pLastAppName,
➥section:=m_pLastSection, _
54:                             Key:=argKey, Default:=argDefault)
55:         Else
56:             m_pCurrentKey = GetSetting(AppName:=m_pLastAppName,
➥section:=m_pLastSection, _
57:                             Key:=argKey, Default:=argDefault)
58:         End If
59:     End If
60:     getRegSetting = m_pCurrentKey
61:     Exit Function
62: getRegSettingErr:
63:     Err.Raise vbError + 1002, "CRegistry",
➥"Please enter both the Application Name and the Section"
64:
65: End Function
66: Public Function getAllRegSettings(argAppName As String, _
67: argSection As String, Optional ByRef argListViewObj)
68:     'Dim localRegSettings(0, 0)
69:     Dim cnt As Long, objColHdr As ColumnHeader, objListItem As
        ➥ListItem
70:     Dim localRegSettings As Variant, arrayRef
71:     Const SPACING As Byte = 30
72:     On Error GoTo getAllRegSettingsErr
73:     localRegSettings = GetAllSettings(AppName:=argAppName,
➥section:=argSection)
74:     If Not IsArray(localRegSettings) Then Exit Function
```

continues

14

LISTING 14.1. CONTINUED

```
75:    If Not IsMissing(argListObj) Then
76:
77:        'Eventually, this code needs to be replaced by a list box
        ➡class
78:        argListObj.AddItem "Key Setting" & Space(11 + (SPACING - 11))
        ➡&"Key Value"
79:        argListObj.AddItem ""
80:        Set objColHdr = argListViewObj.ColumnHeaders.Add(, , "Key", _
81:            argListViewObj.Width / 3)
82:        Set objColHdr = argListViewObj.ColumnHeaders.Add(, ,
        ➡"Setting", _
83:            argListViewObj.Width / 3)
84:        argListViewObj.View = lvwReport
85:        For cnt = LBound(localRegSettings, 1) To UBound
➡(localRegSettings, 1)
86:            argListObj.AddItem localRegSettings(cnt, 0) _
87:            & Space(Len(localRegSettings(cnt, 0)) +
➡(SPACING - Len(localRegSettings(cnt, 0)))) & _
88:                localRegSettings(cnt, 1)
89:            Set objListItem.SubItems(1) =
➡argListViewObj.ListItems.Add(, , _
90:                localRegSettings(cnt, 0))
91:            Set objListItem.SubItems(2) =
➡argListViewObj.ListItems.Add(, , _
92:                localRegSettings(cnt, 1))
93:        Next cnt
94:    Else 'return the list to the caller
95:        getAllRegSettings = localRegSettings
96:    End If
97:    Exit Function
98: getAllRegSettingsErr:
99:    MsgBox "Please provide the correct Section"
100:    Exit Function
101: End Function
102:
103: Public Function deleteRegSetting(argAppName As String, _
104: argSection As String, Optional argKey)
105:    If Not IsMissing(argKey) Then
106:        DeleteSetting argAppName, argSection, argKey
107:    Else
108:        DeleteSetting argAppName, argSection
109:    End If
110: End Function
111:
112: Public Function initializeRegistry()
113:    On Error GoTo initializeRegistryErr
114:    m_returns = Shell("c:\winnt\regedit.exe", vbMinimizedFocus
        ➡'vbHide)
```

```
115:      Exit Function
116: initializeRegistryErr:
117:      'Err.Raise vbError + 1010, "initializeRegistry",
↦"Registry is corrupt or missing"
118:      MsgBox "Registry is corrupt or missing", 64, "initializeRegistry"
119:      Exit Function
120: End Function
121:
122: Public Function findFirstItem(argString As String)
123:      'Finds the first occurrence of an item
124:      'Do Copy Key in Registry, then do
125:      'a ClipBoard.GetText to load full
126:      'key into a variable
127:      SendKeys "^F" & argString & "{ENTER}", True 'CTRL+F
128:
129:      'Copy full key name to ClipBoard (ALT+E)
130:      SendKeys "%EC", True
131:      m_returns = getFullRegKeyName
132: End Function
133:
134: Public Function getFullRegKeyName()
135:      'If argString exists, caller wants this method
136:      'to first find the item, then return the
137:      'corresponding full key name
138:
139:      getFullRegKeyName = Clipboard.GetText(vbCFText)
140: End Function
141:
142: Public Function findNextItem()
143:      'Send "F3" keystroke
144:      SendKeys "{F3}", True
145: End Function
```

As you can see, the RegistryFacade class is fairly short. The methods in this class
include the following:

- saveRegSetting

- getRegSetting

- getAllRegSettings

- deleteRegSetting

- initializeRegistry

- findFirstItem

- getFullRegKeyName

- findNextItem

14

The `saveRegSetting` method wraps the call to the corresponding `saveSetting` function. It's responsible for saving or creating an application entry in the Windows Registry. Its arguments are `argAppName`, `argSection`, `argKey`, and `argSetting`.

The `argAppName` argument represents a `String` expression that contains the name of the application or project to which the setting applies. The `argSection` argument is a `String` expression that contains the name of the section where the key setting is being saved. The `argKey` argument is a `String` expression that contains the name of the key setting being saved. Finally, the `argSetting` argument is a `Variant` expression that contains the value that key is being set to.

The `getRegSetting` method calls the `GetSetting` Registry function that returns a key setting value from your application's entry in the Windows Registry. The arguments are similar to the previous method, except for the optional `argDefault` argument. The `argDefault` argument expression, if present, contains the value to return if no value is set in the key setting. If it is missing, Visual Basic assumes the default value is a zero-length string (`""`). Within the method, a `Switch` statement usage simplifies the checking of boolean expressions. Here, you want to make sure the client provides the `AppName` and `Section` values that the Registry needs.

The remainder of the method sets corresponding properties when the Registry item is returned.

The `getAllRegSettings` method calls the `GetAllSettings` Registry method that returns a list of key settings and their respective values from an application's entry in the Windows Registry. Its arguments are the same as the previous methods discussed, except for an optional argument, `argListViewObj`. The argument `argListViewObj` is a list view object that contains the list of settings returned. It needs the corresponding `objColHdr` and `objListItem` objects to populate it. This list view population works only if the variable `localRegSettings` is indeed an array. That's why the following line is needed to prevent the occurrence of an error:

```
If Not IsArray(localRegSettings) Then Exit Function
```

The `deleteRegSetting` method calls `DeleteSetting` Registry method that deletes a section or key setting from your application's entry in the Windows Registry. It has three arguments similar to their counterparts in the other methods. With this method, though, the `argKey` argument is optional. This optional argument is optional because the `DeleteSetting` method does not require it.

The remaining methods are not required at all. They simply enable you to access the Registry using the Shell command. The method `initializeRegistry` executes the Registry's executable to prepare it for `SendKey` operations. The `findFirstItem` method finds the first occurrence of an item, represented by the argument `argString`. The method sends the string via `SendKeys` to the executable. The method `getFullRegKeyName` returns the corresponding full key name that's in the Clipboard. This method works in conjunction with `findFirstItem`.

Using the Older INI File

If the Registry is not where you want to store user preferences, you might consider the traditional initialization file (INI). Many Visual Basic programmers find the INI file more friendly than the Registry, and thus still use it for user preferences and data source names. Listing 14.2 shows the code for the `IniFile` class.

LISTING 14.2. THE CODE FOR THE `IniFile` CLASS.

```
 1: VERSION 1.0 CLASS
 2: BEGIN
 3:    MultiUse = -1   'True
 4: END
 5: Attribute VB_Name = "IniFile"
 6: Attribute VB_GlobalNameSpace = False
 7: Attribute VB_Creatable = False
 8: Attribute VB_PredeclaredId = False
 9: Attribute VB_Exposed = False
10: Rem Purpose: Handles all interaction with INI files
11:
12: '.INI variables
13: Public DSN As String
14: Public mDbConnect As String, mODBCUser As String   'ODBCUser
15: Public mDbName As String     'Database name
16: Public mDRIVE As String
17: Public mPath As String
18: Public mFrmBackColor
19: Public mFontName
20: Public iniFileName As String
21: Public mRetries As Integer
22: Public AppName As String
23: Public AppRev As String
24:
25: Public Sub writeOutputFile(argOutput As String)
26:
27: If OutputFlag = "Y" Then
28:     Open App.Path & "\SomeFile.ini" For Append As #1
29:     Print #1, argOutput
30:     Close #1
31: End If
32:
```

14

continues

LISTING 14.2. CONTINUED

```
33: End Sub
34:
35: Public Function getINI(argHeader As String, argName As String)
36:
37:     Dim sReturn As String
38:     Dim sProfileString As String
39:     Dim iProfile As Integer
40:     Dim iCount As Integer
41:
42:     sReturn = String(120, " ")
43:     iProfile = GetPrivateProfileString(argHeader, argName, "",
➥sReturn, Len(sReturn), iniFileName)
44:     iCount = 1
45:     Do Until iCount = Len(sReturn)
46:         If Asc(Mid$( sReturn, iCount, 1)) > 31 Then sProfileString =
➥final$ & Mid$(sReturn, Count, 1)
47:     iCount = iCount + 1
48:     Loop
49:
50:     GetINI = Trim(sProfileString)
51:
52: End Function
53:
54:
55: Public Sub getSettings()
56:     'The app should look at an ini file by the same name
57:     iniFileName = App.Path & "\SomeFile.ini"
58:     ' Get ini settings --------------------------
59:     AppName = GetINI("YourApp", "Name")
60:     AppRev = GetINI("YourApp ", "Version")
61:
62:     'Get connection information
63:     DSN = GetINI("ODBC", "DSN")
64:     mDbName = GetINI("ODBC", "dbname")
65:     mDbConnect = GetINI("ODBC", "dbconnect")
66:     mODBCUser = GetINI("ODBC", "username")
67:     mRetries = Val(GetINI("ODBC", "retries"))
68:
69:     'Get user preference settings
70:     mDRIVE = GetINI("Preferences", "Favorite Macro")
71:     mFrmBackColor = GetINI("Screen", "Favorite Form Color")
72:     'Get the Application font
73:     mFontName = GetINI("Screen", "Favorite Font Name")
74: End Sub
```

The writeOutputFile method accepts an argument, argOutput, that represents the contents of a new INI file. The getINI method retrieves a particular item from an INI file based on the INI file header value represented by the argument `argHeader` and the name of the item held in the argument, `argName`. For instance, if you have an INI file with a header such as User Preferences, you might then have an item with the name Favorite Font Name. Passing these two values in results in the actual font name. The `getSettings` method is a convenient method for getting every setting in the INI file.

Logging User Interactions with the Application

Over the life of your application, your user will make a combination of significant and not-so-significant transactions. Depending on your particular situation, you might opt to track every transaction or just the important ones. Of all the user transactions, the most important ones tend to be those that involve logging in and out of an application and interacting with database records.

Undo operations are also important for auditing purposes, at least as a training tool for managers and new employees. In addition, you might want to record the user's ID, start time of transaction, end time of transaction, and possibly the identifier for the transaction or task the user performed. A sequence of these transactions leaves a nice audit trail for any authorized individual.

Logging Errors and Exceptions

Logging errors and exceptions are also important for customer support and troubleshooting. The same important scenarios for logging transactions mentioned in the previous section are also the ones that tend to create the most problems for users.

Logging Memory Allocations/Deallocations

If you want even more detail, you might also record the allocation and deallocation of memory for your significant variables, particularly your business objects and subsystem interface objects. Sometimes, it is helpful to log the stack of function calls, but keep in mind that the more information you log, the more work your application must do. This can cost you in some performance if you abuse this valuable tool. Sticking to the significant transactions won't harm performance, so use this as a criteria for logging transactions.

The Internal Application Manager Subsystem Object Model

This subsystem is relatively simple to implement, though it can be tedious at times (see Figure 14.2). Generally, you model your application to create global objects in the `CApplication` class. For each allocation of memory, the instance of `CApplication`'s

14

class instance, named theApplication for example, invokes the addTrans2MemLog method of the theAppTransactions object. When a user requests a connection to the database, the controller class of the form invokes the addTrans2MemLog method as well. At any time your client has trouble with the application, for instance, invoke the showLog method of the theAppTransactions object.

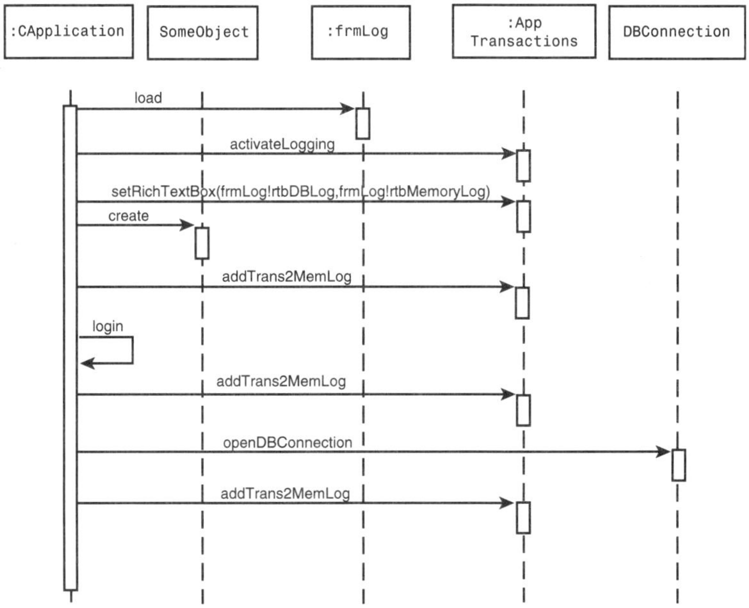

FIGURE 14.2.

Typical sequence of events for logging application transactions and memory allocations.

Modeling the Internal Application Manager Subsystem Class

The class model is exactly the same as Figure 14.1. There are no special accommodations for any application.

The methods of the CApplication class include the following:

* initializeSystem
* getAppState
* setAppState

- login

- logoff

- terminateSystem

The `initializeSystem` method is responsible for safely starting up the system, including global variables. It is equivalent to the `Form_Load` or `Class_Initialize` events. The `terminateSystem` method is responsible for doing the reverse of the `initializeSystem` method. The `terminateSystem` method is equivalent to the `Form_Unload` and `Class_Terminate` events. The `getAppState` method is an accessor that returns the state of the application at any point to the client. The `setAppState` mutator method enables a client to set the state of the application. Ideally, the application's state should only be updated by subsystem interface classes as such classes will have a better understanding of the state of the application than any underlying class. The login and logoff methods are purely optional and are meant to delegate their respective duties to the Workgroup and User Security Subsystem.

The class `AppTransactions` has the following methods:

- activateLogging

- addTrans2List

- addTrans2MemLog

- addTrans2Text

- deactivateLogging

- setListBox

- hideLog

- printLog

- saveLog

- setRichTextBox

- showLog

The `activateLogging` and `deactivateLogging` methods are responsible for activating and deactivating, respectively, the recording of transactions and memory allocations for variables. These methods are helpful when you want to manage whether targeted application events are being logged. For instance, if you notice performance degradation in certain environments, you can turn off the logging feature by accessing these methods.

The `addTrans2List`, `addTrans2MemLog`, and `addTrans2Text` methods are three of the same kinds of methods that are responsible for logging transactions and memory allocations. I already discussed the `addTrans2MemLog` method. What was not revealed was that

14

this method logs events to a Rich Text Box that is contained in the form, frmLog. The Rich Text Box was chosen as the preferred approach because of its ease of creating and accessing files. You'll learn more about this nice little feature of the Rich Text Box in Chapter 17, " The File Operations Subsystem." If you want to use another Rich Text Box control, first invoke the setRichTextBox method, passing in the control.

The methods addTrans2List logs events to a list box on any form. Invoke the setListBox first, passing in the list box to house the events. The showLog and hideLog methods, respectively, show and hide the form, frmLog. The printLog method prints the contents of the Rich Text Box on the form, frmLog. The saveLog method saves the contents of the Rich Text Box on frmLog.

Returns

The CApplication class's initializeSystem method returns a Byte. This Byte value can be any special numeric identifier that indicates the state of the application initialization process. The values are yours to implement.

The Properties

The CApplication class has a State property that is accessed and set via the getState and setState methods. The AppTransactions class has a property, pTransLogIsOn, that is a boolean. It lets clients know whether events are being logged. This is useful in those classes with methods that process errors but might or might not want to have them recorded.

Incorporating the Subsystem into the Samsona Bank Teller System Example

After the many conversations with the branch manager of the Second Bank of Carrollton, you're relieved that you don't have much to discuss in how to implement this subsystem. She tells you that because the auditors run queries on the existing database for some transactions, not every event needs logging. She does want the login and logoff events recorded, as well as new account openings, deposits, and withdrawals. That's all.

In the modMain module, you need the following declaration:

```
Global theApplication As New CApplication
```

▼ From the same module, the following declarations

```
Global theSession As New CSession
Global theUser As New User
Global theMDIController As New MDIController
Global theCancelTransaction As New CancelTransaction
Global theCheckAccountStatus As New CheckAccountStatus
Global theCloseAccount As New closeAccount
Global theDepositFunds As New DepositFunds
Global theMaintainAccount As New MaintainAccount
Global theMaintainBankProducts As New MaintainBankProducts
Global theMaintainCustomer As New MaintainCustomer
Global theMaintainUsers As New MaintainUsers
Global theMaintainWorkgroups As New MaintainWorkgroups
Global theMDIController As New MDIController
Global theOpenAccount As New OpenAccount
Global theTransactionProcessor As New TransactionProcessor
Global theWithdrawFunds As New WithdrawFunds
```

need to be converted to `Public` and moved to `CApplication` as in Listing 14.3.

LISTING 14.3. DECLARATIONS.

```
 1: Public theSession As New CSession
 2: Public theUser As New User
 3: Public theMDIController As New MDIController
 4: Public theSomeWorkgroupProxy As SomeWorkgroupProxy
 5: Public theCancelTransaction As New CancelTransaction
 6: Public theCheckAccountStatus As New CheckAccountStatus
 7: Public theCloseAccount As New closeAccount
 8: Public theDepositFunds As New DepositFunds
 9: Public theMaintainAccount As New MaintainAccount
10: Public theMaintainBankProducts As New MaintainBankProducts
11: Public theMaintainCustomer As New MaintainCustomer
12: Public theMaintainUsers As New MaintainUsers
13: Public theMaintainWorkgroups As New MaintainWorkgroups
14: Public theMDIController As New MDIController
15: Public theOpenAccount As New OpenAccount
16: Public theTransactionProcessor As New TransactionProcessor
17: Public theWithdrawFunds As New WithdrawFunds
```

Every use of these objects now needs to be prefixed with the parent object, `theApplication`. The same conversion needs to occur for the module, `modWorkflow`. These changes are incorporated in the source code on the CD-ROM. Only object variables are affected.

▼ The `initializeSystem` method of `CApplication` looks like Listing 14.4 now.

14

▼ **LISTING 14.4.** THE initializeSystem METHOD OF CApplication.

```
 1:
 2: Public Function initializeSystem() As Byte
 3:     Dim returns
 4:     Set theAppTransactions = New AppTransactions
 5:     m_returns = theAppTransactions.setRichTextBox(frmLog!rtbDBLog,
➥frmLog!rtbMemoryLog)
 6:     Set theSession = New CSession
 7:     theAppTransactions.activateLogging
 8:     theMDIController.showForm
 9:     theSession.showForm
10:     'theAppTransactions.deactivateLogging
11:     theAppTransactions.addTrans2MemLog _
12:         "Allocated memory for theAppTransactions in
➥CApplication.initializeSystem"
13:     theAppTransactions.addTrans2MemLog _
14:         "Allocated memory for theSession in
             ➥CApplication.initializeSystem"
15:     theAppTransactions.addTrans2MemLog _
16:         "Allocated memory for ifcDBConnection in " & TypeName(Me) &
➥".initializeSystem"
17:     m_returns = theAppTransactions.addTrans2Text("Starting up the " &
➥App.EXEName & " system")
18: 'Connect to the database
19:     'returns = ifcDBConnection.OpenConnection("", App.Path &
➥"\bank.mdb", False)
20: End Function
```

Listing 14.5 shows the clickLogin method of the controller class, CSession. The
notable line of code is the logging of the user's ID and time stamp.

LISTING 14.5. THE clickLogin METHOD OF THE CONTROLLER CLASS, CSession.

```
 1: Public Sub clickedLogin()
 2:     Dim returns
 3:     Set theEncryptor = New SHA1Encryption
 4:     theApplication.theUser.UserID = theForm.txtUserID
 5:     theApplication.theUser.UserPassword =
➥theEncryptor.encrypt(theForm.txtPassword)
 6:
 7:     isLoggedIn = authenticate
 8:     If isLoggedIn Then
 9:         'Normally, you
10:         theAppTransactions.addTrans2MemLog _
11:             "User " & theApplication.theUser.UserID &
➥" has logged in at " & Now$
12:
▼ 13:           theApplication.theMDIController.enableProcessMenu
```

```
14:       End If
15:       'Normally, you would check the database
16:       'to see to which workgroup a user belongs
17:       Set theApplication.theSomeWorkgroupProxy = New
          ➥SomeWorkgroupProxy
18:       theApplication.theSomeWorkgroupProxy.startProcess
19:
20:       'MsgBox theApplication.theUser.UserID & vbNewLine _
21:       '    & theApplication.theUser.UserPassword & vbNewLine &
               ➥isLoggedIn
22:       'Note that the encrypted password should be persisted
23: End Sub
24:
```

The closeAccount method of the CloseAccount class looks like Listing 14.6.

LISTING 14.6. THE closeAccount METHOD.

```
1: Public Sub closeAccount()
2:     On Error GoTo closeAccountErr
3:
4:     'your code goes here...
5:     theApplication.theAppTransactions.addTrans2MemLog "Closed
       ➥Account"
6:     Exit Sub
7: closeAccountErr:
8:     Call RaiseError(MyUnhandledError, "CloseAccount:closeAccount
       ➥Method")
9: End Sub
10:
```

Listing 14.7 shows the deposit method for the DepositFunds class.

LISTING 14.7. THE deposit METHOD.

```
1: Public Sub deposit()
2:     On Error GoTo depositErr
3:
4:     'your code goes here...
5:     theApplication.theAppTransactions.addTrans2MemLog "Deposited
       ➥funds"
6:     Exit Sub
7: depositErr:
8:     Call RaiseError(MyUnhandledError, "DepositFunds:deposit
       ➥Method")
9: End Sub
10:
```

14

▼ Listing 14.8 shows the openAccount method of the OpenAccount class.

LISTING 14.8. THE openAccount METHOD.

```
 1: Public Sub openAccount()
 2:     On Error GoTo openAccountErr
 3:
 4:     'your code goes here...
 5:     theApplication.theAppTransactions.addTrans2MemLog "Deposited
        ➥funds"
 6:     Exit Sub
 7: openAccountErr:
 8:     Call RaiseError(MyUnhandledError, "OpenAccount:openAccount
        ➥Method")
 9: End Sub
10:
```

Finally, Listing 14.9 shows the withdraw method of the WithdrawFunds class.

LISTING 14.9. THE withdraw METHOD.

```
 1: Public Sub withdraw()
 2:     On Error GoTo withdrawErr
 3:
 4:     'your code goes here...
 5:     theApplication.theAppTransactions.addTrans2MemLog "Withdrew
        ➥funds"
 6:     Exit Sub
 7: withdrawErr:
 8:     Call RaiseError(MyUnhandledError, "WithdrawFunds:withdraw
        ➥Method")
 9: End Sub
```
▲
```
10:
```

Summary

This chapter presented you with an overview of the Internal Application Manager
Subsystem. You learned the purpose of this subsystem. You learned how to manage
application state issues for Internet and desktop applications and application settings and
user preferences. This chapter also discusses how to use the Windows 95 Registry and
VB5 and the older INI file. Logging user interactions with the application, errors and
exceptions, and memory allocations/deallocations is also covered. You learned how to
manage the classes in the subsystem, as well as their methods, properties, arguments, and
returns. Finally, you incorporated the subsystem into the Samsona Bank Teller System
example.

Q&A

Q **Why would you need an Internal Application Manager Subsystem?**

A Developing applications for any purpose requires some ongoing understanding of how they behave at runtime in different environments. In particular, your application needs to record important transactions that occur between the user and the application.

Q **How would you declare objects in the General Declarations section of `CApplication`?**

A Within `CApplication`, you don't declare each object variable as `Global` but as `Public`; Visual Basic doesn't allow you to declare global variables within classes. Only code modules can hold global declarations.

Q **How can would-be entrepreneurs and commercial software establishments benefit from such a subsystem?**

A If you're an active or would-be entrepreneur, or commercial software establishment, implementing this subsystem adds to the benefits of using classes with regard to troubleshooting and customer support.

Q **What events concerning variables are possibly important to log?**

A If you want even more detail, you might also record the allocation and deallocation of memory for your significant variables, particularly your business objects and subsystem interface objects. Sometimes, it is helpful to log the stack of function calls, but keep in mind that the more information you log, the more work your application must do.

Q **What is the responsibility of the `initializeSystem` method?**

A The `initializeSystem` method is responsible for safely starting up the system, including global variables. It is equivalent to the `Form_Load` or `Class_Initialize` events.

Workshop

The workshop includes quiz questions to help gauge your grasp of the material. You'll find the answers to this quiz in Appendix A, "Answers." Even if you feel that you totally understand the concepts presented here, you should work through the quiz anyway. The last section contains exercises for you to work through to help reinforce your learning.

14

Quiz

1. What are the biggest benefits of this subsystem?

2. What kinds of database operations are candidates for logging?

3. In what ways can you store application or user settings?

4. What kinds of information are potentially useful to record with every log item?

5. What is a potential downfall of logging too much information?

Exercises

1. Using the classes CApplication, AppTransactions, and the form frmLog, create a simple project with a form and a command button. Name the button cmdDone and caption it Done. Create a controller class for this form and call it CForm1. In CForm1, create a method, showForm, that has the line Form1.Show. Create another method, clickedDoneBtn. Add a module, modMain, and add a Main subroutine to it. Declare a new instance of CForm1, theForm1. In Sub Main, insert theForm1.showForm. In the form's cmdDone Click event, insert the code necessary to log the clicking event.

2. Using the code in exercise 1, display the form frmLog to ensure that everything is working properly.

3. Using exercise 1 again, log the event of the clickedDoneBtn method in a list box.

WEEK 2

In Review

In Week 2, you learned about self-testing objects, breaking up applications into subsystems, and refining use cases. This week's lessons also discuss the subsystems for the graphical user interface, workgroup and security, and internal application management.

In the first lesson of the week, you learned how to build objects that test themselves by having methods that test their own preconditions, including making sure that the data or class type of an incoming parameter is of the type expected. Also presented in this lesson was advice on how to debug your classes as well as version control tips for classes and subsystems of classes using Visual SourceSafe.

On Day 9, "Breaking Up an Application into Subsystems," you delved deeply into the process of breaking up a proposed application into subsystems, including components. You learned how to identify and use design patterns for subsystems and their interactions and how to define, name, and apply the design pattern. Finally, you learned the particulars of describing the solution provided by the design pattern, about listing the consequences of using the design pattern, and how to use and reuse design patterns for subsystems, including analyzing and designing subsystem interfaces.

In the next lesson, you learned the art of refining use cases as application and subsystem architecture blueprints. You learned about revisiting use cases in your environment, the problem statement, and the use-case model. This lesson also showed you how to refine user requirements into a better use-case model, as well as the art of working with end users, business analysts, executives, and project managers. You also learned specifically how to incorporate in the design models new discoveries in the way the end user uses your VB application. Moreover, you gained insight into preserving the artifacts of use-case analysis and development in general. Finally, you acquired knowledge toward assessing terminology and traceability, including domain-specific terminology for the Samsona Bank Teller example and related traceability issues involved in refining use cases.

Then you learned the basics of the Graphical User Interface Subsystem. Specifically, you learned how to use the modeling techniques for GUIs and understood the encapsulation of data presentation into a separate class. Finally, you became familiar with some ideas behind ergonomics and internationalization with resource files.

On the next day, you learned how to implement a Graphical User Interface Subsystem. You placed the core logic you generally insert in forms into classes that control the interaction between the forms and the rest of the application. You became familiar with the Facade design pattern, which is a role that can be played by both the form and the controller class. Finally, you received detailed treatment for incorporating the Graphical User Interface Subsystem into the Samsona Bank Teller System example.

On Day 13, "The Workgroup and User Security Subsystem," you learned about the Workgroup and User Security Subsystem. In particular, you learned the purpose of this necessary subsystem and related security issues, including a class for encrypting the password instead of relying solely on asterisk characters. Then you incorporated the subsystem into the Samsona Bank Teller System example.

On the last day of the week, the concept of the Internal Application Manager is used as a mechanism for controlling the initializing and terminating of the application, as well as managing the states an application goes through during a typical session. In particular, you learned the use of an encrypted settings file for more secure applications. Then you studied logging as a way to create a history of user interactions with the application, errors and exceptions, and memory allocations/deallocations.

WEEK 3

At a Glance

In Week 3's lessons, you learn about the rest of the subsystems for the hands-on example. After learning guidelines on identifying business rules, you implement the business rules required by your organization for your application. On the next day, you learn about the Reporting and Printing Subsystem and learn guidelines for planning cyclical and ad hoc reporting uses, as well as working with Microsoft Access, the SelPrint method of the Rich Text Box, and Crystal Reports.

As the week goes on, you learn how to create classes that handle file operations such as open and close, as well as loading values into controls and navigating records saved in files. This knowledge leads directly into learning about the Error-Processing and Exception-Handling Subsystem.

The main study of the subsystems wraps up on Day 19, "The Database Access Subsystem," in which you learn about the Database Access Subsystem and, in particular, how to use ADO, DAO, and RDO to communicate with the database, as well as how to save information from the graphical user interface and business classes.

On the last two days, you wrap up the whole project by learning the anatomy of a complete Visual Basic system, including how subsystems invoke the methods of other subsystems. Finally, you learn how to cope with Visual Basic projects, as well as some project management tips for developing effective software for corporate and commercial clients.

15 15 16 17 18 19 20 21

DAY 15

The Business Rules Subsystem

This chapter presents you with an overview of the Business Rules Subsystem. In particular, you learn the following:

- The purpose of this subsystem
- Practical concepts toward implementing policy management in your application
- Helpful guidelines for identifying your business rules and enterprise objects
- How you can work effectively with your key project stakeholders
- How to unearth existing implementations of business rules in your environment
- The classes you would need to implement in the subsystem, as well as their methods and properties, arguments, and returns
- Practical guidelines for implementing the Business Rules Subsystem
- How to incorporate the subsystem into the Samsona Bank Teller System example

Overview of the Business Rules Subsystem

The most complex part of developing any Visual Basic application is the design and implementation of the set of rules that make the application valuable to the user. The general expression for these rules is *business rules*. Business rule concepts have been floating around the software development and business management world for years. In its three-tier application model, Microsoft describes the middle tier as the *business tier*. It is this tier that is addressed in this chapter.

NEW TERM *Business rules* are the policies implemented and enforced in the application that provide measurable value to the user(s) of the application.

Nonetheless, don't let the expression *business rule* throw you off. A more abstract, generic expression is *domain rule*. I mention this because when some developers read the expression *business rule*, they automatically associate that with only business applications, and no doubt for good reason. Nonprofit and scientific organizations also use applications for their respective domains, so the expression *domain rule* is more universal, but not as popular as the expression *business rule*.

A business rule can be as simple as, for example, requiring that a bank customer have a valid account with a positive balance in it in order to make a withdrawal. Or it can be as complex as requiring that a bank customer wanting a revolving line of credit have an existing checking account in good standing, good credit, $250,000 net worth, and income that exceeds $100,000 a year.

For nonbusiness applications, business rules translate into domain rules. The same concept applies. An application that tracks the distance of some object must implement the known rule that distance equals rate times time (D=r*t). More complex domain rules are involved in applications that manage space shuttle projects.

Because business and domain rules can scale up to be quite complex, object-oriented programming concepts are very effective in comprehending the magnitude of what's involved in enforcing them. For example, recall the bank customer wanting the revolving line of credit. At first glance, it might be tempting for you to simply dive right in and code. However, consider that the revolving line of credit itself might have behavior and attributes that you would discover upon further evaluation. The process of checking for an existing account might involve several tasks not previously known. To calculate the net worth of an individual can be quite involved. The income could be implemented as an attribute if the bank's rule requires taking the customer at his or her word on the loan application, but other banks might require extensive income verification procedures. The bank customer, herself, might exhibit behavior relative to extending a line of credit. Each of these concerns would greatly benefit you by being encapsulated in business classes that enforce business rules.

Thus, throughout the remainder of this chapter, you can substitute business rule terminology with domain rule terminology if that helps.

15

Understanding the Purpose of This Subsystem

The Business Rules Subsystem enforces the policy of the user with respect to the user's organizational goals. The business classes and components that make up this subsystem have the main goal of providing one or more solutions to one or more organizational problems. For simpler applications, this subsystem can be implemented with only one class residing on the client machine. For more complex applications involving a number of groups of users within an organization, business classes can reside on any number of distributed computers. For instance, for a multinational banking corporation using a reasonable distributed application, classes that enforce the rules for clearing checks can reside on the workgroup servers for those groups that handle automated clearinghouse operations.

To build a sound, reusable subsystem of business classes, especially in a distributed architecture such as is typical in large, modern organizations, takes considerable time. In fact, don't worry yourself with designing perfect business classes the first time around. It may take as little as a couple of projects over a year or two to as many as three to five years to get a reasonable return on investment, although you can certainly deploy business objects as soon as you have them designed, tested, and implemented. During the first few iterations of your applications, expect a number of increments to be necessary for developing business classes. After the entire project is complete, your application will evolve with maintenance and cyclical requests for new features to be added. Each evolutionary cycle after the final project iteration release is popularly known as a *version change*, where the version number is incremented.

In more advanced issues, developing business classes with relational databases as part of the architecture of your environment can be tricky. Object databases such as ObjectStore (which has an ActiveX component for Visual Basic developers) don't require a separation of data from the objects themselves. However, relational databases, which still dominate the information storage and retrieval market, do require data disassembly. The problem then becomes how to effectively get the data out of business classes and into relational databases without compromising encapsulation rules. The bulk of the answer lies in design patterns. The lesson for Day 19, "The Database Access Subsystem," introduces you to some patterns/mechanisms for handling data in business classes using Visual Basic.

Concepts in Policy Management

The more academic name for business rule enforcement is *policy management*. Policy management doesn't necessarily have to be solely enforced in your Visual Basic application. Business policy management, in fact, is realized—at least in part—in the application you develop. A well-managed organization has a set of policy rules in place to ensure that the organization's customer base and shareholders are perpetually satisfied.

Due to the increase of technology in the world of information processing, a well-managed organization is also one that is competitive with its peers in its industry. Thus, in recent years, when software applications written in languages such as Visual Basic gave organizations a competitive edge on peers without any software automation in place, the rush for applications soared. Underlying this rush is the fact that part of the organization's business policy management infrastructure became embedded in applications as opposed to residing solely in organizational manuals and the minds of employees.

Business policy management in applications requires an infrastructure for ensuring that organizational policies are properly enforced. This involves the collaboration of the Graphical User Interface and Database (or Persistence) Subsystems. Concerning the involvement of the Graphical User Interface Subsystem, business policy management is not necessarily to be confused with formatting and typographical error rules. For instance, a rule governing whether or not a user entered a special character where only date values should go is generally not viewed as a business rule. However, if the organization requires that a date value be entered and persisted to a database with a slash (/) instead of a dash (–), this is an organizational policy.

> **Note**
>
> Keep in mind that all Graphical User Interface (GUI) rules are enforced in each form's corresponding controller class. This makes it easy to reuse GUI rules from form to form, and project to project.

Remember the rather intriguing adage, "All rules are meant to be broken"? The underlying notion in this adage should guide you in implementing your or the organization's policy. Each time that the user or some client object violates a rule, a class in the Business Rules Subsystem must raise an error. (See the lesson for Day 18, "The Error-Processing and Exception-Handling Subsystem," for more on raising errors.) When you raise an error regarding business rules, this is similar to raising an exception. An *exception* is an abnormal path that occurs in the processing of business rules.

15

When you incorporate business rules concerning workgroups and users, scheduled jobs, and so forth, the Business Rules Subsystem can become very complex. In fact, the bulk of the time consumed on software development projects is in the elaboration of the logic incorporated in business classes. All nonpolicy subsystems are pretty standard and highly reusable almost immediately upon implementing them. However, business classes are defined from a number of sources, including the memory and experiences of employees. Designing and implementing the Business Rules Subsystem, therefore, requires great patience on the part of the Visual Basic development staff.

Guidelines for Identifying Business Rules and Enterprise Objects

The identification of business rules starts with use cases and business process models primarily. But in the absence of these artifacts, you can discover business rules by creating use cases, which involves talking to the users. Day 2, "Fundamental Object-Oriented Analysis," and Day 10, "Refining Use Cases as Application and Subsystem Architecture Blueprints," discuss use cases. You can also simply interview users and search through operations manuals and user manuals for legacy or peer applications.

WORKING WITH KEY STAKEHOLDERS

Trying to document business rules is very difficult. In fact, if you're not careful, you can consume lots of time trying to identify all of them. And even if you are fortunate enough to have identified them all, they may change, as organizations are very dynamic. Thus, you must work with key project stakeholders on a regular basis to ensure that the assumptions you make about business rules are valid. The stakeholders you should work with include the following:

- Project manager, process owner, or similar people
- Users
- Upper executives or the executive sponsor, if appropriate
- Developers already on-board at the organization or who have extensive experience in the problem your application is attempting to solve
- Business analysts, or equivalent, whose job it is to maintain documents and models that reasonably reflect the current state of business rules and process in the organization

---

Unearthing Existing Implementations of Business Rules

Discovering business and domain rules lies at the heart of what every application developer does when analyzing, designing, and programming. Unearthing new rules is an activity ideally suited for interviewing users and creating use cases as a result of the interviews. However, not all rules are known to the users collectively.

Some rules are as dynamic as the organizations for which they exist. If you've developed applications for others besides yourself, recall how they wanted to change rules periodically. The longer an application is used by users, the more the rules the application originally enforced change. This is why users implement a lot of workarounds and hacks with older applications. As a result, you have to unearth these kinds of existing rules in order to understand how to solve the same problem given the new rules. Truly, some rules are meant to be broken, and the applications have to adjust accordingly.

Modeling the Business Rules Subsystem Object Model

Throughout this book, you have already seen a number of sequence diagrams that showed the steps involved in each use case. These sequence diagrams, in effect, show you the interaction of the business classes (or candidate classes if they have not been well-defined yet). To reproduce them here would be redundant. Feel free to revisit them.

Modeling the Business Rules Subsystem Class Hierarchy Model

Although there have been some class diagrams introduced with a subset of the classes involved in the Business Rules Subsystem, it would be helpful now to see them in their entirety. It is safe to do this here because the Second Bank of Carrollton example is quite simple, with a relatively small number of classes.

Figure 15.1 shows the major packages of classes that are typical in a banking organization. Banking class packages were used as part of the ongoing Second Bank of Carrollton example. Figure 15.2 shows the business classes that make up the family of bank products for the Second Bank of Carrollton. Figure 15.3 is a diagram illustrating the class in the Business Rules Subsystem. The next section describes the classes and packages in the subsystem.

FIGURE 15.1.

The major packages of classes that are typical in a banking organization.

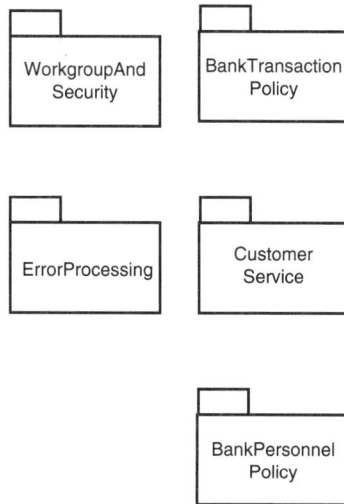

15

FIGURE 15.2.

The business classes that make up the family of bank products.

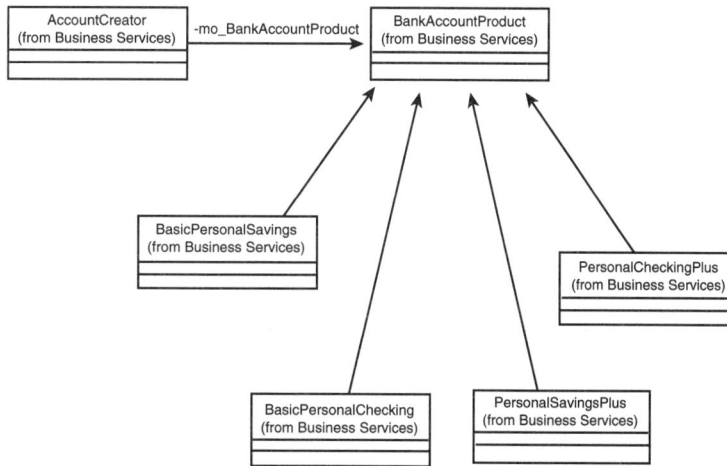

FIGURE 15.3.

*A diagram of the class-
es in the Business
Rules Subsystem.*

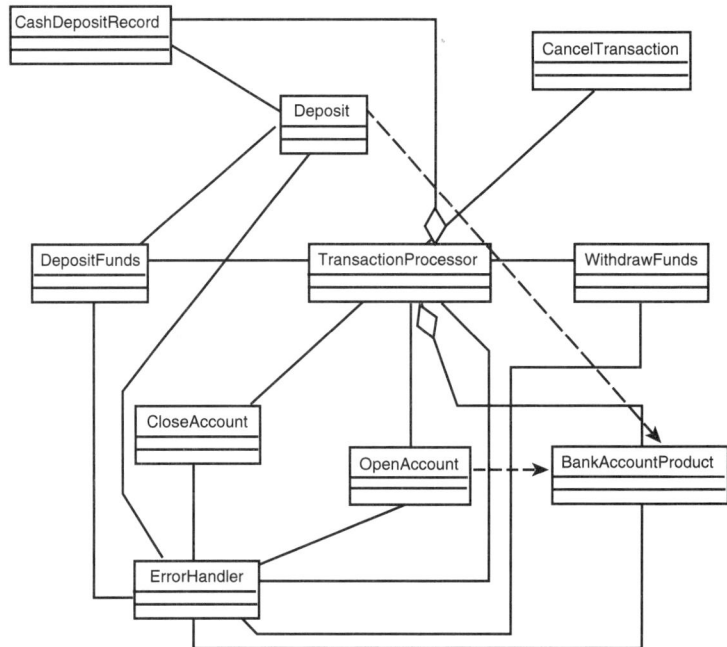

Describing the Packages and Classes in the Subsystem

The packages diagrammed in Figure 15.1 are

- WorkgroupAndSecurity
- BankTransactionPolicy
- ErrorProcessing
- CustomerService
- BankPersonnelPolicy

The packages WorkgroupAndSecurity and ErrorProcessing are discussed in detail in the lessons for Days 13, "The Workgroup and User Security Subsystem," and 18, respectively. The BankTransactionPolicy package includes the classes necessary to handle each banking transaction, including the following:

- WithdrawFunds
- DepositFunds
- OpenAccount

- `CloseAccount`
- `CancelTransaction`
- `CashDepositRecord`

The `WithdrawFunds` class encapsulates the business policy related to withdrawal transactions. Similarly, the `DepositFunds` class encapsulates the business policy related to deposit transactions. For every deposit, the `CashDepositRecord` class must be used to make sure a cash deposit doesn't exceed $10,000. If it does, a Cash Deposit Record form must be filled out by the bank teller online. The `OpenAccount` class enforces banking policy related to opening accounts. Of course, if an initial deposit is in the form of more than $10,000 cash, the `CashDepositRecord` class is used again. The `CloseAccount` class handles all rules related to closing an account, including making sure that if the account being closed is the last one the customer has with the bank, the customer has no outstanding debts with the bank. If the customer does have debts, the bank teller is notified, and the account is tracked until the debt is paid.

These classes, which have been discussed in earlier lessons in this book, work in conjunction with the classes in the bank account product family, including the following:

- `BankAccountProduct`
- `BasicPersonalChecking`
- `BasicPersonalSavings`
- `PersonalCheckingPlus`
- `PersonalSavingsPlus`
- `AccountCreator`

As mentioned in the lesson for Day 3, `AccountCreator` has the responsibility of creating the desired bank product when a bank teller, on behalf of a customer, opens an account. The `BankAccountProduct` class is an interface class that must be implemented by one of the other product classes.

Describing the Methods

The `CashDepositRecord` has a public interface method, `exceedsLimit`, that checks the amount of the deposit. Listing 15.1 in this lesson shows the code in it, as well as the supporting code in `ErrorHandler`, the `Enum eBusinessRules` in `modErrorHandling`, and the code in the `Deposit` and `DepositFunds` classes. The other business rule enforcement code is too lengthy to reproduce as a code listing in this chapter, but the code follows the same general pattern as that of enforcing the $10,000 cash deposit limit. The next paragraph describes the methods involved in this rule.

After the bank teller clicks the Done button on the deposit form, frmDeposit, the
DepositFunds controller class processes the button click. The actual button-click processing is not as important as the actual rule enforcement, but the following code snippet
shows the code in DepositFunds' clickedDoneBtn method:

```
Public Sub clickedDoneBtn()
    On Error GoTo clickedDoneBtnErr

    'your code goes here...
    processDeposit
    Unload theForm
    Set theForm = Nothing

    Exit Sub
clickedDoneBtnErr:
    'Call RaiseError(MyUnhandledError, "DepositFunds:clickedDoneBtn
    'Method")
    theErrorHandler.handleErrors Err
End Sub
```

The clickedDoneBtn method invokes the processDeposit method. This latter method
logs the transaction properly and then creates a Deposit object, theDeposit, based on
the values entered by the bank teller. These values include AccountID and Amount. It then
calls the exceedsLimit method of the CashDepositRecord object,
theCashDepositRecord, passing a reference to theDeposit. Note that this call is always
made regardless of whether the deposit was a cash deposit or if it even exceeded the
limit. This is not a requirement, but a pattern that encapsulates the conditional checking
for the deposit in the CashDepositRecord class. That way, if the government decides
later that the limit rules for cash deposits need to be more complex (that's the government for you), you can simply go to this class and modify the code in the exceedsLimit
method, with no other parts of your application being affected.

In the exceedsLimit method of the CashDepositRecord class, the amount of the deposit
is checked (assuming it's a cash deposit). If the amount exceeds the number 10000, the
handleErrors method of the ErrorHandler object, theErrorHandler, is invoked. The
transaction object, argTransObject, is passed, along with an enumerated constant,
eBusinessRules.CheckDepositAmount. This Enum value is a message ID letting
ErrorHandler know that this is a business rule exception, not a regular error. Finally, the
policy violation is brought to the attention of the bank teller, and the teller is shown the
form that contains the online Cash Deposit Record form. If you enforce your policies
with object interactions similar to the ones just described, the development and ongoing
maintenance activities associated with your application will be much easier.

Practical Guidelines for Implementing the Business Rules Subsystem

15

REAL WORLD

Most of the classes described here have been implemented. For Day 18's lesson, you will implement the ErrorHandler class for the example. The Branch Manager of the Second Bank of Carrollton has already provided the business policy management information you need, represented by the use cases and sequence diagrams.

Listing 15.1 contains subsystem code for the Samsona Bank Teller System example. The code for Listing 15.1 can be found on the CD-ROM in the \Day15 folder.

LISTING 15.1. CODE THAT SHOWS THE ENFORCEMENT OF THE RULE FOR CASH DEPOSITS.

```
 1: 'Global declarations in modErrorHandling
 2: Global theErrorHandler As New ErrorHandler
 3: Global theCashDepositRecord As CashDepositRecord
 4: Public Enum eBusinessRules
 5:     CheckDepositAmount
 6: End Enum
 7:
 8: 'The DepositFunds class
 9: Private theForm As frmDeposit
10: Private theDeposit As Deposit
11: Private Enum eDeposit
12:     AccountID
13:     Amount
14: End Enum
15: Private Sub Class_Terminate()
16:     #If DebugMode Then
17:     'the class is being destroyed
18:         Debug.Print "'" & TypeName(Me) & "' instance " &
➥CStr(mlClassDebugID) & " is terminating"
19:     #End If
20:     Set theForm = Nothing
21:     Set theDeposit = Nothing
22: End Sub
23: '##ModelId=34FDB8C302E4
24: Private Sub Class_Initialize()
25:     #If DebugMode Then
26:         'get the next available class ID, and print out
27:         'that the class was created successfully
28:         mlClassDebugID = GetNextClassDebugID()
29:         Debug.Print "'" & TypeName(Me) & "' instance " &
➥CStr(mlClassDebugID) & " created"
30:     #End If
31:     Set theForm = frmDeposit
```

continues

```
32:      Set theDeposit = New Deposit
33: End Sub
34: Public Sub processDeposit()
35:      On Error GoTo processDepositErr
36:      'your code goes here...
37:      If theSomeWorkgroupProxy.CurrProcess.isCurrTaskComplete Then
38:          theApplication.theAppTransactions.addTrans2MemLog "Deposited
➥funds"
39:          theTransactionProcessor.theTransaction.TellerID =
➥theUser.UserID
40:          theTransactionProcessor.theTransaction.TransID = depositFunds
41:          theTransactionProcessor.theTransaction.DateTimeStamp = Now
42:          TransactionGroup.Add theTransactionProcessor.theTransaction.
➥TellerID, _
43:              theTransactionProcessor.theTransaction.TransID, _
44:              theTransactionProcessor.theTransaction.DateTimeStamp
45:          Set theCashDepositRecord = New CashDepositRecord
46:          Set theDeposit = New Deposit
47:          theDeposit.AccountID = theForm.txtDeposit(eDeposit.AccountID)
48:          theDeposit.Amount = theForm.txtDeposit(eDeposit.Amount)
49:          theCashDepositRecord.exceedsLimit theDeposit
50:      End If
51:      Exit Sub
52: processDepositErr:
53:      'Call RaiseError(MyUnhandledError, "DepositFunds:deposit Method")
54:      theErrorHandler.handleErrors Err
55: End Sub
56: 'The ErrorHandler class
57: Private Enum eBusinessRuleViolations
58:      DepositLimitExceed = 1010
59: End Enum
60: Public Sub handleErrors(argErrObject As Object, _
61: Optional argMethodName As String, Optional argMsg As Integer)
62:      Set mvarCurrErrObject = argErrObject
63:      If Not IsMissing(argMethodName) Then
64:          msMethodName = argMethodName
65:      End If
66:      'handleDBErrors
67:      handleFileErrors
68:      handleGUIErrors
69:      handleMathErrors
70:      handleNetworkErros
71:      handlePrintErrors
72:      If Not IsMissing(argMsg) Then
73:          enforceBusinessRules argMsg
74:      End If
75:      handleUnknownErrors
76: End Sub
77: Private Sub enforceBusinessRules(argMsg As Integer)
```

```
78:     If argMsg = eBusinessRules.CheckDepositAmount Then
79:      'This method can handle the message
80:         Raise vbObjectError +
➥eBusinessRuleViolations.DepositLimitExceed, _
81:             "DepositFunds:deposit Method", _
82:             "Govt limit for cash deposits exceeded. Please fill out
➥Cash Deposit Record"
83:      End If
84: End Sub
85: Private Sub enforceBusinessRules(argMsg As Integer)
86:     If argMsg = eBusinessRules.CheckDepositAmount Then
87:      'This method can handle the message
88:         Raise vbObjectError +
➥eBusinessRuleViolations.DepositLimitExceed, _
89:             "Govt limit for cash deposits exceeded. Please fill out
➥Cash Deposit Record"
90:      End If
91: End Sub
92: 'The CashDepositRecord class
93: Private mvartheForm As Object 'local copy
94: Private theForm As frmCashDepositRecord
95: Friend Property Set theForm(ByVal vData As Object)
96: 'used when assigning an Object to the property, on the left side
➥of a Set statement.
97: 'Syntax: Set x.theForm = Form1
98:     Set mvartheForm = vData
99: End Property
100: Friend Property Get theForm() As Object
101: 'used when retrieving value of a property, on the right side
➥of an assignment.
102: 'Syntax: Debug.Print X.theForm
103:     Set theForm = mvartheForm
104: End Property
105: Public Sub showForm()
106:     theForm.Show
107: End Sub
108: Public Sub printInfo()
109: End Sub
110: #End If
111: Public Function exceedsLimit(argTransObject As Deposit) As Boolean
112:     If argTransObject.Amount > 10000 Then
113:         If theAppTransactions.pTransLogIsOn Then
114:             theAppTransactions.addTrans2Text _
115:                 "Deposit amount for account " _
116:                 & argTransObject.AccountID _
117:                 & " exceeded government limit"
118:         End If
119:         theErrorHandler.handleErrors argTransObject, V _
120:             eBusinessRules.CheckDepositAmount
121:         showForm
122:     End If
```

continues

▼ **LISTING 15.1.** CONTINUED

```
123: End Function
124: Private Sub Class_Initialize()
125:     #If DebugMode Then
126:         'get the next available class ID, and print out
127:         'that the class was created successfully
128:         mlClassDebugID = GetNextClassDebugID()
129:         Debug.Print "'" & TypeName(Me) & "' instance "
➥& mlClassDebugID & " created"
130:     #End If
131:     Set theForm = New frmCashDepositRecord
132: End Sub
```
▲

Summary

This chapter presented you with an overview of the Business Rules Subsystem. Specifically, you learned the purpose of this subsystem, concepts in business policy management, guidelines for identifying business rules and enterprise objects, and some advice on working with key stakeholders. You also learned about unearthing existing implementations of business rules, given the dynamic nature of organizations, large and small. Finally, you were presented with the classes and implementations in the subsystem, including a code listing.

Tomorrow, you'll learn about the subsystem responsible for reporting and printing.

Q&A

Q What's the most complex part of developing an application?

A The most complex part of developing any Visual Basic application is the design and implementation of the set of rules that make the application valuable to the user. The general expression for these rules is *business rules*.

Q What's a more abstract expression for business rule?

A A more abstract, generic expression is *domain rule*.

Q True or False: For simpler applications, the Business Rules Subsystem can be implemented with only one class residing on the client machine. For more complex applications involving a number of groups of users within an organization, business classes can reside on any number of distributed computers.

A True.

Q Is business policy management only embedded in applications?

A No. Business policy management doesn't necessarily have to be solely enforced in your Visual Basic application. Policy management, in fact, is realized—at least in part—in the application you develop. A well-managed organization has a set of policy rules in place to ensure that the organization's customer base and shareholders are perpetually satisfied.

Q What's the name of the enumerated constant passed to the `handleErrors` method of the `ErrorHandler` class?

A `eBusinessRules.CheckDepositAmount`.

Workshop

The workshop includes quiz questions to help gauge your grasp of the material. You'll find the answers to this quiz in Appendix A, "Answers." Even if you feel that you totally understand the concepts presented here, you should work through the quiz anyway. The last section include an exercise for you to work through to help reinforce your learning.

Quiz

1. What's a business rule?
2. Are domain rules only for business applications?
3. What's the purpose of the Business Rules Subsystem?
4. True or False: To build a sound, reusable subsystem of business classes, especially in a distributed architecture such as is typical in large, modern organizations, takes a small amount of time.
5. What is tricky about developing business classes in an environment that uses a relational database?

Exercise

In the `DepositFunds` class, insert code to check for the type of deposit. Use this code in the `processDeposit` method.

WEEK 3

DAY 16

The Reporting and Printing Subsystem

This chapter presents you with an overview of the Reporting and Printing Subsystem. In particular, you learn some powerful techniques for making your reporting and printing code effective and reusable in the form of a subsystem. You also get guidelines for planning cyclical and ad hoc reporting tasks. You learn about the three more readily available forms of printing and reporting available in Visual Basic: Crystal Reports, Access, and the Rich Text Box. This lesson presents you with helpful classes that should prove immediately beneficial in making your applications flexible when you need to dynamically choose a reporting option for changing user reporting needs. Perhaps the best feature of this lesson is that if you have a favorite reporting or printing control or body of code, you can easily implement it in this subsystem by simply following the pattern of class associations (methods and properties accessed by classes) in the lesson's sample code.

An Overview of the Reporting and Printing Subsystem

Visual Basic offers you several mechanisms for designing and creating reports. These mechanisms, which are the key areas of concern in this subsystem, include

- Crystal Reports
- Access Reports
- Rich Text Box Reports

The pivotal class methods for these three reporting mechanisms include those operations that open the report, print the report, and save the report. These operations are members of an interface class, IReporting. I discuss this class throughout the remainder of this chapter.

Understanding the Purpose of This Subsystem

The more popularly known approach of the three reporting mechanisms is Crystal Reports. However, the Rich Text Box also offers nice functionality for reporting, though it requires a bit more coding. Using Microsoft Access Reports is also very powerful and very easy to use. The Reporting and Printing Subsystem provides a common interface to each of the three to encapsulate much of the implementation of reporting details. The following three sections provide you with some helpful, straightforward background on each of the three reporting mechanisms.

Rich Text Box Reporting

Reporting and printing with the Rich Text Box control is relatively easy, though it requires some coding from you. Of course, you can simply print the contents of the Rich Text Box with the following code:

```
theRichTextBox.SelPrint Printer.hDC
```

where theRichTextBox is a reference to a Rich Text Box, SelPrint is the method you invoke to print the contents of the control, and Printer.hDC is the handle to the default printer. However, your users might expect at least a little more visual appeal than plain text as they view the contents either online or in print form. What is the developer to do?

The Rich Text Box offers several methods and properties to help you add some visual appeal to the body information you present to the user. The most helpful include

16

```
SelStart
SelLength
SelText
SelBold
SelColor
SelFontSize
SelFontName
SelColor
SelTabCount
SelTabs
```

The `SelStart` property, in conjunction with `SelLength` and `SelText`, allows you to format a specified sequence of characters or words in the control. These properties are ideal for visually setting apart the header columns from the remainder of the information in your Rich Text Box. `SelStart` specifies the starting position, `SelLength` specifies the length of the text you want selected, and `SelText` represents the actual text in your selection. Thus, given a string variable, `sHeading`, that contained the column headings for the top row of your Rich Text Box control, the property settings might look like Listing 16.1.

LISTING 16.1. VISUALLY SETTING APART HEADER COLUMNS IN A RICH TEXT BOX.

```
1: With theRichTextBox
2:    SelStart = 0
3:    SelLength = Len(sHeading)
4:    MsgBox .SelText
5:    SelBold = True
6:    SelColor = vbBlue
7:    SelFontSize = 18
8:    SelFontName = "Times New Roman"
9: End With
```

Notice the introduction of the properties, `SelBold`, `SelColor`, `SelFontSize`, and `SelFontName`. The property names are self-explanatory. `SelBold` makes the selected text bold. `SelColor` sets the selected color to whatever you specify. `SelFontSize` and `SelFontName`, respectively, change the size and name of the font the selected text has as attributes.

The `SelTabCount` property tells the Rich Text Box how many tab positions to put in the control. For as many tab positions you place in the control, the control has a collection of these tabs encapsulated in the `SelTabs` property.

Other helpful properties include the `SelBullet` property, which inserts a bullet at the beginning of the selected text. The `SelItalic`, `SelStrikethru`, and `SelUnderline` properties, like the `SelBold` property, change how the selected text appears to the user.

Access Reporting

Perhaps unknown to many Visual Basic developers, Microsoft Access offers a very powerful and easy-to-use object library for creating, modifying, and deleting reports. Although you can certainly create and delete Access reports through the ActiveX object library via Visual Basic, it's easier to create the reports in Access itself if you and your users have a copy of it. Access 95, 97, and beyond make it easy to create reports with its report wizards. However, for the purposes of this lesson, I concentrate on implementing the classes necessary to open and print existing reports that will be the more common operations you'll perform with Access Reports.

You can activate references to the Access object library by choosing Project | References from the Visual Basic menu. You must have Access installed on your machine, of course (although Visual Basic does ship with an Access object library). When it's activated, simply browse the objects in the library, named Access, in Object Browser. The typical declarations you might use for Access-based reporting include something like the following:

```
Private theAccessServer As Access.Application
Private theAccessReporter As Access.Report
```

where `theAccessServer` and `theAccessReporter` are your objects, `Access.Application` is the class of the Microsoft Application itself, and `Access.Report` is a class of every Access report. Each report is part of a `Reports` collection you can also access in Visual Basic.

The most common method in the Access object library you'll use is `DoCmd`. For you Access VBA developers, you'll recognize this command as one you use when programming in Access VBA. The main drawback with using Access is that your clients generally need to have Access installed on their machines. However, VideoSoft, a third-party vendor of Visual Basic controls, has a fairly new component called VS Reports. It is an amazingly useful tool that lets you distribute Access reports with your applications without your clients having to have Access installed. It is very reasonably priced. The vendor can be reached at `www.videosoft.com`.

Crystal Reporting

Crystal Reports is a third-party control in Visual Basic that allows you to offer some very powerful reporting design and capabilities in your application. However, working with its more advanced features can be cumbersome, especially because Visual Basic tends to ship earlier versions of Crystal Reports. Nonetheless, keeping your reporting requirements as simple as possible without compromising your users' productivity is an ideal strategy.

Figure 16.1 shows the Create Report Expert dialog box you see when creating a new report in Crystal Reports. To use Crystal Reports Report Expert, choose Add-Ins | Report Designer from the menu in Visual Basic.

FIGURE 16.1.

The Create Report Expert dialog box you see when creating a new report in Crystal Reports.

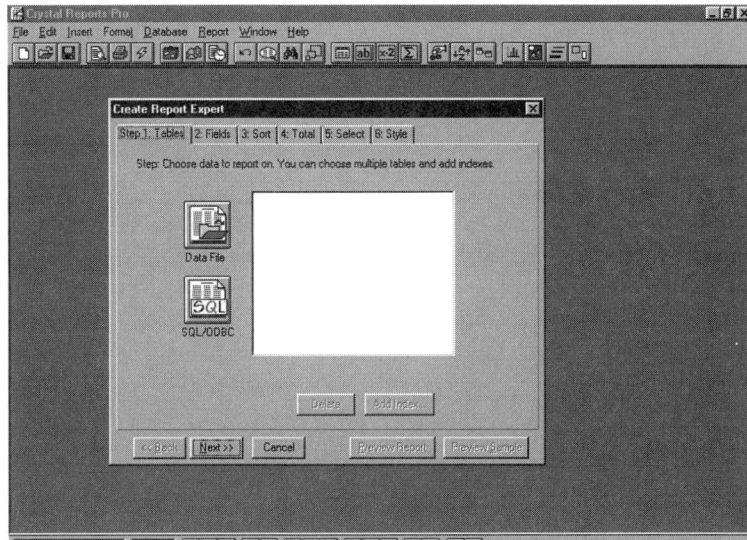

16

Your Crystal Reports control is driven by its Crystal Report Engine. The most popular Report Engine printing operations include a single menu command that produces a single report, a dialog box with a list of several options for printing reports, or a separate component that your application uses. The design of your graphical user interface and underlying subsystem typically depends on one of the following:

- The kinds and total number of reports your application presents to users
- How your users will use your application as indicated by the use cases that indicate the presentation of information in report form
- The underlying printing options you make available with the reports you present to your users

Again, try to keep the presentation of reports simple, at least in the initial versions of your application. Carefully assess the architecture of your application, paying special attention to the Reporting and Printing Subsystem. Design your architecture so that your application, and most importantly your users, will use the underlying Report Engine very productively.

Guidelines for Planning Cyclical and Ad Hoc Reporting Uses

Having users print built-in, canned reports immediately upon clicking a Print button is easy, especially when you design the reports in Access or Crystal Reports. However, giving the user the ability to schedule the printing of reports and customizing the kind of information printed from a report is more difficult.

Scheduling reports to be printed once at some future date and time or cyclically is not as involved as giving users ad hoc reporting abilities. It involves capturing the date and time from the user, saving it to a database, the Registry, or a text file, and continuously checking for the designated date and/or time. After the date and time have arrived, print the report. For this task, it is good to have a controller class called ReportScheduler and a form controlled by this class that has a timer control. The ReportScheduler class would have the following properties:

```
Private mReportDate As Date
Private mReportTime As Date
Private theForm As New frmScheduledReports
Private WithEvents theTimer As Timer
```

and the following methods:

```
Public Sub scheduleReport(argReportName As String, _ argReportDate As
➥Date, argReportTime As Date)
Public Sub cancelReport(argReportID As Long)
Private Sub isTimeToPrint(argReportDate As Date, _ argReportTime As Date)
Private Sub printReport
```

The private properties, ReportDate and ReportTime, respectively, contain the date and time the report is to be printed. The property, theForm, is a reference to the form, frmScheduledReports, which has a Timer control, a list box, or grid control to inform the user of the scheduled reports, and a command button, cmdCancelReport, that allows a user to cancel a scheduled report. The user would have to select a report first. The property, theTimer, is a reference to the Timer control on the form. The WithEvents keyword allows you to maintain the code for the timer's single event, Timer, within the class instead of in the form. This way, you can implement the same timer code from one class for many scheduling-oriented forms. In the ReportScheduler class, in its object list, you will see the theTimer object along with

```
Private Sub theTimer_Timer()

End Sub
```

The scheduleReport method is the public interface method that allows a client to specify the name of the report to be printed (argReportName), as well as the date (argReportDate) and time (argReportTime) the report should be printed. The isTimeToPrint method is responsible for comparing the scheduled date and time with the actual date and time within the theTimer_Timer() event. After the scheduled date and time arrive, it invokes the printReport method. The printReport method prints the report as its due date and time arrive. The cancelReport method allows the user to cancel a scheduled report. When canceled, the report is removed from the list box or grid control (either of which acts as a queue of scheduled reports). Listing 16.2 shows the code you could implement for the ReportScheduler class.

LISTING 16.2. CODE YOU COULD IMPLEMENT FOR THE ReportScheduler CLASS METHODS AND EVENTS.

```
 1: Public Function scheduleReport(argReportName As String, _
    ➥argReportDate As Date, argReportTime As Date) As Long
 2: Dim theFlexGrid As theForm.MSFlexGrid1 Static lCount As Long
 3:     lCount = lCount + 1
 4:     'Add another row for the new report
 5:     theFlexGrid.Rows = theFlexGrid.Rows + 1
 6:     'Make the first column of the last row current
 7:     'in order to add data to the cell
 8:     theFlexGrid.Row = theFlexGrid.Rows
 9:     theFlexGrid.Col = 1
10:     theFlexGrid.Text = lCount 'Assign report ID
11:     theFlexGrid.Col = 2
12:     theFlexGrid.Text = argReportName
13:     'Now add data to the remaining columns
14:     theFlexGrid.Col = 3
15:     theFlexGrid.Text = argReportDate
16:     theFlexGrid.Col = 4
17:     theFlexGrid.Text = argReportTime
18:     scheduleReport = lCount
19: End Function
20:
21: Public Sub cancelReport(argReportID As Long)
22:     Dim lRow As Long, lCol As Long
23:     theFlexGrid.Col = 1
24:     For lRow = 1 To theFlexGrid.Rows
25:       theFlexGrid.Row = lRow
26:       If theFlexGrid.Text = argReportID Then
27:         For lCol = 1 To theFlexGrid.Cols
28:           theFlexGrid.Col = lCol
29:           theFlexGrid.Text = ""
30:         Next lCol
31:       End If
```

continues

LISTING **16.2.** CONTINUED

```
32:    Next lRow
33: End Sub
34:
35: Private Sub isTimeToPrint(argReportDate As Date, _ argReportTime As
    ➥Date)
36:    'Incoming arguments represent Date and Time passed in
37:    Dim dReportDate As Date, dReportTime As Date
38:    Dim sReportName As String
39:    For lRow = 1 To theFlexGrid.Rows
40:      theFlexGrid.Row = lRow
41:      theFlexGrid.Col = 3
42:      dReportDate = theFlexGrid.Text
43:      theFlexGrid.Col = 4
44:      dReportTime = theFlexGrid.Text
45:      If argReportDate = dReportDate And
46:      argReportTime = dReportTime Then
47:          theFlexGrid.Col = 2
48:          sReportName = theFlexGrid.Text
49:          printReport sReportName
50:    Next lRow
51:
52: End Sub
53:
54: Private Sub printReport(argReportName As String)
55:      'Send the report name to the actual reporting class
56:      'responsible for getting and printing reports
57:      theReporting.printReport argReportName
58: End Sub
59:
60: Private Sub theTimer_Timer()
61:      'Periodically invoke isTimeToPrint()
62:      isTimeToPrint Date, Time
63: End Sub
```

Notice the scheduleReport method. It is compatible with all of the grid controls Visual
Basic supports. But the MSFlexGrid control has an AddItem method that would have simplified the code as follows:

```
theFlexGrid.AddItem lCount & vbTab & argReportName & vbTab & argReportDate _
    & vbTab & argReportTime, lCount
```

Then the method cancelReport would look like

```
theFlexGrid.RemoveItem argReportID
```

Designing your application to incorporate ad hoc reporting capabilities, at a minimum,
requires that you accept a query from the user. The user need not be a standard query
language (SQL) expert, but if the user does not know SQL, you must incorporate a query

16

building tool in your application. Crystal Reports offers such a tool, although the version
that ships with Visual Basic might be awkward. If you know at design time the tables
from which the user will choose fields, you could present the user with some user-friendly
list-views of the tables in the database and the fields in each table the user selects. Based
on these selections, build a query and pass that query to either Access or Crystal Reports.
For Crystal Reports, the syntax for setting the query of the active Crystal Reports control is

```
theCrystalControl.SQLQuery = "SELECT SomeColumn FROM SomeTable . . ."
```

where `theCrystalControl` is a reference to a current Crystal Reports control. You set
this reference in the controller class that is responsible for the main reports form you
implement. (`ReportController` for this lesson is the controller class you use.) For
Access Reports objects, the syntax is

```
theAccessReport.RecordSource = "SELECT SomeColumn FROM SomeTable . . ."
```

where `theAccessServer` is an object of type `Access.Report`.

Modeling the Reporting and Printing Subsystem Object Model

Figure 16.2 shows the usual interactions of the objects in this subsystem. A user, represented as Report User, views the main form, `frmReport`, that has a list of reports the user
can choose to open and print. Steps 1 and 2 represent this interaction. In step 3, the user
gets a specific report by selecting the report in a list box and clicking some command
button (let's call it `cmdOpenReport`). Step 4 is the method of the `ReportController` class
that handles the `cmdOpenReport_Click` event. In step 5, `ReportController` invokes the
`openReport` method of the `IReporting` class instance. In step 6, the `IReporting` class
instance invokes the corresponding `openReport` method of its implementation class,
`ReportingClass`, polymorphically. That is, when the `openReport` method of the
`IReporting` class instance is invoked, the compiler routes the method call to the corresponding `openReport` method of the class that implements the `IReporting` interface.
Steps 7 through 10 (printing the report) follow a similar pattern as the previous steps, but
step 11 involves a call to the `PrinterProxy` object to do the actual printing. It's called
`PrinterProxy` because it is a proxy, or stand-in, for the actual printer calls. Actually,
within the `PrinterProxy` are calls to Visual Basic's `Printer` object, the Access Reports
object's print methods, the Crystal Reports print methods, or the actual `SelPrint` method
of the Rich Text Box control. The nice thing about having a `PrinterProxy` object is that
regardless of how you actually use the printer functionality, you know to go to the
`PrinterProxy` class when you encounter problems.

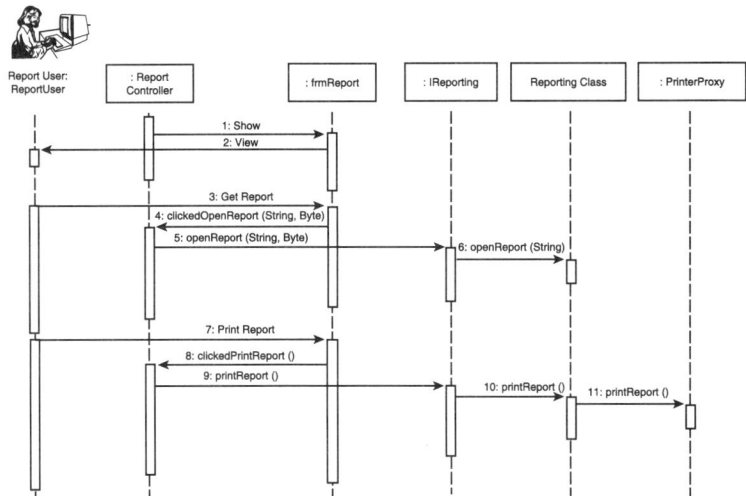

Modeling the Reporting and Printing Subsystem Class Hierarchy Model

Figure 16.3 shows the classes that generally make up the Reporting and Printing Subsystem. The names of the classes are as follows:

```
IReporting
AccessReporting
RichTextReporting
CrystalReporting
ReportController
RichTextFile
RichTextAgent
PrinterProxy
```

Describing the Classes in the Subsystem

`IReporting` is the interface class. It encapsulates the common members (methods and properties) of its implementing classes. Its methods are

```
Public Function openReport(Optional argRptName As String) Public Function
➥printReport(ParamArray argSettings()) _
As Variant
Public Function saveReport(argReportName As String) As Variant
```

FIGURE 16.3.

The classes of the Reporting and Printing Subsystem.

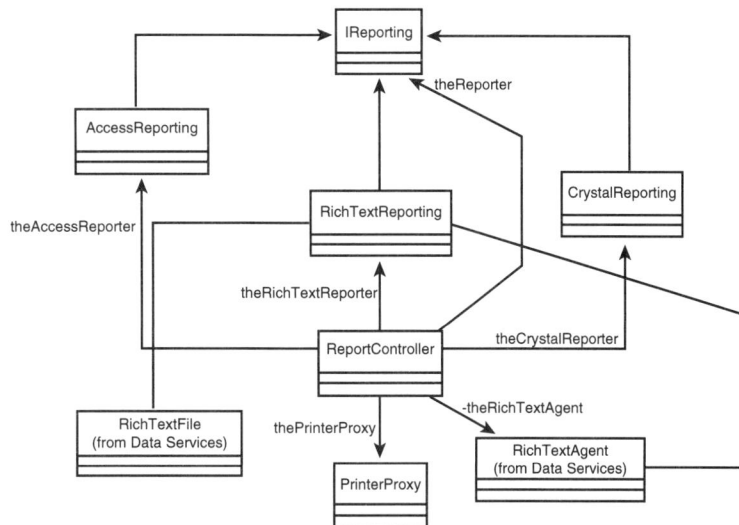

Its properties are

```
ReportName As String
thePrinter As PrinterProxy
```

Its members, as well as those of the other classes, are discussed in the next section.

`AccessReporting` implements the `IReporting` interface. It encapsulates the behavior and state related to Access reports accessed in your application. It has three special methods in addition to those in the `IReporting` interface, including

```
Public Sub setQuery(argQuery As String)
Public Sub displayReportList()
Public Sub setReportList(argComboBox As ComboBox)
```

`RichTextReporting` implements the `IReporting` interface. It encapsulates the behavior and state related to Rich Text Box information used in your application. It has one special method in addition to those in the `IReporting` interface, including

```
Public Sub setRichTextBox(argRichTextBox As RichTextBox)
```

`CrystalReporting` implements the `IReporting` interface. It encapsulates the behavior and state related to Crystal Reports used in your application. It has three special methods in addition to those in the `IReporting` interface, including

```
Public Sub connectToDataSource(argConnString As String)
Public Sub setCrystalControl(argCrystalControl _
As CrystalReport)
Public Sub setQuery(argQuery As String)
```

ReportController is probably best described as the headquarters of all functionality exhibited by this subsystem. It owns a reference to the main report form, frmReport, as well as references to the IReporting class of objects. It has many methods it implements, including

```
Public Sub clickedOpenReport(Optional argReportName _
As String, Optional argReportType As Byte)
Public Sub clickedPrintReport()
Public Sub clickedSaveReport()
Public Sub enableTabStops(argValue As Boolean)
Public Sub hideForm()
Public Sub processToolbar(argButton)
Private Sub setAccessReporting(argMsg As Byte)
Private Sub setCrystalReporting(argMsg As Byte)
Private Sub setRichTextReporting(argMsg As Byte)
Public Sub showForm()
Public Sub updateProgress(argProgressUnit As Long, _
Optional argMessage As String, Optional argProgressTotal _ As Long)
```

RichTextFile is responsible for handling the interactions with the actual Rich Text Box control. Because of its role in other subsystems, please refer to the lesson for Day 17, "The File Operations Subsystem," which describes this class in more detail.

RichTextAgent brokers some of the interactions for the RichTextFile. Because it delegates the same methods as RichTextFile, please refer to the lesson for Day 17, which describes this class in more detail.

PrinterProxy encapsulates any behavior that is directly related to the printer. It has a single public method, printReport. It is in this class where you would add special calls to the printer as discussed earlier. You could even insert low-level API code in this class if your application's requirements call for it.

Methods for the IReporting Class The openReport method is responsible for opening any report. If the information in the report needs to be specially gathered, include that code here. The argRptName argument can be the actual name of the report that Access or Crystal Reports expects, or the filename including the path that the Rich Text Box expects.

The printReport method is responsible for printing the report. It delegates the actual printing to the PrinterProxy, but the best use of PrinterProxy is for accessing members of the Printer object in Visual Basic, including hDC (the device context handle for the printer). Notice the `ParamArray argSettings()` argument. This argument mechanism allows you to overload the polymorphic call to the `printReport` method where an arbitrary number of special settings are required by the underlying implementation class. This is especially important for Access and Crystal Reports, both of which have several special settings you can specify.

The `saveReport` method allows you to save the report to a designated location on disk if disk storage is required.

16

Methods for the `AccessReporting` Class   The `setQuery` method lets you specify the query for the current Access report. `argQuery` is the argument that contains the actual SQL statement. If desired, you can include some code to verify the syntax of the SQL statement, but it's much easier to simply raise errors whenever the syntax is incorrect.

The `displayReportList` method displays a list of Access reports in the Combo Box referenced by the argument `argComboBox`. The list of reports is generated by the `Reports` collection of the `Access.Application` object.

The `setReportList` method sets a local, private reference to the Combo Box object being passed in. The Combo Box must be set before displaying the report list.

Methods for the `RichTextReporting` Class   The `setRichTextBox` method sets a private reference to the Rich Text Box that is to contain the formatted report information.

Methods for the `CrystalReporting` Class   The `connectToDataSource` method established connection to the source of the data, the database. The connection string represented by `argConnString` generally looks like

`"DSN=MyDataSourceName;UID=MyUserID;PWD=MyPassword"`

The `setQuery` method, like the similarly named method for `AccessReporting`, specifies the SQL statement to be used to populate a given report.

Methods for the `ReportController` Class   The `clickedOpenReport` method handles the implementation of the event associated with opening a report. Generally, when the user clicks a command button that triggers the request to open a report, this method accepts responsibility for the fulfillment of that request. The `clickedPrintReport` and `clickedSaveReport`, respectively, handle the request for printing and saving reports in a similar manner.

The `enableTabStops` method disables and enables the tab stops of controls on the form, `frmReport`. Although this method can be used for any reporting implementation, it's best used with `RichTextReporting`.

The `showForm` and `hideForm` methods handle the displaying and hiding of `frmReport` to the user. The `processToolbar` method processes all user interaction with the Toolbar control on `frmReport`. If you don't have a Toolbar control on your form, you can ignore this method. (But review the code in it in order to properly implement similar code in your application. The code can be found on the CD-ROM.)

The methods `setAccessReporting`, `setCrystalReporting`, and `setRichTextReporting` make it convenient for localizing the special `ReportController` behaviors that are specific to each reporting implementation. That way, when you discover errors related to a particular implementation object not being set or something related to the initiating of a particular reporting implementation, you simply review the code in these methods first to find your likely suspects.

The `updateProgress` method is responsible for updating the user with the latest information on how far into the process of opening and/or printing the report the application has gone. This method can also be helpful to you in debugging the application. The argument, `argProgressUnit`, represents the numeric unit that represents the current item being processed. Generally, the unit will be a record. It is used in a loop that processes many records. The `argMessage` argument, which is optional, is used to provide the actual text message to display to the user in one of the Status Panel's Panel controls. It is optional because you generally need to set the message only once per process loop (typically at the beginning). The same is true of the `argProgressTotal` argument. It represents the total number of units being processed. Thus, if you display to the user a message like

```
"Record currently processed: " ¦ 10 ¦ of 100
```

the `"Record currently processed: "` part would correspond to `argMessage`, the number `10` corresponds to `argProgressUnit`, and `100` maps to `argProgressTotal`. The pipe-delimiters each represent a panel control on a Status Bar control. If you don't use a Status Bar control, you would map each to, for instance, a text box, label, or cell in a grid.

Properties of the `IReporting` Class   The `ReportName` property contains the name of the current report being handled by the class. The `thePrinter` property is a private module variable that the class uses for delegating the printing of reports.

> **PRACTICAL GUIDELINES FOR IMPLEMENTING THE REPORTING AND PRINTING SUBSYSTEM**
>
> Perhaps the easiest and most extensible way to implement a reporting mechanism is Microsoft Access. It is very powerful, and it works extremely well with Visual Basic as both implement Microsoft's ActiveX/COM+ architecture. Nevertheless, it is straightforward to replace the implementation of the `IReporting` interface class with `CrystalReporting` or `RichTextReporting` if your customers have needs that demand one of these approaches. The beauty of this subsystem is that its basic interface and structure don't change with different implementations. Simply pull out one of the implementation classes and replace it with another that adheres to the `IReporting` interface.

Incorporating the Subsystem into the Samsona Bank Teller System Example

The branch manager requires only that accounts that required Cash Deposit Records be printed. She has decided that if any bank examiners or auditors need to see other information, they should pester the database administrator for the information. The format of the report should be simple, including only four columns:

Account Number

Customer First Name

Customer Middle Initial

Customer Last Name

You decide to implement `RichTextReporting`. Because you see a need for a class that would handle the formatting of the Rich Text Box separately, you create a `RichTextFormatting` class. You also create a `Customer` class with a corresponding `AllCustomers` collection. The collection is helpful for queuing many customers and their account numbers, or retrieving the account information from the database if you store Cash Deposit Record accounts there. The `Customer` class has the following properties:

```
AccountNumber As String 'local copy
CustomerID As String 'local copy
FirstName As String 'local copy
LastName As String 'local copy
MiddleInitial As String 'local copy
```

▼   The `AllCustomers` collection class has the following methods:

```
Public Function Add(AccountNumber, CustomerID, FirstName _ As String,
➥MiddleInitial As String, LastName As String, _ Optional sKey As String)
➥As Customer

Public Sub buildReport(argFileName As String, _
Optional argRichTextBox As RichTextBox)

Public Sub getFirstObject()

Public Sub getLastObject()

Public Sub getNextObject()

Public Sub getPreviousObject()

Public Sub getCDRReportHeading(argRichTextBox _
As RichTextBox, ByRef argCols)

Public Sub initializeObjects(ParamArray argPropertyStates())

Public Sub Remove(vntIndexKey As Variant)

Public Sub saveAllCustomers()
```

Most of these methods' names clearly explain the purpose of the underlying method. The `initializeObjects` method is a facade to the `Add` method so that it can be used in a loop in the `RichTextReporting` mechanism when creating each object to be added to the collection from a comma-delimited file. Why the facade? Because you don't want `RichTextReporting` to have to know each property in the class. It should know only each column in the comma-delimited file. This helps with encapsulation concerns. The `saveAllCustomers` method works the same as `initializeObjects`, but in reverse, saving each object's data (or state) to the file. The `RichTextFile` handles the details of saving the information. Again, encapsulation of properties is achieved because the `AllCustomers` collection is adding the information to the contents of the Rich Text Box via the `RichTextFile`'s `Contents` property.

The `AllCustomers` class also has the following properties:

```
Public Property Get Count() As Long
Public Property Get CurrObject() As Customer
```
▼   ```Public Property Get Item(vntIndexKey As Variant) As Customer```

▼ The Count and Item properties are typical of collections. The CurrObject property, though seemingly similar to Item, is in fact helpful in cases where a client doesn't know the index of the current Customer object. The property is also helpful when you want to do polymorphic method invocations on any number of Customer objects in the AllCustomers class in a loop through the collection.

Note

> The CurrObject property can be replaced with a private numeric variable that holds the index value of the current Customer object.

16

The code for this subsystem would be too numerous to list here. Please refer to the complete code on the CD-ROM. However, the ReportController class code is listed in Listing 16.3.

LISTING 16.3. THE ReportController CLASS CODE.

```
 1: VERSION 1.0 CLASS
 2: BEGIN
 3:   MultiUse = -1  'True
 4: END
 5: Attribute VB_Name = "ReportController"
 6: Attribute VB_GlobalNameSpace = False
 7: Attribute VB_Creatable = True
 8: Attribute VB_PredeclaredId = False
 9: Attribute VB_Exposed = False
10: Attribute VB_Ext_KEY = "SavedWithClassBuilder" ,"Yes"
11: Attribute VB_Ext_KEY = "Top_Level" ,"Yes"
12: Attribute VB_Ext_KEY = "RVB_UniqueId" ,"3521520F0190"
13: '
14: Option Base 0
15: Private WithEvents theTimer As Timer
16: Attribute theTimer.VB_VarHelpID = -1
17: 'eReporting
18: '##ModelId=3521520F0200
19: Private theReporting As New IReporting
20: '##ModelId=3521520F026E
21: Private theAccessReporter As AccessReporting
22: '##ModelId=3521520F02AA
23: Private theCrystalReporting As CrystalReporting
24: '##ModelId=3521520F0318
25: Private theRichTextReporter As RichTextReporting
```

continues

```
26: '##ModelId=3521520F0386
27: Private thePrinterProxy As PrinterProxy
28: Public theRichTextFormatting As New RichTextFormatting
29:
30: '##ModelId=3521520F03B8
31: Private theReportDB As DAO.Database
32: '##ModelId=35215210000C
33: Private theForm As New frmRTF 'frmReport
34: 'Private theRichTextFormatting As New RichTextFormatting
35:
36: '##ModelId=35215B560294
37: Private Sub Class_Terminate()
38:     #If DebugMode Then
39:     'the class is being destroyed
40:         Debug.Print "'" & TypeName(Me) & "' instance " &
➥CStr(mlClassDebugID) & " is terminating"
41:     #End If
42: End Sub
43:
44: '##ModelId=35215B56017C
45: Private Sub Class_Initialize()
46:     #If DebugMode Then
47:         'get the next available class ID, and print out
48:         'that the class was created successfully
49:         mlClassDebugID = GetNextClassDebugID()
50:         Debug.Print "'" & TypeName(Me) & "' instance " &
➥CStr(mlClassDebugID) & " created"
51:     #End If
52: End Sub
53:
54: '##ModelId=35215210003C
55: Public Sub clickedOpenReport(Optional argReportName As String,
➥Optional argReportType As Byte)
56:     Dim bReportType As Byte
57:     Screen.MousePointer = vbHourglass
58: '    bReportType = eReporting.RichTextReporting
59:     bReportType = eReporting.AccessReporting
60: '    bReportType = eReporting.CrystalReporting
61:
62:     'Only one of these three calls
63:     'will be able to process message
64:     setRichTextReporting bReportType
65:     setAccessReporting bReportType
66:     setCrystalReporting bReportType
▼ 67:
```

```
 68:        'Polymorphic call to openReport() method
 69:        theReporting.openReport theForm.txtReportName
 70:        Screen.MousePointer = vbDefault
 71:
 72: End Sub
 73:
 74: '##ModelId=3521521000AA
 75: Public Sub clickedPrintReport()
 76:        Screen.MousePointer = vbHourglass
 77:        If TypeName(theReporting) <> "Nothing" Then
 78:            'Set thePrinterProxy = New PrinterProxy
 79:            theReporting.printReport 1
 80:        End If
 81:        Screen.MousePointer = vbDefault
 82: End Sub
 83:
 84: '##ModelId=3521521000E6
 85: Public Sub clickedSaveReport()
 86:        If TypeName(theReporting) <> "Nothing" Then
 87:            Screen.MousePointer = vbHourglass
 88:            Dim sPath As String
 89:            'sPath = App.Path & "\Company.rtf"
 90:            Call theReporting.saveReport(theForm.txtReportName)
 91:            Screen.MousePointer = vbDefault
 92:        End If
 93: End Sub
 94:
 95: '##ModelId=352152100118
 96: Public Sub testRichTextReport()
 97:
 98: End Sub
 99:
100: '##ModelId=352152100186
101: Public Sub testAccessReport()
102:
103: End Sub
104:
105: '##ModelId=3521521001C2
106: Public Sub testCrystalReport()
107:
108: End Sub
109:
110: '##ModelId=3521521001F4
111: Private Sub setAccessReporting(argMsg As Byte)
112:        If eReporting.AccessReporting = argMsg Then
113:            Set theAccessReporting = New AccessReporting
```

16

continues

```
114:        Set theReporting = theAccessReporting
115:        theAccessReporting.setReportList theForm.cboReports
116:        'theForm.txtReportName = "AuthorsRpt"
117:        theForm.txtReportName = "LocationPhysiciansRpt"
118:        'theForm.cboReports
119:    End If
120: End Sub
121:
122: '##ModelId=352152100262
123: Private Sub setCrystalReporting(argMsg As Byte)
124:    Dim sConnString As String
125:    On Error GoTo setCrystalReportingErr
126:    sConnString = "DSN = TestDB;UID = sa;PWD = sa"
127:    If eReporting.CrystalReporting = argMsg Then
128:        Set theCrystalReporting = New CrystalReporting
129:        Set theReporting = theCrystalReporting
130:        theCrystalReporting.setCrystalControl
           ➥theForm.CrystalReport1
131:        theCrystalReporting.connectToDataSource sConnString
132:        'theForm.txtReportName = "AuthorsRpt"
133:    End If
134:    Exit Sub
135: setCrystalReportingErr:
136:    MsgBox Err.Number & ": " & Err.Description
137: End Sub
138:
139: '##ModelId=3521521002D0
140: Private Sub setRichTextReporting(argMsg As Byte)
141:    If eReporting.RichTextReporting = argMsg Then
142:        Set theRichTextReporting = New RichTextReporting
143:        Set theReporting = theRichTextReporting
144:        theRichTextReporting.setRichTextBox
           ➥theForm.txtReportContents
145:        'theForm.txtReportName = "AuthorsRpt"
146:        theReporting.ReportName = txtReportName.Text
➥'theForm.txtReportContents.Text
147:        'theReporting.openReport theReporting.ReportName
148:    End If
149: End Sub
150:
151: '##ModelId=35215210030D
152: Public Sub showForm()
153:    'Set theForm = New frmRTF
154:    With theForm
155:        theRichTextFormatting.setupForm .txtReportContents, _
156:            .cmbFontName, .cmbFontSize, .cmbFontColor
157:        'Activates timer (see WithEvents declaration)
▼   158:        Set theTimer = .Timer1
```

```
159:            '.txtReportName = App.Path & "\KEN0001 PCP.txt"
160:            '.txtReportName = "LocationPhysiciansRpt"
161:            .Show
162:        End With
163: End Sub
164:
165: '##ModelId=35215210037A
166: Public Sub hideForm()
167:     Unload theForm
168:     Set theForm = Nothing
169: End Sub
170:
171: Public Sub setNewFontColor()
172:     theRichTextFormatting.setNewFontColor
173: End Sub
174:
175: Public Sub setNewFontName()
176:     theRichTextFormatting.setNewFontName
177: End Sub
178:
179: Public Sub setNewFontSize()
180:     theRichTextFormatting.setNewFontSize
181: End Sub
182:
183: Public Sub processToolbar(argButton) ' As ComctlLib.Button)
184:     'On Error Resume Next
185:     Select Case argButton.Key
186:         Case "Open"
187:             'ToDo: Add 'Open' button code.
188:             clickedOpenReport theForm.txtReportName.Text
189:         Case "Print"
190:             'ToDo: Add 'Print' button code.
191:             clickedPrintReport
192:         Case "Save"
193:             'ToDo: Add 'Save' button code.
194:             clickedSaveReport
195:         Case "Bold"
196:             'ToDo: Add 'Bold' button code.
197:         Case "Italic"
198:             'ToDo: Add 'Italic' button code.
199:         Case "Underline"
200:             'ToDo: Add 'Underline' button code.
201:         Case "Undo"
202:             'ToDo: Add 'Undo' button code.
203:         Case "Redo"
204:             'ToDo: Add 'Redo' button code.
205:     End Select
206: End Sub
207: Public Sub updateProgress(argProgressUnit As Long, _
```

continues

▼ **LISTING 16.3.** CONTINUED

```
208: Optional argMessage As String, Optional argProgressTotal As
➥Long)
209:     'argProgressUnit represents the unit of measure
210:     'that let's the user know what's going on with a
211:     'task. argProgressTotal is the total number of
212:     'unit being processed
213:     If Not IsMissing(argMessage) And Len(argMessage) <> 0 Then
214:         theForm.StatusBar1.Panels(eStatusPanel.Message) _
215:             = argMessage
216:     End If
217:     If Not IsMissing(argProgressTotal) And _
218:     argProgressTotal <> 0 Then
219: theForm.StatusBar1.Panels(eStatusPanel.TotalUnitsProcessed) _
220:             = "Of " & CStr(argProgressTotal) & " records"
221:     End If
222:     theForm.StatusBar1.Panels(eStatusPanel.CurrUnitProcessed)= _
➥argProgressUnit
223:     theForm.Refresh
224: End Sub
225: Private Sub theTimer_Timer()
226:     theForm.StatusBar1.Panels(eStatusPanel.FreeForm).Text = Now
227: End Sub
228: Public Sub setTabs(argTabCount As Byte)
229:     enableTabStops False
230:     theForm.txtReportContents.SelTabCount = argTabCount
231: End Sub
232:
233: Public Sub enableTabStops(argValue As Boolean)
234:     ' Ignore errors for controls without the TabStop property.
235:     On Error Resume Next
236:     ' Switch off the change of focus when pressing TAB.
237:     For Each Control In theForm.Controls
238:         Control.TabStop = argValue
239:     Next Control
240: End Sub
241:
```

Summary

In this lesson, you got an overview of the Reporting and Printing Subsystem. In particular, you learned some powerful techniques for making your reporting and printing code effective as well as reusable. You also received some guidelines for planning cyclical and ad hoc reporting tasks as well as additional tips on making the best of your reporting mechanism. Moreover, you learned about the three more readily available forms of printing and reporting available in Visual Basic: Crystal Reports, Access, and the Rich Text Box. This lesson presented you with helpful classes that should be immediately beneficial in making your applications flexible when you need to dynamically choose a reporting option for changing user reporting needs. Tomorrow, your lesson will give valuable class structures for handling file operations such as Random, Sequential, Binary, and once again, Rich Text Box file operations.

Q&A

Q What are three mechanisms for designing and creating reports in Visual Basic?

A Crystal Reports, Access Reports, and Rich Text Box Reports.

Q What is the more popular reporting mechanism known to Visual Basic developers?

A The more popularly known approach of the three reporting mechanisms is Crystal Reports.

Q What is `Printer.hDC` used for?

A `Printer.hDC` is the handle to the default printer. `hDC` stands for the handle to the device context (for the printer in this case). Use it to print to the physical printer it identifies.

Q What is the ActiveX type for an Access Application object?

A `Access.Application`.

Q What is the ActiveX type for an Access Report object?

A `Access.Report`.

Q What factors are important when designing your graphical user interface and underlying subsystem?

A The kinds and total number of reports your application presents to users; how your users will use your application as indicated by the use cases that indicate the presentation of information in report form; and the underlying printing options you make available with the reports you present to your users.

Workshop

The workshop includes quiz questions to help gauge your grasp of the material. You'll find the answers to this quiz in Appendix A, "Answers." Even if you feel that you totally understand the concepts presented here, you should work through the quiz anyway. The last section contains exercises for you to work through to help reinforce your learning.

Quiz

1. What are pivotal class methods for the three reporting mechanisms discussed in this lesson?

2. What is the benefit of using Microsoft Access for reporting?

3. What is the most common method you'll use in the Access object library?

4. What drives the Crystal Reports control?

5. What are the most popular Report Engine printing operations?

6. What is the chief benefit of the `ReportScheduler` class?

7. How does the Timer control and the `ReportScheduler` class members help the overall `ReportScheduler` class fulfill its responsibilities?

Exercises

1. Using the `ReportScheduler` class mentioned in the middle of this lesson, modify it so that it can handle a collection of scheduled reports.

2. Choose Add-Ins | Report Designer from the Visual Basic menu. Using Crystal Reports, create a new report based on the `biblio.mdb` database that ships with Visual Basic. Design the report so that it retrieves only authors from the Authors table whose last name begins with *M*. Open and print the report using the code on the CD.

3. Using exercise 2, and if you have access to Microsoft Access 95 or 97, create an Access report using Report Wizard. Open and print the report using the code on the CD.

DAY 17

The File Operations Subsystem

This chapter presents you with an overview of the File Operations Subsystem. You learn how to create classes that handle file operations such as open and close, as well as loading values into controls and classes, and navigating records saved in files. In particular, you learn

- The purpose of this subsystem, including treatment of random, sequential, and binary files, and how classes can encapsulate each type

- How you can benefit by using the Rich Text Box versus older file access methods

- The classes in the subsystem, as well as their methods and properties, arguments, and returns

- Practical guidelines for implementing the File Operations Subsystem in order to help you use it effectively

- How to incorporate the subsystem into the Samsona Bank Teller System example

Understanding the Purpose of the File Operations Subsystem

Handling the persistence of information to any source is a primary concern of every software application. Even serious computer and television video games have to save information about player scores to some media, whether it be hard disk or insertable memory cards. In Visual Basic, you need a handful of different classes to handle your application's own persistence needs.

If you've been developing applications in Visual Basic for some time, you're probably familiar with the classic pair of file operation commands:

```
Open FileName For Input As #FileNumber
'Grab some information from the file
Close #FileNumber
```

or

```
Open FileName For Output As #FileNumber
'Persist some info into the file
Close #FileNumber
```

The variable `FileName` can be any valid path and filename. By default, you normally save a file to the same path as that of your application. That is, the `FileName` variable could be set as

```
FileName = App.Path & "\SomeFile.txt"
```

The `App` object has a `Path` property that contains the name of the fully qualified folder in which your application resides. However, it doesn't contain the \ at the end, which is why the file, `SomeFile.txt`, is prefixed with the back slash. Figure 17.1 presents the primary pattern of classes you find in this subsystem. The classes in the class model are discussed later in this lesson.

Because the classes of this subsystem use some of the traditional file operations at which Visual Basic excels, I cover these mechanisms in the following sections. The three types of file access operations Visual Basic supports are

- Random File Management
- Sequential File Management
- Binary File Management

Figure 17.1.

The File Operations Subsystem's pattern of classes.

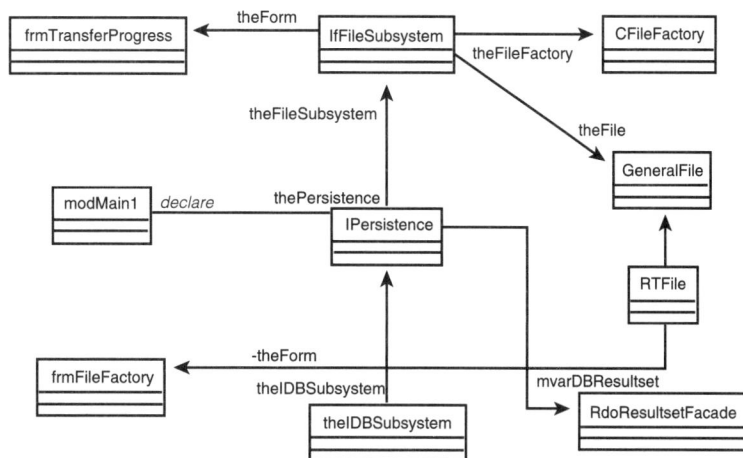

Random File Management

Using Visual Basic's random access file management is good for record-oriented files. Like a spreadsheet or database table, a random access file has rows and columns. A row, which is a record, that has only one column is good for populating list or combo boxes. The sole column can handle data of types such as an integer or fixed-length string. If the file contains a row with more than one column, you can map each row to a user-defined type (UDT). For instance, if you persisted the transactions of a bank teller to a random access file, you can map each row of the file to a UDT named `BankTellerTrans`, which can look like

```
Type BankTellerTrans
     UserID         As String * 12
     TransID        As String * 12
     DateTiemStamp   As Date
     AccountNum     As String * 15
 End Type
```

Declaring the `BankTellerTrans` UDT, or any other variable, should occur before accessing the file. If you're not careful in making sure that a UDT maps properly to each two in the random access file, including data types and column lengths, be prepared for lots of debugging effort. In the case of column lengths, if the column is expecting a string of 12 characters (`As String * 12`), and you only pass in eight, Visual Basic inserts four additional spaces (called *padding*, with each space known as a *trailing* space). If your value is longer than the 12-character limit, the value is truncated. Thus, it is wise to be careful in planning file formats.

Caution

> Before opening a random access file for output, implement code to enforce the lengths of columns. That way, if a string value is longer than what the column expects, you can raise an error or event before potentially losing data. Designing a class for this purpose, therefore, is a good, reusable approach.

Opening Random Access Files

Opening a file for random access is pretty easy. The following syntax is required:

```
Open pathname [For Random] As filenumber Len = reclength
```

Although the Random keyword is the default access type for Visual Basic file operations, it is good to explicitly state them. The length (or size) of each row is determined by the *reclength* value assigned to Len. If the row of information you pass in (as a UDT, for example) is less than *reclength*, an error occurs. If greater, no error occurs, but your management of disk space will not be optimal.

Tip

> An exception to explicitly naming the type of access in an Open statement is when you create a class called something like RandomFile whose purpose is to facilitate random access file operations.

Listing 17.1 gives you an example of opening a file for random access.

LISTING 17.1. OPENING A FILE FOR RANDOM ACCESS.

```
1: Dim iFileNumber As Integer
2: Dim lRecLen As Long
3: Dim Teller1Trans As BankTellerTrans
4: 'Specify the length of each row.
5: lRecLen = Len(Teller1Trans)
6: 'Get the next available file number.
7: iFileNum = FreeFile
8: 'Now open the file.
9: Open "transactions.txt" For Random As iFileNum Len = lRecLen
```

Modifying Random Access Files

The process for modifying a random access file is as follows:

1. Assign rows from the file into variables.

2. Modify the values in the variables.

3. Persist the values in the variables back to the file.

You read about the Open part of step 1 in Listing 17.1. The assignment of rows to variables requires the use of the Get statement as follows:

```
Dim lPosition As Long
. . .
Get #iFileNumber, lPosition, Teller1Trans
```

The Get statement uses iFileNumber to open a file and to assign it the number contained in the variable. You can view iFileNumber as similar to an index that differentiates one open file from another (in those cases where you might have more than one file open simultaneously). lPosition contains the row number of the row to copy. It is like a primary index or row identifier. The Teller1Trans user-defined type receives the contents of the row in columnar fashion. That is, each column is assigned to each member variable of the UDT.

Step 2 represents whatever you want to do to the values in code. In the case of the Teller1Trans UDT, you probably wouldn't want someone to modify it because a transaction is really a historical archive used for auditing (read-only) purposes anyway. However, if you have a UDT that has, say, a LastName variable, and a person got married or simply changed his or her name for whatever reason, or a data entry person made a mistake in typing, you'd definitely want the ability to modify information.

Step 3 involves persisting (or storing) the information modified back to the file. Use the Put statement for this operation. The Put statement is generally coupled with the Get statement in managing random access files. It has a very similar syntax as the Get statement.

To replace records, use a Put statement, specifying the position of the record you want to replace—for example,

```
Put #iFileNumber, lPosition, Teller1Trans
```

The row identified with lPosition will be modified accordingly.

The next section discusses sequential file management. Because much of the same pattern of operation for sequential files is similar to that of random files, the discussion is briefer.

Sequential File Management

Sequential file management is characterized by the following operations:

- Assign characters from a file to some variable via the `Input` statement
- Persist characters to a file from some variable via the `Output` statement
- Persist additional characters to the end of an existing file from some variable via the `Append` statement

Opening a Sequential Access File

Opening a file for random access is also pretty easy. The following syntax is required:

```
Open pathname For [Input ¦ Output ¦ Append] As filenumber [Len =
buffersize]
```

The `Input` keyword works only with files that already exist. Using the keyword otherwise results in an error, so it is good to have a class or class method that is responsible for making sure the file indeed exists and to raise an error or event in case it doesn't. Opening a nonexistent file using the `Output` keyword simply results in a new file. You might even have a class method name, `createNewFile(argFileName)`, with the sole purpose of opening a file for `Output` using the value of the filename in the `argFileName` argument. Although the `Append` keyword has the same effect as the `Output` statement, your code would be more readable and logical if you used this keyword only for existing files. You could have a method named `persistAddedInfo(argFileName)` or `appendInfo(argFileName)` for this purpose.

The optional `Len` argument indicates the number of characters to buffer when copying information between the file and your application. Use the `Close` statement to close the file.

Modifying Sequential Access Files

Modifying sequential access files follows the same pattern as modifying random access files. Once you open a file for sequential access, use either the `Line Input #`, `Input( )`, or `Input #` statement to map values in the file to your variables. A feature of sequential files is that you can read information contained in them either one character at a time or an entire line at a time. Listing 17.2 shows some code that reads a file one line at a time.

LISTING 17.2. CODE THAT READS A FILE ONE LINE AT A TIME.

```
1: Dim vFileContents, sCurrentLine As String
2: Do Until EOF(iFileNum)
3:     Line Input #iFileNumber, NextLine
4:     vFileContents = vFileContents + sCurrentLine + vbNewLine
5: Loop
6:
```

Notice the use of the Visual Basic constant vbNewLine. The Line Input # statement
uses this to identify the end of a line and the beginning of the next. However, the value
of vbNewLine is ignored when values are copied from the line in the file to your variables. Thus, in those situations where you want the vbNewLine value, you need to explicitly add it to your variables in code, not in the file. The Input # statement by itself is
very useful. If you have a number of variables into which you want to read values from a
sequential file, use a syntax like

```
Input #iFileNumber, sLastName, sFirstName, sBankTellerID, sWorkgroup,
sRole
```

The Input function, without the pound sign (#), can copy from one character to the
entire contents of a file into a variable large enough to handle the information. The Text
property of the Rich Text Box control can certainly handle large amounts of information.
String variables also are large enough, but be careful about eating up your computer's
memory. To read the entire contents of a file into a variable, use the following syntax:

```
vFileContents = Input(LOF(iFileNumber), iFileNumber)
```

Persisting Information to a Sequential Access File

Use the Print # statement to store information in your application's variables into a
sequential access file. Having a class named SequentialFile with a method called
something like persistNewInfo(argFileName) might help. The syntax for persisting
information is as follows:

```
Print #iFileNumber, sLotsOfInfo
```

If you have information that needs to be read from variables of different data types and
later needs to be exported to a database such as Access, you might choose the Write #
statement as an alternative to Print #. The Write # statement writes (or persists) a list
of string or numeric values to a given file. The beauty of the Write # statement is that it

automatically separates each value with a comma and puts quotation marks around values of the `String` data type. Applications like Access and Excel read comma-separated value (CSV) files very smoothly, a fact that's helpful if you are a developer for a software development outsourcing firm where clients might send you values using your client software to your server site, and you need to persist the information to a mature database. Listing 17.3 gives an example of the `Write #` statement.

LISTING 17.3. THE `Write #` STATEMENT.

```
1: Dim sCompanyName As String, sglStockPrice As Single
2: sCompanyName = "Samsona Software"
3: sglStockPrice = 100.25
4: Write #iFileNumber sCompanyName, sglStockPrice
5:
```

In Listing 17.3, the variable `sCompanyName` is of the `String` data type. The variable `sglStockPrice` is of the `Single` data type. Given the values assigned to each, the following literal information is persisted to the file:

```
"Samsona Software ",100.25
```

Nevertheless, sequential access files are best for document-style information as opposed to record-style information. Thus, when using the `Write #` and `Input #` statements with sequential access file operations, it is advisable to instead use random or binary access file mechanisms because they are specially designed for record/row-style information.

Binary File Management

Implementing binary access file operations allows you to assume significant responsibility not just for the contents of the file, but also for the way the file stores its information. Binary access file operations are most useful in situations where you must conserve disk space. This is probably of particular concern for commercial software development and outsourcing firms where it is not known how much disk space a client or customer machine might have available for their applications. In addition, it is generally best to use a `Byte` array whenever you persist information to a binary file. If you use `String` variables to persist the information, for instance, the binary file operations in Visual Basic assume the variable value contains string characters instead of actual binary information. Thus, there's a risk of data integrity being lost in making the mapping between `String` and binary data.

Opening Binary Access Files

Opening a file for binary access is, again, pretty easy. It is similar to the other access mechanisms mentioned earlier, except this time, the length of a row is not necessary. The following syntax is required:

```
Open pathname For Binary As filenumber
```

It's probably good to create a class called `BinaryFile` that has an `openFile()` method with this syntax in it.

Binary access file operations, though powerful, are sometimes complex. You have much more control over how information is stored, meaning you've got to be careful about what you store. Let's examine a bank transaction information binary file. Consider the following user-defined type (UDT) named `BankTransaction`:

```
Type BankTransaction
    TransactionID       As Integer
    TellerName          As String * 25
    Description         As String * 50
    MonthlySalary       As Currency
    HireDate            As Long
End Type
Dim SomeTransaction As BankTransaction
```

Each row of `SomeTransaction` information you save to the binary file consumes 49 bytes. For a handful of rows, this is minuscule. But if you must persist thousands of records to a file daily, and the file accumulates over time, you might need to consider better disk space management. Fixed-length strings almost always result in excess bytes of data as Visual Basic pads each `String` variable member with spaces to keep the length fixed. Binary access files are good for disk space management. Let's change the `BankTransaction` UDT as follows:

```
Type BankTransaction
    TransactionID       As Integer
    TellerName          As String
    Description         As String
    MonthlySalary       As Currency
    HireDate            As Long
End Type
```

Of course, the benefit of removing the fixed-length attributes of the `String` variables is that only the precise number of bytes is stored persistently. The disadvantage of binary files is that each row must be accessed sequentially (not to be confused with sequential access files) in order to compute the length of it. Use the `Seek` statement to go to a certain byte position in the file that has variable-length information; however, there's no exact way to get at a particular record.

Using the Rich Text Box Versus Older File Access Methods

Although opening files for random, sequential, or binary access is fairly simple, at times it can be tedious. Not only do you need to know the filename, but you also need to map an opened file with a particular file number. You also have to explicitly close the file when you're finished working with it. Although it's no binary access file mechanism, the Rich Text Box control makes managing files much simpler.

In short, the Rich Text Box control combines the text box, file operations, simple word-processing, and printing and reporting capabilities in one object. As mentioned earlier, the Rich Text Box can hold huge amounts of information, more so than the conventional text box. Plus, it gives you the flexibility to manage .RTF (rich text) and ASCII files (of any extension, but typically .TXT). If you want to store information in row and column format, simply insert commas and the vbNewLine value where you need it. And when you persist information in the comma-separated value (CSV) format, you can open it and read the information in it using the Random Access or Binary Access methods. In fact, as mentioned earlier, in CSV format, you can export the file to Access, Excel, SQL Server, and other databases that accept CSV files.

Moreover, there are no file numbers to remember. Simply invoke the LoadFile and SaveFile methods of the Rich Text Box, specifying the name of the file and the type of file (defaults to .RTF). If you need more than one file open at a time, create one form with a Rich Text Box control, and create a collection of controller class objects (where each object has its own reference to the form). Want to print the contents of the Rich Text Box? Use the SelPrint method. You can even bind the Rich Text Box to any ODBC-compliant data source to accept huge amounts of information, such as what you get with the Text data type field in SQL Server. Changing fonts and text colors, as well as doing searches for specific words, can all be done in Rich Text Boxes without much tedious effort.

The File Operations Subsystem Object Model

Figure 17.2 shows the interaction of classes needed to open a file of any type, be it binary, random, sequential, or rich text. Figure 17.3 shows the interaction of classes needed to close a file of any type. Although at first glance, there seems to be repetition, in fact, the success open and close file events are really delegations to the next class down in the hierarchy. The IPersistence class instance (or object) owns a reference to the IFileSubsystem class instance. This object, in turn, owns a reference to an instance of a GeneralFile interface implementation class such as RandomFile, SequentialFile, BinaryFile, or RichTextFile. One of these classes does the actual grunt work.

FIGURE 17.2.

The interaction of classes needed to open a file of any type.

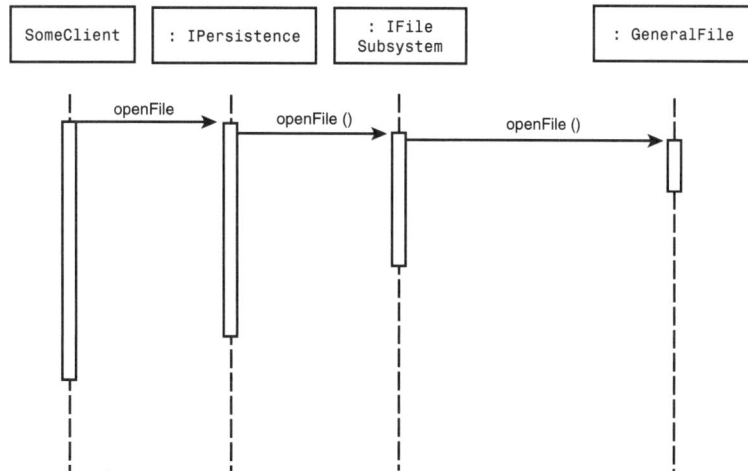

FIGURE 17.3.

The interaction of classes needed to close a file of any type.

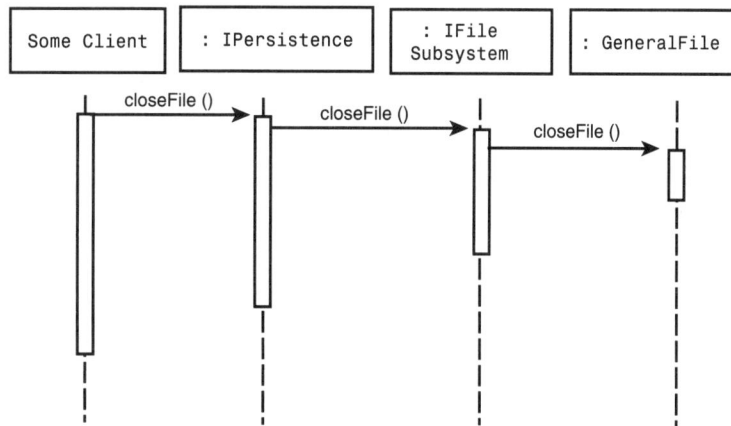

17

The File Operations Subsystem Class Hierarchy Model

In designing and implementing your own classes for this subsystem, it is important to remember that the classes in it will overlap with the Database Access Subsystem. Both the File Operations Subsystem and the Database Access Subsystem are forms of information persistence mechanisms, and in fact popular databases are nothing more than sophisticated file operation systems.

Figure 17.4 shows the hierarchy of classes related to each file.

FIGURE **17.4.**

The hierarchy of file classes.

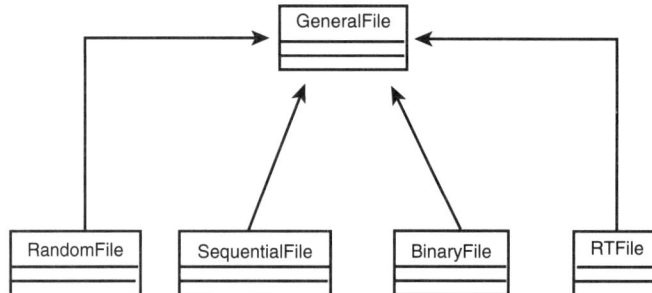

The Classes and Forms of the Subsystem

The forms in the subsystem include

- frmFileFactory
- frmTransferProgress

The frmFileFactory form is not only a visual object for displaying information in files to your users, it is also helpful in debugging your classes in this subsystem to make sure the information is being saved (persisted) to the file in the format you desire. The frmTransferProgress form displays the progress of the number of records copied from or to a file. This form is helpful when dealing with very large files.

The notable classes in this subsystem include

- IPersistence
- IFileSubsystem
- GeneralFile
- RandomFile
- SequentialFile
- BinaryFile
- RichTextFile

The IPersistence class is important as an organizer of any event triggering the persistence of information, whether in a database or regular file. This class is not owned by the subsystem but is the gateway for the flow of events with a given client. The IFileSubsystem class is the interface for the subsystem, making sure that the proper response to an incoming event or message is handled as expected. The TaskProgress controller class controls the frmTaskProgress form.

The `GeneralFile` class is purely an interface class, meaning that its methods and properties are to be implemented by other classes that subscribe to its interface via the `Implements` keyword. It is implemented by the `RandomFile`, `SequentialFile`, `BinaryFile`, and `RichTextFile` classes. The `RandomFile` class encapsulates file operations related to random access files. The `SequentialFile` class encapsulates file operations related to sequential access files. The `BinaryFile` class encapsulates file operations related to binary access files. The `RichTextFile` class encapsulates file operations related to Rich Text Box files. The `RichTextFile` class also includes methods for working with the Rich Text Box. If your implementation of this class becomes complex, you might consider creating helper classes that specialize in selecting a range of text and printing the contents of the file.

Methods

`GeneralFile` family of classes each support the following methods:

- `openFile`
- `closeFile`
- `persistNewInfo`
- `persistAddedInfo`

The `openFile` and `closeFile` methods are self-explanatory. However, each file class implements them differently. That is, the `RandomFile` class opens a file for random access, a `SequentialFile` class for sequential access, and a `BinaryFile` class for binary access. The `RichTextFile` class simply loads a file into the Rich Text Box and assigns the `Contents` property of the `RichTextFile` class to the value of the `Text` property. The `persistNewInfo` saves information to a file that did not exist before, while the `persistAddedInfo` adds information to a previously existing file. For `SequentialFile` objects, the file would have to be opened in `Append` mode.

The notable methods of the `IFileSubsystem` class are

- `copyFile`
- `deleteFile`
- `transferToFile`

The `copyFile` method uses Visual Basic's `FileCopy` statement to copy a file from one place to another. The `deleteFile` method uses Visual Basic's `Kill` statement to delete a file from disk. The `transferToFile` method takes the records in a Remote Data Object (RDO) `Resultset` and persists them to a file.

Arguments

The `copyFile` method of the `IFileSubsystem` class accepts a `String` argument for the source file and a `String` argument for the destination to which the file is to be copied.

The `deleteFile` method of the `IFileSubsystem` class accepts a `String` argument for the file that is to be deleted.

The `transferToFile` method of the `IFileSubsystem` class accepts an RDO `Resultset` object from which to receive records to persist to file.

Practical Guidelines for Implementing the File Operations Subsystem

In most of your applications, you're not going to need all of the `GeneralFile` family of classes. It is likely that you'll need at most two, with the `RichTextFile` class more likely. The `IPersistence` class will be quite busy if your application uses both database information and file information; however, in most cases, your application will only use one or the other.

Incorporating the File Operations Subsystem into the Samsona Bank Teller System Example

The branch manager at the Second Bank of Carrollton instructed you that she needs only a bank teller transaction file to record every withdrawal and deposit process each teller performs. Thus, in the deposit method of the `DepositFunds` class and the withdraw method of the `WithdrawFunds` class, the following steps must be completed upon the successful completion of these transactions:

1. Declare a `Transaction` object, `theTransaction`, as `Public` in the class `TransactionProcessor`.

2. Declare four global constants for the transaction IDs in the `modMain` module:
```
Public Const OPENNEWACCOUNT As Long = 100001
Public Const CLOSEACCOUNT As Long = 100002
Public Const DEPOSITFUNDS As Long = 100003
Public Const WITHDRAWFUNDS As Long = 100004
```

3. Invoke the add method of the `AllTransactions` instance, `TransactionGroup`.

4. In the `terminateSystem` method of the `CApplication` class, insert code to save the collection of `Transaction` objects to a file.

▼ The `AllTransactions` class has the two notable methods: `Add` and `saveAllTransactions`. Listing 17.4 shows this code.

LISTING 17.4. NOTABLE METHODS OF THE `AllTransactions` CLASS.

```
 1:
 2: Public Sub Add(TellerID As String, TransID As Long, DateTimeStamp
➥As Date, Optional sKey As String) ' As Transaction
 3:     'create a new object
 4:     Dim objNewMember As Transaction
 5:     Set objNewMember = New Transaction
 6:     'set the properties passed into the method
 7:     objNewMember.TellerID = TellerID
 8:     objNewMember.TransID = TransID
 9:     objNewMember.DateTimeStamp = DateTimeStamp
10:     If Len(sKey) = 0 Then
11:         mCol.Add objNewMember
12:     Else
13:         mCol.Add objNewMember, sKey
14:     End If
15:     'Set Add = objNewMember
16:     Set objNewMember = Nothing
17: End Sub
18: Public Sub saveAllTransactions()
19: 'Add the state of each Transaction object
20: 'to the RichTextFile text box. This is for caching of
21: 'Transaction objects in memory before saving
22: ' & vbNewLine
23: Dim aTransaction As Transaction
24: theFileSubsystem.theRichTextFile.FileName = App.Path &
    ➥"\Transactions.txt"
25: For Each aTransaction In mCol
26:     theFileSubsystem.theRichTextFile.Contents = _
27:     theFileSubsystem.theRichTextFile.Contents & _
28:     gsSINGLEQUOTE & aTransaction.TellerID & gsSINGLEQUOTE & ","
29:     theFileSubsystem.theRichTextFile.Contents = _
30:     theFileSubsystem.theRichTextFile.Contents & _
31:     aTransaction.TransID & ","
32:     theFileSubsystem.theRichTextFile.Contents = _
33:     theFileSubsystem.theRichTextFile.Contents & _
34:     aTransaction.DateTimeStamp & vbNewLine
35: Next
36: 'theFileSubsystem.theRichTextFile.showContents
37: theFileSubsystem.theRichTextFile.saveFile
38: End Sub
▼ 39:
```

17

▼ Listing 17.5 shows the code for the terminateSystem method of CApplication.

LISTING 17.5. THE terminateSystem METHOD OF CApplication.

```
 1:
 2: Public Sub terminateSystem()
 3:     theAppTransactions.addTrans2Text "Shutting down the " &
    ➥App.EXEName & " system"
 4:     'Set ifcDBConnection = Nothing
 5:     'theAppTransactions.addTrans2MemLog "Deallocated memory for
➥ifcDBConnection in CApplication.terminateSystem"
 6:
 7:     'Save all transactions
 8:     TransactionGroup.saveAllTransactions
 9:
10:     m_returns = ifcDBConnection.closeDBConnection
11:     theAppTransactions.addTrans2MemLog "Deallocated memory for
➥clsApplication in CApplication.terminateSystem"
12:     theAppTransactions.addTrans2MemLog "Deallocated memory for
➥theAppTransactions in CApplication.terminateSystem"
13:
14:     For m_returns = 0 To Forms.Count - 2
15:         theAppTransactions.addTrans2MemLog "Deallocated memory
        ➥for " & Forms(m_returns).Name & " in
        ➥CApplication.terminateSystem"
16:         'Because you are unloading the form that houses the
➥Rich Text Box, you
17:         'must save your log first.
18:     Next
19:     m_returns = theAppTransactions.saveLog
20:     For m_returns = 0 To Forms.Count - 2
21:         If Not IsEmpty(Forms(m_returns)) Then
22:             Unload Forms(m_returns)
23:         End If
24:     Next
25:     Set clsApplication = Nothing
26:     Set theAppTransactions = Nothing
27:     'End
28: End Sub
```

▼ Listing 17.6 shows the deposit method of the DepositFunds class.

▼ **LISTING 17.6.** THE deposit METHOD OF THE DepositFunds CLASS.

```
1: Public Sub Deposit()
2:     On Error GoTo depositErr
3:
4:     'your code goes here...
5:     If theSomeWorkgroupProxy.CurrProcess.isCurrTaskComplete Then
6:         theApplication.theAppTransactions.addTrans2MemLog
        ➥"Deposited funds"
7:         theTransactionProcessor.theTransaction.TellerID =
        ➥theUser.UserID
8:         theTransactionProcessor.theTransaction.TransID =
        ➥DEPOSITFUNDS
9:         theTransactionProcessor.theTransaction.DateTimeStamp = Now
10:         TransactionGroup.Add theTransactionProcessor.
        ➥theTransaction.TellerID, _
11:             theTransactionProcessor.theTransaction.TransID, _
12:             theTransactionProcessor.theTransaction.DateTimeStamp
13:     End If
14:     Exit Sub
15: depositErr:
16:     Call RaiseError(MyUnhandledError, "DepositFunds:deposit
        ➥Method")
17: End Sub
```

Finally, Listing 17.7 shows the code for the withdraw method of the withdrawFunds class. You can find the code in this chapter on the CD-ROM in the \Day17 folder.

LISTING 17.7. THE withdraw METHOD OF THE withdrawFunds CLASS.

```
1: Public Sub withdraw()
2:     On Error GoTo withdrawErr
3:
4:     'your code goes here...
5:
6:     If theSomeWorkgroupProxy.CurrProcess.isCurrTaskComplete Then
7:         theApplication.theAppTransactions.addTrans2MemLog
        ➥"Withdrew funds"
8:         theTransactionProcessor.theTransaction.TellerID =
        ➥theUser.UserID
9:         theTransactionProcessor.theTransaction.TransID =
        ➥WITHDRAWFUNDS
10:         theTransactionProcessor.theTransaction.DateTimeStamp =
        ➥Now
11:         TransactionGroup.Add theTransactionProcessor.
        ➥theTransaction.TellerID, _
```

17

▼

continues

```
12:                    theTransactionProcessor.theTransaction.TransID, _
13:                    theTransactionProcessor.theTransaction.DateTimeStamp
14:     End If
15:     Exit Sub
16: withdrawErr:
17:     Call RaiseError(MyUnhandledError, "WithdrawFunds:withdraw
        ↪Method")
18: End Sub
```
▲

Summary

This chapter presented you with an overview of the File Operations Subsystem. In particular, you learned the purpose of this subsystem, including helpful treatment of the random, sequential, and binary file access mechanisms, as well as how to use the power of
the Rich Text Box versus older file access methods. You also were presented with the
classes in the subsystem, as well as their methods and properties, arguments, and returns.
Notable classes introduced to you included `RandomFile`, `SequentialFile`, `BinaryFile`,
`IPersistence`, `IFileSubsystem`, and `RichTextFile`. You also received practical guidelines for implementing the File Operations Subsystem, as well as how to incorporate the
subsystem into the Samsona Bank Teller System example.

Q&A

**Q What kinds of information are both the random file access and binary file
access mechanisms good for?**

A They are both good for record-oriented information.

Q What is padding?

A Padding is the inserting of blank spaces to a string variable value.

**Q What happens when you try to add more bytes to a random access file column
than Visual Basic expects?**

A An error occurs. Before opening a random access file for output, try to implement
code to enforce the lengths of columns.

Q In opening a sequential access file, what is the purpose of the `Append` keyword?

A The `Append` keyword alerts Visual Basic that the application will add additional
data to a file that already contains information.

Q What value do you use to specify a new line in your file?

A The `vbNewLine` constant.

Q What kinds of applications read comma-separated value (CSV) files?

A Applications like Access, SQL Server, and Excel read comma-separated value (CSV) files very smoothly, a fact that's helpful if you are a developer for a software development outsourcing firm where clients might send you values using your client software to your server site and you need to persist the information to a mature database.

Workshop

The workshop includes quiz questions to help gauge your grasp of the material. You'll find the answers to this quiz in Appendix A, "Answers." Even if you feel that you totally understand the concepts presented here, you should work through the quiz anyway. The last section contains exercises for you to work through to help reinforce your learning.

Quiz

1. What are the three kinds of file management discussed in this chapter?

2. What is the purpose of the `Get` statement for random access files?

3. What are the four classes you could use to implement objects that manage files?

4. What does CSV stand for?

5. What kinds of file operations are best when using the `Write #` and `Input #` statements?

6. What is a benefit of implementing binary access file operations?

7. What is an assumption made about `String` values in binary files?

8. What are the advantages of using the Rich Text Box in managing files?

9. What is the purpose of the `IPersistence`, `GeneralFile`, and `IFileSubsystem` classes?

10. Explain the `persistNewInfo` and `persistAddedInfo` methods of the `GeneralFile` family of classes.

Exercises

1. The `IFileSubsystem` class has the methods `copyFile`, `deleteFile`, and `transferToFile`. Implement a method, `findFile`, that searches for the file indicated by an argument, `argFileName`, that a client passes in. Use the classes in this chapter. This example assumes you have experience with Visual Basic file operations. Open a new Visual Basic project.

2. Open a new Visual Basic project. For the class, RichTextFile, create a method that searches the contents of a file for any word. Use a less-important plain ASCII text file on your hard disk.

3. Open a new Visual Basic project. Using methods similar to RDO's MoveFirst, MoveNext, MovePrevious, and MoveLast, implement methods that assign each column to corresponding variables from a file, displaying the contents in a form. Use the following kinds of information for some arbitrary class, Person:

```
LastName As String
FirstName As String
BirthDate As Date

LastName = "Smith"
FirstName = "John"
BirthDate = #01/31/60#
```

Create a controller class, CPersonController, for the form frmPerson. Declare a private reference to the form. Create a method in CPersonController, initializeSystem, to add the information to a file and then load it back into variables, assigning the variable values to class properties. Display the values of the properties in the form. Add a code module as well as a Sub Main. In Sub Main, call the method initializeSystem.

DAY **18**

The Error-Processing and Exception-Handling Subsystem

This chapter presents an overview of the Error-Processing and Exception-Handling Subsystem. You will learn how to centralize the processing of errors and exception handling in one subsystem. You'll learn that all classes that raise should delegate the actual handling of errors, including displaying messages to users, to classes in this subsystem in order to reduce repetitive code. In particular, this lesson covers

- Why this subsystem is so important for developing serious, reusable application code
- How to effectively raise errors and exceptions, including errors originating in components external to the application as would be the case in distributed applications
- The classes in the subsystem, as well as their methods, properties, arguments, and returns

- Practical guidelines for implementing the Error-Processing and Exception-Handling Subsystem in order to minimize the risk of unnecessary application failure
- How to incorporate the subsystem into the Samsona Bank Teller System example

An Overview of the Error-Processing and Exception-Handling Subsystem

Perhaps it could go without mentioning that a serious application, whether for deployment on the Internet, a corporate intranet, or desktop, requires that all errors and exceptions be properly trapped. A quality application allows no fatal flaws, and few minor bugs. This lesson discusses error processing and exception handling and how to encapsulate these methods in classes.

Error handling includes the trapping and the subsequent chain of responses to errors in your application. Each significant class method and code module function (if any) requires initial error handling. Only the simplest methods that have been well tested or are otherwise no-brainers should be considered candidates for skipping inline error handling. Implementing inline error handling in your methods requires you to do the following:

1. Enable the error trap (equivalent to throwing an exception).
2. Respond to the error (equivalent to catching an exception).
3. Complete the error-handling process and, if possible, continue program execution.

Step 1 activates an error trap by informing the application what inline code to execute as an error occurs. In order to inform Visual Basic of what code to invoke, you use the On Error statement. The On Error statement initiates your error traps, specifying to which label the application should go to perform the beginning of the error-handling routine.

Step 2 implies writing an inline error-handling routine that responds to the errors that occur in a given method. It's in the inline routine that you invoke a method on an object whose class you create at design time to handle the attribute values of the Err object. It's advisable not to do too much complex error handling within a method as this could clutter your method code and make it difficult to debug. Besides, you want to be able to reuse sophisticated error-handling routines throughout your application.

Step 3 marks the completion of error handling and the resuming of code execution, if possible. The Resume statement tells your application to continue process instructions (lines of code) at the line where the error occurred. Visual Basic then retries that line of code. If the error condition has not been properly resolved, then the error-handling operation is initiated again. If your application continually encounters a problem that you feel is truly irrelevant or you just need to move on and debug other areas of your code while in design time, use the `Resume Next` statement. `Resume Next` does not require any special object-oriented treatment, so it won't be discussed further unless it's truly warranted.

The Visual Basic Books Online set includes some simple error-handling code for dealing with division-by-zero errors and other math errors. Let's create a simple class called `ErrorHandler` that has a method that encapsulates this logic. Start a new Visual Basic project. Using the Class Builder utility, create a class named `ErrorHandler`. You can also simply add a class module. Now, create a method named `handleErrors`. Its only argument is `argErrorObj As Object` (or `As ErrObject` if your situation requires early binding). It accepts the error object.

Using the default startup `Form1`, create a class, `FormController`, that controls `Form1`. Declare a private module variable, the `Form As New Form1`. Create a method, `showForm`. Add a code module, `modMain`. The code for `FormController` class is shown in Listing 18.1. The `ErrorHandler` class code is shown in Listing 18.2. `ErrorHandler` is declared globally as

```
Global As theErrorHandler As New ErrorHandler
```

LISTING 18.1. THE showForm METHOD OF THE FormController CLASS.

```
 1: Public Sub showForm
 2: Dim iSomeNumber As Integer
 3: Dim sglAnotherNumber As Single
 4: Dim iResult As Integer
 5: Dim sString As String
 6:
 7: On Error GoTo showFormErr
 8: sglAnotherNumber = 51000.25
 9: iResult = sglAnotherNumber / iSomeNumber
10: Exit Sub
11: showFormErr:
12: End Sub
```

LISTING 18.2. THE handleErrors METHOD OF THE ErrorHandler CLASS. IT IS ACCOMPANIED BY A HELPER METHOD, handleMathErrors.

```
1: Public Sub handleErrors(argErrorObj As Object)
2:     handleMathErrors argErrorObj
3: End Sub
4: Private Sub handleMathErrors(argErrorObj As Object)
5:     sMsg As String
```

continues

18

LISTING 18.2. CONTINUED

```
 6:    'If the following Select statement is able to handle message
 7:    'then the error can be handled by this method
 8:     Select Case argErrorObj.Number
 9:        Case eMathErrors.DivByZero
10:            sMsg = "Division by zero was attempted"
11:        Case eMathErrors.OverFlow
12:            sMsg = "Overflow occurred"
13:        Case eMathErrors.BadCall
14:            sMsg = "Illegal procedure call"
15:     End Select
16:
17: MsgBox sMsg, vbExclamation
18: Resume Next         ' the Exit Function statement.
19: End Sub
20: Private Enum eMathErrors
21:   DivByZero = 11
22:   OverFlow = 6
23:   BadCall = 5
24: End Enum
```

You could reduce the lines of code in Listing 18.2 as follows:

```
Select Case argErrorObject.Number
Case eMathErrors.DivByZero, eMathErrors.OverFlow, eMathErrors.BadCall
    MsgBox argErrorObject.Description, vbExclamation
End Select
```

However, this approach would not make your error-handling subsystem very precise in its treatment. But if your application doesn't require anything beyond what error information Visual Basic provides, then the simplified approach might be preferable.

The Purpose of This Subsystem

Designing and implementing components in Visual Basic can be a complex undertaking. You must create a useful set of interfaces as well as effective implementation classes and methods. More importantly, your components have to successfully handle errors and exceptions that are bound to occur. In particular, you must plan for the following kinds of errors:

- Errors that your component traps but allows the client to handle

- Errors that originate in another component from which your component received and used object references

- Errors that originate in your component that may have been the result of programmer error or some rule violation that must be enforced by your component

Handling errors that originate in your component and that your component must enforce is similar to error handling in standard Visual Basic applications. It would follow a pattern similar to Listings 18.1 and 18.2.

When you design your component to allow a client application to handle an error, you must raise that error. That is, the method in your component that trapped the error tells the compiler to notify the previous method (of the client application) on the call stack that it must catch the error your component is raising up the stack. It's sort of like playing hot potatoes, only you're passing the hot potato up the call stack to the body of code that called your component.

Raising an error involves the `Raise` method. To use the `Raise` method, your method should resemble the code outline in Listing 18.3.

LISTING 18.3. THE `Raise` METHOD IN ACTION.

```
 1: Public Sub doSomething()
 2:      On Error GoTo doSomethingErr
 3:      'Do some code here
 4:      Exit Sub
 5: doSomethingErr:
 6:      Err.Raise _
 7:          Number:=(SOME_ERR_NUMBER + vbObjectError), _
 8:          Source:=COMPONENT_SOURCENAME, _
 9:          Description:="Something's wrong here"
10: End Sub
```

18

You can also use the `Raise` method without error handling. Listing 18.4 shows an example of using the `Raise` method with error handling disabled.

LISTING 18.4. USING THE `Raise` METHOD WITH ERROR HANDLING DISABLED.

```
 1: Public Sub Run()
 2:      ' Use in-line error handling.
 3:      On Error Resume Next
 4:      ' Do something. . .
 5:      ' If the following test fails, raise an error in
 6:      ' the client that called the method.
 7:      ' Disable in-line error handling.
 8:      If SomethingIsWrong Then
 9:        On Error Goto 0
10:        Err.Raise _
11:          Number:=(SOME_ERR_NUMBER + vbObjectError), _
12:          Source:=COMPONENT_SOURCENAME, _
```

continues

LISTING **18.4.** CONTINUED

```
13:            Description:="Something's wrong here"
14:        End If
15:        ' (Run method code continues.)
16: End Sub
```

When you test preconditions such as the validity of argument values, you can simply place the `Err.Raise` statements (similar to Listing 18.4) at the beginning of the method, just before the first `On Error` statement.

When you are using references to foreign objects owned by other components, it is important to handle errors that can result when you invoke methods of those objects. For as many errors as may be generated by the owning component, your component must have access to a list of such errors from the owning component's documentation. This is especially important as you want to gracefully handle errors of foreign objects on behalf of your component's client application. After all, your client application only knows your component and has been developed to handle your component's errors. It wouldn't make sense to pass along errors from your foreign objects to the client application. This would break encapsulation as your client application would then have intimate details of what your component does internally. For commercial development especially, this is unacceptable.

Listing 18.5 shows a snippet of code that uses an error handler for components that use foreign objects owned by another component. Upon encountering an error beyond its ability to properly enforce, the error handler raises an error for the client, complete with its own error numbers and descriptions. In other words, your component becomes a helpful translator for the foreign objects, just as a human language translator translates the words of foreigners.

LISTING **18.5.** USING THE `Raise` METHOD FOR ERRORS ORIGINATING WITH FOREIGN OBJECTS.

```
 1: Public Sub doSomething(argSpeed As Double)
 2:    On Error Goto doSomethingErr
 3:    ' Some code goes here. . .
 4:    '
 5: Exit Sub
 6: doSomethingErr:
 7: Select Case Err.Number
 8: ' Errors your component can handle would go here
 9: '
10: ' --- Errors from some foreign component. ---
11: Case vbObjectError + SOME_FOREIGN_ERR_NUMBER
12:   Err.Raise TRANSLATED_NUMBER + vbObjectError, _
13:   COMPONENT_SOURCENAME, _
```

```
14:   "I'll take the blame for this error"
15:   ' --- Unanticipated errors from foreign
16:   'components. ---
17: Case vbObjectError To (vbObjectError + 65536)
18:   Err.Raise TRANSLATED_NUMBER + vbObjectError, _
19:   CMP_SOURCENAME, LoadResString(ERR_SPN_FAILURE)
20: End Select
21: End Sub
```

Notice the use of the maximum 65535. Some older components may return error numbers in the range 0–65535.

In the preceding example a global constant, the string constant COMPONENT_SOURCENAME, is used for the source argument of the Err object's Raise method. If you raise errors anywhere outside your error handler and neglect to specify the source argument, Visual Basic uses your component's Project Name, combined with the Name property of the class.

Raising Errors and Exceptions

Raising an error involves notifying a client that some systemic error occurred. Raising an exception, while technically the same as raising an error in Visual Basic, is a violation of some policy of which your users inform you. For business applications, the policy violations are enforced by business rules. All policy violations that trigger you to raise an exception should be documented in your use cases, sequence diagrams, and collaboration diagrams.

As mentioned earlier, raising errors and exceptions involves invoking the Raise method of the Err object. As Visual Basic's Online Book advises, when you use the Raise method to generate an error, leave the Err object's other properties unchanged. That way, if the raised error is not easily trapped, you can still display the Source and Description properties to help users take their own measures to resolve the error or exception.

If you find it difficult to tell which class generated which error, activate the Break in Class Module option. To activate it, choose Tools | Options from the menu. You should see the Options dialog box shown in Figure 18.1. Click the General tab and click the Break in Class Module option button. The Break in Class Module option will cause a class module or an object in another application to enter the debugger's Break mode. At this point, you can analyze the error. As expected, any error that originates in a compiled object will not display in the Immediate window while in Break mode. That compiled object will handle its errors by its error handler or will be subsequently trapped by the referencing module.

18

FIGURE 18.1.

The Options dialog box.

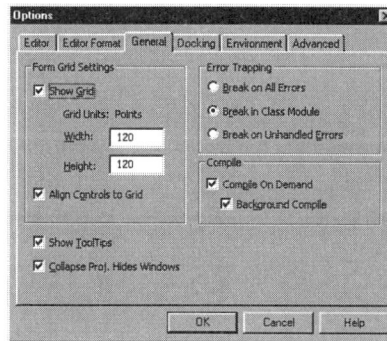

The Error-Processing and Exception-Handling Subsystem Object Model

The Error-Processing and Exception-Handling Subsystem doesn't easily fit into any application tier because it is an integral part of all tiers. However, the exception portion generally falls under the business tier for business applications, or the domain tier as it is known in nonbusiness applications.

Figure 18.2 shows the typical interaction between an object, SomeObject, and the ErrorHandler object. If SomeObject invokes a method, but does not comply with the intrinsic contract between it and ErrorHandler, the latter will raise an error to let SomeObject deal with it. In Figure 18.3, ErrorHandler deals directly with the user so that the user can fix the problem. Figure 18.4 goes a step further. It shows the sequence of events that happens when a foreign object is used by your component, LocalComponent, on behalf of an object, SomeObject, in a client application. Because the LocalComponent used a reference to ForeignObject, it had the responsibility of trapping, interpreting, and raising foreign-originated errors on behalf of SomeObject.

Modeling the Subsystem Class Hierarchy Model

Typically, only one class is involved in simple error- and exception-handling subsystems. However, in a distributed or Web-based architecture, there can be many objects that enforce errors and exceptions. For instance, you might have a business rule engine component that handles all business rule violations on a server machine that is separate from the machine that hosts a component that handles date-formatting errors. With a Web-based system, you may have an object residing on an HTML page that handles local errors while another on the server handles Active Server Pages' problems.

FIGURE 18.2.

Sequence of events for typical error handling.

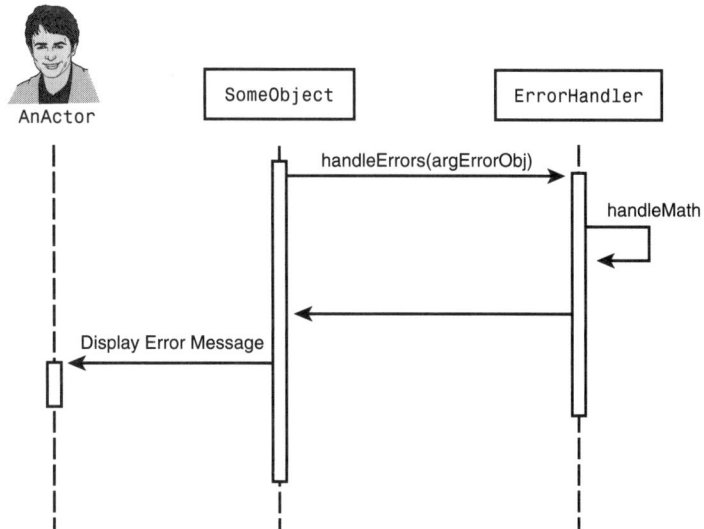

FIGURE 18.3.

Sequence of events for typical error handling that includes notifying the user of a problem for his or her intervention.

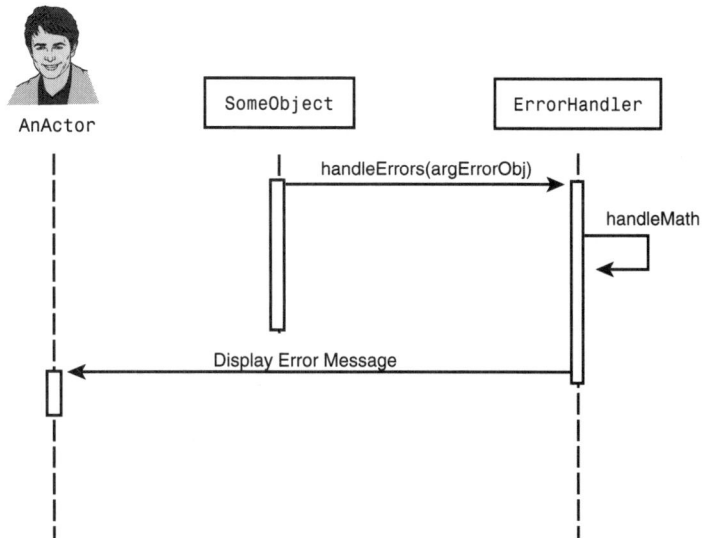

18

FIGURE 18.4.

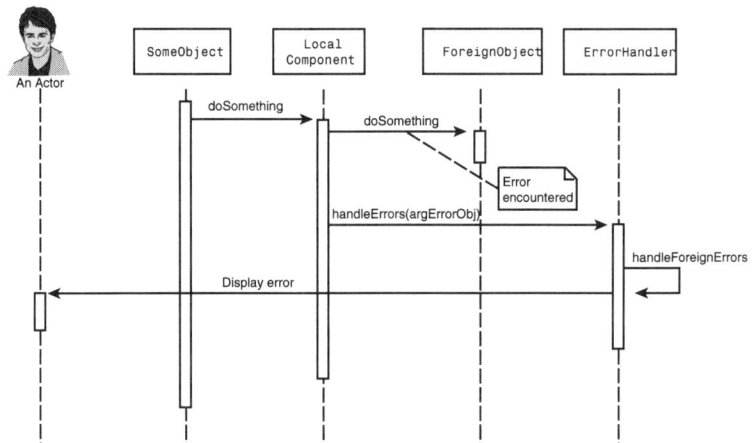

FIGURE 18.4.

Sequence of events for typical error handling involving a foreign object used by a local component. User notification is indicated.

Describing the Classes in the Subsystem

The ErrorHandler class is the only one in this subsystem. In a distributed or Web-based system, similar objects will typically implement the interface of ErrorHandler, and in many cases, delegate some policy enforcement responsibility to ErrorHandler.

Describing the Methods

The handleErrors method is the only public interface method exposed. This is due to the relatively straightforward nature of error handling. Within it are calls to specialized private methods that handle various kinds of errors you deem important. For instance, handleMathErrors handles all errors related to math errors, handleDBErrors handles errors related to the database, while handleNetworkErrors handles network-related errors.

The handleErrors method would look something like this:

```
Public Sub handleErrors(argErrorObject As ErrObject)
    Set LocalErrObject = argErrorObject
    handleMathErrors
    handleDBErrors
    handleNetworkErrors
    handleUnknownErrors
End Sub
```

The argument, argErrorObject, contains a reference to an incoming Err object from a client object. The LocalErrObject is a module-level variable to temporarily hold a reference to the argument. Each of the private methods are invoked, but only the method to which the error applies can handle the error. For instance, `handleMathErrors` might look like the following:

```
Private Sub handleMathErrors
    If LocalErrObject.Number = DIVISION_BY_ZERO Then
        'Do something about the error here
    End If
End Sub
```

If `LocalErrObject.Number` does not equal the arbitrary constant `DIVISION_BY_ZERO`, then the compiler essentially skips it and goes to the next method in the call stack (the list of methods in `handleErrors`). If none of the methods can handle it, the `handleUnknownErrors` method is the catch-all, alerting the client to an unknown error.

Practical Guidelines for Implementing the Error-Processing and Exception-Handling Subsystem

To reiterate, be sure that all significant methods and global functions make calls to the `ErrorHandler` object for complete error handling. Having a centralized object handle as many errors as is possible makes maintaining the code behind your applications easier. Plus, there's less chance of duplicating error-handling code unnecessarily.

18

Incorporating the Subsystem into the Samsona Bank Teller System Example

REAL WORLD

For the Second Bank of Carrollton, you decided you need to place calls to `ErrorHandler` in all of the methods that are involved in banking transactions. Listing 18.6 shows the deposit method of the `DepositFunds` class. In the exercises at the end of this lesson, you will implement the method calls for the other banking methods.

LISTING 18.6. ERROR HANDLING ORIGINATING IN THE DEPOSIT METHOD OF THE `DepositFunds` CLASS.

```
1:
2: Public Sub Deposit()
3:     On Error GoTo depositErr
4:     'your code goes here...
5:     If theSomeWorkgroupProxy.CurrProcess.isCurrTaskComplete Then
6:         theApplication.theAppTransactions.addTrans2MemLog
              ➥"Deposited funds"
```

continues

▼ **LISTING 18.6.** CONTINUED

```
  7:          theTransactionProcessor.theTransaction.TellerID =
             ➥theUser.UserID
  8:          theTransactionProcessor.theTransaction.TransID =
             ➥DEPOSITFUNDS
  9:          theTransactionProcessor.theTransaction.DateTimeStamp =
             ➥Now
 10:          TransactionGroup.Add
             ➥theTransactionProcessor.theTransaction.TellerID, _
 11:              theTransactionProcessor.theTransaction.TransID, _
 12:              theTransactionProcessor.theTransaction.DateTimeStamp
 13:      End If
 14:      Exit Sub
 15: depositErr:
 16:      theErrorHandler.handleErrors(Err)
 17: End Sub
```

The code for this lesson is disbursed across too many methods for all of them to be listed
here. Refer to the CD-ROM for all of the source code. You will add some error-handling
calls in the exercises. However, Listing 18.7 shows how ErrorHandler collaborates with
modErrorHandling and the DBRdoConnection class to trap and process errors related to
connecting to an RDO source.

LISTING 18.7. ErrorHandler COLLABORATES WITH modErrorHandling AND THE
DBRdoConnection CLASS TO TRAP AND PROCESS ERRORS RELATED TO CONNECTING TO AN RDO
SOURCE.

```
  1:
  2: 'Declared in modErrorHandling module
  3: 'Used by the handleDBErrors method of
  4: 'ErrorHandler
  5: Public Enum eDBErrors
  6:     RDOErr
  7:     DAOErr
  8:     ADOErr
  9: End Enum
 10: 'Declared in DBRdoConnection
 11: Public Function executeSQL(argSQL As String)
 12:     On Error GoTo executeSQLErr
 13:     Dim iErrCnt As Integer
 14:     ms_SQL = argSQL
 15:     If theAppTransactions.pTransLogIsOn Then
 16:         theAppTransactions.addTrans2Text "Attempting to execute SQL
            ➥string==> " & ms_SQL
 17:     End If
 18:     'Returns the number of records affected
```

```
19:     'If repSQLEngine.TransactionState <> TRANSACTION_ROLLBACK Then
20:         m_returns = beginDBTrans
21:         m_pConnection.Execute ms_SQL
22:         m_returns = m_pConnection.RowsAffected
23:         If m_returns >= 0 Then
24:             executeSQL = m_returns
25:         End If
26:     'End If
27:     executeSQL = rdoEngine.rdoErrors(0).SQLRetcode
28:     If Switch(executeSQL = 0, True, executeSQL = 1, True) Then
29:         'Operation successful
30:         If theAppTransactions.pTransLogIsOn Then
31:             theAppTransactions.addTrans2Text "Processing of SQL was
                ➥successful"
32:         End If
33:         commitDBTrans
34:     End If
35:     Exit Function
36: executeSQLErr:
37:     m_returns = rollbackDBTrans
38:     theErrorHandler.handleErrors Err
39:     theErrorHandler.handleDBErrors rdoEngine.rdoErrors,
        ➥eDBErrors.RDOErr
40:     'theAppTransactions.activateLogging
41: End Function
42: 'Declared in ErrorHandler
43: Public Sub handleDBErrors(argMsg As Byte, _
44: argObject As Object)
45:     handleDaoErrors argMsg, argObject
46:     handleRdoErrors argMsg, argObject
47: End Sub
48: Private Sub handleDaoErrors(argMsg As Byte, _
49:  argObject As DAO.Errors)
50:     If argMsg = eDBErrors.DAOErr Then
51:         Dim theDAOError As DAO.Error
52:         For Each theDAOError In argObject
53:             theAppTransactions.addTrans2Text _
54:                 theDAOError.Number & theRDOError.Source _
55:                 & theDAOError.Description
56:         Next
57:         theAppTransactions.addTrans2Text _
58:             "Processing of SQL was not successful"
59:         theAppTransactions.showLog
60:     End If
61: End Sub
62: Private Sub handleRdoErrors(argMsg As Byte, _
63: argObject As rdoErrors)
64:     If argMsg = eDBErrors.RDOErr Then
65:         Dim theRDOError As rdoError
```

18

continues

LISTING 18.7. CONTINUED

```
66:          For Each theRDOError In argObject
67:              theAppTransactions.addTrans2Text _
68:                  theRDOError.Number & theRDOError.Source _
69:                  & theRDOError.Description
70:          Next
71:          theAppTransactions.addTrans2Text _
72:              "Processing of SQL was not successful"
73:          theAppTransactions.showLog
74:      End If
75: End Sub
```

Summary

This lesson presented you with an overview of the Error-Processing and Exception-Handling Subsystem. In particular, you learned the purpose of this subsystem and how to raise errors and exceptions. The classes in the subsystem, as well as their methods, properties, arguments, and returns, were presented, and you learned how to implement the Error-Processing and Exception-Handling Subsystem.

Q&A

Q What kinds of actions are included in error handling?

A Error handling includes the trapping and the subsequent chain of responses to errors in your application.

Q Should even the simplest methods have error handling?

A Every significant class method and code module function (if any) requires initial error handling. Only the simplest methods that have been well tested or are otherwise a no-brainer should be considered for not having inline error handling.

Q What does the `Resume` statement do?

A The `Resume` statement tells your application to continue process instructions (lines of code) at the line where the error occurred. Visual Basic then retries that line of code. If the error condition has not been properly resolved, then the error-handling operation is initiated again.

Q When should you use the `Resume Next` statement?

A When you feel your application continually encounters a problem that you feel is truly irrelevant or you just need to move on and debug other areas of your code while in design time. `Resume Next` does not require any special object-oriented treatment, so it won't be discussed further unless it's truly warranted.

Q When must you raise an error?

A When you design your component to allow a client application to handle an error, you must raise that error. That is, the method in your component that trapped the error tells the compiler to notify the previous method (of the client application) on the call stack that it must catch the error your component is raising up the stack. It's sort of like playing hot potatoes, only you're passing the hot potato up the call stack to the body of code that called your component. Raising an error involves the `Raise` method.

Workshop

The workshop includes quiz questions to help gauge your grasp of the material. You'll find the answers to this quiz in Appendix A, "Answers." Even if you feel that you totally understand the concepts presented here, you should work through the quiz anyway. The last section contains exercises for you to work through to help reinforce your learning.

Quiz

1. True or False: Every significant class method and code module function (if any) requires initial error handling.

2. What three steps are typically involved in implementing inline error handling in your methods?

3. What statement initiates your error traps?

4. Is it okay to do very complex error handling in every method?

5. What are the various kinds of methods for which you must plan?

Exercises

1. Copy the code for the Samsona Bank Teller System from the CD-ROM to somewhere on your hard disk. Add error-handling code, similar to Listing 18.6, to the withdraw method of the `WithdrawFunds` class.

2. Based on exercise 1, add error-handling code to the public methods of the following classes: `Process`, `Role`, `User`, `SecurityPolicy`, `TransactionProcessor`, `OpenAccount`, `CloseAccount`.

DAY 19

The Database Access Subsystem

This chapter presents you with an overview of the Database Access Subsystem. In particular, this chapter covers the following:

- Understanding the purpose of the Database Access Subsystem
- Implementing a common interface for different database models
- Understanding ADO
- Understanding DAO
- Understanding RDO
- Understanding ODBC
- Keeping data controls in their proper perspective
- The classes in the subsystem, as well as their methods, properties, arguments, and returns
- Practical guidelines for implementing the Database Access Subsystem

- Incorporating the subsystem into the Samsona Bank Teller System example
- The subsystem code listings for the Samsona Bank Teller System example

An Overview of the Database Access Subsystem

Every application you develop with Visual Basic will likely have a need to persistently store information. However, there is a need to have common code with which to store that information properly. By *common*, it's meant that the code should be reusable and independent of any underlying data access mechanism. Simply inserting data controls on a form isn't adequate because you generally have more than one form with data controls on it or, to complicate matters, several data controls on each form. What's needed is a common, reusable, centralized subsystem dedicated to all your application's storage needs without adding too much complexity. The Database Access Subsystem presented today offers you the power and flexibility to store your application's information with less duplication of code.

The Database Access Subsystem centers on implementing an adaptable framework for data access in an object-oriented way. Of the many ways you can access a database in Visual Basic, the three more popularly used are

- ActiveX Data Objects (ADO)
- Remote Data Objects (RDO)
- Data Access Objects (DAO)

Of the three approaches, the ActiveX Data Object framework has become the prominent one that Microsoft promotes as the standard for Visual Basic and its other development languages. Nonetheless, Remote Data Objects, which offer a friendly facade to the ODBC API, still remains popular. To a lesser extent, Data Access Objects also have a large following among Visual Basic and Visual C++ developers. In every case, the idea you should firmly understand is that it is important to have an interface generic enough to be used easily in either approach. Later, I will also discuss advanced issues in each approach, with more emphasis on ADO and RDO. Concentrating first on the common interface for all three will help reinforce the importance of coding easily and seamlessly for all three.

Understanding the Purpose of This Subsystem

The subsystem decouples the typical database access interface from its particular implementation so that you can freely choose your favorite mechanism without much change to the rest of your application. It handles the persistence of your objects or other variables that aren't properties of objects (though it's advisable to have important variables housed as properties in objects).

Implementing a Common Interface for Different Database Models

IDatabase is the common interface shared by objects that participate in the various data access mechanisms Visual Basic developers use. IDatabase is owned by the IPersistence interface class. By *owned*, it's meant that you would access a method of an IDatabase object as follows:

```
thePersistence.theDatabase.Connect()
```

The spirit of this lesson coincides with Microsoft's push toward its Universal Data Access umbrella: Microsoft Universal Data Access (UDA). UDA is a new Microsoft architecture that promises to provide efficient access to a variety of data formats—relational and nonrelational—on different platforms across your enterprise. UDA gives you a developer-friendly programming interface that can be used with Visual Basic.

Microsoft stated that UDA is based on open industry specifications, therefore supporting more than just Microsoft platforms. In many ways, like its predecessor ODBC, UDA works with all of today's major database platforms. This feature enables you to seamlessly migrate data from one database product to another, compared with more complex migration strategies in place today. Also, if you have an environment mixed with newer and older database technologies, UDA gives you the ability to leverage and extend current persistence storage repositories.

Figure 19.1 illustrates how each UDA component fits into the overall UDA architecture. ADO offers developers an interface to persistent information. Remote Data Service (RDS), which was known as the *Active Data Connector*, is a client-side component used by ADO to provide the following features:

- Opening and managing database cursors
- Remote object invocation
- Explicit access to remote recordsets

19

FIGURE **19.1.**

The framework of the Universal Data Access architecture.

FIGURE **19.1.**

The framework of the Universal Data Access architecture.

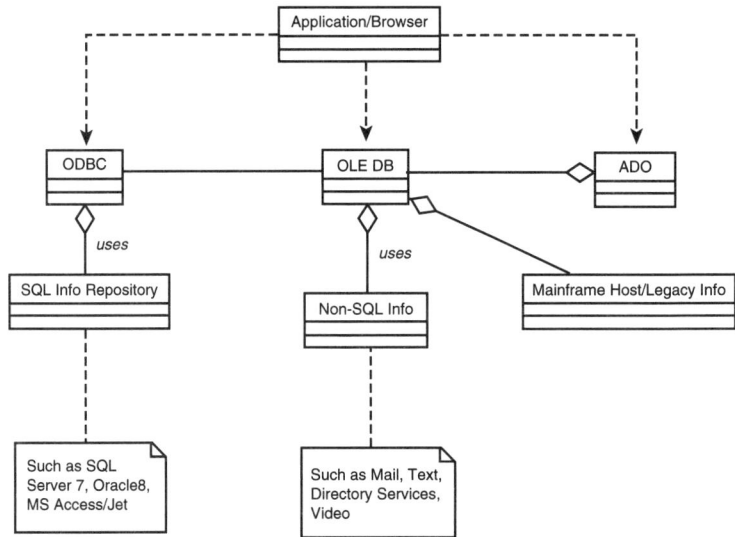

OLE DB (OLE Database) provides the low-level interface to persistent information across the enterprise. This is facilitated by the fact that ADO interacts seamlessly with OLE DB. Earlier, ODBC was mentioned as the predecessor of UDA. Although true in the long run, in the immediate future you can expect ODBC to be the mechanism of choice when you need to work with older drivers from a development standpoint.

UDA, centered on ADO, is closely coupled with Microsoft's other rising star, the Microsoft Distributed InterNet Applications architecture (Windows DNA). The name *Windows DNA* might look like Windows Open System Architecture (WOSA) from days gone by. DNA is sort of the WOSA of the Internet for Microsoft's Windows platforms. DNA offers powerful features in integrating Windows with the Internet, including services for business rules, your graphical user interface, and, of course, persistence of information. DNA's persistence is driven by UDA. As a developer, you utilize UDA through what Microsoft calls Microsoft Data Access Components (MDACs). MDACs include ADO, OLE DB, RDS, and ODBC.

Understanding ADO

Microsoft designed ADO for several critical reasons, including the following:

- To address your unique Internet development needs
- To assist you when you need to access special kinds of persistent information not limited to relational data
- To assist you in developing faster, smaller, and more efficient applications

The latest release of ADO is the standard for database access for Microsoft Visual Studio languages. ADO presents a common facade for developing one data access subsystem for either desktop or Internet deployment. ADO supports several different development needs, including the needs of the Graphical User Interface Subsystem and the Business Rule Subsystem, as well as packaged tools, programming languages, and browsers.

According to Microsoft, ADO will eventually be a superset of RDO. For now, it doesn't quite support every powerful feature of RDO. ADO is the object-based interface to OLE DB. By using a DAO-like data access interface, developers can now access an even broader variety of data sources—using both OLE DB service providers and existing ODBC drivers through its OLE DB for ODBC intermediate interface. ADO's most serious shortcoming at this point is its scope. ADO 1.5 implements only part of RDO's full range of functionality. Later versions will implement a superset of both RDO and DAO.

You'll find the key benefits of ADO to be ease of use, high speed, low memory overhead, and a small disk footprint. Among many usability and technical features, ADO supports certain critical features for building client/server and Web-based applications, including

- Hierarchy-less data access objects. Unlike DAO or RDO, there's no hierarchy of objects to browse in order to create objects. That is, an ADO recordset object doesn't need a database object initialized first in order to access information from a database. This is very helpful when you have a recordset with a query that can be activated against two or more database servers.
- Stored procedures that enable you to pass In and Out parameters, return values, and multiple recordsets.
- Batch updating that helps improve performance by locally caching changes to data and then writing them all to the server in a single update.
- Free-threaded objects for efficient Web server applications.
- Different cursor types.
- Support for limits on the number of returned rows.
- Support for various query goals you can implement for performance tuning.

19

New Term An *In parameter* is similar to an In argument in which the argument variable is to be used locally without modifying it. An *Out parameter* is an argument variable that is modified by the stored procedure.

As with ODBC, not all ADO vendor drivers support every feature of ADO. Microsoft keeps you abreast of what ADO features are supported at `www.microsoft.com/data/ado`.

The notable objects exposed by ADO and in common with, or similar to, DAO and RDO are the following:

```
ADODB.Connection
ADODB.Error
ADODB.Errors
ADODB.Field/ ADOR.Field
ADODB.Fields/ADOR.Fields
ADODB.Recordset/ADOR.Recordset
ADODB.Command.CommandText
```

Understanding DAO

If you've programmed database applications in Visual Basic for only a few months, you've no doubt worked with Data Access Objects (DAO). DAO is the first object library/data access mechanism that provides an interface to the Microsoft Jet database engine to access native Jet databases as well as other kinds of data sources. If you used the Data control, you will recognize that its data access architecture is based on DAO. It's probably safe to say that DAO is one of the most popularly used data access mechanism available to Visual Basic developers. ODBCDirect, in fact, is derived from DAO, exposing many RDO functions.

Data Access Objects are mainly designed for optimum use with Microsoft Access, due to both DAO and Access supporting the Jet database engine. Among Visual Basic developers, DAO has lost ground to RDO since early 1997.

The Data Access Objects (version 3.5) in common with, or similar to, counterparts in ADO and RDO include

```
DAO.Connection
DAO.Connections
DAO.Database
DAO.Databases
DAO.Error
DAO.Errors
DAO.Field
DAO.Fields
DAO.QueryDef.SQL
DAO.Recordset
DAO.Recordsets
```

Understanding RDO

By far, the most popular data access mechanism among experienced, heavyweight Visual Basic developers is RDO (Remote Data Objects). Like ADO and DAO, RDO is object-based, providing a relatively tight, lightweight interface to ODBC. Unlike its underlying ODBC API calls, RDO is very user-friendly, making developing serious database-oriented applications fast and relatively easy.

If you've worked with DAO, working with RDO won't be much more complex, even though it offers more powerful, faster features. The underlying mechanisms of the complex ODBC architecture are controllable through RDO.

RDO, and its DAO Data control alternative—the Remote Data control, lets your applications access ODBC data sources without using a local query processor. Without localizing a query processor, your applications enjoy higher performance and more flexibility when accessing remote database engines. Other key features of RDO include

- Executing action queries (INSERT, UPDATE, or DELETE queries, to name more notable ones) that implement data manipulation or data definition operations
- Creating resultsets (or recordsets) with or without cursors of varying complexities
- Enabling synchronous, asynchronous, or event-driven asynchronous processing (the latter two features ensure your application isn't blocked while the server is processing lengthy queries, among other reasons)
- Executing stored procedures that return resultsets (or recordsets) with or without output parameters and return values
- Enabling you to limit the number of rows returned or processed
- Running general queries and processing any number of resultsets

19

There are only a few, minor drawbacks to RDO, compared with DAO. RDO isn't as effective as Jet-based DAO in accessing Jet or ISAM databases. Also, RDO can access relational databases only through existing ODBC drivers. Of course, these drawbacks are more than outweighed by the fact that you can access databases more powerful than Access, including SQL Server, Oracle, DB2, Sybase, Informix, and other ODBC-compliant, relational DBMS customers. In addition, RDO provides the objects, properties, and methods you need in order to implement code to handle more sophisticated aspects of stored procedures and complex resultsets.

The Remote Data Objects in common or similar to counterparts in ADO and RDO include

```
RDO.rdoConnection
RDO.rdoConnections
RDO.rdoError
```

```
RDO.rdoErrors
RDO.rdoField
RDO.rdoFields
RDO.rdoQuery
RDO.rdoResultset
RDO.rdoResultsets
```

Understanding ODBC

The Open Database Connectivity Application Programming Interface (ODBC API) has generally been an alternative mechanism that serious Visual Basic developers use to improve upon the data access speed lacking in connecting to ODBC data sources through earlier versions of Visual Basic. The ODBC API is the most popular architecture for accessing a heterogeneous variety of database servers and runs on environments such as 16-bit Windows, 32-bit Windows 95 and Windows NT, and others. The ODBC API, always complex, has become even more so as Microsoft has addressed the growing needs of today's information storage and retrieval needs. RDO, in fact, was created as a result of developer complaints about the complexity of the ODBC API. Added to that was the headache of maintaining ODBC API code as the application evolved. Designing and implementing your own classes can encapsulate this detail, but RDO and ADO are robust enough to not justify the need to do so. Also, if you use RDO, you can pass the hDbc handle of the rdoConnection object to an ODBC API function that requires it. If you're still determined, however, to create your own raw ODBC API classes, the next section provides some assistance in how to begin designing and implementing them well.

General ODBC API Operations   Working with the ODBC API generally requires the following:

- Establishing the environment by allocating an environment handle (hEnv) using ODBC's SQLAllocEnv.

- Establishing the environment by allocating a database connection handle (hDbc) using ODBC's SQLAllocConnect. You also need a valid data source name (DSN), user ID, and password for databases that require them.

- Establishing the environment by allocating a SQL/database command statement handle (hStmt).

- Working with the actual data by binding columns, opening and closing cursors, and moving through sets of records.

- Deallocating a SQL/database command statement handle (hStmt).

- Deallocating a database connection handle (hDbc).

- Deallocating an environment handle (hEnv).

Upon allocating environment and connection handles, you can open one or more connections to remote database servers by using a different connection handle (hDbc) for each database connection. Sophisticated enterprise applications you write in Visual Basic might require that you open more than one connection to support simultaneous action queries. For less sophisticated applications, only one connection is sufficient. You have to weigh having more than one hDbc handle allocated versus simply allocating more than one hStmt handle—one for each SQL statement in which the fulfillment of a query doesn't depend on the fulfillment of another.

Tip

Use the ODBC's SQLGetInfo function to verify whether your database driver supports multiple active statements on a single connection before allocating more than one hStmt handle. Otherwise, you might receive an error.

Using the SQLConnect function in the ODBC API, you pass it a data source name, user ID, and password as arguments. Internally, SQLConnect changes the state of the newly acquired hDbc to Connected. The returned values you need to check for include SQL_SUCCESS, SQL_SUCCESS_WITH_INFO, and SQL_ERROR. Other connection functions you can use include SQLDriverConnect and SQLBrowseConnect.

SQLDriverConnect accepts DSN connection strings—for example,

`"DSN=MyDSN;UID=MyID;PWD=MyPWD"`

To set the ODBC connection time-out, use the SQLSetConnectionOption function. Your application will receive an error if the syntax of the string is missing a parameter or has a misspelling. Check for the SQL_ERROR return value if the user cancels the connection request or if the driver manager is unable to connect to the data source.

19

Using SQLBrowseConnect, you can obtain a list of available drivers, data sources, and other parameters. Your application chooses from available data items. Ideally, you can list these data items in a list box to let a user select one.

To make your use of the ODBC API as painless as possible, create classes with the following names:

```
ODBCEnvironment
ODBCConnection
ODBCResultset
```

`ODBCEnvironment` essentially encapsulates behavior and information related to the ODBC environment. An environment handle must be allocated before you can do anything with the ODBC API. Its property is `EnvHandle As Long`. Its methods are `allocateEnvironment()` and `deallocateEnvironment()`, which set `EnvHandle`. After declaring the `SQLAllocEnv` in the ODBC DLL, the `allocateEnvironment` method will contain the following code:

```
Dim iReturnCode as integer
iReturnCode = SQLAllocEnv(mvarEnvHandle)
```

You could invoke this method in the `Class_Initialize` event because the returned environment handle supports multiple connections to data sources. If `SQLAllocEnv` returns `SQL_SUCCEED`, the ODBC driver manager is initialized. Memory is allocated to store information about the environment. If this function call fails, the ODBC DLLs didn't correctly initialize.

`ODBCConnection` encapsulates the behavior and information related to the connection. Properties include `DbcHandle As Long` and `Status As Byte`. Its methods are `openConnection()` and `closeConnection()`.

`ODBCResultset` encapsulates behavior and information related to the sets of records with which your application works. Properties include `StmtHandle As Long`, `SQL As String`, `Status As Byte`, and `RecordCount As Long`.

Establishing a Connection   Establishing a connection is essential before proceeding with further ODBC calls. The `ODBCConnection` class has a property, `ConnHandle As Long`, to hold the `hDbc` value of the current connection.

The `openConnection` method of the `ODBCConnection` class has the following contents:

```
Public Sub openConnection(argConnStr As String)
Dim lHdbc As Long, lHenv As Long, vRetCode
vRetCode = SQLAllocConnect(ByVal lHenv, lHdbc)
theODBCEnvironment.EnvHandle = lHenv
ConnHandle = lHdbc
```

`vRetCode` receives the return code value of the call. If `vRetCode = SQL_SUCCEED`, the connection handle is allocated some space in memory. If unsuccessful, a call to the `SQLError` function gives you the reason for the failure. `theODBCEnvironment` is an instance of the class `ODBCEnvironment`.

Working with ODBC Results   Using the ODBC API to handle information in the database can become complex. If you didn't understand the operations of cursors before, the ODBC API isn't going to give you much comfort. Nonetheless, you need to firmly understand how to work with cursors and how to modify your resultsets. For every SQL command you send to the database via the ODBC API, you must work with the result-set(s) subsequently generated, regardless of whether the resultset contains any records. Because you use a statement handle (`hStmt`) for each resultset, you must process the rows in them before using that statement handle again.

With regard to the ODBC API, your use of the `SELECT` statement in a query results in a cursor being associated with that query. To apply a name to that cursor, use the `SQLSetCursorName`. At times you might need to configure certain information regarding resultset columns. Use the ODBC functions `SQLDescribeCol`, `SQLColAttributes`, and `SQLNumResultCol` to determine the characteristics of the resultset. In the `ODBCResultset` class, you would have the following method:

```
Public Sub configureAttributes(ParamArray argAttribs())
```

The `ParamArray` argument, `argAttribs()`, gives you the flexibility to send in a varying number of arguments that contain attribute values for the three ODBC functions.

The `ODBCResultset` class would also have the following method for working with results:

```
Public Sub openDBResultset()
```

The `openDBResultset` method uses any number of the following ODBC API functions to get data from the data source and into Visual Basic variables:

- `SQLBindCol`
- `SQLFetch`
- `SQLExtendedFetch`
- `SQLGetData`

19

`SQLBindCol` assigns a variable to one or more selected columns that make up the result-set. You place data into the desired variable with either the `SQLFetch` or `SQLExtendedFetch` function. The `SQLGetData` function fetches character data from a specific column into a Visual Basic string variable. `SQLGetNumericData` obtains non-`String` data from a specific column in the data source and assigns it to a Visual Basic variable. To set the column attributes for each column, pass in the appropriate function arguments of the relevant ODBC function.

> **Note**
>
> In accessing ODBC drivers, your application architecture needs to be designed carefully. You should pay special attention to the SQLBindCol function. Although you can pass the address of a string variable to SQLBindCol, strings in Visual Basic are moved in memory without notice. This could render your use of SQLBindCol ineffective (and even cause application problems) if you don't explicitly lock the memory space of the variable. You could also use Byte arrays that aren't subject to Visual Basic's need to reallocate string variable memory spaces.
>
> In the openDBResultset, you would have a private method, bindColumn, that is called from within the public interface method, openDBResultset. One reason for having a separate method is that the SQLBindCol method requires many methods, some of which might necessitate special code on your part. Having this separate method, then, would better organize your typically complex ODBC code. In an appropriate module (you should probably name it modODBC), you would have the following declaration:
>
> ```
> Declare Function SQLBindCol Lib "odbc.dll" _
> Alias "SqlBindCol" _
> (ByVal hstmt As Long, ByVal icol As Integer, _
> ByVal fCType As Integer, rgbValue As Any, _
> ByVal cbValueMax As Long, pcbValue As Long) _
> As Integer
> ```
>
> Fortunately, the class structures you use for wrapping ODBC API calls behind facades are the same class structures you can use for wrapping VBSQL and Oracle Objects calls. For the sake of brevity, these data access mechanisms aren't detailed in this chapter. Nevertheless, it shouldn't be at all difficult because popular data access mechanisms in the industry have much the same look and feel.

Keeping Data Controls in Their Proper Perspective

When you begin developing applications in Visual Basic and are faced with a pressing deadline, Data controls are electronic lifesavers. Just place a control on a form, set a few attributes on bound controls, and you've created powerful access to an ODBC-compliant or Jet-based data source. Your customers are happy, your project manager is happy, and you're happy…or are you?

Sometimes, the seeming ease of the Data control can be quickly eclipsed by the awkwardness of reusing database code across many forms and the failure of the Data control's underlying mechanism.

If, on a form, you have a grid that has one SQL statement and a collection of text boxes that has another SQL statement, you need two Data controls. Typically, the code to manage both is duplicated. If the Data control fails for reasons beyond your control, you're stuck until the vendor offers a solution. You can mitigate the risk of code duplication, at least, by passing a reference to the Data control to a common class. However, the better, more scalable and reusable solution is to use ADO, RDO, DAO, VBSQL, ODBC API, or third-party tools such as Oracle Objects for Visual Basic. That way, you can create a common mechanism to handle each platform, encapsulating your application from changes in data access implementation code. Data controls can't optimally offer this kind of scalability. Nonetheless, when you have an independent mechanism in place, there's no harm in using Data controls; you have something to fall back on if the Data control fails.

Modeling the Database Access Object Model

Given that this subsystem is part of the critical path of any application you develop, it's complex. In fact, much of its functionality is so complex that there isn't enough space in this chapter to cover every issue you might face. RDO alone offers more services than both DAO and ADO. Nevertheless, this section explains the key interactions between the objects in this subsystem. Figure 19.2 shows the interactions in a sequence diagram. Because the interactions can be complicated at times, it's useful to use Visual Basic's Call Stack dialog box to verify the sequence of method calls.

> **Tip**
>
> When you create sequence diagrams for complex object interactions, use Visual Basic's Call Stack dialog box to view a list of method invocations. The call stack list isn't always exhaustive, but it's informative. To use it, choose View Call Stack (Ctrl+L) from the Visual Basic menu.

19

The interaction in Figure 19.2 involves using the ActiveX Data Objects mechanism. The code module modMain has a method, Sub Main, that is the startup method for the application. It invokes the initializeDB method of CDatabaseForm (the class instance: theDatabaseForm). The initializeDB method accepts a Byte argument that contains the Ado value of the following enum:

```
Public Enum eDataAccess
    Ado
    Dao
    Rdo
End Enum
```

FIGURE **19.2.**

The sequence diagram showing the interactions between the objects in the subsystem.

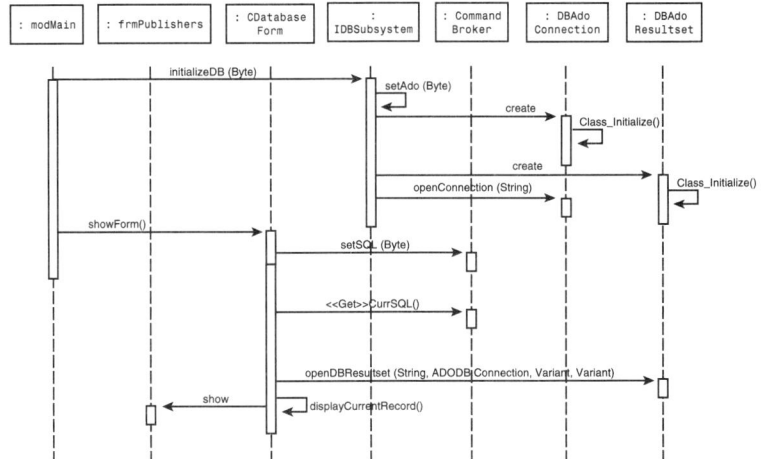

The instance of IDSubsystem, theDBSubsystem, calls the setAdo method, passing the value eDataAccess.Ado. The method then creates instances of DBAdoConnection and DBAdoResultset. The instances are, at design time, each typed as Object. This late type binding (not using the New keyword with a specific class type) is necessary so that the generic DBConnection and DBResultset object properties of IDBSubsystem can be bound in memory to the mechanisms for Ado, Rdo, or Dao with minimal code changes. In creating each instance, the Class_Initialize event is triggered. The object, theDBSubsystem, then invokes the openConnection method of the instance of DBAdoConnection, passing in a connection string argument that contains enough information to open a data source.

When the connection to the data source via Ado is successfully completed, Sub Main in modMain invokes the showForm method of theDatabaseForm form controller object. The controller object then invokes the setSQL method of the instance of CommandBroker, theCommandBroker, to set the string value of the current SQL statement to use. Again, the eDataAccess.Ado value is passed in so that the appropriate SQL command is used. Dao and Ado can use the same SQL syntax, particularly when it comes to columns with spaces in the name (such as [First Name]). This method assigns the requested SQL statement housed on CommandBroker to its property, CurrSQL. The property has the <<Get>> stereotype, meaning that the type of property is a Get type (or stereotype in a strict sense) property.

With the SQL statement set, theDatabaseForm invokes the openDBResultset method of DBResultset, which is a generic object property referencing DBAdoResultset. The first argument in the argument list is the SQL command statement, referenced by `theCommandBroker.CurrSQL`. The second argument, which is optional, represents an `Ado` connection. The remaining arguments are optional flags that you can use for additional purposes.

Finally, the object `theDatabaseForm` invokes its own `displayCurrentRecord` method to display the desired record that you make current. By default, for any opened set of records, the first record is made the current record. Then, using its private `theForm` object reference to, in this case, the `frmPublishers` form, `theDatabaseForm` invokes the `Show` method of the actual form reference. Because `IDBSubsystem` is a common facade for the three data access mechanisms, the same object interactions just described can be easily used with `Dao` and `Rdo` by replacing the `eDataAccess.Ado` parameters with either `eDataAccess.Dao` or `eDataAccess.Rdo`, respectively. When implementing `IDBSubsystem` within `IPersistence` (when necessary), simply declare the former within the General Declarations section of the latter as follows:

`Public theDBSubsystem As IDBSubsystem`

and then access as follows (assuming an object variable, `thePersistence`):

`thePersistence.theDBSubsystem.DBConnection.openConnection _ sConnStr`

The Database Access Class Hierarchy Model

Figure 19.3 shows the classes that make up the Database Access Subsystem.

FIGURE 19.3.

The classes in the Database Access Subsystem.

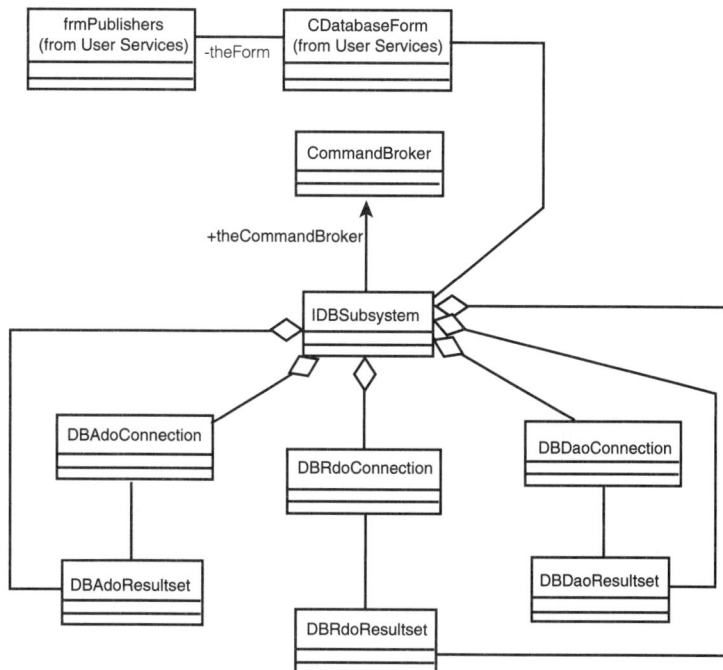

The names of the classes are as follows:

```
CDatabaseForm
CommandBroker
IDBSubsystem
DBAdoConnection
DBAdoResultset
DBRdoConnection
DBRdoResultset
DBDaoConnection
DBDaoResultset
```

The Classes in the Subsystem

CDatabaseForm is a form controller that, in this case, owns a private reference, theForm, to the form frmPublishers. The role it plays with respect to IDBSubsystem is the same as the role played by any form controller that needs data access services. Its methods include

```
Private Sub ClearDataFields()
Public Sub clickedAddNewRecord()
Public Sub clickedCancel()
Public Sub clickedDeleteRecord()
Public Sub clickedDone()
Public Sub clickedEditRecord()
Public Sub clickedFirstRecord()
Public Sub clickedLastRecord()
Public Sub clickedNextRecord()
Public Sub clickedPrevRecord()
Public Sub clickedUpdate()
Public Sub displayCurrentRecord()
Public Sub hideForm()
Public Sub processChangedField()
Public Sub processKeyDown(argKeyCode As Integer, argShift _
  As Integer)
Public Sub processKeyPress(argIndex As Integer, _
  argKeyAscii As Integer)
Public Sub processLostFocus(argIndex As Integer)
Public Sub resizeForm()
Private Sub setButtons(bVal As Boolean)
Public Sub showForm()
Private Sub syncGrid()
Public Function setFieldVal(rvntFieldVal As Variant) _
  As Variant
```

Though most of the methods here don't require a detailed description of exactly what each does, because their names accurately describe them, some of these methods do require explanation.

The clearDataFields method clears each field on the form. Because it uses a text box collection to iterate through the fields, you can easily reuse this method (and the others) with essentially any form that displays data to users in text boxes. It can be easily customized to labels, grids, list boxes, and other data-aware controls. The methods prefixed with clicked refer to any clickable control that requires further processing. The method displayCurrentRecord displays the current record to the user. ProcessChangedField sets flags whenever the user changes the value of a field. This is helpful for edit/update operations. The methods processKeyDown, processKeyPress, and processLostFocus process the similarly named events in the form that relate to changing field values and updating resultsets (or recordsets). SetButtons enables and disables buttons on the form, based on how users interact with data-aware controls. SyncGrid synchronizes the contents of the MS Grid (or MS Flex Grid) control to keep its slave data in sync with the master record in the fields. Finally, setFieldVal handles the setting of each field on behalf of displayCurrentRecord.

CommandBroker has the following members:

```
Public Property Get CurrSQL() As String
Public Sub setTestSQL(argDataAccess As Byte)
```

CurrSQL contains the current SQL statement. SetTestSQL is used to acquire dummy SQL commands by which to test the database subsystem.

IDBSubsystem has the following members:

```
Public Property Get DBConnection() As Object
Public Property Get DBResultset() As Object
Public Sub initializeDB(Optional argDataAccess As Byte)
Private Sub setAdo(argDataAccess As Byte)
Private Sub setDao(argDataAccess As Byte)
Private Sub setRdo(argDataAccess As Byte)
Public Sub setDataControl(argDataControl As Object)
```

19

DBConnection is a generic object reference that can be adapted to the connection classes for Ado, Rdo, and Dao. DBResultset plays the same adapter role for the resultset classes of Ado, Rdo, and Dao. InitializeDB initializes the database environment for the entire application. The argument argDataAccess is a value that specifies which data access mechanism (eDataAccess enum value for Ado, Rdo, and Dao) to use.

DefaultDriverName and DefaultServerName are used to specify the default driver name of the ODBC driver and the default server name of the database server. These are helpful when doing connections that don't require a data source name (DSN) as part of the connection string. The methods setAdo, setRdo, and setDao establish which data access mechanism (specified by the argDataAccess argument of initializeDB) to use. Finally, the setDataControl method accepts an argument, argDataControl, that is a reference to a Data control to be synchronized in CDatabaseForm's syncGrid method.

`DBAdoConnection`, `DBRdoConnection`, and `DBDaoConnection` each have the following
members:

```
Public Function beginDBTrans() As Variant
Public Sub closeDBConnection(Optional argConnection)
Public Sub commitDBTrans()
Public Property Get DefaultDriverName() As String
Public Property Get DefaultServerName() As String
Public Function executeSQL(argSQL As String) As Variant
Public Function executeSQL(argSQL As String) As Variant
Public Sub openConnection(argConnStr As String)
Public Property Get pDBConnection() As Database
Public Function rollbackDBTrans() As Variant
Public Function setColumn(argCol As Object) As Variant
```

The methods `beginDBTrans`, `commitDBTrans`, and `rollbackDBTrans` handle any operations that are grouped as transactions. The methods `openConnection` and
`closeDBConnection` open and close, respectively, the connection to the database. As
mentioned for `IDBSubsystem`, `DefaultDriverName`, and `DefaultServerName` are used to
specify the default driver name of the ODBC driver and the default server name of the
database server. `ExecuteSQL` directly executes a SQL statement against a specified connection referenced by `pDBConnection`. Finally, `setColumn` sets a reference to a column
specified by the `argCol` object argument.

`DBAdoResultset`, `DBRdoResultset`, and `DBDaoResultset` have the following members:

```
Public Sub addNewRecord()
Public Sub CancelTrans()
Public pChangedByCode As Boolean
Public pBookMark As Variant
Public pEditFlag As Boolean
Public pAddNewFlag As Boolean
Public pDataChanged As Boolean
Public Property Get DBColumn() As Object
Public Sub getFirstRec()
Public Sub getLastRec()
Public Sub getNextRec()
Public Sub getPreviousRec()
Public Function getRecordCount() As Long
Public Sub openDBResultset(argSQL As String, _
  Optional argDBConnection As ADODB.Connection)
Public Property Get pBOF() As Boolean
Public Property Get pCurrentSQL() As String
Public Property Get pEOF() As Boolean
Public Sub prepareForChange()
Public Property Get pResultset() As Object
Public Property Get pSQLTimeout() As Integer
Public Property Get RSFields() As Object
Public Sub startEditMode()
```

```
Public Sub updateOneRecord(Optional argClientObject _
 As Object)
```

addNewRecord facilitates the adding of records to the underlying data source.
CancelTrans cancels a transaction. In the case of Ado, you can cancel a batch operation
or update operation. pChangedByCode and pDataChanged are boolean flags that alert the
subsystems in the application that either the application (pChangedByCode) or the user
(pDataChange) changed a data-aware field.

pBookMark is a bookmark for the resultset. DBColumn is a reference to a particular column
in the resultset. PEditFlag prepares the environment for editing a record in the resultset.
pAddNewFlag, in conjunction with addNewRecord, prepares the environment for adding a
new record to the underlying database via the resultset. The methods getFirstRec,
getLastRec, getNextRec, and getPreviousRec are used to navigate through the resultset. They are typically invoked by the clickedFirst...LastRecord methods of
CDatabaseForm. getRecordCount obtains the numeric total of all the records in the
resultset. openDBResultset opens the resultset against the connection object referenced
by the argument, argDBConnection. The argument argSQL is the SQL statement used to
open the resultset. The property pCurrentSQL holds the value of argSQL. The properties
pBOF and pEOF specify whether the resultset is at the beginning or end of the set.

The method prepareForChange prepares the environment for a change to data fields by
the application code. The property pResultset is a reference to the resultset object.
pSQLTimeout establishes the time-out value that determines how long the resultset should
take in obtaining records. RSFields contains a reference to the columns in the resultset.
The method startEditMode prepares the environment for editing a record, working in
conjunction with pEditFlag. Finally, updateOneRecord prepares the environment for
updating a single record to the underlying database. You can create a corresponding
method to update a batch of records.

Practical Guidelines for Implementing Database Access in Code

Where possible, you should start using ActiveX Data Objects in your database applications. ADO will become the standard mechanism for Visual Basic, particularly because
of its strong Internet capabilities. RDO will still remain a dominant force for some time
because it works so well with the ODBC API. However, ADO will catch up with it soon.
Moreover, it's helpful if you compile this subsystem into its own ActiveX component
because it can quickly become large and complex. Debugging it with subsystems from
other parts of the application in one project will prove to be a constant source of frustration because you'll likely feel overwhelmed by all the many classes and lines of code. A

huge project full of a dizzying number of classes and lines of code is difficult to maintain, and you'll quickly lose the benefits of object-oriented programming.

Incorporating the Subsystem into the Samsona Bank Teller System Example

▼ REAL WORLD

The branch manager has a simple requirement: "Make sure that we can save all our account transactions, customer information, and cash deposit records." Because you're using a relational database, you sit down with a database administrator at the bank to come up with an acceptable database schema. The tables resulting from these conversations are named `tblAccount`, `tblBankProduct`, `tblTransaction_Archive`, `tblCustomer`, and `tblCash_Deposit_Record`. The branch manager makes things easy on you this time, requiring only that you provide a mechanism for obtaining and inserting records. The update operations will be handled by her in-house development staff.

The code listings for this section would be too numerous to present here. However, it is worthwhile to list the code for both the `DBAdoConnection` and `DBAdoResultset` classes. Listing 19.1 shows the code for `DBAdoConnection`, and Listing 19.2 shows the code for `DBAdoResultset`. Grab a cup of your favorite beverage because the listings are full of helpful class methods—quite a few of them. You can also access them on the CD-ROM. They're presented here as a convenience so that you can become acquainted with the kind of data access code you should try to use and expand on when developing your applications.

LISTING 19.1. THE CODE FOR THE `DBAdoConnection` CLASS.

```
 1: VERSION 1.0 CLASS
 2: BEGIN
 3:   MultiUse = -1  'True
 4: END
 5: Attribute VB_Name = "DBAdoConnection"
 6: Attribute VB_GlobalNameSpace = True
 7: Attribute VB_Creatable = True
 8: Attribute VB_PredeclaredId = False
 9: Attribute VB_Exposed = False
10: Attribute VB_Ext_KEY = "SavedWithClassBuilder" ,"Yes"
11: Attribute VB_Ext_KEY = "Top_Level" ,"Yes"
12: Attribute VB_Ext_KEY = "RVB_UniqueId" ,"352AB4C70302"
13: 'local variable(s) to hold property value(s)
14: '##ModelId=352AB4C8010F
15: Private mvarpTblColumns As ADODB.Fields 'local copy
16: '##ModelId=352AB4C801B0
17: Private mvarpResultset As ADOR.Recordset 'local copy
```

```
18: '##ModelId=352AB4C801B3
19: Private mvarpDBConnection As ADODB.Connection 'local copy
20: '##ModelId=352AB4C80258
21: Private mvarDBConnect As String 'local copy
22: 'local variable(s) to hold property value(s)
23: '##ModelId=352AB4C802C6
24: Private mvarDefaultDriverName As String 'local copy
25: 'local variable(s) to hold property value(s)
26: '##ModelId=352AB4C80366
27: Private mvarDefaultServerName As String 'local copy
28: '##ModelId=352AB4C90136
29: Public Property Let DefaultServerName(ByVal vData As String)
30: 'used when assigning a value to the property, on the left side of an
➥assignment.
31: 'Syntax: X.DefaultServerName = 5
32:     mvarDefaultServerName = vData
33: End Property
34:
35:
36: '##ModelId=352AB4C803D4
37: Public Property Get DefaultServerName() As String
38: 'used when retrieving value of a property, on the right side of an
➥assignment.
39: 'Syntax: Debug.Print X.DefaultServerName
40:     DefaultServerName = mvarDefaultServerName
41: End Property
42:
43:
44:
45: '##ModelId=352AB4CA0014
46: Public Property Let DefaultDriverName(ByVal vData As String)
47: 'used when assigning a value to the property, on the left side of an
➥assignment.
48: 'Syntax: X.DefaultDriverName = 5
49:     mvarDefaultDriverName = vData
50: End Property
51:
52:
53: '##ModelId=352AB4C902EE
54: Public Property Get DefaultDriverName() As String
55: 'used when retrieving value of ODBC driver name.
56: 'Syntax: Debug.Print X.DefaultDriverName
57:     DefaultDriverName = mvarDefaultDriverName
58: End Property
59:
60:
61:
62: '##ModelId=352AB4CA0316
63: Public Property Let DBConnect(ByVal vData As String)
```

19

continues

```
64: 'used when assigning a value to the property, on the left side of an
➡assignment.
65: 'Syntax: X.DBConnect = 5
66:     mvarDBConnect = vData
67: End Property
68:
69:
70: '##ModelId=352AB4CA01CC
71: Public Property Get DBConnect() As String
72: 'used when retrieving value of a property, on the right side of an
➡assignment.
73: 'Syntax: Debug.Print X.DBConnect
74:     DBConnect = mvarDBConnect
75: End Property
76:
77:
78:
79: '##ModelId=352AB4CB026C
80: Public Property Set pDBConnection(ByVal vData As Object)
81: 'used when assigning an Object to the property, on the left side of a
➡Set statement.
82: 'Syntax: Set x.pDBConnection = Form1
83:     Set mvarpDBConnection = vData
84: End Property
85:
86:
87: '##ModelId=352AB4CB0154
88: Public Property Get pDBConnection() As ADODB.Connection
89: 'used when retrieving value of a property, on the right side of an
➡assignment.
90: 'Syntax: Debug.Print X.pDBConnection
91:     Set pDBConnection = mvarpDBConnection
92: End Property
93:
94:
95:
96: '##ModelId=352AB4CC003C 'Executes a SQL statement
97: Public Function executeSQL(argSQL As String) As Variant
98:     Dim lRecordsAffected As Long
99:     With mvarpDBConnection
100:        .Execute argSQL, lRecordsAffected
101:     End With
102:     MsgBox "Records affected; " & CStr(lRecordsAffected)
103: End Function
104:
105: '##ModelId=352AB4CC01B8 'Opens a connection using DSN
106: Public Sub openConnectionWithDSN(argConnStr As String) 'As Variant
▼ 107:     On Error GoTo openConnectionErr
```

```
▼  108:      Set mvarpDBConnection = New ADODB.Connection
   109:      With mvarpDBConnection
   110:          ' Open a connection using an ODBC DSN.
   111:          .ConnectionString = argConnStr '"DSN=Pubs;UID=sa;PWD=;"
   112:          .ConnectionTimeout = 30
   113:          .Open
   114:          ' Find out if the attempt to connect worked.
   115:          If .State = adStateOpen Then
   116: '            MsgBox "Connection successfully established"
   117: '          Else
   118: '            MsgBox "Connection not successfully established"
   119:          End If
   120:      End With
   121:      Exit Sub
   122: openConnectionErr:
   123: '      For Each m_rdoError In rdoErrors
   124: '          clsAppTransactions.addTrans2Text m_rdoError.Number '&
➥m_rdoError.Source & m_rdoError.Description
   125: '              'rdoEngine.rdoErrors(iErrCnt).Number &
'rdoEngine.rdoErrors
➥(iErrCnt).Source & 'rdoEngine.rdoErrors(iErrCnt).Description
   126: '      Next
   127: '      clsAppTransactions.addTrans2Text "Connection to database was not
➥successful"
   128: '      clsAppTransactions.showLog
   129: '      openConnection = gFAILURE
   130:      MsgBox CStr(Err.Number) & ": " & Err.Description
   131:      Set mvarpDBConnection = Nothing
   132: End Sub
   133:
   134: '##ModelId=352AB4CD0064
   135: Public Property Let pTblColumns(ByVal vData As rdoColumns)
   136: 'used when assigning a value to the property, on the left side of an
➥assignment.
   137: 'Syntax: X.pTblColumns = 5
   138:      mvarpTblColumns = vData
   139: End Property
   140:
   141:
   142: '##ModelId=352AB4CC0334
   143: Public Property Get pTblColumns() As rdoColumns
   144: 'used when retrieving value of a property, on the right side of an
➥assignment.
   145: 'Syntax: Debug.Print X.pTblColumns
   146:      Set pTblColumns = mvarpTblColumns
   147: End Property
   148:
   149:
   150:
▼  151: '##ModelId=352AB4CD028A
```

19

continues

```
152: Public Function getRecordCount() As Variant
153: End Function
154:
155: '##ModelId=352AB4CD0366
156: Public Function setColumn(argCol As rdoColumn) As Variant
157: End Function
158:
159: '##ModelId=352AB4CE00FA
160: Public Function openTable() As Variant
161: End Function
162:
163: '##ModelId=352AB4CE01D6
164: Public Function rollbackDBTrans() As Variant
165: End Function
166:
167: '##ModelId=352AB4CE02EE
168: Public Function beginDBTrans() As Variant
169: End Function
170:
171: '##ModelId=352AB4CE03CA
172: Public Sub commitDBTrans()
173: End Sub
174:
175: '##ModelId=352AB4CF00BE
176: Public Sub closeDBConnection(Optional argConnection) ' As Variant
177:     ' Close the connection.
178:     mvarpDBConnection.Close
179: End Sub
180:
181: '##ModelId=352AB4CF0276
182: Public Sub openConnection(argConnStr As String)
183:     'openConnectionNoDSN argConnStr
184:     openConnectionWithDSN argConnStr
185: End Sub
186:
187:
188: '##ModelId=352AB4D0000A 'Opens connection without DSN
189: Public Sub openConnectionNoDSN(argConnStr As String) 'As Variant
190:     Dim sConnStr As String
191:     On Error GoTo openConnectionErr
192:     Set mvarpDBConnection = New ADODB.Connection
193:     sConnStr = "driver=" & mvarDefaultDriverName & ";" & argConnStr
194:
195:     With mvarpDBConnection
196:         ' Open a connection using an ODBC DSN.
197:         'cnn.ConnectionString = "driver={SQL Server};" &
➥"server=rgreennt;uid=sa;pwd=;database=pubs"
198:             'Set the provider property to the OLE DB Provider for ODBC.
```
▼

```
▼  199:          .Provider = "MSDASQL"
   200:          .ConnectionString = argConnStr '"DSN=Pubs;UID=sa;PWD=;"
   201:          .ConnectionTimeout = 30
   202:          .Open
   203:          ' Find out if the attempt to connect worked.
   204:          If .State = adStateOpen Then
   205: '            MsgBox "Connection successfully established"
   206: '        Else
   207: '            MsgBox "Connection not successfully established"
   208:          End If
   209:      End With
   210:      Exit Sub
   211: openConnectionErr:
   212: MsgBox CStr(Err.Number) & ": " & Err.Description
   213:      Set mvarpDBConnection = Nothing
   214:
   215: End Sub
   216:
   217: '##ModelId=352AB4D001C2
   218: Private Sub Class_Initialize()
   219: '      mvarDefaultDriverName = "{SQL Server}"
   220: '      mvarDefaultServerName = "rc01_srvr"
   221:       mvarDefaultDriverName = "{MS Access}"
   222:       mvarDefaultServerName = ""
   223: End Sub
   224:
```

LISTING 19.2. THE CODE FOR THE DBAdoResultset CLASS.

```
    1: VERSION 1.0 CLASS
    2: BEGIN
    3:    MultiUse = -1  'True
    4: END
    5: Attribute VB_Name = "DBAdoResultset"
    6: Attribute VB_GlobalNameSpace = True
    7: Attribute VB_Creatable = True
    8: Attribute VB_PredeclaredId = False
    9: Attribute VB_Exposed = False
   10: Attribute VB_Ext_KEY = "SavedWithClassBuilder" ,"Yes"
   11: Attribute VB_Ext_KEY = "Member0" ,"DBColumn"
   12: Attribute VB_Ext_KEY = "Top_Level" ,"Yes"
   13: Attribute VB_Ext_KEY = "RVB_UniqueId" ,"352AB4DC0096"
   14: 'local variable(s) to hold property value(s)
   15: '##ModelId=352AB4DC0212
   16: Private mvarpSQLTimeout As Integer 'local copy
   17: '##ModelId=352AB4DC0280
   18: Private mvarpCurrentSQL As String 'local copy
   19: '##ModelId=352AB4DC02BC
▼  20: Private mvarpPreviousSQL As String 'local copy
```

19

continues

```
21: 'Private mvarpResultset As ADOR.Recordset 'local copy
22: '##ModelId=352AB4DC02EE
23: Private mvarpResultset As ADOR.Recordset 'local copy
24: '##ModelId=352AB4DC035C
25: Private mvarpTblColumns As Object 'local copy
26: '##ModelId=352AB4DC03CA
27: Private mvarpEOF As Boolean 'local copy
28: '##ModelId=352AB4DD008C
29: Private mvarpBOF As Boolean 'local copy
30: 'Private mvarhasBeenChanged As Boolean 'local copy
31: 'Private mvarisBeingEdited As Boolean 'local copy
32: 'Private mvarhasBeenAdded As Boolean 'local copy
33: 'Private mvarChangedByCode As Boolean 'local copy
34: '##ModelId=352AB4DD00FA
35: Private mvarpBookmark As Variant 'local copy
36: '##ModelId=352AB4DD019C
37: Private mvarDBColumn As ADOR.Field 'local copy
38: '##ModelId=352AB4DD0208
39: Public pChangedByCode As Boolean
40: '##ModelId=352AB4DD0276
41: Public mvBookMark As Variant
42: '##ModelId=352AB4DD0320
43: Public pEditFlag As Boolean
44: '##ModelId=352AB4DD038E
45: Public pAddNewFlag As Boolean
46: '##ModelId=352AB4DD03C0
47: Public pDataChanged As Boolean
48: 'local variable(s) to hold property value(s)
49: '##ModelId=352AB4DD03C1
50: Private mvarRSFields As Object 'local copy
51: '##ModelId=352AB4DE0082
52: Public Property Get RSFields() As Object
53: 'used when retrieving value of a property, on the right side of an
➥assignment.
54: 'Syntax: Debug.Print X.RSFields
55:     Set mvarRSFields = mvarpResultset.Fields
56:     Set RSFields = mvarRSFields
57: End Property
58:
59:
60:
61:
62: '##ModelId=352AB4DE01CC
63: Public Property Set DBColumn(ByVal vData As Object)
64: 'used when assigning an Object to the property, on the left side of a
➥Set statement.
65: 'Syntax: Set x.DBColumn = Form1
66:     Set mvarDBColumn = vData
67: End Property
```

```
68:
69:
70: '##ModelId=352AB4DE0122
71: Public Property Get DBColumn() As Object
72: 'used when retrieving value of a property, on the right side of an
➥assignment.
73: 'Syntax: Debug.Print X.DBColumn
74:     Set DBColumn = mvarDBColumn
75: End Property
76:
77:
78:
79: '##ModelId=352AB4DF000A
80: Public Sub openDBResultset(argSQL As String, Optional argDBConnection
➥As ADODB.Connection, Optional argFlag, Optional argRSType) 'As Variant
81:
82:     On Error GoTo openDBResultsetErr
83:     Set mvarpResultset = argDBConnection.Execute(argSQL)
84:         'mvarpResultset.Open argSQL, argDBConnection
85:     Exit Sub
86: openDBResultsetErr:
87:     MsgBox "Error # " & Err.Number & ": " & Err.Description &
➥" Source:" & Err.Source
88: End Sub
89: '##ModelId=352AB4DF0370
90: Public Sub prepareForChange()
91:    If pChangedByCode Then Exit Sub
92:    'just set the flag if data is changed
93:    'it gets reset to false when a new record is displayed
94:    pDataChanged = True
95: End Sub
96:
97:
98:
99:
100:
101: '##ModelId=352AB4E001AE
102: Public Property Let pBookmark(ByVal vData As Variant)
103: 'used when assigning a value to the property, on the left side
➥of an assignment.
104: 'Syntax: X.pBookmark = 5
105:     mvarpBookmark = vData
106: End Property
107:
108:
109: '##ModelId=352AB4E00366
110: Public Property Set pBookmark(ByVal vData As Object)
111: 'used when assigning an Object to the property, on the left side of a
➥Set statement.
```

19

continues

```
112: 'Syntax: Set x.pBookmark = Form1
113:     Set mvarpBookmark = vData
114: End Property
115:
116:
117: '##ModelId=352AB4E00064
118: Public Property Get pBookmark() As Variant
119: 'used when retrieving value of a property, on the right side of an
➥assignment.
120: 'Syntax: Debug.Print X.pBookmark
121:     If IsObject(mvarpBookmark) Then
122:         Set pBookmark = mvarpBookmark
123:     Else
124:         pBookmark = mvarpBookmark
125:     End If
126: End Property
127:
128:
129:
130: '##ModelId=352AB4E103CA
131: Public Property Let ChangedByCode(ByVal vData As Boolean)
132: 'used when assigning a value to the property, on the left side of an
➥assignment.
133: 'Syntax: X.ChangedByCode = 5
134:     mvarChangedByCode = vData
135: End Property
136:
137:
138: '##ModelId=352AB4E101E0
139: Public Property Get ChangedByCode() As Boolean
140: 'used when retrieving value of a property, on the right side of an
➥assignment.
141: 'Syntax: Debug.Print X.ChangedByCode
142:     ChangedByCode = mvarChangedByCode
143: End Property
144:
145:
146:
147: '##ModelId=352AB4E202B2
148: Public Property Let hasBeenAdded(ByVal vData As Boolean)
149: 'used when assigning a value to the property, on the left side of an
➥assignment.
150: 'Syntax: X.hasBeenAdded = 5
151:     mvarhasBeenAdded = vData
152: End Property
153:
154:
155: '##ModelId=352AB4E2019A
156: Public Property Get hasBeenAdded() As Boolean
```

```
▼  157: 'used when retrieving value of a property, on the right side of an
      ➥assignment.
   158: 'Syntax: Debug.Print X.hasBeenAdded
   159:     hasBeenAdded = mvarhasBeenAdded
   160: End Property
   161:
   162:
   163:
   164: '##ModelId=352AB4E30190
   165: Public Property Let isBeingEdited(ByVal vData As Boolean)
   166: 'used when assigning a value to the property, on the left side of an
      ➥assignment.
   167: 'Syntax: X.isBeingEdited = 5
   168:     mvarisBeingEdited = vData
   169: End Property
   170:
   171:
   172: '##ModelId=352AB4E3000A
   173: Public Property Get isBeingEdited() As Boolean
   174: 'used when retrieving value of a property, on the right side of an
      ➥assignment.
   175: 'Syntax: Debug.Print X.isBeingEdited
   176:     isBeingEdited = mvarisBeingEdited
   177: End Property
   178:
   179:
   180:
   181: '##ModelId=352AB4E4003C
   182: Public Property Let hasBeenChanged(ByVal vData As Boolean)
   183: 'used when assigning a value to the property, on the left side of an
      ➥assignment.
   184: 'Syntax: X.hasBeenChanged = 5
   185:     mvarhasBeenChanged = vData
   186: End Property
   187:
   188:
   189: '##ModelId=352AB4E3030C
   190: Public Property Get hasBeenChanged() As Boolean
   191: 'used when retrieving value of a property, on the right side of an
      ➥assignment.
   192: 'Syntax: Debug.Print X.hasBeenChanged
   193:     hasBeenChanged = mvarhasBeenChanged
   194: End Property
   195:
   196:
   197:
   198: '##ModelId=352AB4E40226
   199: Public Function getSpecificRecord(ParamArray argKeys()) As Boolean
   200: End Function
▼  201:
```

19

continues

▼ **LISTING 19.2.** CONTINUED

```
202: '##ModelId=352AB4E403DE
203: Public Sub queryAgain()
204: End Sub
205:
206: '##ModelId=352AB4E501EA
207: Public Property Let pBOF(ByVal vData As Boolean)
208: 'used when assigning a value to the property, on the left side of an
➥assignment.
209: 'Syntax: X.pBOF = 5
210:     mvarpBOF = vData
211: End Property
212:
213:
214: '##ModelId=352AB4E500D2
215: Public Property Get pBOF() As Boolean
216: 'used when retrieving value of a property, on the right side of an
➥assignment.
217: 'Syntax: Debug.Print X.pBOF
218:     pBOF = mvarpBOF
219: End Property
220:
221:
222:
223: '##ModelId=352AB4E600C8
224: Public Property Let pEOF(ByVal vData As Boolean)
225: 'used when assigning a value to the property, on the left side of an
➥assignment.
226: 'Syntax: X.pEOF = 5
227:     mvarpEOF = vData
228: End Property
229:
230:
231: '##ModelId=352AB4E503A2
232: Public Property Get pEOF() As Boolean
233: 'used when retrieving value of a property, on the right side of an
➥assignment.
234: 'Syntax: Debug.Print X.pEOF
235:     pEOF = mvarpEOF
236: End Property
237:
238:
239:
240: '##ModelId=352AB4E6038E
241: Public Property Set pTblColumns(ByVal vData As Object)
242: 'used when assigning an Object to the property, on the left side of a
➥Set statement.
243: 'Syntax: Set x.pTblColumns = Form1
244:     Set mvarpTblColumns = vData
```
▼

```
▼ 245: End Property
  246:
  247:
  248: '##ModelId=352AB4E60280
  249: Public Property Get pTblColumns() As Object
  250: 'used when retrieving value of a property, on the right side of an
  ➥assignment.
  251: 'Syntax: Debug.Print X.pTblColumns
  252:     Set pTblColumns = mvarpTblColumns
  253: End Property
  254:
  255:
  256:
  257: '##ModelId=352AB4E70352
  258: Public Property Set pResultset(ByVal vData As Object)
  259: 'used when assigning an Object to the property, on the left side of a
  ➥Set statement.
  260: 'Syntax: Set x.pResultset = Form1
  261:     Set mvarpResultset = vData
  262: End Property
  263:
  264:
  265: '##ModelId=352AB4E700F0
  266: Public Property Get pResultset() As ADOR.Recordset
  267: 'used when retrieving value of a property, on the right side of an
  ➥assignment.
  268: 'Syntax: Debug.Print X.pResultset
  269:     Set pResultset = mvarpResultset
  270: End Property
  271:
  272:
  273:
  274: '##ModelId=352AB4EA0172
  275: Public Property Let pPreviousSQL(ByVal vData As String)
  276: 'used when assigning a value to the property, on the left side of an
  ➥assignment.
  277: 'Syntax: X.pPreviousSQL = 5
  278:     mvarpPreviousSQL = vData
  279: End Property
  280:
  281:
  282: '##ModelId=352AB4E90370
  283: Public Property Get pPreviousSQL() As String
  284: 'used when retrieving value of a property, on the right side of an
  ➥assignment.
  285: 'Syntax: Debug.Print X.pPreviousSQL
  286:     pPreviousSQL = mvarpPreviousSQL
  287: End Property
  288:
▼ 289:
```

19

continues

```
290:
291: '##ModelId=352AB4EB005A
292: Public Property Let pCurrentSQL(ByVal vData As String)
293: 'used when assigning a value to the property, on the left side of an
➥assignment.
294: 'Syntax: X.pCurrentSQL = 5
295:     mvarpCurrentSQL = vData
296: End Property
297:
298:
299: '##ModelId=352AB4EA032A
300: Public Property Get pCurrentSQL() As String
301: 'used when retrieving value of a property, on the right side of an
➥assignment.
302: 'Syntax: Debug.Print X.pCurrentSQL
303:     pCurrentSQL = mvarpCurrentSQL
304: End Property
305:
306:
307:
308: '##ModelId=352AB4EC0082
309: Public Property Let pSQLTimeout(ByVal vData As Integer)
310: 'used when assigning a value to the property, on the left side of an
➥assignment.
311: 'Syntax: X.pSQLTimeout = 5
312:     mvarpSQLTimeout = vData
313: End Property
314:
315:
316: '##ModelId=352AB4EB01A4
317: Public Property Get pSQLTimeout() As Integer
318: 'used when retrieving value of a property, on the right side of an
➥assignment.
319: 'Syntax: Debug.Print X.pSQLTimeout
320:     pSQLTimeout = mvarpSQLTimeout
321: End Property
322:
323:
324:
325: '##ModelId=352AB4EC0316
326: Public Function getRecordCount() As Long
327:     getRecordCount = mvarpResultset.RecordCount
328: End Function
329:
330: '##ModelId=352AB4ED00E6
331: Public Sub getLastRec()
332:    'On Error GoTo GoLastError
333:
```

```
▼ 334:     With mvarpResultset
  335:         Do Until .EOF
  336:             .MoveNext
  337:              If .EOF Then Exit Do
  338:         Loop
  339:     End With
  340: '    mvarpEOF = True
  341: '    mvarpBOF = False
  342:    pDataChanged = False
  343:
  344:    Exit Sub
  345:
  346: GoLastError:
  347:    MsgBox Err.Description
  348: End Sub
  349:
  350: '##ModelId=352AB4ED01C2
  351: Public Sub getFirstRec()
  352:    On Error GoTo GoFirstError
  353:
  354:     With mvarpResultset
  355:          .MoveFirst
  356:     End With
  357: '    pBOF = True
  358: '    pEOF = False
  359:    'displayCurrentRecord
  360:    pDataChanged = False
  361:
  362:    Screen.MousePointer = vbDefault
  363:    Exit Sub
  364:
  365: GoFirstError:
  366:    MsgBox Err.Description
  367: End Sub
  368:
  369: '##ModelId=352AB4ED026C
  370: Public Sub getPreviousRec()
  371:    On Error GoTo GoPrevError
  372:
  373:     With mvarpResultset
  374:         If Not .BOF Then .MovePrevious
  375:         If .BOF And .RecordCount > 0 Then
  376:           Beep
  377:           'moved off the end so go back
  378:            .MoveFirst
  379:         End If
  380:     End With
  381:     'mvarpBOF = True
  382:    pDataChanged = False
▼ 383:
```

continues

```
384:    Exit Sub
385:
386: GoPrevError:
387:    MsgBox Err.Description
388: End Sub
389:
390: '##ModelId=352AB4ED033E
391: Public Sub getNextRec()
392:    On Error GoTo GoNextError
393:      With mvarpResultset
394:          If Not .EOF Then .MoveNext
395:          If .EOF And .RecordCount > 0 Then
396:            Beep
397:             'moved off the end so go back
398:            .MoveLast
399:          End If
400:      End With
401:       'mvarpEOF = True
402:    pDataChanged = False
403:
404:    Exit Sub
405: GoNextError:
406:    MsgBox Err.Description
407: End Sub
408: '##ModelId=352AB4ED03AC
409: Public Function openDBTable(argTableName As String) As Variant
410: End Function
411:
412: '##ModelId=352AB4EE014A
413: Public Sub updateManyRecords()
414: End Sub
415:
416: '##ModelId=352AB4EE01EA
417: Public Sub updateBySQL()
418: End Sub
419:
420: '##ModelId=352AB4EE02C6
421: Public Sub startEditMode()
422:    On Error GoTo EditErr
423:
424:    Screen.MousePointer = vbHourglass
425:    .Edit
426:    pEditFlag = True
427:    mvBookMark = .Bookmark
428:
429:    Exit Sub
430:
431: EditErr:
```

```
▼  432:    Screen.MousePointer = vbDefault
   433:    MsgBox Err.Description
   434: End Sub
   435:
   436: '##ModelId=352AB4EF0096 'Updates a single record to DB
   437: Public Sub updateOneRecord(Optional argClientObject As Object)
   438:    On Error GoTo UpdateErr
   439:
   440:    With mvarpResultset
   441:      .Update
   442:
   443:      If pAddNewFlag Then
   444:        .MoveLast                'move to the new record
   445:        mvarpEOF = True
   446:      End If
   447:    End With
   448:
   449:    pEditFlag = False
   450:    pAddNewFlag = False
   451:    pDataChanged = False
   452:    Exit Sub
   453:
   454: UpdateErr:
   455:    MsgBox Err.Description
   456: End Sub
   457:
   458:
   459: '##ModelId=352AB4EF021C
   460: Public Sub addNewRecord()
   461:    On Error GoTo AddErr
   462:    With mvarpResultset
   463:      .AddNew
   464:      lblStatus.Caption = "Add record"
   465:      pAddNewFlag = True
   466:      If .RecordCount > 0 Then
   467:        mvBookMark = .Bookmark
   468:      Else
   469:        mvBookMark = vbNullString
   470:      End If
   471:    End With
   472:
   473:    Exit Sub
   474: AddErr:
   475:    MsgBox Err.Description
   476: End Sub
   477:
   478: '##ModelId=352AB4EF02F8
   479: Public Sub addBySQL()
   480: End Sub
▼  481:
```

19

continues

```
482: '##ModelId=352AB4F0001E
483: Public Sub CancelTrans()
484: End Sub
485:
486:
```
▲

Summary

This chapter describes the Database Access Subsystem and its purpose. In particular, it explains ADO, DAO, RDO, and ODBC. You learned about the classes in the Database Access Subsystem, as well as their methods, properties, arguments, and returns. The chapter presents practical guidelines for implementing this subsystem in code and discusses how to incorporate it into the Samsona Bank Teller System example, providing subsystem code listings for the Bank example.

Tomorrow, you learn how to bring all the parts of your application together to make your application complete. That is, you learn how to make your subsystems communicate with one another to support the various ways your users use your application.

Q&A

Q What are the three popular data access mechanisms supported in Visual Basic?

A ActiveX Data Objects (ADO), Remote Data Objects (RDO), and Data Access Objects (DAO).

Q Which data access mechanism has Microsoft embraced as the future standard?

A ActiveX Data Objects.

Q What is the main goal of this lesson?

A To present a common interface for any data access mechanism supported in Visual Basic, especially ADO, RDO, and DAO.

Q What is `IDatabase` in this subsystem?

A `IDatabase` is the common interface shared by objects that participate in the various data access mechanisms Visual Basic developers use.

Q True or False: Microsoft doesn't expect ADO to be a superset of RDO.

A False. According to Microsoft, ADO will eventually be a superset of RDO.

Q What is DAO?

A Data Access Objects. DAO is the first object library/data access mechanism that provided an interface to the Microsoft Jet database engine to access native Jet databases as well as other kinds of data sources.

Q What is a benefit of RDO in query processing?

A RDO—and its DAO Data control alternative, the Remote Data control—lets your applications access ODBC data sources without using a local query processor. Without localizing a query processor, your applications enjoy faster performance and more flexibility when accessing remote database engines.

Workshop

The workshop includes quiz questions to help gauge your grasp of the material. You'll find the answers to this quiz in Appendix A, "Answers." Even if you feel that you understand the concepts presented here, you should work through the quiz. The last section contains exercises to help reinforce your learning.

Quiz

1. What does UDA stand for? What is its purpose?
2. What features does the Remote Data Services (RDS) component provide for ADO?
3. What are three reasons ADO was created by Microsoft?
4. True or False: RDO enables you to limit the number of rows returned or processed.
5. What are the advantages and disadvantages of using the ODBC API?
6. What are the general operations involved in working with the ODBC API?
7. What are the advantages and disadvantages of using Data controls?

19

Exercises

1. Using the code on the CD-ROM, create and implement collection classes for the connection classes (`DBAdoConnection`, `DBRdoConnection`, and `DBDaoConnection`) and the resultset classes (`DBAdoResultset`, `DBRdoResultset`, and `DBDaoResultset`).
2. Using the `updateOneRecord` method of `DBAdoResultset` (the code is on the CD-ROM), create a corresponding method to update a batch of records. (Hint: Think of ways you might update a group of records in a loop.)

DAY 20

The Anatomy of a Complete Visual Basic System

This chapter presents you with an overview of a complete Visual Basic system. In particular, you learn about

- Different ways subsystems interact to augment application behavior
- Interfacing between the Graphical User Interface and the Database Access Subsystems
- Interfacing between the Reporting and Printing and the Graphical User Interface Subsystems
- Interfacing between the Workgroup and User Security Subsystem and between the Data Access and Internal Application Manager Subsystems
- Interfacing between the Internal Application Manager Subsystem and all subsystems

- Identifying the need for other subsystems
- Deploying the Samsona Bank Teller System example

Different Ways Subsystems Interact to Augment Application Behavior

After reading the previous 19 chapters, you have realized by now that an application is at its best when its expected behavior is compartmentalized into subsystems. Subsystems, in turn, are compartmentalized into classes. Finally, classes are compartmentalized into methods, properties, and events. These various compartments communicate with one another through a common interface. At the subsystem level, the interfaces are represented by interface classes. At the class level, members communicate through argument lists accessed when methods, property methods, or events are invoked.

The most critical communications, however, occur between subsystems. Subsystem interface classes are important because changes to them can cause a debugging and maintenance nightmare. It would be beneficial, then, to briefly discuss the major interfaces with respect to their intercommunications.

Interfacing Between the Graphical User Interface and the Database Access Subsystems

The Graphical User Interface Subsystem and the Database Access Subsystem typically don't need to communicate directly with one another. Data controls are an exception. Nonetheless, it's important to describe how information in the Graphical User Interface Subsystem is eventually channeled to or from the Database Access Subsystem.

The forms themselves should not communicate directly with the database because the code that makes this communication happen tends to be duplicated or otherwise difficult to maintain. A healthy decoupling between the two subsystems is a result of using form controller classes, business or domain classes, and data access (or persistence) classes.

Forms only invoke methods of their respective form controllers. Therefore, when you click a command button in the form, a method in the form controller is dedicated to processing the click event of that button. If you want to implement code to respond to the resizing of the form, the form delegates the response to a dedicated method in its controller. If the form's labels and text boxes need to be filled with data from the database, the form calls some method in its controller that is responsible for obtaining the data it needs. The story doesn't end here.

When the form requests that its controller obtain the data it needs to display to the user, the form controller communicates with business (or domain classes, for nonbusiness applications), including collection classes. Business classes manage the data that is meaningful to the user. In fact, business classes are typically based on the user's business knowledge, as well as on any business rules in the organization.

Often, applications deal with several records at a time, for which collections of business classes are useful. Business class collections are, in a sense, queues or stores of data out of which form controllers request information to display. Collections can very well be seen as mini object-oriented databases that help shield (or encapsulate) the rest of the application from the relational database. Behind this shield, however, is even more of the story.

Business classes, and their collections, communicate with Database Access classes to get data into and out of the database. The Business Rules Subsystem, then, communicates with the Database Access Subsystem through interface classes such as `IPersistence`, or in less complex applications, the `IDBSubssytem` interface class. As you saw on Day 19, "The Database Access Subsystem," the Database Access Subsystem classes communicate with the database itself through any number of data access mechanisms, including ADO, RDO, DAO, ODBC API, VBSQL (SQL Server `DBLIB` and `SQLOLE` objects), data controls, and third-party data access mechanisms such as Oracle Objects. In addition, if you're developing a distributed Visual Basic application, you would have a proxy class that locally represents a remote subsystem (therefore, the word *proxy*). If you deploy the Business Rules Subsystem on a workgroup server, and the Database Access Subsystem on a separate enterprise server, you might find it convenient to create a data access proxy class, `DBProxy`, that handles the information persistence needs of the workgroup server on behalf of the enterprise server. In a fully qualified sense, `DBProxy` is a proxy interface class. This interface proxy class could also be helpful on regular two-tier client/server applications in which you create an ActiveX component to handle data access on the server (or even locally).

Although it's certainly wise from a code reuse standpoint to not enable forms to directly communicate with the Database Access Subsystem, form controllers at times need to communicate with it. In fact, form controller classes aren't monopolized exclusively by the Graphical User Interface Subsystem in every situation. Sometimes a controller class can be the communication hub, of sorts, between the form business rules and the Database Access Subsystem. This is helpful when you're moving data in and out of a database, one record at a time, and no business rule processing occurs. Typical applications that might face this scenario include pure data entry applications in which the user is keying in information on a client machine, and that information is to be processed later

20

by some server subsystem independent of the client. Listing 20.1 shows a form controller method, showForm, that displays information to the user with a SQL statement.

LISTING 20.1. AN EXAMPLE OF A FORM CONTROLLER THAT DIRECTLY CONTROLS THE FLOW OF INFORMATION FROM THE DATABASE ACCESS SUBSYSTEM TO THE GRAPHICAL USER INTERFACE SUBSYSTEM.

```
 1:
 2: Public Sub showForm()
 3:     Dim sSQL As String
 4:     sSQL = sSQL & "SELECT [PubID],[Name],[Company Name],[Telephone]"
 5:     sSQL = sSQL & " FROM [Publishers] Order by [PubID]"
 6:
 7:     With theDBSubsystem
 8:         sSQL = .theCommandBroker.CurrSQL
 9:         .DBResultset.openDBResultset sSQL,
             ➥theDBSubsystem.DBConnection.pDBConnection
10:     End With
11:     Set theForm = New frmPublishers
12:     displayCurrentRecord
13:     theForm.Show
14: End Sub
15:
```

theDBSubsystem is the instance of the data access interface class, IDBSubsystem. theCommandBroker is the class instance of CommandBroker, which is responsible for managing the references to SQL statements, ADO Command objects, RDO rdoQuery objects, and similar objects. DBResultset is the resultset (or recordset) object reference owned by theDBSubsystem. DBConnection is the reference to the connection object facade also owned by theDBSubsystem. DBConnection, in turn, has the property, pDBConnection, which is the actual connection object reference. theForm is the reference to frmPublishers. Finally, displayCurrentRecord is the controller's method responsible for displaying the current record. The controller classes in the Second Bank of Carrollton example follow this general pattern.

NEW TERM   A *proxy class* is a class that acts as a stand-in for a remote subsystem or component.

Interfacing Between the Reporting and Printing and the Graphical User Interface Subsystems

When a user requests a report in a GUI-based system, he or she typically selects a report on a form. The form delegates the request to its controller. From there, the form controller, part of the Graphical User Interface (and often Business Rules) Subsystem, communicates with the interface class of the Reporting and Printing Subsystem, IReporting. Depending on the adapter implementation class chosen (such as AccessReporting, CrystalReporting, or RichTextReporting), the report is opened or built and then sent to the PrinterProxy class for actual printing.

Listing 20.2 shows the important methods involved in the communication between the two subsystems for the purpose of requesting a report. Listing 20.3 shows the printing requests as they are implemented between the subsystems. In the Second Bank of Carrollton example, the CashDepositRecord class communicates with IReporting in the manner of these two listings.

LISTING 20.2. THE CLASS METHODS IN THE COMMUNICATION BETWEEN THE TWO SUBSYSTEMS. THE INTERACTION OF THESE METHODS IS NECESSARY FOR REQUESTING A REPORT.

```
 1: 'In a form controller class, such as CashDepositRecord
 2: Public Sub clickedOpenReport(Optional argReportName As String,
    ➥Optional argReportType As Byte)
 3:     Dim bReportType As Byte
 4:     Screen.MousePointer = vbHourglass
 5:     bReportType = eReporting.RichTextReporting 'Implemented
 6: '   bReportType = eReporting.AccessReporting 'Not implemented
 7: '   bReportType = eReporting.CrystalReporting 'Not implemented
 8:
 9:     'Only one of these three calls
10:     'will be able to process message
11:     setRichTextReporting bReportType
12:     setAccessReporting bReportType
13:     setCrystalReporting bReportType
14:
15:     'Polymorphic call to openReport() method
16:     theReporting.openReport theForm.txtReportName
17:     Screen.MousePointer = vbDefault
18:
19: End Sub
20:
21: 'In RichTextReporting. . .
22: Private Function IReporting_openReport(Optional _
23: argRptName As String) ', _
24: Optional argContents) As Variant
25:     'If Not IsMissing(argContents) Then mvarContents = argContents
26:     'theReportController.showForm
27:     mvarReportName = argRptName
28:      EveryCashDepositRecord.buildReport mvarReportName,
           ➥theRichTextBox
29: End Function
```

continues

20

LISTING **20.2.** CONTINUED

```
30: 'In a business rule collection object such as EveryCashDepositRecord
31: Public Sub buildReport(argFileName As String, _
32: Optional argRichTextBox As RichTextBox)
33:     Dim objObject As Customer, sFileName As String,
        ➥objRichTextBox As RichTextBox
34:     Dim sMsg As String, lRecCount As Long, sTempFile As String
35:     Dim bCol(3) As Byte
36:
37:     Set objRichTextBox = argRichTextBox
38:     sFileName = argFileName
39:     theReportController.setTabs 5
40:     'Assists this class in creating an object for each record
41:     'in the file
42:     sMsg = "Building report information"
43:     theReportController.updateProgress 0, sMsg, Me.Count
44:     theFileSubsystem.populatePCPhysicians sFileName, Me
45:
46:     sMsg = "Records processed"
47:     theReportController.updateProgress 0, sMsg, Me.Count
48:
49:     bCol(0) = 12
50:     bCol(1) = 20
51:     bCol(2) = 5
52:     bCol(3) = 20
53:
54:     objRichTextBox.SelTabs(0) = bCol(0)
55:     objRichTextBox.SelTabs(1) = bCol(1)
56:     objRichTextBox.SelTabs(2) = bCol(2)
57:     objRichTextBox.SelTabs(3) = bCol(3)
58:
59:     'Set temporary report file
60:     sTempFile = App.Path & "\report.tmp"
61:     Open sTempFile For Append As #1
62:     Width #1, 80
63:     For Each objObject In Me
64:         lRecCount = lRecCount + 1
65:         objRichTextBox.TabStop = True
66:         With objRichTextBox
67:             If objObject.CustomerID = "" Then
68:                 objObject.CustomerID = String(7, "?")
69:             End If
70:             If objObject.FirstName = "" Then
71:                 objObject.FirstName = String$(12, "?") '"--"
72:             End If
73:             If objObject.MiddleInitial = "" Then
74:                 objObject.MiddleInitial = "----"
75:             End If
```

```
76:                    If objObject.LastName = "" Then
77:                        objObject.LastName = String$(12, "?")
78:                    End If
79:
80:                Print #1, objObject.CustomerID & Space$(bCol(0) -
                    ➥Len(objObject.CustomerID)); _
81:                    Tab; objObject.FirstName & Space$(bCol(1) -
                        ➥Len(objObject.FirstName)); _
82:                    Tab; objObject.MiddleInitial & Space$(bCol(2) -
                        ➥Len(objObject.MiddleInitial)); Tab; _
83:                    objObject.LastName & Space$(bCol(3) -
                        ➥Len(objObject.LastName)); Tab '; vbNewLine
84:            End With
85:            theReportController.updateProgress lRecCount
86:        Next
87:        Close #1
88:
89:        objRichTextBox.LoadFile sTempFile, rtfText
90:        theRichTextAgent.deleteFile sTempFile
91:        theReportController.enableTabStops True
92:        getCDRReportHeading objRichTextBox, bCol
93: End Sub
94: Public Sub getCDRReportHeading(argRichTextBox As RichTextBox,
                                ➥ByRef argCols)
95:        'theRichTextBox
96:        Dim sHeading As String, sCol(3) As String
97:        sCol(0) = "CustomerID"
98:        sCol(1) = "First Name"
99:        sCol(2) = "MI"
100:       sCol(3) = "Last Name"
101:
102:       sHeading = sCol(0) & "   " _
103:           & sCol(1) & "   " _
104:           & sCol(2) & "   " _
105:           & sCol(3)
106:       'Dim FoundPos As Long
107:       With argRichTextBox
108:           '.LoadFile App.Path & "\KEN0001 PCP.txt"
109:           .Text = sHeading & vbNewLine & String(60, "_") _
110:               & vbNewLine & vbNewLine & .Text
111:           .SelStart = 0
112:           .SelLength = Len(sHeading)
113:           .SelBold = True
114:           .SelColor = vbBlue
115:           .SelFontSize = 18
116:           .SelFontName = "Bookshelf Symbol 2"
117:           .Refresh
118:       End With
119: End Sub
```

20

LISTING 20.3. PRINTING A REPORT. THE REPORTING AND PRINTING AND THE GRAPHICAL USER
INTERFACE SUBSYSTEMS COMMUNICATE TO CARRY OUT THE PRINTING.

```
 1: 'In the form controller
 2: Public Sub clickedPrintReport()
 3:     Screen.MousePointer = vbHourglass
 4:     If TypeName(theReporting) <> "Nothing" Then
 5:         'Set thePrinterProxy = New PrinterProxy
 6:         theReporting.printReport 1
 7:     End If
 8:     Screen.MousePointer = vbDefault
 9: End Sub
10:
11: 'In RochTextReporting
12: Private Function IReporting_printReport(ParamArray argSettings()) As
    ➥Variant
13:     thePrinterProxy.printReport theRichTextBox, ,
        ➥eReporting.RichTextReporting 'Print to actual Printer
14: End Function
15: 'In PrinterProxy
16: Public Sub printReport(ParamArray argObject())
17: 'argObject(0) = Object
18: 'argObject(1) = Message
19: If Not IsMissing(argObject(0)) Then
20:     Select Case argObject(1)
21:         Case eReporting.AccessReporting
22:         Case eReporting.CrystalReporting
23:         Case eReporting.RichTextReporting
24:             argObject(0).SelPrint Printer.hDC 'Physical printing done
                ➥now
25:     End Select
26: End If
27: End Sub
```

Interfacing Between the Workgroup and User Security Subsystem and the Database Access and Internal Application Manager Subsystems

Perhaps the most complex part of creating commercial and corporate applications is determining whether the user is supposed to use the application (known as *authorization*). In addition, you have to verify exactly what roles the user can perform and assign role controller classes to keep track of all the various roles the user can play (known as *authentication*). Authorization and authentication involve the sometimes complex communication between the Workgroup and User Security, Database Access, and Internal Application Manager subsystems. Listing 20.4 shows the sequence of interactions between these subsystems, from the initialization of the application to the completed authorization and authentication.

LISTING 20.4. THE SEQUENCE OF INTERACTIONS BETWEEN THESE SUBSYSTEMS, FROM THE INITIALIZA-TION OF THE APPLICATION TO THE COMPLETED AUTHORIZATION AND AUTHENTICATION.

```
 1: 'In modMain
 2: Public Sub Main()
 3:     Dim bState As Byte
 4:     bState = theApplication.initializeSystem
 5: End Sub
 6: 'In CApplication
 7: Public Function initializeSystem() As Byte
 8:     Dim returns
 9:     Set theAppTransactions = New AppTransactions
10:
11:     m_returns = theAppTransactions.setRichTextBox(frmLog!rtbDBLog, _
                        ➥frmLog!rtbMemoryLog)
12:     Set theSession = New CSession
13:     theAppTransactions.activateLogging
14:     theMDIController.showForm
15:     theSession.showForm
16:     'theAppTransactions.deactivateLogging
17:     theAppTransactions.addTrans2MemLog _
18:         "Allocated memory for theAppTransactions in
            ➥CApplication.initializeSystem"
19:     theAppTransactions.addTrans2MemLog _
20:         "Allocated memory for theSession in
            ➥CApplication.initializeSystem"
21:     theAppTransactions.addTrans2MemLog _
22:         "Allocated memory for ifcDBConnection in " & TypeName(Me) &
            ➥".initializeSystem"
23:     m_returns = theAppTransactions.addTrans2Text("Starting up the " &
                        ➥App.EXEName & " system")
24:
25:     'Connect to the database
26:     'returns = ifcDBConnection.OpenConnection("", App.Path &
                        ➥"\bank.mdb", False)
27: End Function
28:
29: 'In CSession
30: 'Show the login form
31: Public Sub showForm()
32:     theForm.Show
33: End Sub
34: 'When the user fills in the UserID and Password, and then
35: 'clicks 'Login', the following method is invoked
36: Public Sub clickedLogin()
37:     Dim returns
38:     Set theEncryptor = New SHA1Encryption
39:     theApplication.theUser.UserID = theForm.txtUserID
40:     theApplication.theUser.UserPassword = theEncryptor.encrypt
                                    ➥(theForm.txtPassword)
```

continues

20

LISTING 20.4. CONTINUED

```
41:
42:        'Connect to database and login here. Data Access
43:        'subsystem usage simplified here to avoid a
44:        'clutter of code
45:        Dim sConn As String
46:        Set theDBConnection = New DBAdoConnection
47:        sCOnn = "DSN=CorporateDB;UID=JSmith;PWD=greetings"
48:        theDBConnection.OpenConnectionWithDSN sConn
49:        If theDBConnection.isConnected Then
50:            isLoggedIn = authenticated
51:        End If
52:        If isLoggedIn Then
53:            'Normally, you
54:            theAppTransactions.addTrans2MemLog _
55:                "User " & theApplication.theUser.UserID &
                    ➡" has logged in at " & Now$
56:
57:            theApplication.theMDIController.enableProcessMenu
58:        End If
59:        'Normally, you would check the database
60:        'to see to which workgroup a user belongs
61:        Set theApplication.theSomeWorkgroupProxy = New SomeWorkgroupProxy
62:        theApplication.theSomeWorkgroupProxy.startProcess
63:
64:        'MsgBox theApplication.theUser.UserID & vbNewLine _
65:        '        & theApplication.theUser.UserPassword & vbNewLine &
                    ➡isLoggedIn
66:        'Note that the encrypted password should be persisted
67: End Sub
68:
69: 'In DBAdoConnection
70: Public Sub openConnectionWithDSN(argConnStr As String) 'As Variant
71:        On Error GoTo openConnectionErr
72:        Set mvarpDBConnection = New ADODB.Connection
73:        With mvarpDBConnection
74:            ' Open a connection using an ODBC DSN.
75:            .ConnectionString = argConnStr '"DSN=Pubs;UID=sa;PWD=;"
76:            .ConnectionTimeout = 30
77:            .Open
78:            ' Find out if the attempt to connect worked.
79: '          If .State = adStateOpen Then
80: '              MsgBox "Connection successfully established"
81: '          Else
82: '              MsgBox "Connection not successfully established"
83: '          End If
84:        End With
85:        Exit Sub
86: openConnectionErr:
87: '    For Each m_rdoError In rdoErrors
```

```
88: '        clsAppTransactions.addTrans2Text m_rdoError.Number &
            ➥m_rdoError.Source & m_rdoError.Description
89: '           'rdoEngine.rdoErrors(iErrCnt).Number &
               ➥'rdoEngine.rdoErrors
        ➥(iErrCnt).Source & 'rdoEngine.rdoErrors(iErrCnt).Description
90: '    Next
91: '    clsAppTransactions.addTrans2Text "Connection to database was
            ➥not successful"
92: '    clsAppTransactions.showLog
93: '    openConnection = gFAILURE
94:     MsgBox CStr(Err.Number) & ": " & Err.Description
95:     Set mvarpDBConnection = Nothing
96: End Sub
97: 'In the WorkgroupProxy
98: 'Initialize the class instance
99: Private Sub Class_Initialize()
100:     #If DebugMode Then
101:         'get the next available class ID, and print out
102:         'that the class was created successfully
103:         mlClassDebugID = GetNextClassDebugID()
104:         Debug.Print "'" & TypeName(Me) & "' instance " &
            ➥mlClassDebugID & " created"
105:     #End If
106:     '*****************
107:     If Not theSession.isLoggedIn Then
108:         'Normally, process in error subsystem
109:         MsgBox "User not logged in"
110:         Set theSomeWorkgroupProxy = Nothing
111:     Else
112:         miLastProcessCompleted = -1
113:         'startProcess
114:         'determineRoles
115:     End If
116: End Sub
117: 'Start the initial process
118: Public Sub startProcess()
119:     'Set CurrProcess = New Process
120:     If miLastProcessCompleted = -1 Then
121:         Set CurrProcess = AllProcesses.Add(eProcess.DoProcess1)
122:     End If
123:     'startProcess
124:     determineRoles
125: End Sub
126: 'Determine which roles the user can perform
127: Private Sub determineRoles()
128:     Dim arrRoles
129:     'Involves accessing the role IDs of the roles
130:     'the user can perform in this workgroup
131:     'lookup roles by user id
132:     'theUser.UserID
```

20

continues

LISTING 20.4. CONTINUED

```
133:
134:       'Create role objects based on number
135:       'of records returned. For now, we'll
136:       'just mock up the roles
137:       arrRoles = Array("Worker", "Manager")
138:       AllRoles.Add CStr(arrRoles(eRole.WorkerRole - 1)),
          ➥CStr(eRole.WorkerRole)
139:       AllRoles.Add CStr(arrRoles(eRole.ManagerRole - 1)),
          ➥CStr(eRole.ManagerRole)
140:
141:       'Set current role to the first role
142:       Set CurrRole = AllRoles.Item(eRole.WorkerRole)
143:       MsgBox CurrRole.RoleID
144: End Sub
145: 'In the collection, AllRoles
146: 'Add the roles the user performs
147: Public Sub Add(RoleID As String, _
148: Optional sKey As String) 'As Role
149: 'Public Sub Add(Key As String, _
150: RoleID As String, Optional sKey As String) 'As Role      'create a new
     ➥object
151:
152:       Dim objNewMember As Role
153:
154:       'Determine which object is being created
155:       Select Case RoleID
156:           Case "Worker"
157:               Set objNewMember = New WorkerRole
158:           Case "Manager"
159:               Set objNewMember = New ManagerRole
160:       End Select
161:
162:       'set the properties passed into the method
163:       'objNewMember.Key = Key
164:       'If IsObject(AllForms) Then
165:       '    Set objNewMember.AllForms = AllForms
166:       'Else
167:       '    objNewMember.AllForms = AllForms
168:       'End If
169:       objNewMember.RoleID = RoleID
170:       If Len(sKey) = 0 Then
171:           mCol.Add objNewMember
172:       Else
173:           mCol.Add objNewMember, sKey
174:       End If
175:
176:       ''return the object created
177:       'Set Add = objNewMember
```

```
178:     Set objNewMember = Nothing
179: End Sub
180:
```

Interfacing Between the Internal Application Manager Subsystem and All Subsystems

Notice in Listing 20.4 how the Internal Application Manager Subsystem controls the initialization of the system. It's also actively involved in tracking state changes that applications typically go through. In any subsystem in which you expect a class to affect the state of another subsystem, it's advisable to include this subsystem in the actual tracking and recording of such changes.

Identifying the Need for Other Subsystems

So far, you have been introduced to many critical application subsystems that all Visual Basic applications require in order to be useful to the user and easily maintained by you, the developer. However, the list of all possible subsystems you might need isn't complete.

For instance, you might need a help subsystem that would be responsible for implementing user help for the application. You might also create an application setup subsystem to handle installation and configuration issues, particularly if you use an API for custom installations. In a broader sense, there are those industry-specific subsystems that have proven elusive to standardize in any one book. The development of these subsystems is the challenge you are presented with.

> Although it's difficult to document industry-standard subsystems, there are some interesting projects by major software manufacturing companies in this area. Microsoft has been pushing its COM solutions (along with SAP business components) towards industry-specific subsystems. Sun Microsystems has also gone after this previously neglected market. Most notable of all, though, is IBM's San Francisco project. It is based on Java, but the design patterns and object interactions embodied in the project can be adapted to Visual Basic or accessed via COM-Java bridges. For more information on the San Francisco project, visit www.ibm.com/java/sanfrancisco.

20

Deploying the Samsona Bank Teller System Example

◀ REAL WORLD After the classes and subsystems are developed, implementing the Samsona Bank Teller System requires making the subsystem interface classes properly communicate. This involves heavy subsystem interface testing, logging arguments passed between them and expected returns or application state changes. When that is completed, the testing and quality assurance specialists perform their tasks, working with you and your team iteratively to resolve major flaws discovered. Because you planned your project's iterations and increments, the quality assurance cycles are quick and effective, although several of your developers are at times wary of some of the seemingly insignificant bugs. After the program is tested by the quality assurance team, a couple of tellers conduct user acceptance testing, also in an iterative manner, helping you resolve usability issues. After the users accept the application, you treat your team to a much deserved dinner at a top restaurant.

The branch manager at the Second Bank of Carrollton is pleased that you were able to finish the application on time and within budget. She realizes that there will be some bugs in the application, so she requests that you document possible trouble spots and any advice and tips on debugging and evolving the code. You assure her that this is standard procedure for your consulting firm, Samsona Software.

You explain to her that you will document how the subsystems in the applications interact as well as advise developers about where in the code to look when particular errors occur. In fact, you add that your firm also provides application administrators with guidelines for installing and configuring the application for the various clients. Also, at no extra charge, your firm will provide a specialist to the bank to set up an intranet Web site to help keep the developers informed of code updates, peer tips, and links to Samsona's Web site. One of the developers who will maintain the application happens to walk by, overhearing part of your conversation. She asks whether you will be available for further questions, whereupon you give her an extra business card. You exchange handshakes and sign-offs with the bank developers and teller staff and go home.

▲ If you'd like to view the code listing for the Samsona Bank Teller System, please refer to the code on the CD-ROM that accompanies this book.

Summary

This chapter is an overview of the anatomy of a complete Visual Basic system. In particular, it examines the different ways subsystems interact to augment application behavior, describing the interfacing between the Graphical User Interface and Database Access Subsystems, between the Reporting and Printing and Graphical User Interface Subsystems, between the Workgroup and User Security Subsystems, between the Database Access and Internal Application Manager Subsystems, and between the Internal Application Manager Subsystem and all the subsystems. You learned how to identify the need for other subsystems. Finally, the deployment of the Samsona Bank Teller System is carried out.

For tomorrow's lesson, which is the last one, you go beyond technical details to understand how to make object-oriented programming in Visual Basic more successful in a commercial or corporate environment. That is, you learn how to round out your technical knowledge with advice on how to maximize your surroundings so that you can better concentrate on Visual Basic development and the power of Visual Basic. Focusing on programming rather than on politics or other stressful factors is very important in discovering and designing robust, lasting classes.

Q&A

Q **True or False: An application is at its best when its expected behavior is compartmentalized into subsystems. Subsystems, in turn, are compartmentalized into classes.**

A True

Q **Do the Graphical User Interface Subsystem and the Database Access Subsystem always need to interact directly?**

A The Graphical User Interface Subsystem and the Database Access Subsystem typically don't need to communicate directly with one another. Data controls are an exception.

Q **What are the various data access mechanisms that the Database Access Subsystem encapsulates from the other subsystems in the application?**

A The Database Access Subsystem classes communicate with the database itself through any number of data access mechanisms, including Ado, Rdo, Dao, ODBC API, VBSQL (SQL Server DBLIB and SQLOLE objects), data controls, and third-party data access mechanisms such as Oracle Objects.

20

Q What does a proxy class do for the application?

A If you're developing a distributed Visual Basic application, you would have a proxy class that locally represents a remote subsystem. For example, if you deploy the Business Rules Subsystem on a workgroup server, and the Database Access Subsystem on a separate enterprise server, you might find it convenient to create a data access proxy class, DBProxy, that handles the information persistence needs of the workgroup server on behalf of the enterprise server.

Workshop

The workshop includes quiz questions to help gauge your grasp of the material. You'll find the answers to this quiz in Appendix A, "Answers." Even if you feel that you understand the concepts presented here, you should work through the quiz. The last section contains exercises to help reinforce your learning.

Quiz

1. What is the compartmental hierarchy for subsystems and their members?

2. Why are subsystem interface classes so important?

3. What is a good way to decouple an actual form in the Graphical User Interface Subsystem from direct communications with the Database Access Subsystem?

4. What's the importance of collections of business classes in the Business Rules Subsystem?

5. Explain the nature of the form controller in subsystem-to-subsystem communications.

Exercises

1. Open a new Visual Basic project (Standard EXE). Create a broker class that works with the Security Subsystem in this book and a Graphical User Interface Subsystem to process the ID and password of a user. The Graphical User Interface Subsystem consists of a form, Form1, and a controller class, CForm1.

2. Using exercise 1, create a facade class, PrinterFacade, that retrieves the hDc handle of the physical printer on behalf of CForm1.

DAY **21**

Coping with Visual Basic Projects: A Primer on Visual Basic Project Management in the Enterprise

Congratulations! This chapter rounds out your understanding of object-oriented programming in Visual Basic by presenting you with some issues and advice for using Visual Basic in large corporate and commercial environments. If you're experienced with corporate politics and how some large companies view Visual Basic, you should find this chapter to be a refresher, and you might find some helpful advice. If you're a new college graduate or are still in college but want to know what kind of Visual Basic development environment in which you can reasonably expect to work, this chapter will prove invaluable.

A Sample Scenario Using the Samsona Bank Teller Project

◄ REAL WORLD

The branch manager at the Second Bank of Carrollton is pleased with the application you delivered. She only noticed a few minor details to change to improve teller productivity, and she was willing to look past the few bugs she noticed. Overall, the project was a success. She shakes your hand. "It's a good thing I didn't listen to that other programming consultant who berated Visual Basic as a toy language that would never create anything of worth. I admit I was a bit wary of Visual Basic, but in hindsight, I'm glad I gave it a shot. Thank you."

You grin, having heard other statements about Visual Basic that have become irrelevant now. "I'm glad that he isn't working here anymore," you say, feeling confident.

She raises an eyebrow. "Well, I didn't mean to imply that *she* was gone." Gulp! "I just didn't listen to her when I made this judgment. Actually, our corporate bank office is going to hire her on as a permanent employee, and we hoped you would spend two or three weeks training her and her staff of 15 programmers. They will extend the application to work at all of our branches. Sometimes, they can be a funny bunch—a little competitive, but all in all, they're great to work with. Some are C++ programmers; others are a mix of COBOL and Visual Basic programmers and one Pascal programmer."

The weeks of training the programmers were grueling, to say the least. A couple of the C++ programmers chuckled about having to learn Visual Basic, although another was happy to leave the memory management nightmares of C++. One of the COBOL programmers wondered why people were moving to the inferior PC platform when the mainframe was so much more reliable (and on some points, you agreed with the underlying sentiment). The Visual Basic programmers had only recently worked with earlier versions of the language so were awed by all of the new and confusing things you were able to do in the newest version.

There were arguments among the trainees about some of the topics you discussed. A senior C++ programmer walked out on a couple of training sessions, frustrated. Later, one of the Visual Basic programmers informed you that the C++ programmer had strongly recommended that Visual Basic not be used, claiming that no serious programmer uses it. The programmer had frequently complained to the team leader, who was also a Pascal programmer—and the one who advised the branch manager against Visual Basic. However, the other Visual Basic programmers had reassured the branch manager that Visual Basic had matured immensely and was quite capable of handling very complex business applications. They also said that Visual Basic had gotten wide industry acclaim, including positive comments from the C++/Ada-inclined world of object-oriented

▼ programming.

▼ To sum up, you experienced some viruses on your on-site computer, and one day you couldn't log in at all to correct a problem that a user complained about. You became a bit paranoid, trying to balance that feeling with giving the perpetrators (if any) the benefit of the doubt. In the end, you survived, handing over the project to the team members. You received some gratification in the fact that the branch manager had given equal weight to
▲ the advisories of the Visual Basic programmers.

An Overview and Discussion of Visual Basic, Project Management, and the Development Process

The example you just read fictionalizes a scenario that you have probably seen played out in newly converted Visual Basic development shops around the world. If, by chance, you're relatively new to Visual Basic, or have only worked with it in small environments, you probably have not experienced anything of the magnitude in the example. However, pick up any number of programming and computer technology magazines, and you'll find people—including Visual Basic programmers—making comments about Visual Basic not being as serious as C++ or some other languages. Although there are some features in other languages that Visual Basic doesn't support, there are some features in Visual Basic that others don't support, including rapid development, helpful and built-in memory management, and user-friendliness. In short, every language has its niche in the market, and selecting one over another is like choosing a hammer over a screwdriver. Different problems require different tools. Other than perhaps creating a language compiler, there's not much you can't accomplish with Visual Basic compared with other languages. In the area of business applications, there's no business problem for which you can't provide a solution in Visual Basic. However, you can't provide that solution without a way to manage your project, regardless of its complexity.

Managing a Visual Basic project is no different from managing projects in other languages. As mentioned earlier in this book, you have to analyze and assess the problem you're trying to tackle, design one or more solutions to that problem, and pick the best one to implement in code and then test it in an iterative and incremental manner. If you don't approach software development in this regard, your chances for solving the original problem that led to your development effort will be very slim and possibly nil. Generally speaking, effective object-oriented code is designed without being heavily dependent on any specific programming language.

21

Technology changes too quickly to avoid the sometimes tedious task of organizing the methods you choose for programming. The latest version of Visual Basic is full of so many features that many die-hard Visual Basic programmers still have not had time to digest it all. (These same feelings of being overwhelmed have been experienced by C++, Java, and Smalltalk programmers as well.) Given that you can usually handle only seven (plus or minus) points of complexity, it is strongly advisable to approach all your Visual Basic development efforts with the utmost organization and methodology.

Understanding the Ideal Visual Basic Project

Okay, so there are no ideal projects. However, there are some project environments that are closer to ideal than others. As with any project, a factor that will increase the chances of successfully delivering a product written in Visual Basic is to have access to a Visual Basic developer who has experience in the best features of Visual Basic, including its object-oriented programming features. Having a good library of classes and components is also helpful. That is, with preexisting classes and components, you not only reuse your code, you also reuse your labor, thereby minimizing the time it takes to develop the next solution.

As a Visual Basic developer, you want to be in the company of fellow Visual Basic developers, unless you have the guts to stand alone with programmers in more "serious" languages. Seriously, though, having team members who are unbiased with regard to programming languages helps you concentrate on the really important issue, which is to design and implement a quality solution to a persistent problem in the appropriate programming language. These days, Visual Basic is so powerful in both rapid application development and object-oriented programming simultaneously that you'll be able to speak proudly of being a Visual Basic developer. Coupled with the power in Visual Basic is the incredible time savings in delivering a serious solution to any complex problem, a fact that makes the language the most effective in minimizing wasted resources.

Finally, having a good manager, whether in a large bureaucratic corporation or a small start-up, is very critical. The next section discusses what qualities a manager should exhibit when managing a Visual Basic project.

Effectively Managing the Visual Basic Project

In the example earlier in this chapter, you read how the branch manager listened to everyone on the team. For better or for worse, a good Visual Basic project manager must give an ear to every comment and criticism, positive and negative. Like a judge, the project manager must determine the best approach without alienating too many team members. Of course, this doesn't mean that the project manager must be indecisive or vague. As with the branch manager, an effective manager must be willing to make sometimes unpopular, seemingly unwise decisions.

Important factors to consider in managing a Visual Basic project successfully are as follows:

- Give developers inexperienced with the powerful, overwhelming new features in Visual Basic the right resources to help them succeed, including acquiring an outside mentor if necessary.

- Track and maintain domain terminology so that developers are not later sidetracked on ambiguity in users' terms.

- Plan for the one- to three-month learning curve when hiring new developers on a fairly large project. (For smaller projects, the learning curve is typically shorter.)

- When reengineering an undocumented legacy system into a Visual Basic application, be sure to allow time to help users separate (within reason) the navigation of windows from the actual tasks they are trying to accomplish.

- Emphasize the necessity of having clearly defined project team roles. This helps avoid confusion as to which project tasks, component, and subsystem are assigned to which developers.

- Avoid scope creep, or the unnoticed increase in the project's requirements.

- Select, follow, and when necessary, customize an object-oriented methodology for the Visual Basic project (based on deadline pressures, budgets, and so on).

- When developing a large Visual Basic project with more than one team, each tasked with developing a complex component or subsystem, develop a plan for coordinating the delivery of each team's expected product; this includes version control and compilation issues.

- Make sure developers are physically seated within a reasonably close proximity to one another; the farther apart developers must sit, the less chance the Visual Basic project has for success.

- Acquire Visual Basic and other development tools early enough in the project so that developers have a chance to get acclimated to the environment and toy with prototypes well before crunch time.

- When a project grows too large, break it up into smaller projects. Visual Basic offers you the powerful feature of grouping many projects into one project group. You would then control the code through tools such as SourceSafe. The design models would then be broken out into categories in Visual Modeler or Rational Rose.

- Build an intranet Web site to make available documentation, code, and executables related to all Visual Basic projects in your domain.

21

There are many other concepts and advisories you can use to increase the chance of success for your Visual Basic application. This list encapsulates the crux of these things.

Migrating to Project Auditing from Project Management

If you've developed software for any length of time for commercial, corporate, or nonprofit organizations, you might have worked under a project manager. The project manager traditionally is responsible for making sure that the software needed by the organization is delivered on time with no budget overruns. Of course, this scenario seldom occurs, especially without an organized methodology, but project managers are strictly tasked with making it happen. Unfortunately, this strategy often leads to excess stress and higher turnover among project personnel. You can perhaps name many other factors about traditional project management that had sometimes adversely impacted your development efforts.

A better approach might be to re-orient the role of the project manager. Let's face it, as mentioned earlier, technology changes rapidly, with Visual Basic being no exception in technological changes. Project managers today seldom get involved in the daily grunt work of software development. Instead of imposing a traditionalist software development process on today's developers, project managers should become more like project auditors.

A project auditor is like a project manager who audits the development process at certain realistic milestones to gauge whether progress is being made at an acceptable pace given the very high risks of successfully developing quality software. For all it's worth, I must admit that developing software is in some cases riskier than gambling in Las Vegas, and in some ways resembles the risk of highly speculative, wildcat oil drilling.

One way that modern oil companies have mitigated the risks of pouring huge amounts of money into drilling for oil in places where none exists is to budget a certain amount of money for exploration and research using the latest petroleum and geological research technology. Yes, it's a lot of money, but much of the oil industry learned that the money spent on analytical research has consistently proven to be far cheaper than blindly drilling for oil.

Similarly, software development project moneyholders should realistically budget some money for problem assessment and solution exploration by well-respected technical experts in order to come up with an intelligent estimate of the effort necessary to elaborate, construct, and deploy a product. For these three phases, the managers would then audit the project at predetermined milestones to see if progress is being made at a reasonable pace. If not, look for ways to improve the situation; if that doesn't help, simply shelve all of the knowledge gained for possible work later and give notice to the team members to pursue other contracts or internal jobs. Something along these lines is more realistic and in line with other industries. That is the best approach to making the role of project manager more compatible with what we've learned about software development over the last half century.

Tips on Choosing an Effective Methodology for the System and the Project

Without a methodology, a software development project is doomed to fail. It has been reported that from anywhere between 70 percent to 85 percent of software development projects fail to adequately meet their original requirements or to deliver quality. In the majority of these cases, a lack of a foundation of methods based on an industry-accepted methodology underlined the problems.

If you've used Visual Basic for a while but had not seriously considered learning a methodology—or couldn't afford the typically expensive training—this book helps to bring you what today's object-oriented methodologies have to offer. If necessary, periodically reread the first four chapters, as well as other books on the subject, so that you can make a better, more informed decision about implementing object-oriented technology. At the same time, when working with other developers as part of a team, avoid the temptation to force your favorite methodology on the other team members. This approach tends to alienate other members, decreasing the chances for success of the methodology and the project as a whole. If you don't feel quite up to making the decision to use an object-oriented methodology but feel it could benefit your project, seek the advice and assistance of an experienced mentor.

Rethinking What Developer Productivity Means

Developer productivity has traditionally been measured by expecting a developer to create the largest body of code that meets most of the requirements in the shortest amount of time. However, experience has shown that this criteria is simply insufficient. The best measure of productivity is where the Visual Basic developer

- Has discovered designs in code that can be reusable, thus reducing the lines of code
- Creates classes that facilitate reusability of code
- Develops code in an iterative, incremental way where each increment and iteration compartmentalizes the complexity of the problem being solved

21

The Visual Basic language itself is already geared toward making developers more productive. But language technology alone is not enough. It must be combined with a sound methodology and process implementation, which boosts developer productivity and, in some cases, morale.

Staffing the Visual Basic Project with Quality and Productivity in Mind

The previous section mentioned factors that improved developer productivity. Another important issue in productivity and software quality in general is whether to hire many or fewer developers on complex projects. The ideal number of developers to have on a team is in the range of four to six. This is not just a computer science finding but an idea made prominent by leading psychological and behavioral researchers. The larger the team, the more prone to political infighting, division, and diminishing returns. If you happen to be on a project currently that is staffed with 15 to 20 (or more) developers under one project, you should strongly consider breaking it up into smaller projects. As mentioned earlier, Visual Basic supports the grouping and management of many projects, so all of the smaller projects can be, like distributed architectures, decentralized yet managed by the project group. If you're developing software as part of an enterprise team, implementing this approach quickly becomes important.

Creating Better Enterprise Teams and Roles

For large and growing organizations, trying to scale up one small development team to handle growing computer needs is similar to a mayor trying to maintain a small-town presence of police officers for a city that has grown into an international metropolis. You can probably imagine the resulting rise in crime as the police force would be overwhelmed. The same holds true for a development staff. As an organization grows, development tasks and projects need to be specialized with developers duly assigned to them. For large organizations, enterprise teams are also needed to maintain common and reusable classes so that future projects are developed and implemented in optimal delivery cycles. This section addresses specialized roles. For larger organizations, you might have a team of developers performing these roles.

The Technology Reviewer

If you work for a company that is not accustomed to having a formal methodology and process in place, you're probably responsible not just for the development, but the review of technology as well. Sometimes, you have time to do this. However, at other times, time is so precious that you don't have time to review the latest technology. In the short run, this might not impact you, unless you're working with antiquated technology. However, in the long run, the organization stands to lose a competitive advantage with its peers in its industry. That is, if your organization's peers have successfully separated the task of reviewing new technology from the task of developing software, they increase their chances of boosting worker productivity from the use of the new stuff. By the time your organization decides to separate the tasks, it might be too far behind.

When possible, try to convince management to consider creating a technology review team, or at least a technology review individual. Avoid the temptation to overindulge in new technology reviews when you have pressing deadlines. It might seem harmless to do so in the initial "honeymoon" of a new project, but this lost time tends to come back to haunt you later. If your organization cannot afford to have a distinct technology review team, explain to them that reviewing new technology can sometimes have an adverse impact on project deadlines.

The Object and Application Repository Caretaker

Related to the previous section, having an object and application repository caretaker ensures that objects you develop get published in a corporate development repository. Generally, this caretaker will interact with you at the end of your iterations, when your objects are typically ready for publication. Nonetheless, it is advisable to work with the caretaker at the actual end of the project.

Why at the end of the project and not the beginning? Although you can achieve reuse of use cases early in the analysis phase, there's no way to gauge reuse of implemented objects up front until you've elaborated the use cases into design diagrams and models and then in code. The coding is where you judge where code reuse begins and ends. Before that, the analysis and design cannot dictate reuse accurately in code, only reuse in analysis and design. Not realizing this important point can cause frustration with the object-oriented programming process. Some developers who try to achieve reuse too soon generally find that what they analyzed and designed was not a good basis for judging code reuse. In general, you achieve or identify patterns of use case reuse in analysis, design reuse in design, and code reuse during construction or implementation. Added to this is the fact that even when judging code reuse, you don't know it's reusable until you've used the classes over several projects.

The Enterprise Architecture and Reuse Team

Similar to the team in the previous section, the enterprise architecture and reuse team looks for opportunities of reuse among all of the repositories across an enterprise. This

21

team manages all of the object-oriented models of the enterprise and tries to optimize them for future use. This strategy helps to maximize the organization's return on investment (ROI).

The Enterprise Business Process Team

Like the enterprise architecture and reuse team, the enterprise business process team looks for opportunities of reuse among the enterprise's business processes and process models. The work of this team provides the artifacts needed by the other software development teams, which increases the productivity of their efforts.

The Documentation Specialist

A documentation specialist is tasked with managing all of the documentation that results from your analysis and design activities. This would include use cases and supplementary documents such as application performance requirements, information storage and retrieval specifications, and quality assurance specifications. Moreover, this person would also maintain user guides and programmer references.

The Testing and Quality Assurance Specialist

The testing and quality assurance specialist, as the name implies, ensures the quality of the applications developed by testing them. This person increases productivity by helping developers find weaknesses in their designs and class implementations. It is important to appreciate the work of this specialist so that your Visual Basic applications are delivered with optimal quality.

NEW WINE IN OLD WINESKINS: AVOIDING THE BATTLES BETWEEN THE OLD SCHOOL AND THE NEW SCHOOL TEAM MEMBERS

In the example earlier in this chapter, you got the feel for the dichotomy that sometimes exists between users of new languages versus old languages. Similarly, traditional project management has been at odds with the latest advances in software development technology as some managers have not actively kept current with the latest techniques and methodologies. In the Bible, a quote of Jesus Christ states that you cannot pour new wine into old wineskins. Well, this certainly has application in software development.

The most popular battle in the development industry today rages in the area of development methodology. In particular, developers and project managers have taken sides on whether waterfall is still king versus the iterative, incremental approach, which marks an improvement over the older approaches. The idea to keep in mind is that object-oriented programming is an improvement over traditional waterfall methods because the former has addressed the concerns of how to perform analysis, design, and implementation without losing traceability between artifacts and the original requirements. It also addresses the decrease in software usability that tended to result from not iteratively revisiting earlier phases of a project before delivering a product to the user. Some older, relatively static ideas of analysis, design, and code implementation simply do not fit well into a dynamic, cyclical, discovery-oriented development process.

Confronting the Myth About Prototypes

To prototype or not to prototype: that is the controversy. Smaller projects naturally take an informal approach to developing prototypes, whereas others are very sensitive about making the decision to develop them. In that environment where there has been a generally positive relationship between users and developers, prototypes tend to be successful in promoting a better understanding of user requirements, thus bolstering the credibility of the use cases that formalize them. However, where there's a lack of trust between the two camps, prototypes can serve to be pawns in a political battle between users, developers, and executives. In politically charged environments, it's best to postpone the introduction of prototypes to users until the requirements are reasonably well understood. Given that, it does not automatically follow that you should always introduce prototypes to users as soon as possible.

Prevailing False Assumptions About Visual Basic

Despite the attitudes of some in the general software industry, Visual Basic is the most successful and well-accepted language in the history of programming languages because it is both powerful and allows the rapid implementation of object-oriented designs. Visual Basic is certainly not a toy language anymore. It offers several helpful approaches to database connectivity and Internet development unparalleled by most programming languages. And it accommodates the widest ranges of experiences among its developer-consumer than most other languages. From beginning programmers (who have hailed from some very noncomputer backgrounds) to the most advanced computer scientists, Visual Basic is like the Statue of Liberty, welcoming all the tired masses who hunger for easier development into her environment. By the way, if you do hail from a nonprogramming background, be sure to reread the first four chapters to develop an understanding of the fundamentals of effective software development in Visual Basic.

21

Worshipping the God of Lapsed Visual Basic Project Schedules

At first glance, you might be overwhelmed by the kinds of classes, objects, and subsystems—described in this book—that Visual Basic is capable of supporting. Don't be. The information contained in this book is intended to provide you with an honestly working skeleton (with sample "flesh") that you can use to provide a reasonable, instant architecture upon which to build your Visual Basic application. The skeleton is to help you concentrate more on your client's business rules and the low-level APIs you've been required to work with at the client site. This skeleton, then, is by no means an exhaustive application architecture but a skeletal architecture that has some flesh, but needs for you, the developer, to flesh it out completely and rapidly.

Try not to interpret the adverb "rapidly" loosely. Rapid development without an architecture, purpose, focus, cooperation, and coordination is meaningless at best, and doomed to failure at worst. It seems that 9 out of 10 projects, in some way, fit this description. In fact, you're probably on such a project now. You know this kind of project, where in the interview, you're assured that you'll have plenty of time to deliver something (as long as you meet the deadlines), that the requirements have already been gathered, and on and on. And then, when you get onboard the project, everything is like a honeymoon for a couple of weeks, but suddenly, out of the blue, some unseen force pushes your head into your desk and tells you, "Get that code hammered out and delivered by close of business tomorrow!" That unseen force is what you might call the *god of lapsed project schedules*.

This god is a fierce god. Because this terrible god often demands human sacrifices (that is, your spouse, children, parents, friends, your sanity, and so on), most programmers don't have time to lift their heads up and expect more out of life. And this god claims its adherents early in their careers, even before they leave college. That's right, think back to the times you had to have a program finished before a midterm or a final exam, and you begged your professor for more time, only to be politely rebuffed. You might not have realized it then, but that was the god of lapsed project schedules introducing itself to you, trying to claim your soul. Just because you graduated didn't mean he left you alone. Oh, no. In fact, he already claims more adherents than any system development methodology in the industry today. If you're not careful, you or someone you know might become the next faithful adherent in a seeming conspiracy to convert every new programmer to this unseen religion.

This god is also a very complex god, with numerous and varied ways for his adherents to express their obedience. What this god doesn't like is the efficient programmer, system analyst, architect, tester, and technical writer. He can't stand having too much time on his hands by developers having completed their tasks ahead of schedule, because that means that the programmer might wake up from her slumber and think! He despises systems with architectures because, like the truth, a project backbone will set the programmer free from his grasp. He frowns on documentation, because he knows that with better programmer documentation, his gospel won't have room to grow in the future (that is, no room for errors that could lead to lapsed schedules).

Sharing Development Costs with Other Enterprise Business Groups

It makes sense to share development costs with other enterprise business groups that have some requirements and classes in common. Perhaps it might make too much sense. The idea of maximizing an organization's return on investment for a group of related projects, though increasing in the amount of attention given it, has still not taken hold. Organization's hire accountants to look for ways to cut costs and increase profits in most departments and business groups, yet virtually ignore doing the same for software development projects. If you or your fellow developers notice that your efforts are being duplicated by another team, try mentioning this to your project manager. The shared efforts will not only reduce costs and relieve you of perhaps some complex coding efforts, it can also increase your value to your manager. Object-oriented programming offers the best approach for discovering opportunities for sharing development costs.

Summary

This chapter helped you understand various key issues with regard to developing object-oriented Visual Basic applications in corporate and commercial environments. In particular, you received an overview and discussion of Visual Basic, project management, and the development process, as well as tips on choosing an effective methodology for the system and the project. You also learned the importance of making the methodology decision, as well as rethinking what developer productivity means. You were presented with advice on staffing the Visual Basic project with quality and productivity in mind, choosing better but fewer team members, creating better enterprise teams and developer roles, and confronting the myth about prototypes.

Well, I hope you had a very enlightening and effective three weeks of lessons. Learning how to break an application up into major subsystems is a very productive but complex undertaking, so be sure to keep this book handy for future reference when you encounter productivity bottlenecks in your projects. With the powerful lessons on object-oriented programming you received, you're now well ahead in the object technology paradigm shift that is revolutionizing the way we develop software.

21

Q&A

Q True or False: Different problems require different tools. Other than perhaps creating a language compiler, there's not much that you cannot accomplish with Visual Basic compared with other languages.

A True.

Q True or False: Managing a Visual Basic project is very different from managing projects in other languages.

A False.

Q What is a project auditor?

A A project auditor is like a project manager who audits the development process at certain realistic milestones to gauge whether progress is being made at an acceptable pace given the very high risks of successfully developed quality software.

Q What is the main reason to have a small number of developers on a team?

A The ideal number of developers to have on a team is in the range of four to six. The larger the team, the more prone to political infighting, division, and subject to diminishing returns.

Q Name a benefit of creating a technology review team.

A Your development time can be better spent developing the actual software as opposed to reviewing technology. Also, your organization increases its competitive advantage relative to its industry peers.

Workshop

The workshop includes quiz questions to help gauge your grasp of the material. You'll find the answers to this quiz in Appendix A, "Answers." Even if you feel that you totally understand the concepts presented here, you should work through the quiz anyway.

Quiz

1. Why is it strongly advisable to approach all your Visual Basic development efforts with the utmost organization and methodology?

2. What factor increases the chances of successfully delivering a product written in Visual Basic?

3. What are the important factors to consider in managing a Visual Basic project successfully?

4. How is software development similar to wildcat oil drilling?

5. What is the best measure of developer productivity?

21

WEEK 3

In Review

In the final week, you learned about the subsystems for business rules, reporting and printing, error processing and exception handling, and database access. Finally, you learned how each subsystem generally communicates with other subsystems in the entire application.

The week starts with an overview of the Business Rules Subsystem, including how to implement business rules required by your organization for your application. In particular, you learned about concepts in policy management, how to work with key stakeholders, and how to unearth existing implementations of business rules.

On Day 16, "The Reporting and Printing Subsystem," you learned about the Reporting and Printing Subsystem, along with guidelines for planning cyclical and ad hoc reporting uses. You also learned about working with Microsoft Access, the SelPrint method of the Rich Text Box, and Crystal Reports.

On the next day, you learned how to create classes that handle file operations such as open and close, as well as how to load values into controls and navigate records saved in files. You learned the use of the Rich Text Box versus older file access methods.

Then you learned about the Error-Processing and Exception-Handling Subsystem. You learned about raising errors and exceptions and then how to incorporate the subsystem into the Samsona Bank Teller System example.

On Day 19, "The Database Access Subsystem," you learned about the Database Access Subsystem and how to use ADO,

DAO, and RDO to communicate with the database, as well as how to save information from the graphical user interface and business classes.

On the next-to-last day, you learned the anatomy of a complete Visual Basic system. You examined different ways subsystems interact to augment application behavior. You studied the interface between the Graphical User Interface and the Database Access Subsystems; between the Reporting and Printing Subsystem and the Graphical User Interface subsystem; between the Workgroup and User Security, Database Access, and Internal Application Manager Subsystems; and finally between the Internal Application Manager Subsystem and all subsystems.

Then you wrapped up the week by learning how to cope with Visual Basic projects, as well as some project management tips for effectively developing software for corporate and commercial clients.

APPENDIX A

Answers

This appendix provides the answers to the quizzes at the end of each chapter.

Day 1

1. What is one of the chief benefits of object-oriented programming?

   One chief benefit of OOP is that it facilitates better team development. This is important for users of Visual Basic. OOP represents a better-organized way to reuse code in chunks called *objects*.

2. What is the importance of behavior?

   A conceptual behavior eventually provides the foundation for actual class methods. An object's action or reaction is a manifestation of that object's behavior. Behavior exhibited by an object at any given time can lead to changes in the object's state.

3. Describe the roles that the keywords `Public` and `Private` play in encapsulation.

   The keyword `Public` means that the member is accessible to all modules, both within the project and in external projects. The keyword `Private` means that the member is accessible only by other members within the class module. This does not mean that you can't pass the value of the private property to an external module via a public property or method, however.

Day 2

1. What is at least one benefit of object-oriented analysis?

   Object-oriented analysis provides the best early gauge of the feasibility of successfully completing an object-oriented programming project. Analysis helps to find a solution to a business problem, turning a picture in someone's head into a high-level, often user-friendly model that can evolve into an application.

2. What is a methodology?

   A methodology is an organized, disciplined system for doing something in an orderly manner. It's the implementation of a body of methods to achieve a measurable goal. It is, in other words, a strategy for developing a solution that includes a set of scientific methods.

3. Describe the importance of use cases in analysis.

   Taken together, the application's use cases provide the scope of your project and help you understand how the user will use the application.

4. What are the three primary roles performed during analysis?

   Requirements gatherer, object-oriented analyst, and architect.

Day 3

1. How can executives and managers better facilitate the object-oriented design process?

   Executives and managers, typically accustomed to the mainframe application development processes, have seldom established their IS and IT departments as they would other business groups. It would be helpful if groupings within IS/IT operations were taken as seriously as other important business groups. There should be a separation between a designer role and the programmer role, between the architect and the project manager. Generally, programmers are expected to double as designers (and sometimes analysts, architects, testers, documenters, and so on). Also, executives and managers should consider breaking up the phases of the project so that each phase has realistic schedules tied to goals, instead of having one large goal for all the phases. This would give you the focus to concentrate on one project phase, instead of all of them.

A

2. What is at least one benefit of having clearly defined roles for project team members?

Team members are able to focus on a smaller set of deliverables, thus optimizing their productivity.

3. What are some advantages and disadvantages of creating and viewing design artifacts?

Some advantages include the following: When you're finished with the last design iteration (there can be many iterations through the design phase, depending on the complexity of your proposed system), you will have enough of a detailed system specification to develop the system without having to make assumptions about the system architecture or user motivations. The problems discovered during the actual development phase should be minor and should require minor iterations through the design phase to update the corresponding models. At the same time, minor updates in design models should lead to very minor updates in the analysis models—such as changes in the name of a class or class member or the addition of an argument to a private method. Major changes—such as drastic changes in the way objects communicate, the addition of a new subsystem or package, and changes to the graphical user interface or interfaces between systems—should not occur during the development phase. If such changes weren't addressed during design before development, this might suggest inadequate skill sets among domain experts, analysts, architects, or designers. In any event, such modifications should be deferred to a future release of the system, if possible. If it's not possible, the development phase must be postponed while the design flaws are revisited in the design phase.

Some disadvantages include the following: Maintaining design artifacts can be tedious, particularly when you're checking for traceability between user requirements and design classes.

4. Who are the Three Amigos? Briefly explain their respective methodologies.

Grady Booch, Ivar Jacobson, and Jim Rumbaugh. The Booch method poses questions for designers to use in the elaboration of class structures and relationships. The questions follow the following format: (a) Candidate Class A "is a" type of Class B; (b) Candidate Class A "has a" Class B type of object; and (c) Candidate Class A "uses" Class B.

Jacobson came up with the Objectory method, which is based on the object-oriented software engineering methodology he created. The OOSE design approach models the behavior of the system as documented by the use cases into logical parts, also known as classes. At the core of the design model in OOSE are three types of classes (whose instances are objects): entity, interface, and control.

Jim Rumbaugh developed the Object Modeling Technique (OMT) to help developers capture the design specification of a proposed system. OMT is primarily based on entity/relationship modeling and emphasizes modeling classes, inheritance, and encapsulated behavior. The OMT process includes analysis, system design, object design, coding, and testing.

5. What is traceability? Why is it important?

    Traceability is the attribute of a project artifact that enables following business-related entity classes from the actual code to the lowest class models up to the high analysis models and the project documentation itself. Master test cases and test scripts also refer to the same class, object, and actor names as other artifacts of the project life cycle. Make sure to keep all artifacts (documents, models, diagrams, and code files) in sync when it comes to business domain terminology. Failing to do so often results in unnecessary confusion and stress down the road.

6. Explain what a design pattern is and how it benefits software development practices in general.

    Design patterns are repeated ways that objects communicate with each other to carry out a system goal. The purpose of design patterns within the OO community is to make available a repository of problems and solutions to help software deal with common redundant issues. Identifying design patterns facilitates communication of in-depth knowledge and experience about these recurring problems and deciding how best to implement solutions. Having this at the disposal of developers, especially Visual Basic developers, results in well-structured system architectures that provide rapid reuse for the client and are understandable to fellow developers.

Day 4

1. What is the role of OOP in solution development?

    To provide you with a way to implement a particular design structure of collaborating class instances. This design structure is typically elaborated in a mix of class models, interaction diagrams such as sequence and collaboration diagrams, and state diagrams.

2. What is a long-term benefit of encapsulation?

    Encapsulation contributes to the ease of an application's maintenance and evolution over time. Encapsulation is often referred to as information hiding because of the goal of hiding internal information about the object and how it implements its class interface.

3. How are the terms *type* and *interface* related?

   A type is realized through the interface of a class. For instance, a checking account is a type of bank account. Notice the use of the word *type*. An interface of a class describes its type. For example, when you say CheckingAccount is a type of BankAccount, you are saying that the former inherits the interface of BankAccount. So if BankAccount has a public method deposit, CheckingAccount implements that same method in its own unique way, if necessary.

4. How do you realize interface inheritance in Visual Basic?

   You realize interface inheritance by using the Implements *<name of interface class>* keyword in the class module of the implementation class.

5. What's the difference between collection and aggregate objects?

   An aggregate object is composed of one or more objects that are an integral part of that object. A collection of objects holds references to one or more objects that are loosely coupled. That is, a collection can hold references to any kind of object, and the lifetime of those objects are not dependent on the collection itself.

6. What are methods, accessors, and mutators?

   Methods are nicely encapsulated series of code instructions that enable access to implemented behavior. Accessors give an object's clients access to its property value. Mutators give an object's clients access to set its property values.

7. What's the difference between a subsystem and a category?

   The logical representation of a subsystem is called a category, although this some-times leads to confusion between the two. The distinction between the two is a relic of C++ programming, with the separate header and implementation files that map to one logical class. For Visual Basic, a class interface and implementation are stored in one file, so there is no real distinction. Thus, a subsystem of five class files maps directly to a category of five classes.

8. What is a class diagram? a sequence diagram?

   A class diagram shows the unique identity of one or more classes, their behaviors, and any inheritance, delegation, or aggregation relationships. Scenario diagrams (along with collaboration diagrams) capture how the instances of these classes interact at runtime to carry out some system behavior. Because of the easy-to-follow nature of these types of models, complex systems can be broken down into simpler abstractions. Together, they provide the architectural expression of the proposed system.

Day 5

1. What are helper methods?

   Helper methods offload some of a public method's responsibilities.

2. What is the best way to manage your runtime object creatures?

   To implement tactics to reduce the amount of memory space your application needs.

3. What's wrong with variants as return types?

   Variants require more memory than other types because of the underlying mapping to specific types.

4. What's a good way to help manage memory use?

   To track and eliminate unused methods and attributes and to avoid variants.

5. What are the best ways to achieve reuse?

   The best ways to achieve reuse are by having well-defined class interfaces in which each interface has only a few, well-encapsulated public methods; by elaborating abstractions from unambiguous terms and concepts in the domain; with uncomplicated class inheritance relationships or delegation; with well-documented use cases that themselves can be reused; and commitment from fellow team members to practice good object-oriented programming.

6. What is an implementation class?

   Any class that implements its own interface or the interface of another class is an implementation class.

7. What should you do when you discover design flaws in construction?

   Revisit those diagrams and pinpoint applicationwide ramifications of those flaws.

8. What is aggregation?

   Aggregation represents a tightly or loosely coupled ownership relationship between an aggregate object and the objects it's aggregating. By *ownership*, it is meant that the aggregate object owns either the lifetime of an object (composition) or the exclusive use of services (containment) of an object. Aggregation is best defined by the distinction between composition and containment.

9. What responsibility does a composite object have?

   A composite object is responsible for creating and destroying the object of which it is composed. In some cases, the composite object specifies that another object be delegated such responsibility, as in the case of object factories and garbage collectors.

10. Briefly explain containment.

    Containment is similar to composition, except that the containing object is not
    responsible for the life of the contained object. Thus, an object can create another
    object for its exclusive use but can't pass the object to another for the other's use.
    This is the case with collections in which a containing object creates an object,
    populates it with data from a graphical user interface, and then passes that object to
    a collection. A collection object contains objects.

Day 6

1. What is another name for a general code module?

   Class utility.

2. What is the value of the Make index tab in the Project Properties dialog box?

   It's valuable for version management and protection of copyrights if you plan to
   sell your component commercially.

3. What is required when testing a component?

   Testing any component requires a plan with clear goals.

4. What is a master test plan?

   In its simplest form, a master test plan summarizes the goal of the testing effort,
   the resources required to test the software, and the actual test cases to be examined.

5. What is the importance of a test script?

   A well-written test script is the realization of a test case, given a set of conditions
   and assumptions.

Day 7

1. What advantages and disadvantages must you consider when deciding whether to
   acquire third-party controls?

   The advantages are decreased development time (and therefore reduced development costs) and reuse over many projects. Buying a third-party control is like buying "canned" labor: the third-party vendor has put its labor force's time and energy
   into that control so that you don't have to put your time and energy into reproducing the same code. What's more, you can reuse that canned time and energy over
   many projects, thus receiving increasing returns on investment over time.

   The disadvantages are that many controls have been poorly documented, rendering
   the controls almost useless. Other controls are awkward or require too many

function calls and declarations, making development and maintenance tasks almost as painful as developing the code yourself. Some vendor technical support staffs are overwhelmed by calls and emails so that it's difficult to reach them for help. Other vendors have vanished entirely after releasing a first version, and more than a few have simply gone bankrupt. Technical support, in these cases, is an impossibility.

2. What are better ways of incorporating controls that are still useful?

   - By creating a component committee

   - By formulating an evaluation and selection criteria

   - By pricing components versus in-house component development

3. Describe one or more benefits of having a separate committee evaluate third-party controls for use in an enterprise?

   A separate committee (either in-house or an independent, external organization) composed of one or more developers and testing experts can dedicate exclusive time to evaluating third-party controls. The committee can also test the documentation for accuracy. It can evaluate the vendor's response to technical support and general questions about the control. Finally, the committee can test the control by creating test applications that incorporate the controls. To be even more thorough, the committee can have the quality assurance and testing team test the test application to make sure the component can handle a full production environment. A thorough committee might even investigate the financial soundness and commercial health of the third-party vendor when it has decided on a control but is unsure whether the company might be around long. If this latter approach is taken, the committee would look at whether the vendor is constantly in debt, no matter how large or small.

4. What questions should you ask in evaluating third-party controls?

   How long has the vendor been in business? How easy is it to use the control? How much does the control cost relative to developing the code yourself? Can you reuse this control to obtain a fair return on investment? Is the control well documented? How responsive is technical support? Will the vendor be around to provide technical support?

5. For what purposes must organizations pay up-front costs in seeking return on investment through component reusability?

   - To assess the applications with which to achieve reuse

   - To properly define the application's architecture so that the component has a role to play within it

- To reorganize, when necessary, the domain that will use the application so as to optimize the usefulness of the application and the components in it
- To make sure all project teams are aware of (and trained in) the control or component being evaluated or implemented so that all opportunities for reuse are available

6. What is a strategy for incorporating third-party controls over a period of time?

Incorporating third-party controls and components early on involves cost and little reuse. Plan on little benefit over the first few months and possibly the first year or two. In time, reuse of the control will increase the return on investment substantially—and incrementally, as increases in technology, competition, and upgrades of the controls reduce the increase of returns on investment.

7. What strategies might you use in evaluating third-party controls if you don't have an evaluation committee?

- Accepting proposals from in-house developers
- Accepting proposals directly from third-party vendors
- Measuring use cases against proposals

Day 8

1. What testing activities should you, as an object-oriented Visual Basic developer, know?

Distributed portability testing, integration testing, graphical user interface testing, regression testing, positive testing, negative testing, and beta testing.

2. What's the importance of code inspections?

Inspections give a chance for your peers and architects to review your code and design models, praise the good parts, and offer constructive, positive criticism of discovered flaws.

3. What two method responsibilities are examples, respectively, of precondition and postcondition processing?

Argument data type checking and return data type checking.

4. When is it necessary to check the data type of an argument?

When the argument is of the Variant type and your local processing requires a specific type for a given private method.

5. Why is the development of business applications complex?

Developing business applications is quite complex because many business rules tend to be somewhat confusing or vague at times. This is specifically true for companies where business processes are very dynamic, sometimes volatile.

6. What features in Microsoft Visual SourceSafe support parallel iterative development?

In the SourceSafe Admin server, you can disallow access rights to nonowners of a given project folder. In the SourceSafe client, you can cloak a project so that projects you don't own do not get copied to your local hard disk.

Day 9

1. What fundamental concepts should a subsystem-based application model reflect?

It should reflect the concept that each subsystem must have well-defined interface classes acting as ambassadors, facades, or mediators; encapsulate any platform-specific or legacy-specific dependencies from its core services; ensure type-safety either by self-testing objects or delegating type-checking to the Visual Basic compiler; have an interface that is easy to review by developer-users to plan for use; and be efficient in terms of memory and other resources.

2. What is a helpful prefix you should use for the name of an abstract component?

Abstract-

3. How can you decrease the dependency between two subsystems?

Avoid making client classes and subsystems invoking operations on implementation classes. Instead, try to use the services of interface classes.

4. What is involved in analyzing and designing a subsystem interface?

Analysis for interface classes involves elaborating a business abstraction or concept often. This usually means analyzing use cases for key concepts, but also includes (but is not limited to) assessing application performance requirements; interactions with external and remote applications, servers, and components; user-interface requirements; and real-time, embedded system requirements. You should design a subsystem interface in the form of interface classes.

5. What is one of the most popular kinds of applications? What typical behaviors does it exhibit?

(a) Order entry. *(b)* An order entry system typically exhibits behaviors related to capturing an order for some product or service, enforcing rules related to the product or service being ordered, and submitting subsequent auxiliary order fulfillment requests to back office workers/workgroups.

Day 10

1. What are two ways you can structure an iteration plan?

   If you choose the Objectory Process (the official UML process), analysis, design, and construction can be decomposed into iterations, with one or more increments per iteration.

2. What are the benefits of revisiting your use cases?

   Revisiting use cases helps to continually verify that the system is still on track to fulfill the requirements or user expectations of the Visual Basic application. This revisitation also helps to ensure that the use case model remains robust and easily extensible as discoveries about the problem and solution are made. Always keep in mind that the importance of updating the content of the use cases is that the use case model not only defines the behavior of the application but also provides a basis for the development process of your project itself.

3. Why is it important to involve your users in the refining of your use cases?

   Involving users in the refining of your use cases and sequence diagrams goes a long way toward filling in gaps in business activities you've modeled. Users also help to validate your assumptions about how your Visual Basic application will solve their problems. At the end of each iteration, you should plan on user review and testing.

4. Explain the financial implications of elaborating business processes while developing your applications.

   The development work you're doing has implications for the bottom line—increased revenues or reduced cost. Executives want their investment in your skills to deliver a solution that means increased profits. The term for this in financial circles is *return on investment* (ROI). However, the funny thing about this financial expectation is that some executives analyze the ROI for only a single project. A real return on investment should be measured across several software development projects. Executives should be looking for how a component developed in project A can be effectively reused in succeeding projects B, C, D, E, and so on. Reuse of components is like having a part of a project that pays for itself over and over again. Because reusable objects and components provide a lasting return on investment, they should be valued across many projects, not just one. The labor of a skilled developer (such as you) can be encapsulated in a reusable component and implemented repeatedly, providing diminishing costs. This line of thinking should be the basis of your discussion with curious managers and executives, should you ever be summoned to speak to them about the progress of your project.

5. What four factors should you take into account when assessing the state of your development efforts?

   - The number of interface and implementation classes

   - Of the interface classes, the number of classes that implement them

   - The number of public methods per class

   - Coupling between objects

Day 11

1. What are some benefits of scenario scripts?

   Scenario scripts provide you with a guideline for the behavior and features of each form. This practice of scripting your forms also encourages reuse of forms by not only other team members but also other teams.

2. What design pattern is useful for implementing the undo operations for an Undo button?

   The Memento design pattern.

3. What are some negative aspects of naming buttons *OK* and *Cancel*?

   The word *OK*, which is not a verb, is sometimes ambiguous because it doesn't indicate a business process being complete. In general, command buttons should have names in verb form that indicate some action or event. At times, the name *Cancel* is ambiguous because it doesn't specifically indicate what is being canceled. Cancel buttons are more appropriate for small forms that have only a progress bar control indicating some process is underway that can be canceled. In most circumstances, however, what is typically called the Cancel button should instead be called *Close*.

4. What are the main requirements of an undo operation?

   - Cancellation of a transaction.

   - Repopulation of previous data into display controls such as text boxes, labels, combo and list boxes, and grids.

Day 12

1. Describe one way you can design the form to automatically tab to the next data entry field?

   Set the tab stop values of each of the form objects. For grids and spreadsheets, be sure to enable the user to tab to the next logical column in the row. When necessary, design your GUI form to automatically tab to the next logical data entry item.

A

2. How should you treat calculated fields with regard to user data entry?

Make calculate fields read-only. To provide the user a visual clue, make the background color different from the other fields. Labels are good for read-only fields.

3. What's the best way to document the steps necessary to start up an application?

Scenario scripts. Every application has an implied use of the system for starting up the system and shutting it down. Although you can certainly have formal use cases for these business tasks, scenario scripts are acceptable.

4. What is the relationship between a GUI control event and a controller class method?

The events of each of the GUI controls on each form have a corresponding method in their respective controllers.

5. What is a way to break up a large controller class?

Create helper classes for your controllers so that these controllers don't become too large.

6. What two packages should you create in Visual Modeler to help you separate forms from controller classes?

In Visual Modeler, create a package named Forms and another named Controllers.

7. What's the purpose of the Facade pattern?

It provides a mechanism for better organizing the interfaces between one subsystem and another. Facades are like faces between subsystems—interfaces, to be exact. As you create the Graphical User Interface Subsystem, you need to decouple it from the other subsystems with which it interacts. For the Graphical User Interface Subsystem, controller classes perform this role well.

8. Can a controller class be responsible for more than one form?

Yes.

9. How does one form display another form?

A form displays another form by invoking the showForm method of the other form.

Day 13

1. What security features should you implement in your commercial or industrial applications?

Companies expect your applications, if deployed on the Web, to have some security mechanisms built in them to

- Allow only paying customers into restricted areas on the site geared for premium content

- Allow only employees of the company to access the Web site remotely
- Completely disallow general, unrestricted access

2. What are some factors to look for with regard to application sabotage?

   Disgruntled employees will exploit weaknesses and errors in your application to get revenge on a boss or for some slight they experienced. Further, forcing users to use a system that is either flawed or, for reasons unknown to you, undesirable, only exaggerates the problem.

3. What are the general steps involved in a typical task?

   The general steps involved in a typical task within a workflow include the following:

   - Choose and start an associated task, which can include starting a software application.
   - Implement the work for that task, which can include creating one or more records or documents.
   - Delegate the work to the proper role or workgroup.

4. Why is it generally wise not to tightly couple a workgroup with a traditional department or a role with a user?

   Because the structure of companies changes often.

5. Briefly explain the order sequence of roles in a workgroup.

   Some processes require that several roles be ordered in sequence in order to create a finished product. Your application should let the user define such a sequence. In this strategy, the sequence is as follows:

   1. A time-sensitive task is assigned to the first user of the first role in the workgroup.
   2. If the user is not able to do the task by the task's deadline, your application automatically routes the task to the next user with the same role.

   The ordered sequence should be defined in the database. That way, your application simply looks up the sequence and applies the routing based on the information it receives. You can do the same thing for weighted workgroups, where the ordered sequence is dependent on which role and user has the greatest weight (a percentage value that represents relative importance).

Day 14

1. What are the biggest benefits of this subsystem?

   The biggest benefit of this subsystem lies in two areas: *(a)* Security and *(b)* Troubleshooting and Customer Support.

2. What kinds of database operations are candidates for logging?

   Every add, update, delete, and read operation aimed at the database can be logged properly in a hidden file or straight to a database. Every login attempt can also be recorded.

3. In what ways can you store application or user settings?

   Your application might require that some user preferences be recorded and remembered the next time the user uses the application. For such requirements, the controller class CApplication will be tasked with enforcing these preferences in conjunction with the Graphical User Interface subsystem. You can record these preferences to a database, regular file, an INI (initialization) file, or the Registry.

4. What kinds of information are potentially useful to record with every log item?

   You might want to record the user's ID, start time of transaction, end time of transaction, and possibly the identifier for the transaction or task the user performed. A sequence of these transactions leaves a nice audit trail for any authorized individual.

5. What is a potential downfall of logging too much information?

   Your application might encounter performance degradation if it is a very data-intensive system.

Day 15

1. What's a business rule?

   The policy implemented and enforced in the application that provides measurable value to the user(s) of the application.

2. Are domain rules only for business applications?

   No. Nonprofit and scientific organizations also use applications for their respective domains, so the expression domain rule is more universal, but not as popular as the expression business rule.

3. What's the purpose of the Business Rules Subsystem?

   The Business Rules Subsystem enforces the policy of the user with respect to the user's organizational goals. The business classes and components that make up this subsystem have the main goal of providing one or more solutions to one or more organizational problems.

4. True or False: To build a sound, reusable subsystem of business classes, especially in a distributed architecture such as is typical in large, modern organizations, takes a small amount of time.

False. To build a sound, reusable subsystem of business classes, especially in a distributed architecture such as is typical in large, modern organizations, takes considerable time. In fact, the bulk of the time consumed on software development projects is in the elaboration of the logic incorporated in business classes. All non-policy subsystems are pretty standard and highly reusable almost immediately upon implementing them. However, business classes are defined from a number of sources, including the memory and experiences of employees. Designing and implementing the Business Rules Subsystem, therefore, requires great patience on the part of the Visual Basic development staff.

5. What is tricky about developing business classes in an environment that uses a relational database?

Developing business classes with relational databases as part of the architecture of your environment can be tricky. Object databases don't require a separation of data from the objects themselves. However, relational databases, which still dominate the market, do require data disassembly. The problem then becomes how to effectively get the data out of business classes and into relational databases without compromising encapsulation rules? The bulk of the answer lies in design patterns. Day 19, "The Database Access Subsystem," introduces you to some patterns/mechanisms for handling data in business classes using Visual Basic.

Day 16

1. What are pivotal class methods for the three reporting mechanisms discussed in this lesson?

The pivotal class methods for these three reporting mechanisms include those operations that open the report, print the report, and save the report. These operations are members of an interface class, IReporting.

2. What is the benefit of using Microsoft Access for reporting?

Microsoft Access offers a very powerful and easy-to-use object library for creating, modifying, and deleting reports. Although you can certainly create and delete Access reports through the ActiveX object library via Visual Basic, it's easier to create the reports in Access itself if you and your users have a copy of it. Access 95, 97, and beyond make it easy to create reports with its report wizards.

A

3. What is the most common method you'll use in the Access object library?

   The most common method in the Access object library you'll use is DoCmd.

4. What drives the Crystal Reports control?

   Your Crystal Reports control is driven by its Crystal Report Engine.

5. What are the most popular Report Engine printing operations?

   The most popular Report Engine printing operations include a single menu command that produces a single report, a dialog box with a list of several options for printing reports, or a separate component that your application uses.

6. What is the chief benefit of the ReportScheduler class?

   Scheduling reports. Scheduling reports to be printed once at some future date and time or cyclically is not as involved as giving users ad hoc reporting abilities. It involves capturing the date and time from the user, saving it to a database, the Registry, or a text file, and continuously checking for the designated date and/or time. After the date and time have arrived, print the report. For this task, it is good to have a controller class called ReportScheduler and a form controlled by this class that has a timer control.

7. How does the Timer control and the ReportScheduler class members help the overall ReportScheduler class fulfill its responsibilities?

   The private properties, ReportDate and ReportTime, respectively, contain the date and time the report is to be printed. The property, theForm, is a reference to the form, frmScheduledReports, which has a Timer control, a list box, or grid control to inform the user of the scheduled reports, and a command button, cmdCancelReport, that allows a user to cancel a scheduled report. The user would have to select a report first. The property, theTimer, is a reference to the Timer control on the form. The WithEvents keyword allows you to maintain the code for the timer's single event, Timer, within the class instead of in the form.

Day 17

1. What are the three kinds of file management discussed in this chapter?

   Random File Management, Sequential File Management, Binary File Management.

2. What is the purpose of the Get statement for random access files?

   The Get statement uses iFileNumber to open a file and assign it the number contained in the variable.

3. What are the four classes you can use to implement objects that manage files?

   The four classes are `SequentialFile`, `RandomFile`, `BinaryFile`, and `RichTextFile`.

4. What does CSV stand for?

   CSV stands for comma-separated value.

5. What kinds of file operations are best when using the `Write #` and `Input #` statements?

   Random or binary access file mechanisms.

6. What is a benefit of implementing binary access file operations?

   Implementing binary access file operations allows you to assume significant responsibility not just for the contents of the file, but also for the way the file stores its information. Binary access file operations are most useful in situations where you must conserve disk space.

7. What is an assumption made about `String` values in binary files?

   If you use `String` variables to persist the information, for instance, the binary file operations in Visual Basic assume that the variable value contains string characters instead of actual binary information. Thus, there's a risk of data integrity being lost in making the mapping between `String` and binary data.

8. What are the advantages of using the Rich Text Box in managing files?

   The Rich Text Box control makes managing files much simpler. In short, the Rich Text Box control combines the text box, file operations, simple word-processing, and printing and reporting capabilities in one object. As mentioned earlier, the Rich Text Box can hold huge amounts of information, more so than the conventional text box. Plus, it gives you the flexibility to manage `.RTF` (rich text) and ASCII files (of any extension, but typically `.TXT`). If you want to store information in row and column format, simply insert commas and the `vbNewLine` value where you need it. And when you persist information in the comma-separated value (CSV) format, you can open it and read the information in it using the Random Access or Binary Access methods. In fact, as mentioned earlier, in CSV format, you can export the file to Access, Excel, as well as SQL Server and other databases that accept CSV files.

9. What is the purpose of the `IPersistence`, `GeneralFile`, and `IFileSubsystem` classes?

   The `IPersistence` class is important as an organizer of any event triggering the persistence of information, whether in a database or regular file. This class is not owned by the subsystem but is the gateway for the flow of events with a given

A

client. The IFileSubsystem class is the interface for the subsystem, making sure that the proper response to an incoming event or message is handled as expected. The IPersistence class instance (or object) owns a reference to the IFileSubsystem class instance. This object, in turn, owns a reference to an instance of a GeneralFile interface implementation class such as RandomFile, SequentialFile, BinaryFile, or RichTextFile. One of these classes does the actual grunt work. Note that the GeneralFile class is purely an interface class that abstracts the common interface between the four implementation classes.

10. Explain the persistNewInfo and persistAddedInfo methods of the GeneralFile family of classes.

The persistNewInfo method saves information to a file that did not exist before, whereas the persistAddedInfo method adds information to a previously existing file. For SequentialFile objects, the file has to be opened in Append mode.

Day 18

1. True or False: Every significant class method and code module function (if any) requires initial error handling.

True

2. What three steps are typically involved in implementing inline error handling in your methods?

The steps are as follows:

1. Enable the error trap (equivalent to throwing an exception).

2. Respond to the error (equivalent to catching an exception).

3. Complete the error-handling process and, if possible, continue program execution.

3. What statement initiates your error traps?

The On Error statement initiates your error traps, specifying to which label the application should go to perform the beginning of the error-handling routine.

4. Is it okay to do very complex error handling in every method?

No. It's advisable not to do too much complex error handling within a method as this could clutter your method code and make it difficult to debug. Besides, you want to be able to reuse sophisticated error-handling routines throughout your application.

5. What are the various kinds of methods for which you must plan?

You must plan for the following kinds of errors:

- Errors that your component traps but allows the client to handle.

- Errors that originate in another component from which your component received and used object references.

- Errors that originate in your component that may have been the result of programmer error or some rule violation that must be enforced by your component.

Day 19

1. What does UDA stand for? What is its purpose?

Microsoft Universal Data Access. UDA is a new Microsoft architecture that promises to provide efficient access to a variety of data formats—relational and nonrelational—on different platforms across your enterprise. UDA gives you a developer-friendly programming interface that can be used with Visual Basic.

2. What features does the Remote Data Services (RDS) component provide for ADO?

The Remote Data Services is a client-side component used by ADO to provide for opening and managing database cursors, remote object invocation, and explicit access to remote recordsets.

3. What are three reasons ADO was created by Microsoft?

Microsoft designed ADO to assist in the following ways:

- To address your unique Internet development needs

- To access special kinds of persistent information not limited to relational data

- To develop faster, smaller, and more efficient applications

4. True or False: RDO enables you to limit the number of rows returned or processed.

True

5. What are the advantages and disadvantages of using the ODBC API?

The chief advantage includes speed due to less overhead than other data access mechanisms. Disadvantages include a high level of complexity and difficulty in maintaining code.

6. What are the general operations involved in working with the ODBC API?

- Establishing the environment by allocating an environment handle (hEnv) using ODBC's SQLAllocEnv.

A

- Establishing the environment by allocating a database connection handle (hDbc) using ODBC's SQLAllocConnect. You also need a valid data source name (DSN), user ID, and password for databases that require them.

- Establishing the environment by allocating a SQL/database command statement handle (hStmt).

- Working with the actual data by binding columns, opening and closing cursors, and moving through sets of records.

- Deallocating a SQL/database command statement handle (hStmt).

- Deallocating a database connection handle (hDbc).

- Deallocating an environment handle (hEnv).

7. What are the advantages and disadvantages of using Data controls?

The advantages include ease of implementation, ease of maintenance when data access is relatively straightforward, and rapid development. Disadvantages include susceptibility to data control failure, less code reuse, and less ease of code duplication.

Day 20

1. What is the compartmental hierarchy for subsystems and their members?

Subsystems are compartmentalized into classes. Classes are compartmentalized into methods, properties, and events. Subsystem compartments communicate with one another through a common interface.

2. Why are subsystem interface classes so important?

Subsystem interface classes are important because changes to them can cause a debugging and maintenance nightmare.

3. What is a good way to decouple an actual form in the Graphical User Interface Subsystem from direct communications with the Database Access Subsystem?

By using form controller classes, business or domain classes, and data access (or persistence) classes.

4. What's the importance of collections of business classes in the Business Rules Subsystem?

Often, applications deal with several records at a time, for which collections of business classes are useful. Business class collections are, in a sense, queues or stores of data out of which form controllers request information to display. Collections can very well be seen as mini–object-oriented databases that help shield (or encapsulate) the rest of the application from the relational database.

5. Explain the nature of the form controller in subsystem-to-subsystem communications.

Although it is certainly wise from a code reuse standpoint to not allow forms to directly communicate with the Database Access Subsystem, form controllers at times need to communicate with it. In fact, form controller classes aren't monopolized exclusively by the Graphical User Interface Subsystem in every situation. Sometimes a controller class can be the communication hub between the form business rules and the Database Access Subsystem. This is helpful when you're moving data in and out of a database, one record at a time, and no business rule processing occurs. Typical applications that might face this scenario include pure data entry applications in which the user is keying in information on a client machine, and that information is to be processed later by some server subsystem independent of the client.

Day 21

1. Why is it strongly advisable to approach all your Visual Basic development efforts with the utmost organization and methodology?

You can usually handle only seven (plus or minus two) points of complexity.

2. What factor increases the chances of successfully delivering a product written in Visual Basic?

A factor that will increase the chances of successfully delivering a product written in Visual Basic is to have access to a Visual Basic developer who has experience in the best features of Visual Basic, including its object-oriented programming features. Having a good library of classes and components is also helpful.

3. What are the important factors to consider in managing a Visual Basic project successfully?

- Give developers inexperienced with the powerful, overwhelming new features in Visual Basic the right resources to help them succeed, including acquiring an outside mentor if necessary.

- Track and maintain domain terminology so that developers are not later side-tracked on ambiguity in terms users use.

- Plan for the one- to three-month learning curve when hiring new developers on a fairly large project. (For smaller projects, the learning curve is typically shorter.)

- When reengineering an undocumented legacy system into a Visual Basic application, be sure to allow time to help users separate (within reason) the navigation of windows from the actual tasks they are trying to accomplish.

- Emphasize the necessity of having clearly defined project team roles; this helps avoid confusion as to which project tasks, components, and subsystems are assigned to which developers.

- Avoid scope creep, or the unnoticed increase in the project's requirements.

- Select, follow, and, when necessary, customize an object-oriented methodology for the Visual Basic project (based on deadline pressures, budgets, and so on).

- When developing a large Visual Basic project with more than one team, each tasked with developing a complex component or subsystem, develop a plan for coordinating the delivery of each team's expected product; this includes version control and compilation issues.

- Make sure developers are physically seated within a reasonably close proximity to one another; the farther apart developers must sit, the less chance the Visual Basic project has for success.

- Acquire Visual Basic and other development tools early enough in the project so that developers have a chance to get acclimated to the environment and toy with prototypes well before crunch time.

- When a project grows too large, break it up into smaller projects. Visual Basic offers you the powerful feature of grouping many projects into one project group.

- Build an intranet Web site to make available documentation, code, and executables related to all Visual Basic projects in your domain.

4. How is software development similar to wildcat oil drilling?

Developing software is in some cases riskier than gambling in Las Vegas, and in some ways resembles the risk of highly speculative, wildcat oil drilling.

One way that modern oil companies have mitigated the risks of pouring huge amounts of money into drilling for oil in places where none exists is to budget a certain amount of money for exploration and research using the latest petroleum and geological research technology. Yes, it's a lot of money, but much of the oil industry learned that the money spent on analytical research has consistently proven to be far cheaper than blindly drilling for oil.

Similarly, software development project moneyholders should realistically budget some money for problem assessment and solution exploration by well-respected technical experts in order to come up with an intelligent estimate of the effort necessary to elaborate, construct, and deploy a product. For these three phases, the managers would then audit the project at predetermined milestones to see if progress is being made at a reasonable pace. If not, look for ways to improve the situation; if that doesn't help, simply shelve all of the knowledge gained for possible work later and give notice to the team members to pursue other contracts or internal jobs. Something along these lines is more realistic and in line with other industries.

5. What is the best measure of developer productivity?

The best measure of productivity is where the Visual Basic developer

- Has discovered designs in code that can be reusable, thus reducing the lines of code.

- Creates classes that facilitate reusability of code.

- Develops code in an iterative, incremental way where each increment and iteration compartmentalizes the complexity of the problem being solved.

Index

Symbols

(pound) sign, 381
#define statement, 258
\ (backslash), 376

A

abnormal paths, 141
abnormal scenarios, 51
abstract classes, 12-13
abstract components (subsystems), 201
access
  children's, 286, 289
  components, sharing, 192
  concurrency/multiple users, 173
  control checkpoints, 288

enforcing rights, 286
  owners and non-owners
    unauthorized, 287-289
    violations, 173
  files, 376-384
  Rich Text Box control, 384
  security
    encrypting passwords, 287, 301
  setting permissions, 193
  subsystem, sharing, 192
Access (Microsoft)
  DAO, 416
  exporting comma-separated values (CSVs) to, 382-384
  exporting sequential access files to, 381
  logging runtime errors using, 188
Access reporting, 354

accessors, 101
AccessReporting class, 363
AccountCreator class, 343
AccountTransactionsGroup class, 303
activateLogging method, 323
activating debug mode, 185
ActiveX
  components
    abstract components, 201
    concrete components, 202
    object-oriented testing services, 143
    test components, 143-148
    test planning, 139-142
  DLLs
    building, 134-139
    DLL project, 132

M

m1ClassDebugID property, 185
MaintainAccount class, 274
MaintainBankProducts class, 273
MaintainCustomer class, 274
maintaining
  applications, 337
  domain terminology, 469
MaintainUsers class, 274
MaintainWorkgroups class, 274
maintenance tasks, 188
ManagerRole class, 296
ManagerRole role, 303
managing, 309
  business rules/policies in applications, 338
  files
    binary access, 382-383
    random access, 377-380
    Rich Text Box control, 384
    sequential access, 380-382
  policy enforcement, 338, 343-347
  projects
    approaches, 468-470
    auditing approach, 470-471
    avoiding increased requirements (scope creep), 469
    coordinating subsystem development teams, 469
    corporate environments, 465-467
    defining team-member roles, 469
    ideal components, 468, 472
    incremental/iterative code development, 471
    intranet Web communications, 469
    learning curves, 469
    managers, 468-471
    mentorship, 469
    object-oriented methodology, 469-471, 474
    overview, 467-471, 475
    physical proximity, 469
    productivity, 472
    prototypes, 475
    reengineering time, 469
    sample scenario, 466-467
    schedule changes, 476-477
    sharing costs, 477
    subdividing, 469
    tracking/maintaining domain terminology, 469
    traditional approach, 470
    waterfall methodology, 474
    Windows navigation time, 469
  tasks, 299-300
  workgroups, 298-299
Mandelbrot Set Web site, 158
math methods, error handling, 397-398
MDIController class, 273

members (classes), 14-16
Memento class, 250
memory
  components, 114
  logging allocations, 321
  reclaiming, 113
  reducing requirements, 113
mentorship, 469
messages, 27-28
Method Builder dialog box, 24-25
method calls, 181
methodology
  analysis paralysis, 35
  object-oriented, 471, 474
  OOSE, 35
  overview, 34-35
  Rumbaugh, Jim, 37
  waterfall, 474
methods
  AccessReporting class, 363
  activateLogging, 323
  Add, 303
  adjustBalance(), 147, 180, 244
  AppTransactions class, 323
  arguments, 174-175, 254
  authenticate, 303
  BankTransactionPolicy, 344
  CApplication class, 322
  CashDepositRecord, 343
  checking unattended sessions, 289-290
  clickedAddBtn(), 254
  clickedCancelBtn(), 249
  clickedControl, 297
  clickedDoneBtn(), 248-249, 344

Sams Teach Yourself More Visual Basic 5 in 21 Days

—Lowell Mauer

Using the formula of the best-selling *Sams Teach Yourself* series, this comprehensive guide teaches readers everything they need to know about Visual Basic—quickly and easily. With the book's logical, easy-to-follow format, readers will be developing dynamic Visual Basic programs in no time. This book explores the newest features of Visual Basic and advanced programming techniques in detail. Workshops, Q&A sections, and Do's and Don'ts make learning easy and fun. The CD-ROM is loaded with all the source code from the book, third-party utilities, and sample scripts.

Price: $29.99 USA/$42.95 CAN   *Casual–Accomplished–Expert*
ISBN: 0-672-31062-7   *650 pages*

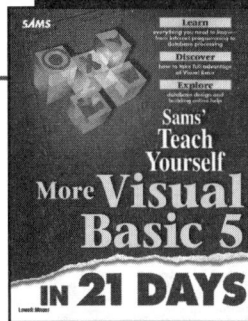

Visual Basic 5 Unleashed, Professional Reference Edition

—Rob Thayer

The *Unleashed* series takes you beyond the average discussions of a technology, giving you practical advice and in-depth coverage, and this book in particular is a powerful resource. Use the comprehensive index, legends, and table of contents to find everything you need. With these extensive guides, you'll obtain the skills, understanding, and breadth of knowledge to unleash the full potential of Visual Basic 5.

The book's CD-ROM includes powerful software: source code and examples from the book, Microsoft Visual Basic Control Creation Edition (see the Microsoft Visual Basic Control Creation Edition end user license inside the book before installing the software), and Macmillan Computer Publishing's Visual Basic Knowledgebase—a collection of topic-oriented issues with resource information gathered from multiple Visual Basic bestsellers. You can create bug-free applications with BoundChecker, CodeReview, and FailSafe from NuMega Technologies; design applications that exploit Internet capabilities with the Crescent Division of Progress Software's Internet ToolPak; make your applications Internet-ready with Dart Communications' PowerTCP; and incorporate graphic tools in your programs using ImageLib Corporate Suite from SkyLine Tools. The CD-ROM also includes the Microsoft Internet Explorer logo, the Microsoft Internet Explorer 4 browser, and Visual Basic F.A.

With this book, you will learn to use the Microsoft Visual Data Tools; discover how to mail-enable applications with MAPI; delve into Visual SourceSafe; implement OLE drag-and-drop capabilities into controls; learn VB variable types, data structures, collections, and enumerations; use message boxes and input dialogs; discover using the common dialog control; implement polymorphism for your objects; and learn algorithms for Visual Basic programmers—including sorts, encryption, and compression. You will also reuse and share components with the Template Manager; manage your database with the Visual Data Manager; enhance add-ins and flexible add-in registration; learn how to create telephony-enabled applications with TAPI; make use of the ActiveX Data Objects; and learn to add and control Remote Data Objects.

Price: $59.99 USA/$84.95 CAN   *Intermediate–Advanced*
ISBN: 0-672-31297-2   *1,200 pages*

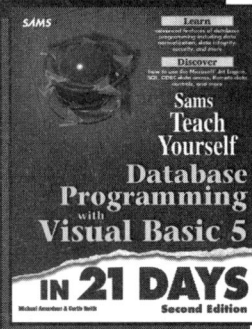

Sams Teach Yourself Database Programming with Visual Basic 5 in 21 Days, Second Edition

—Michael Amundsen and Curtis Smith

Visual Basic, the 32-bit programming language from Microsoft, is used by programmers to create Windows and Windows 95 applications. You can also use it to program World Wide Web applications, so this book shows you how to design, develop, and deploy Visual Basic applications for the Web. This book is presented in a daily format, with each week focusing on a different area of database development, and is written by a Microsoft Certified Visual Basic Professional. The CD-ROM includes chapter examples, function libraries, the Microsoft Access/Jet 2.5 compatibility layer, and the WHAT6 Help Authoring Tool.

Price: $45.00 USA/$63.95 CAN   *New–Casual–Advanced*
ISBN: 0-672-31018-X   *1,080 pages*

Dan Appleman's Visual Basic 5.0 Programmer's Guide to the Win32 API

—Daniel Appleman

No other book on the market can compete with this complete guide to the Win32 API. This book is already being hailed as the definitive reference for Visual Basic programmers because it contains a wealth of background information on how Windows works. It includes the API Toolkit and Desaware API Class Library. The CD-ROM contains source code examples and video annotations by the author in the full-text, searchable edition of the book.

Price: $59.99 USA/$84.95 CAN   *Beginning–Advanced*
ISBN: 1-56276-446-2   *1,584 pages*

Add to Your Sams Library Today with the Best Books for Programming, Operating Systems, and New Technologies

The easiest way to order is to pick up the phone and call

1-800-428-5331

between 9:00 a.m. and 5:00 p.m. EST.

For faster service please have your credit card available.

ISBN	Quantity	Description of Item	Unit Cost	Total Cost
0-672-31062-7		Sams Teach Yourself More Visual Basic 5 in 21 Days	$29.99	
0-672-31297-2		Visual Basic 5 Unleashed, Professional Reference Edition	$59.99	
0-672-31018-X		Sams Teach Yourself Database Programming with Visual Basic 5 in 21 Days, Second Edition	$45.00	
1-56276-446-2		Dan Appleman's Visual Basic 5.0 Programmer's Guide to the Win32 API	$59.99	
		Shipping and Handling: See information below.		
		TOTAL		

Shipping and Handling: $4.00 for the first book, and $1.75 for each additional book. If you need to have it NOW, we can ship the product to you in 24 hours for an additional charge of approximately $18.00, and you will receive your item overnight or in two days. Overseas shipping and handling adds $2.00 per book. Prices subject to change. Call for availability and pricing information on latest editions.

201 W. 103rd Street, Indianapolis, Indiana 46290

1-800-428-5331 — Orders   1-800-835-3202 — Fax   1-800-858-7674 — Customer Service

Book ISBN 0-672-31299-9

What's on the CD-ROM

The companion CD-ROM contains all the author's source code and examples from the book, as well as many third-party software products.

Windows 95/NT 4 Installation Instructions

1. Insert the CD-ROM into your CD-ROM drive.
2. From the Windows 95 desktop, double-click the My Computer icon.
3. Double-click the icon representing your CD-ROM drive.
4. Double-click the icon titled SETUP.EXE to run the installation program.
5. The installation program creates a program group with the book's name as the group name. This group contains icons to browse the CD-ROM.

Note
If Windows 95 is installed on your computer and you have the AutoPlay feature enabled, the SETUP.EXE program starts automatically when you insert the CD-ROM into your CD-ROM drive.

System Requirements

This CD-ROM contains the Microsoft Visual Basic® Control Creation Edition. Some of the features of Visual Basic 5 discussed in this book might not be usable with the Control Creation Edition. The Control Creation Edition is provided to allow you to become familiar with the Visual Basic environment and to create your own ActiveX controls.

The following are the minimum system requirements for the Visual Basic Control Creation Edition:

- A personal computer with a 486 or higher processor
- Microsoft Windows 95 or Windows NT Workstation 4.0 or higher
- 8MB of memory (12MB recommended) if running Windows NT Workstation
- The following hard disk space:

  Typical installation: 20MB

  Minimum installation: 14MB

  CD-ROM installation (tools run from the CD-ROM): 14MB

  Total tools and information on the CD-ROM: 50MB

- A CD-ROM drive
- A VGA or higher-resolution monitor (SVGA recommended)

jurisdiction of the courts of the Province of Ontario and further agrees to commence any litigation which may arise hereunder in the courts located in the Judicial District of York, Province of Ontario.

If this product was acquired outside the United States, then local law may apply.

Should you have any questions concerning this EULA, or if you desire to contact Microsoft for any reason, please contact the Microsoft subsidiary serving your country, or write: Microsoft Sales Information Center/One Microsoft Way/Redmond, WA 98052-6399.

LIMITED WARRANTY

NO WARRANTIES. Microsoft expressly disclaims any warranty for the SOFTWARE PRODUCT. The SOFTWARE PRODUCT and any related documentation is provided "as is" without warranty of any kind, either express or implied, including, without limitation, the implied warranties or merchantability, fitness for a particular purpose, or noninfringement. The entire risk arising out of use or performance of the SOFTWARE PRODUCT remains with you.

NO LIABILITY FOR DAMAGES. In no event shall Microsoft or its suppliers be liable for any damages whatsoever (including, without limitation, damages for loss of business profits, business interruption, loss of business information, or any other pecuniary loss) arising out of the use of or inability to use this Microsoft product, even if Microsoft has been advised of the possibility of such damages. Because some states/jurisdictions do not allow the exclusion or limitation of liability for consequential or incidental damages, the above limitation may not apply to you.

4. **COPYRIGHT.** All title and copyrights in and to the SOFTWARE PRODUCT (including but not limited to any images, photographs, animations, video, audio, music, text, and "applets" incorporated into the SOFTWARE PRODUCT), the accompanying printed materials, and any copies of the SOFTWARE PRODUCT are owned by Microsoft or its suppliers. The SOFTWARE PRODUCT is protected by copyright laws and international treaty provisions. Therefore, you must treat the SOFTWARE PRODUCT like any other copyrighted material except that you may install the SOFTWARE PRODUCT on a single computer provided you keep the original solely for backup or archival purposes. You may not copy the printed materials accompanying the SOFTWARE PRODUCT.

5. **DUAL-MEDIA SOFTWARE.** You may receive the SOFTWARE PRODUCT in more than one medium. Regardless of the type or size of medium you receive, you may use only one medium that is appropriate for your single computer. You may not use or install the other medium on another computer. You may not loan, rent, lease, or otherwise transfer the other medium to another user, except as part of the permanent transfer (as provided above) of the SOFTWARE PRODUCT.

6. **U.S. GOVERNMENT RESTRICTED RIGHTS.** The SOFTWARE PRODUCT and documentation are provided with RESTRICTED RIGHTS. Use, duplication, or disclosure by the Government is subject to restrictions as set forth in subparagraph (c)(1)(ii) of the Rights in Technical Data and Computer Software clause at DFARS 252.227-7013 or subparagraphs (c)(1) and (2) of the Commercial Computer Software—Restricted Rights at 48 CFR 52.227-19, as applicable. Manufacturer is Microsoft Corporation/One Microsoft Way/Redmond, WA 98052-6399.

7. **EXPORT RESTRICTIONS.** You agree that neither you nor your customers intend to or will, directly or indirectly, export or transmit (i) the SOFTWARE or related documentation and technical data or (ii) your software product as described in Section 1(b) of this License (or any part thereof), or process, or service that is the direct product of the SOFTWARE, to any country to which such export or transmission is restricted by any applicable U.S. regulation or statute, without the prior written consent, if required, of the Bureau of Export Administration of the U.S. Department of Commerce, or such other governmental entity as may have jurisdiction over such export or transmission.

MISCELLANEOUS

If you acquired this product in the United States, this EULA is governed by the laws of the State of Washington.

If you acquired this product in Canada, this EULA is governed by the laws of the Province of Ontario, Canada. Each of the parties hereto irrevocably attorns to the

←

b. **Limitations on Reverse Engineering, Decompilation, and Disassembly.** You may not reverse engineer, decompile, or disassemble the SOFTWARE PRODUCT, except and only to the extent that such activity is expressly permitted by applicable law notwithstanding this limitation.

c. **Separation of Components.** The SOFTWARE PRODUCT is licensed as a single product. Its component parts may not be separated for use by more than one user.

d. **Rental.** You may not rent, lease, or lend the SOFTWARE PRODUCT.

e. **Support Services.** Microsoft may provide you with support services related to the SOFTWARE PRODUCT ("Support Services"). Use of Support Services is governed by the Microsoft policies and programs described in the user manual, in "online" documentation, and/or in other Microsoft-provided materials. Any supplemental software code provided to you as part of the Support Services shall be considered part of the SOFTWARE PRODUCT and subject to the terms and conditions of this EULA. With respect to technical information you provide to Microsoft as part of the Support Services, Microsoft may use such information for its business purposes, including for product support and development. Microsoft will not utilize such technical information in a form that personally identifies you.

f. **Software Transfer.** You may permanently transfer all of your rights under this EULA, provided you retain no copies, you transfer all of the SOFTWARE PRODUCT (including all component parts, the media and printed materials, any upgrades, this EULA, and, if applicable, the Certificate of Authenticity), **and** the recipient agrees to the terms of this EULA. If the SOFTWARE PRODUCT is an upgrade, any transfer must include all prior versions of the SOFTWARE PRODUCT.

g. **Termination.** Without prejudice to any other rights, Microsoft may terminate this EULA if you fail to comply with the terms and conditions of this EULA. In such event, you must destroy all copies of the SOFTWARE PRODUCT and all of its component parts.

3. **UPGRADES.** If the SOFTWARE PRODUCT is labeled as an upgrade, you must be properly licensed to use a product identified by Microsoft as being eligible for the upgrade in order to use the SOFTWARE PRODUCT. A SOFTWARE PRODUCT labeled as an upgrade replaces and/or supplements the product that formed the basis for your eligibility for the upgrade. You may use the resulting upgraded product only in accordance with the terms of this EULA. If the SOFTWARE PRODUCT is an upgrade of a component of a package of software programs that you licensed as a single product, the SOFTWARE PRODUCT may be used and transferred only as part of that single product package and may not be separated for use on more than one computer.

c. **Redistributable Components.**

(i) **Sample Code.** In addition to the rights granted in Section 1, Microsoft grants you the right to use and modify the source code version of those portions of the SOFTWARE designated as "Sample Code" ("SAMPLE CODE") for the sole purposes of designing, developing, and testing your software product(s), and to reproduce and distribute the SAMPLE CODE, along with any modifications thereof, only in object code form provided that you comply with Section d(iii), below.

(ii) **Redistributable Components.** In addition to the rights granted in Section 1, Microsoft grants you a nonexclusive royalty-free right to reproduce and distribute the object code version of any portion of the SOFTWARE listed in the SOFTWARE file REDIST.TXT ("REDISTRIBUTABLE SOFTWARE"), provided you comply with Section d (iii), below.

(iii) **Redistribution Requirements.** If you redistribute the SAMPLE CODE or REDISTRIBUTABLE SOFTWARE (collectively, "REDISTRIBUTA-BLES"), you agree to: (A) distribute the REDISTRIBUTABLES in object code only in conjunction with and as a part of a software application product developed by you that adds significant and primary functionality to the SOFTWARE and that is developed to operate on the Windows or Windows NT environment ("Application"); (B) not use Microsoft's name, logo, or trademarks to market your software application product; (C) include a valid copyright notice on your software product; (D) indemnify, hold harmless, and defend Microsoft from and against any claims or lawsuits, including attorney's fees, that arise or result from the use or distribution of your software application product; (E) not permit further distribution of the REDISTRIB-UTABLES by your end user. The following **exceptions** apply to subsection (iii) (E), above: (1) you may permit further redistribution of the REDIS-TRIBUTABLES by your distributors to your end-user customers if your distributors only distribute the REDISTRIBUTABLES in conjunction with, and as part of, your Application and you and your distributors comply with all other terms of this EULA; and (2) you may permit your end users to reproduce and distribute the object code version of the files designated by ".ocx" file extensions ("Controls") only in conjunction with and as a part of an Application and/or Web page that adds significant and primary functionality to the Controls, and such end user complies with all other terms of this EULA.

2. **DESCRIPTION OF OTHER RIGHTS AND LIMITATIONS.**

a. **Not for Resale Software.** If the SOFTWARE PRODUCT is labeled "Not for Resale" or "NFR," then, notwithstanding other sections of this EULA, you may not resell, or otherwise transfer for value, the SOFTWARE PRODUCT.

←

END-USER LICENSE AGREEMENT FOR MICROSOFT SOFTWARE

Microsoft Visual Basic, Control Creation Edition

IMPORTANT—READ CAREFULLY: This Microsoft End-User License Agreement ("EULA") is a legal agreement between you (either an individual or a single entity) and Microsoft Corporation for the Microsoft software product identified above, which includes computer software and may include associated media, printed materials, and "online" or electronic documentation ("SOFTWARE PRODUCT"). By installing, copying, or otherwise using the SOFTWARE PRODUCT, you agree to be bound by the terms of this EULA. If you do not agree to the terms of this EULA, do not install or use the SOFTWARE PRODUCT; you may, however, return it to your place of purchase for a full refund.

SOFTWARE PRODUCT LICENSE

The SOFTWARE PRODUCT is protected by copyright laws and international copyright treaties, as well as other intellectual property laws and treaties. The SOFTWARE PRODUCT is licensed, not sold.

1. **GRANT OF LICENSE.** This EULA grants you the following rights:

    a. **Software Product.** Microsoft grants to you as an individual, a personal, nonexclusive license to make and use copies of the SOFTWARE for the sole purposes of designing, developing, and testing your software product(s) that are designed to operate in conjunction with any Microsoft operating system product. You may install copies of the SOFTWARE on an unlimited number of computers provided that you are the only individual using the SOFTWARE. If you are an entity, Microsoft grants you the right to designate one individual within your organization to have the right to use the SOFTWARE in the manner provided above.

    b. **Electronic Documents.** Solely with respect to electronic documents included with the SOFTWARE, you may make an unlimited number of copies (either in hardcopy or electronic form), provided that such copies shall be used only for internal purposes and are not republished or distributed to any third party.